REVOLUTION
AND GENOCIDE

ROBERT MELSON

REVOLUTION AND GENOCIDE

On the Origins of the Armenian Genocide and the Holocaust

With a Foreword by
LEO KUPER

THE UNIVERSITY OF CHICAGO PRESS
Chicago and London

THE UNIVERSITY OF CHICAGO PRESS, CHICAGO 60637
THE UNIVERSITY OF CHICAGO PRESS, LTD., LONDON
© 1992 by the University of Chicago
All rights reserved. Published 1992
Paperback edition 1996
Printed in the United States of America
01 00 99 98 97 96   5 4 3 2

ISBN (cloth): 0–226–51990–2
ISBN (paper): 0–226–51991–0

Library of Congress Cataloging-in-Publication Data

Melson, Robert, 1937–
    Revolution and genocide : the origins of the Armenian genocide and
the Holocaust / Robert Melson : with a foreword by Leo Kuper.
        p. cm.
    Includes bibliographical references and index.
    1. Armenian massacres, 1915–1923. 2. Holocaust, Jewish.
1939–1945. 3. Genocide—Case studies. I. Title.
DS195.5.M45   1992
956.6'2023—dc20

The epigraph in the Preface is from *W. H. Auden: Collected Poems*, by W. H. Auden, edited by Edward Mendelson. Copyright © 1975 by Edward Mendelson, William Meredith, and Monroe K. Spears, Executors of the Estate of W. H. Auden. Reprinted by permission of Random House, Inc. Also reprinted by permission from *The English Auden*, edited by Edward Mendelson, Faber and Faber Ltd.

Robert Melson, "A Theoretical Inquiry into the Armenian Massacres of 1894–96," *Comparative Studies in Society and History* 24, no. 3 (July 1982): 481–509, with some revisions, appears as Chapter 2. Reprinted by permission of Cambridge University Press.

Chapter 5 is based on Robert Melson, "Provocation or Nationalism: A Critical Inquiry into the Armenian Genocide of 1915," in *The Armenian Genocide in Perspective*, edited by Richard G. Hovannisian (New Brunswick, N.J.: Transaction Press, 1986), 61–84. Reprinted with permission.

To Gail, as always

In Memory of ז"ל

My Grandparents

Sylvia Sara Blumenfeld Mendelsohn (d. Davos, 1916)

Julius Joel Mendelsohn (d. Stanislawov, 1941)

Stefania Bathsheba Gromb Ponczek (d. Treblinka, 1942)

Leon Leib Judah Ponczek (d. Treblinka, 1942)

and My Teacher

Professor Daniel Lerner (1917–1980)

and My Friend

Professor Larry Axel (1946–1991)

CONTENTS

FOREWORD

The expectation that victims of oppression, when liberated, would transcend their own trauma in compassion for the suffering of others seems unrealistic in retrospect. So I was intrigued to meet at the home of an Armenian colleague a survivor of the Holocaust, who had devoted a significant part of his academic career to pioneering studies of the Armenian genocide. Professor Melson's traumatic experiences in the Holocaust go back to early childhood when he and his parents, in October 1941, escaped annihilation by a Nazi extermination squad, which massacred most of the Jews of the small Polish town in which they lived; his parents had refused to go to the appointed place of assembly. Thereafter, acquiring false papers and assuming the identity of Polish aristocrats, they managed to survive to the end of the war. Other members of his family were less fortunate.

This direct experience of the Holocaust has left its marked imprint on his academic orientation, and in particular on his preoccupation with total genocide, the subject of the present volume. If I recall correctly, at one time he defined genocide, within an encompassing concern for massacre, as total genocide. His experience is also reflected in his discussion of the particularist approach to the Holocaust, which emphasizes the incomparable uniqueness of that event, and the universalist perspective, which subsumes it under the category of genocide.

Reading his comments, one cannot fail to be impressed by the distinctive qualities in his academic approach; the analytical attention to detail, the fair presentation of both perspectives, the careful examination of the pros and cons of these diametrically opposed points of view, and his final resolution of the issue. From my own point of view, growing up in the racially oppressive police state of South Africa which preceded apartheid, and with the experience of an indigenous Nazi movement, and experience also in World War II, I tend to equate the particularist orientation with an alienating ethnocentrism.

The universalist definition of genocide by Raphael Lemkin, who pioneered the concept, seems to me perfectly acceptable—"a coordinated plan of different actions aiming at the destruction of essential foundations of the life of the national groups, with the aim of annihilating the groups themselves."

So, too, the definition in the UN Convention on the Prevention of the Crime of Genocide, derived in the process of lengthy debates, incorporating the varied experiences of the annihilation of peoples, represented a universalistic approach. The inclusion of the Holocaust within the general comprehensive concept of genocide does not imply equating it with other genocides, or even comparing it with other genocides. Each genocide contains its unique aspect together with the general defining characteristic of genocide at a high level of abstraction.

Professor Melson, in his own approach to problems of definition, reverts to his initial concern with mass killing. From a humanitarian point of view, this is the basic issue and not precision in the specific labeling. Defining the victims broadly as a *"social collectivity or category* usually a communal group, a class or political faction," he develops a typology, moving from massacre or pogrom through partial genocide and total genocide to the Holocaust as "a specific historical instance of total genocide."

This typology seems an admirable one. There is a problem, however, in the general definition, which if applied might deprive genocide of its unique horror. Presumably the definition chosen from the abundant offerings in the field would depend on the objective. If it is to activate the UN machinery for the Prevention and Punishment of the Crime of Genocide, or to extend domestic jurisdiction to punishment of this international crime, one would fall back on the internationally accepted legal definition.

A further formative influence on Professor Melson's theoretical orientation and the present study was a brief experience as an Africanist in Nigeria shortly before the military coup in 1966 and a major massacre of Ibos. Rejecting communalism (or tribalism or primordial sentiment) as the precipitating cause, he argues that it is the process of change (such as urbanization, mass education, the diffusion of the mass media, and the development of increasingly efficient and productive commercial networks) that give rise to a new social mobilization. As a result, men come to desire precisely the same things, and they engage in conflict not because they are different but because they are essentially the same (Robert Melson and Howard Wolpe, "Modernization and the Politics of Communalism," *American Political Science Review* 64, no. 4 [1970], Proposition 1, p. 1114).

So, too, it is not ideology in isolation that is the propelling force in genocide but the broad socioeconomic political context within which ideology becomes effectively motivating. Nor is the Holocaust to be explained simply as a manifestation of deep-rooted German antisemitism with its long history of Jewish victimization and dehumanization. "But," as he comments in a personal communication, "antisemitism existed in Imperial Germany without its leading to genocide, and Jewish victimization and dehumanization had a long history prior to the Holocaust." Revolution was the catalyst that transformed German antisemitism into total domestic genocide, not ideology, nor the needs and dynamics of party organizations and bureaucratic structures that developed and manned the machinery of destruction. However influential these factors may have been, they neglect, as an explanation of the Holocaust, the circumstances enabling the Nazis to come to power and implement their ideology as the public policy of the state. The effective precipitating causes were the revolutionary interregnum in Germany, which enabled the Nazis to become the effective rulers, and World War II. The revolutionary regime, in redefining German political culture and the identity of the new political community, rendered excluded groups vulnerable to genocide.

The same themes of war and revolution are analyzed in the transformation of the traditional conditional tolerance of the Ottoman Empire into the narrow, chauvinistic, and xenophobic Turkish nationalism of the ruling revolutionary Committee of Union and Progress. In the process, and in the overall context of the disintegration of the Ottoman Empire and military defeat, Armenians became redundant. Indeed, they were viewed as enemies, particularly dangerous, since they occupied the heartland of Turkey and straddled the boundary with Russia. The provocation thesis, that Armenians, by reason of their revolutionary and provocative behavior were in fact the agents of their own destruction, offers a parallel to the Nazi ideology of Jews engaged in an international conspiracy against the Third Reich.

This analytical procedure linking revolution to total domestic genocide is applied briefly also to the annihilation of the Kulaks in Soviet Russia under Stalin and to the "autogenocide" in Kampuchea. Drawing on his conclusions in the Armenian and Nazi case studies, and the confirming evidence in the destruction of the Kulaks and in the Cambodian "autogenocide," Professor Melson analyzes, in a final chapter, the processes linking revolution, war, and total domestic genocide (presumably in plural societies). But the argument is carefully qualified, since there are revolutions and wars that do not produce genocide. Revolution and war, though necessary conditions, are not sufficient in themselves. They are only potentially genocidal, depending on many variables that influence the final result.

Ideology, in interaction with structural conditions, is one of these variables, particularly in the manner in which the excluded groups are defined. Is the taint ineradicable as in antisemitic and racial ideologies, or the perception of the Armenians in the ideology of Turkish nationalism, or of social background as in Stalinism and the Khmer Rouge annihilation of the middle classes, the compradore bourgeoisie? Or can the excluded group be reeducated or treated by other measures less drastic, such as territorial segregation or expulsion?

A further significant variable related impending war to the probability of genocide, when the excluded group is believed to have links to the enemy either through its diaspora or through betrayal, as in the Armenian case. And the Nazi view of Russia and communism as tools of the "Jewish World Conspiracy" rendered all Jews everywhere, and above all in Russia, targets for annihilation. Charges of international conspiracy were, of course, common in Stalinist Russia against excluded groups or individuals or those categorized as enemies of the people, or against the Kulaks, or Ukrainian leaders during the Great Famine. The personality of the leaders is also significant, whether motivated by paranoid fantasies or firmly opposed to the final solution of annihilation. A further variable is the vulnerability of the victims, which renders them an ideal target for persecution and as scapegoats.

This study is distinctive for the quality of its scholarship and the originality of its contribution. This is the first study that links the Holocaust and the Armenian Genocide as examples of total domestic genocide and explores the role of revolution and war. These often appear in the literature in narrative form. Professor Melson's contribution, however, lies in the exploration of the manner in which they may facilitate total domestic genocide by providing "ideological vanguards with an opportunity to come to power and to refashion the identity of the society and the system of legitimation." The general principles he advances should open up a rich and creative field for future research.

Professor Melson concludes his study with a quotation from the Algerian French writer Camus who risked his life to bring about conciliation between the warring parties in his native country, and who provided us with the ordeal of Sisyphus as symbolic of the endless struggle against oppression and for justice, of which his own life was a most eloquent expression. "Nothing," he wrote, "is given to men and the little they can conquer is paid with unjust deaths. But man's greatness lies elsewhere. It lies in his decision to be stronger than his condition. And if his condition is unjust, he has only one way of overcoming it, which is to be just himself."

Reflecting on this quotation, I remembered that Professor Melson had told me that he concluded his course on the Holocaust with reference to Philip Hallie's book *Lest Innocent Blood Be Shed*. This was the story of the French Huguenot village of Le Chambon which rescued many Jewish refugees during the Vichy and Nazi occupations. The moral lessons to his class were "to draw out the generous, universal, loving aspect of your tradition. Love the stranger as yourself."

I then settled down to read Hallie's book. It was most impressive, a welcome correction to my opening comments expressing the somewhat jaundiced view of extreme suffering as alienating. Here were the descendants of the Protestants, who had experienced the most horrendous persecution of their faith, responding to the desperate need of others at great risk to their own survival. It was enough for them to see the need in the eyes of those they rescued.

This book and Professor Melson's life and career and human concern recalled to me Lifton and Markusen's concept of Species Mentality, which they contrasted with Genocidal Mentality. They described Species Mentality as "an expansion of collective awareness, an altered sense of self, that embraces our reality as members of a single species."

May Species Mentality prevail in a world torn by lethal ethnic conflict, and by religious persecution, with starvation used as a genocidal weapon, and a vigorous arms trade in more and more deadly annihilatory weapons.

Leo Kuper
Professor Emeritus
University of California, Los Angeles

October 1991

PREFACE

Defenseless under the night
Our world in stupor lies;
Yet, dotted everywhere,
Ironic points of light
Flash out wherever the Just
Exchange their messages:
May I, composed like them
Of eros and of dust,
Beleaguered by the same
Negation and Despair,
Show an affirming flame.

W. H. Auden
"September 1, 1939"

This book compares the Holocaust to the Armenian Genocide in order to try to answer the questions, Why did genocide happen in these two instances, and why does it happen at all? Our goal is to identify some of the deadly intentions and circumstances that turn ordinary human beings into killers and their victims.

Although the Holocaust stands apart in modern consciousness as the apotheosis of mass destruction, the Armenian Genocide resembles it in significant ways. As in the case of the Final Solution, a regime formulated a public policy whose intent was the physical destruction of the Armenian community and its elimination from the society, culture, and politics of the Ottoman Empire. Both the Holocaust and the Armenian Genocide were the quintessential examples of total domestic genocide, what the United Nations has called "genocide-in-whole" to distinguish such instances from "genocide-in-part."

This book seeks to compare the histories of these two instances, including their suggestive similarities and significant differences. The main aims of this work are to help clarify their common causes and to formulate a credible explanatory framework for genocide-in-whole or total domestic genocide. Indeed, this study proposes that such mass murder may best be understood as a complex process that is set in motion by revolution and war.

Revolutionary governments that come to power after the breakdown of old regimes need to create a new order that will support the revolutionary state. Desiring to reconstruct the polity according to their own views, revolutionary vanguards are likely to label some groups as the "people," "the class," "the nation," or "the race," that is, those who support the revolution and from whom the new regime derives its legitimacy. By the same token, revolutionary regimes are also likely to label other groups as the "enemies of the revolution and the people." Such enemies may become candidates for repression and even genocide.

The likelihood that the outcome of a revolution will include genocide increases with war when the domestic "enemies of the revolution" come to be identified with external foes of the revolutionary regime. Especially vulnerable are communal groups and classes that are despised by society at large while, at the same time, they seem able to succeed in the modern world. When a revolutionary regime can identify such "problem" collectivities with its domestic and international enemies, in the absence of other alternatives it may turn to "final solutions."

Clearly it is not the case that every revolution leads to genocide or that every genocide in history has occurred because of revolution. It is likely, however, as this work tries to show, that in the modern world total genocides have mainly been launched by revolutionary states seeking to transform society in their image. In addition to the Armenian Genocide and the Holocaust, the two other examples that may be cited are the destruction of the Kulaks by the Stalinists and the "autogenocide" of the Khmer Rouge.

In our era not only have millions of innocent human beings been slaughtered, usually by their own governments espousing bizarre worldviews, but genocide has revealed to us aspects of human behavior so terrible that one begins to question the worth of the human enterprise. After experiencing or otherwise becoming aware of genocidal bestiality and irrationality, one begins to dream of a world without people, a primordial world of plants and animals where pain exists but cruelty does not, where killing occurs out of necessity—not out of malice, paranoid fantasy, or blind commitment to a political faith. Despite the understandable dread one feels in dealing with such a topic, one needs to face up to the fact that genocide, mass murder, is part of human history, and thus in principle explainable in broadly historical terms.

There is, however, a danger implicit in the search for understanding the mainsprings of the Holocaust and genocide. In our eagerness for closure, for putting the past behind us, we run the danger of oversimplifying the events and thereby trivializing them. Writing of the casual manner in which terms like "genocide," "holocaust," and "Auschwitz" have been used in our time, Peter Gay has remarked: "Such trivializing of the awesome is itself evidence that the world is a beastly place—impatient with precision, anxious to set memories aside, callous, heartlessly forgetful."[1]

Indeed, for some survivors of genocide the very attempt at explanation is a form of transgression, if not violence. This is so because they believe that events like the Holocaust or the Armenian Genocide are inherently inexplicable—the product of heinous, radically evil minds and spirits. Moreover, the very attempt at explanation may be both a distancing of oneself from the victims and an expression of empathy for the killers. Understanding may be an attempt at affirming life beyond the murders, but it is an affirmation that—given the horror—may be both false and a sacrilege.

I come to the question of genocide both through personal experience and scholarly reflection. On 12 October 1941, *Einsatzgruppe D*, a special formation of the SS and other units, massacred most of the Jews in the little Polish town of Stanislawov. My parents and I were those who survived; I was four years old at the time. We survived because my parents mistrusted the Germans' motives and refused to go to the place of assembly. Later, because we looked Slavic, we were able to acquire false papers of identity and to pass as non-Jews until the end of the war. Most other Jews were less lucky. My grandparents, my mother's parents, living in Warsaw perished in Treblinka. My grandfather, my father's father, had been killed by the Gestapo even before the massacre of 12 October. Other relatives who were killed I never knew or do not remember.

When I became older and tried to think about what had happened to my family and to all those who had been killed for no reason other than the accident of their birth, I would become so overcome that I simply could not sustain thinking about what others called "the Holocaust." The memory was a trauma, a "wounding experience," not to be "understood" but simply endured.

In 1966, when I was in my late twenties, thousands of Ibos were massacred in Northern Nigeria. Later, during the civil war that lasted from 1967 until 1970, some one million, perhaps as many as two million, people starved to death. They perished because the Federal Military Government (FMG) refused to lift the blockade that would have relieved the defenders, and the Biafrans refused to surrender.

In 1965, a year before the onset of these massacres, I had returned to America from Nigeria where I had done my fieldwork on the country's labor movement as part of the requirement for a doctorate in political science at the Massachusetts Institute of Technology. As did so many of my generation growing up in the late 1950s and 1960s, I had hoped that Africa, the Third World, would avoid the recent horrors of Europe. Gail Freedman, who was then finishing up at Radcliffe, had joined me in Ibadan, where we were married. It was a promising and happy time.

Soon after we returned to America, the killings began. Their reality was brought home to me in a nondescript hotel room in New York. At a meeting of the African Studies Association, I ran into a Nigerian acquaintance, a trade unionist I knew from Lagos. We went up to his room with some other people, and over a beer I asked him about Gogo Chu Nzeribe, a trade unionist I had interviewed and respected. "Gogo? Haven't you heard? Some troops came to his house in Ikeja and clubbed him to death." The conversation continued to swirl about me, but I no longer heard. Gogo was dead. When I had first met him he had seemed indestructible. Not tall, but solid and broad, with the shoulders of a linebacker. He was very canny, very smart about Nigeria and the world. He had an explosive sense of humor and a certain generosity of spirit. When that night I heard that he had been killed, it was as if the twenty years after the Second World War had been compressed into a few minutes. I felt as if the war had never ended, and it was no use trying to escape it in Africa or elsewhere.

When I realized that Ibos like Gogo were being slaughtered for no other reason than their ethnicity, I could not help making the connection between my family's experience and their own. I wholeheartedly supported the Biafran secession and was convinced that, should it fail, Ibos would be massacred by the Nigerians. Thankfully, I and others who thought like I did were wrong. The Nigerians were not Nazis, and the Ibos were not Jews. When the Nigerians proved victorious, their peace terms were humane and generous. But from then on I knew I had to return to the Holocaust to try to make sense of it both at the level of personal emotion and in some broader comparative intellectual perspective.

Thinking through what had happened in Biafra I realized that this instance of mass death was in some essential ways not comparable to the Holocaust—for one thing the FMG had no intention of exterminating the Ibos or of destroying them as a collectivity. Indeed, when I tried to find instances of comparison for the Holocaust, I settled not on Biafra but on the Armenian Genocide as the case that most closely resembled it.

In 1977, seven years after the end of the Biafran war, and again in 1983, I spent a portion of a sabbatical year at the Harry S. Truman Institute of the Hebrew University, Jerusalem. It was there in an office that overlooked the Judean desert and the Dead Sea that I started in earnest on the work of comparing the Holocaust to the Armenian Genocide. It felt like an appropriate place for such a project.

In Jerusalem I had the opportunity to discuss my work with scholars like Professors Israel Guttman, Shmuel Almog, Yehuda Bauer, and the late Shmuel Ettinger, some of them survivors who had devoted their lives to the study of the Holocaust and antisemitism. I also took the opportunity to reacquaint myself with Professor S. N. Eisenstadt, my old teacher from MIT and Harvard, who is the preeminent authority on comparative historical sociology—a field crucial to this study. At other times I was shown about the Armenian quarter in Jerusalem by George Hintlian, secretary to the patriarchate. There I was introduced to Professor Vahakn N. Dadrian, a lifetime student of the Armenian Genocide, who has been a mentor and a colleague ever since. These scholars' lucid and skeptical questions have kept me busy for years.

In the spring of 1990, together with other researchers from around the world, I was invited by the Academy of Sciences of the Armenian Soviet Socialist Republic to Yerevan to participate in a commemorative scholarly conference on the Armenian Genocide. On 24 April, the day that Armenians memorialize the genocide, I stood in silence with my colleagues from the conference among thousands of people who were commemorating their dead and the loss of their lands.

I have sketched out a portion of the personal road I traveled before coming to this study in order to help clarify my motives. These do not spring from a desire to trivialize the Holocaust by spuriously universalizing human suffering and denying its unique and perhaps unfathomable characteristics. Nor do they arise out of a personal animus against any group or nation.

Having completed this study—one writes the preface at the end of a work—I am more convinced than ever that the capacity to perpetrate genocide is not limited to one culture or one people but is an inherent potential of the human condition. The task before us is to explain those special political and other circumstances that turn ordinary men and women into killers and victims.

Partial explanations like the one I propose in this book will not bring the dead back to life, nor undo the cruelty, but at least they may help us—I mean all of us who have been struck forever by the terrible knowledge of these events—to deal with our memories and to become, in Auden's phrase, "an affirming flame." Beyond that—are we expecting too much?—by linking causes to effects, valid explanations may serve as warnings of human crimes and disasters to come.

Acknowledgments

I wish to acknowledge with many thanks support from the Memorial Foundation for Jewish Culture; the Purdue University Center for Humanistic Study; the Purdue University Jewish Studies Program; the Harry S. Truman Institute, Hebrew University; the Center for International Affairs, Harvard University; and the Center for International Studies, MIT. Without such financial and institutional help this study could not have been completed.

In this context I would like especially to thank a number of friends and colleagues who helped with institutional and/or financial arrangements: David A. Caputo, Naomi Chazan, Samuel P. Huntington, Edy Kaufman, Moshe Ma'oz, Dalia Shemer, Myron Weiner, and Zvi Schiffrin.

My professional training is in comparative politics. I cannot claim to be an expert in Armenian, Ottoman, Turkish, Jewish, and German history—all areas crucial to this study. I am most grateful to the following friends and colleagues who steered me to the appropriate literatures and who invested their valuable time in criticizing various parts of the manuscript. Their help was invaluable, and without it I could not have completed this book. It goes without saying that they did not always agree with my interpretations, and if there are any errors and mistakes in the manuscript they are my own.

For help with Armenian, Ottoman, and Turkish history, I wish to thank Victor Azarya, Kevork Bardakjian, Vahakn N. Dadrian, Alan Fisher, George Hintlian, Richard G. Hovannisian, Gerard J. Libaridian, James Reid, Ronald G. Suny, Manoog Young, and Marvin Zonis.

For help with Jewish and German history, I wish to thank Shmuel Almog, the late Larry Axel, Yehuda Bauer, Christopher R. Browning,

Todd M. Endelman, the late Shmuel Ettinger, Erich Goldhagen, Israel Guttman, Steven Katz, Jacques Kornberg, Richard S. Levy, and Gordon Mork.

Still other friends and scholars helped in clarifying some of the comparative, theoretical, legal, moral, or even personal aspects of this work. Among these I wish to thank Michel Abitbol, Robert Bartlett, Louis René Beres, Herta R. Bernbach, David A. Caputo, Frank Chalk, Israel W. Charny, Naomi Chazan, Fritz Cohen, Karl W. Deutsch, Mark U. Edwards, Jr., S. N. Eisenstadt, Joseph Haberer, Myron Q. Hale, David Hawk, Walter Hirsch, Willard R. Johnson, Kurt Jonassohn, Steven Kaplan, Edy Kaufman, Leo Kuper, Robert McDaniel, Richard E. Melson, Eric Nordlinger, Lucian W. Pye, Dov Ronen, Richard L. Sklar, Gregory H. Stanton, William Shaffer, Roger W. Smith, Michael A. Weinstein, Frank L. Wilson, Gordon Young, and Shimshon Zelniker.

Helen Fein was one of the two principal readers of this manuscript for the University of Chicago Press. I would like to thank her and the first reader for incisive comments that helped to strengthen this work. In this connection I am most grateful to John Tryneski and Lila Weinberg, senior editor and senior manuscript editor at the University of Chicago Press, and to Randy Petilos, editorial associate, for shepherding this book to completion. Evan Ellis, graduate assistant at Purdue University, helped with the copyediting.

From this list I would like especially to single out Richard G. Hovannisian, Jacques Kornberg, and Richard S. Levy who spent hours of their valuable time critiquing the manuscript and making extensive suggestions for revision. Though I did not always agree with their comments, they taught me lessons in collegial generosity and personal and professional integrity.

Finally, I thank my wife, Gail Freedman Melson, for helping me to edit the book and to clarify its intellectual content. Her love, intelligence, and good humor, and those of my children, Sara and Josh, helped this family to complete a long and difficult project.

ONE

Introduction: Overview and Major Themes

Men make their own history, but they do not make it as they please; they do not make it under circumstances chosen by themselves, but under circumstances directly encountered, given, and transmitted from the past.

Karl Marx[1]

It may be that, without the pressure of social forces political ideas are still born: what is certain is that these forces, unless they clothe themselves in ideas remain blind and undirected.

Isaiah Berlin[2]

The twentieth century has been a murderous era. Tens of millions of noncombatants have been killed, not necessarily for what they did or failed to do but for their collective identity and their ascribed group membership. Indeed, not long after the Second World War, even as a few survivors, scholars, and others tried to grasp the enormity of Nazi crimes, they became aware of fresh instances of mass murder as well as other catastrophes that have come to light from the recent past. Among the mass destructions that followed the war one thinks of the communal, class, and political massacres in Indonesia, Biafra, Burundi, and Rwanda, Lebanon, Sudan, and Ethiopia, and especially of the Cambodian "auto-genocide." Among mass murders that preceded the war one recalls the destruction of the Kulaks, the Ukrainian famine, the daily dying in the Gulag, and the Armenian Genocide.[3]

Although the Holocaust stands apart in modern consciousness as the apotheosis of mass destruction and is in many ways wholly unique, it

1

bears enough similarity to recent acts of mass murder to warrant a comparative study of the phenomenon. This is the basic assumption of the essay that follows. Needless to say, the point of such comparison is not to diminish the events themselves, certainly not to relativize the crimes of the perpetrators, but rather to try to shed light on the empirical conditions, the underlying pattern of empirical similarity, that led to genocide in the past and may lead to it in the future.

This Introduction is meant as an overview and overture. Some of the major themes that are only sketchily raised here will be taken up again in greater detail in what follows. The chapter is divided into eight sections. The first argues that the Armenian Genocide resembles the Holocaust in significant ways. The second touches on the comparative historical method. The third section briefly discusses several explanations that have been proposed for genocide. The fourth briefly presents a conceptual framework suggesting that genocide, including the Holocaust, is related to revolution. The fifth and sixth sections define genocide and revolution. The seventh discusses the uniqueness of the Holocaust and the claim that it cannot be compared to any other event. Finally, the eighth section outlines the plan of the study.

The Armenian Genocide and the Holocaust

The Armenian Genocide and the Holocaust were the quintessential instances of genocide in the modern era. [4] Three reasons may be cited for this claim. First, these were instances of what we shall call "total genocide" or what the United Nations has called "genocide-in-whole" to distinguish such instances from massacre and "genocide-in-part." [5] Both catastrophes were the products of state-initiated policies whose intended and actual results were the elimination of the Armenian community from the Ottoman Empire and of the Jewish community from most of Europe, respectively. Second, both victimized groups were ethnoreligious communal minorities that had been partially integrated and assimilated into the larger society. Their destruction was not only a war against foreign strangers, it was a mass murder that commenced with an attack on an internal domestic segment of the state's own society. Thus the Armenian Genocide and the Holocaust were instances not only of total genocide but of what we shall refer to as *total domestic genocide*—to differentiate these two cases from the genocide of foreign groups, that is, foreign with regard to the borders of the state. Third, Armenians and Jews were unmistakably communal or ethnic groups, not classes or political groups whose inclusion under the UN definition of genocide has generated some controversy. These three points need some elaboration.

As will be discussed in Chapter 5, the Armenian Genocide resembles the Holocaust in that it was an instance of a policy whose intent was to destroy a communal group by killing its members and obliterating its identity in all of its aspects. This was an instance of total genocide that differed from other instances of partial genocide or communal massacre like that of the Ibos in Northern Nigeria, the Hutu in Burundi, the Muslims and Hindus in India, or the Palestinians and Christians in Lebanon.

Furthermore, in distinguishing the Armenian Genocide and the Holocaust from other cases of genocide, one needs to recall that history records other examples of peoples who were exterminated or whose identities were wiped out by force. For the most part, however, these other instances of mass murder of peoples and the destruction of their identities were the products of invading armies wishing to seize their land, to enslave them, or to convert them to their religions. Many examples might be cited, such as the depredations of the Athenians against Melos, of the Romans against Carthage, of Tamerlane, Genghis Khan, and the European colonization of the New World, Africa, and Tasmania.[6] In none of these instances, however, did a state devise a public policy designed to destroy a major communal component of its own society.

The men of Melos were not Athenians; the Carthagenians were not Romans; Native Americans, Africans, and Tasmanians were not Europeans; but the Armenians had been an ancient community integral to the Ottoman Empire preceding modern Turkey, and the Jews had been emancipated citizens of Imperial Germany since 1871. To destroy such partially assimilated and integrated communities, the perpetrators had to devise ideological excuses and methods of mass murder that had not been previously used. Though the Nazis pursued the Jews in areas beyond Germany, it was their original attempt to destroy German Jews that made the Holocaust a domestic genocide that spread to the international arena. Thus the Armenian Genocide and the Holocaust were instances of total and domestic genocide.

Last, both the Armenian Genocide and the Holocaust bear striking resemblance to the total destruction of classes like the Kulaks and the urban Cambodians.[7] Initially, these have not been used as primary instances of comparison to the Holocaust because they are examples of the destruction of classes rather than of communal groups, and under some

definitions they would not qualify as "genocide." Under a broader definition of genocide that will be formulated here, however, these two examples will be used in Chapter 9 as confirming cases for propositions
derived from an analysis of the Armenian Genocide and the Holocaust.

Thus, it is because of their intrinsic importance as well as their essential similarity and their joint difference from other instances of destruction that we have chosen these two cases for examination and comparison. The point of this comparison is to find suggestive parallels
between the two cases that might generate an explanatory framework
that would apply to these two instances and to others like them. It should
be noted at the outset, however, that emphasizing their similarity in no
way implies that the Armenian Genocide and the Holocaust were equivalent events. Indeed, as will be shown, there were significant differences
not only between these two examples of total domestic genocide and
other instances of mass murder, but there were notable and instructive
differences between these two cases as well.

Comparative History

The main goal of this study is not to add new historical information
to what is already known. What is sought is a conceptual framework from
which might be derived some credible and insightful propositions that
would apply not only to the two instances under investigation but to
others as well. The procedures of this study, therefore, employ the methods of comparative history as applied to a few selected cases. In such an
endeavor "the investigator assumes that causal regularities—at least regularities of limited scope—may be found in history."[8] On the one hand,
this approach tries to avoid "the interpretive tendency to attribute self-
contained significance to each individual context";[9] on the other hand,
unlike grand theory building whose test is its universality, comparative
history concerns itself with propositions valid only within specific historical time periods. The time period that brackets the present essay is
that of capitalism and the emergence of the modern state.[10]

By analyzing more than one case, comparative analysis hopes to
suggest general patterns. At the same time it should be noted that there
are limits to what comparative analysis of a few cases can do. It cannot
prove that its propositions are valid, it can only suggest their truth.
Furthermore, it must rely on histories written by others. Since such histories for the most part were not written with comparative analysis in
mind, there is always the danger of gross oversimplification and the omission of essential elements. This is certainly a pitfall of the present study.

4

In brief, the approach offered here relies on the comparative historical method—one informed by political and social science—that empirically compares selected cases of total domestic genocide and seeks to arrive at an explanation that would fit such cases and others like them. To this end the Armenian Genocide and the Holocaust have been selected as emblematic of total domestic genocide in the modern period. Other cases that will be discussed as confirming examples are the destruction of the Kulaks by the Stalinist regime and the "autogenocide" in Cambodia. The extermination of the Gypsies by the Nazis also constitutes a total genocide as that will be defined.

In limiting the base of comparison to instances of total domestic genocide, this approach differs from some statistical studies that use cross-national data and enlarge the number of cases.[11] We have chosen to reduce the sample of cases to "total domestic genocides" as against "massacres," "politicides," and "partial genocides," as these will be defined below, because in this study we are concerned with explaining the narrower complex phenomenon known as "total domestic genocide" rather than the broader phenomenon of genocide in general.[12] Nevertheless, it is hoped that by shedding light on the narrower range of cases more general studies will also be illuminated.

Explanations for Genocide

The major explanations for the Holocaust, the Armenian Genocide, and for genocide in general are complex and cannot be given justice in a brief introduction. In taking an overview, however, one is struck by how often four kinds of factors are stressed. Two of these apply especially to the Holocaust, one to the Armenian Genocide, and one to genocide in general. When explaining the Holocaust, one explanation centers primarily on Nazi ideology, which itself had "roots" in racism and earlier forms of antisemitism. Meanwhile, an alternative explanation of the same phenomena stresses that, although Hitler's ideology may have been important for legitimating decisions, the main sources of the Final Solution derived from the exigencies and the cumulative radicalization of the machinery of destruction whose main task was to solve the "Jewish Problem." Neither the "intentionalist" nor the "functionalist," as the first and second approaches have been labeled, would argue that it was the Jewish victims themselves who provoked the Holocaust.[13]

Surprisingly, however, that is precisely what some respected analyses of the Armenian Genocide imply. A number of influential studies of Ottoman and Turkish history have suggested that the Armenian Genocide had little to do with the ideology of the Young Turks and the Committee of Union and Progress (CUP) that came to power in 1908, or with the exigencies and dynamics of the organizations that were saddled with solving the "Armenian Question." Instead, they assert that its origins lay in the provocative behavior of the victims themselves.[14] Finally, other scholarly works of the general phenomenon of genocide have emphasized the role of the modern national state and society. As a variation on the theme, some have emphasized the connection between genocide and the totalitarian state.[15]

Thus the ideology of the perpetrators, the functional needs and dynamics of the organizations actually carrying out the genocide, the provocative behavior of the victims, and the role of the modern state and society are often cited as principal factors in explanations of genocide. It may be pointed out that such explanations are not necessarily wrong, but they are insufficient to account for genocide. We shall touch on each of these explanations below.

Ideology

The motivations and other causes leading to the Holocaust remain a puzzle. The principal reason for the mystery lies in the irrationality of the motives: Why did the Nazis want to destroy the Jews? The question is simple enough, but the answers suggested are not. Unless one believed as the Nazis did that the Jews were masters of the Communist and capitalist worlds, that they had caused the First World War and Germany's defeat, and that they were an imminent threat to every German, there were few practical or instrumental reasons for killing Jews, and many reasons for not doing so.

In Germany, Jews constituted less than 1 percent of the population. Though they were seldom accepted as equals, a majority had acculturated and assimilated to German culture and society. While some were Communists—as were other Germans—most Jews supported socialist, liberal, conservative, and even nationalist parties, excluding the Nazis. In the Great War many had served with distinction or fallen on behalf of the Fatherland. Why then the hatred and contempt for Jews? Why the fear and horror that they provoked? Why the murders? Indeed, why is it that in the war's most crucial battle, which was to turn the tide against Germany, troop trains were diverted from Stalingrad to the Final Solution? Why at this juncture did genocide take precedence even over winning the war with Russia?[16]

The usual explanation for this state of affairs is "ideology." The

Nazis did not act in a rational, instrumental manner when it came to the Jews because they were driven by racialist antisemitism. To understand the origins of the Holocaust, therefore, one would need to uncover the sources and the appeal of this worldview; for it was not what the Jews did or failed to do that mattered, it was what the Germans imagined them to be that determined their fate.

No doubt ideology played an indispensable role in the Holocaust. It provided the conceptual framework, the cognitive map, the "warrant for genocide" that gave the Nazis the illusion that they had located the sources of defeat, crisis, and disintegration besetting Germany.[17] It also provided part of the élan that the Nazis needed to fight the enemy they had discovered or, better yet, whom they had constructed. In a revealing comment, after reading the notorious forgery *The Protocols of the Elders of Zion*, Himmler wrote in his diary, "This [is] a book that explains everything and tells us whom we must fight next time."[18]

Relying on ideology alone as the main explanation for historical events, however, raises at least three important questions: (1) What is the source of the ideology itself? Where did it come from? (2) Why was it believed? And this is most important: (3) What if anything does ideology have to do with action and behavior? What was the connection between antisemitism and genocide?

Ideology and Policy

The question of how Nazi antisemitism actually became translated into a public policy of destruction called the "Final Solution" has in recent years divided historians into "intentionalists," those who emphasize the ideology and role of the führer, and "functionalists," those who stress the needs and dynamics of organizations.[19] Although this is not the place to explore the details of the debate, its general outlines may be sketched out.

Intentionalists, like Dawidowicz and Fleming, trace the origins of the Holocaust straight to Hitler's intentions as articulated in his pathological antisemitism.[20] Though they admit that the Third Reich was not as monolithic as it appeared to outsiders; nevertheless, so goes the argument, the führer dominated the major institutions of the party, the SS, the government, the army, and industry. Without his vision and will these structures would not have become the machinery of destruction that implemented the Final Solution.

Intentionalists recognize that in its early stages of operations Hitler's machinery of destruction may have tried other policies, like expulsion and deportation, but these were stopgap measures. They derived not from Hitler's vacillations, or from the system experimenting with various other "options" short of extermination, but from the führer waiting for an opportune moment to carry out his fixed objectives. That moment came with the invasion of Russia. According to Hitler's chiliastic and Manichean worldview, war with Russia meant, in effect, the final battle with the "Jewish World Conspiracy." Such a war was no ordinary struggle but a titanic conflict between the forces of good and evil. The defeat of Russia and the extermination of the Jews would bring on the Thousand Year Reich and the triumph of the good.[21]

First, special forces, *Einsatzgruppen*, were dispatched to destroy Russian Jewry. They followed the army and massacred the Jews by mass shootings over open graves. Shortly after, as the policy of extermination was extended to all of occupied Europe and even beyond, death camps were built. Here the killing could proceed in a more organized, efficient, and secret manner.

It is no great surprise, say the intentionalists, that there does not seem to exist a document signed by Hitler specifically ordering the Final Solution. The führer did not work that way. He seldom put his more important orders in writing. Instead, he relied on oral directives to trusted henchmen like Himmler. Nor is it a mystery that he was not involved in all the details of the genocide. These he left to his subordinates, but without him and his charismatic persona, his inflexible will, and his pathological antisemitism, there would have been no Holocaust.

The Needs and Dynamics of Organizations

The functionalists give the story a different twist. They do not dismiss Hitler, nor antisemitism, but they see Hitler as a rather distant figure whose ideology allowed him to set a general framework for action rather than to specify particular policies. They shift their focus of attention away from the führer and the elite levels of the institutional system to the middle and lower strata that were intent on translating general and sometimes vague directives into practical actions.

The bureaucrats, party hacks, and SS stalwarts from the nether world of the Third Reich arrived at the Final Solution in order to meet both what they thought were Hitler's expectations and to resolve organizational problems, once other less drastic measures like deportations became impossible to implement. Indeed, the picture drawn by the functionalists is that of a Third Reich careening toward the Final Solution, not because it was finely tuned to do so by Hitler but because of a vicious competition among institutional spheres to "solve" the Jewish Question in the most efficient and expeditious manner. Echoing an argument made earlier by Raul Hilberg and Hannah Arendt, the functionalists argued that an amoral professionalism and a perverted devotion to duty were as likely to account for the Final Solution as was antisemitism. [22]

Although intentionalists and functionalists both have attempted to explain how the decision to implement the Final Solution might have been formulated, two things need to be pointed out about their controversy: first, their arguments are not mutually exclusive; and second, neither position, nor even both together, provide an adequate and complete explanation for the origins of the Holocaust.

We shall discuss this point more fully in Chapter 7, but it is impossible to account for the Holocaust without including both antisemitism as an ideology, especially as formulated in Hitler's writings and pronouncements, and the enthusiastic cooperation of those who at every level manned the machinery of destruction. Both elements were crucial to the Final Solution. The Nazis' worldview as articulated by the führer provided the mandate for the formulation of general policy and the revolutionary creed that guided the actions of his true believers. By the same token, the Nazi fanatics and opportunists in charge of the Jewish Question not only translated Hitler's intentions, or what they thought were his desires, into policy, they also anticipated his wishes and devised some of the methods of destruction that were later given his stamp of approval.

There can be no denying that antisemitism as an ideology, with Hitler as its fanatical exponent, and the machinery of destruction both played necessary roles in the Holocaust. Consider the counterfactual alternative: Would there have been a Holocaust without antisemitism, or without Hitler, or without the party and bureaucratic structures that implemented the destruction? The problem with identifying Hitler's intentions and the exigencies and dynamics of the machinery of destruction with a causal analysis of the Holocaust is that these neglect other essential factors. Chief among these are the circumstances under which the Nazis were able to come to power and to implement their ideological preferences into a public policy of the German state.

For the Holocaust to become a policy of the Third Reich, it was not enough for Hitler to wish to destroy the Jews, nor even for a party and a bureaucracy to implement or to anticipate his wishes. Without state power Hitler would have remained a harmless crank, and without the opportune context provided by the German revolution and the Second

World War, the institutional spheres of the German state and society would not have been organized into a machinery of destruction against the Jews. As will be suggested in Chapters 6 and 7, it was the German revolution that destroyed the systems of legitimate authority that had existed under Imperial Germany and the Weimar Republic and propelled the Nazis to power. Moreover, it was the vacuum in legitimate authority created by the revolution that allowed the Nazis to substitute their own myth of legitimacy resting on antisemitism, racism, and *Lebensraum*. Acting in the name of that new authority, the Nazi regime then perpetrated world war and genocide.

Thus the causal analysis of the Holocaust points to historical, structural, and contextual factors transcending both Nazi ideology and Hitler's personality as the intentionalists stress, and the exigencies of the machinery of destruction that the functionalists emphasize. As will be suggested below, on the one hand, it points to an analysis of a revolutionary interregnum in Germany that allowed the Nazis to come to power and to transform German political culture; and, on the other hand, to the world war that radicalized German intentions and their policies toward the Jews. We shall return to these points presently; meanwhile, we shall encounter other problems in the explanations that have been advanced for the Armenian Genocide.

The Provocation Thesis

Though we shall discuss the provocation thesis more fully in Chapter 5, its main features can be sketched out here: in contrast to works that trace the causes of genocide to the motives and ideology of the perpetrators, a number of influential studies dealing with the Armenian Genocide continue to derive it from the supposedly provocative behavior of the victims themselves. [23] Briefly, it is contended that the Armenian Genocide was due to the intolerable threat that the Armenians posed to the Ottoman Empire and to the Committee of Union and Progress which came to power in 1908.

The provocation thesis assumes that the issue between the Turks and Armenians was that of two national movements in desperate conflict over the eastern provinces of Turkey, an area that each considered to be the very heartland of its people. In this view Armenians were a Christian national minority living, unfortunately for them, on both sides of the Turkish-Russian border. Like the other minorities of the Ottoman Empire, they got caught up in the nationalism of the period and began to make demands for self-determination. Hence, like the Serbs, Bulgarians, Albanians, and Greeks, and later the Arabs, their desire for self-determination would necessarily lead to secession. Whereas the departure of the other nationalities was a blow to the power and prestige of the Ottoman Empire, the secession of Armenia would mean the death of Turkey. This was the situation even before the war with Russia.

Once the First World War began, however, and Russian troops were poised to invade Turkey, the frightening possibility appeared that the Armenians would join the Russians, and Turkey would be destroyed. Hence, the Armenian danger had to be eliminated. It was this threatening situation that, while not justifying them, created the conditions for the deportations of the Armenians to the Syrian desert and their ensuing destruction. A major component of the threat that drove the Young Turks to commit genocide, so goes the argument, was Armenian nationalism; hence, it can be said that Armenians provoked their own fate.

The discussion in Chapter 5 will show that the problem with the provocation thesis derives from its exaggerating the extent and threat of Armenian nationalism, while underestimating the role that Turkish nationalism and the ideology of Pan-Turkism played in the genocide. Some accounts of the Turkish revolution that commenced in 1908 stress its role in transforming Ottoman and Muslim into Turkish identity.[24] The Young Turks ushered in a nationalist revolution wherein both the Ottomanism and the Pan-Islam of the old regime were swept away by Turkish nationalism. The people who had been formerly Muslim Ottomans living in Turkey came to view themselves as "Turks." It may be assumed that this transformation in the identity of the majority had fateful consequences for the minority.

When Muslim Ottomans had become Turks, they came to perceive Armenians not as a millet, a traditional Ottoman community, the most loyal in the realm, but as a separate nation just like they had become. Thus the alleged popularity and intensity of Armenian nationalism was in part a projection of the Young Turks themselves. Indeed, it may be suggested that the intolerable threat that the Young Turks experienced derived not from Armenian actions but from their own constructions about the Armenians. Moreover, it should be noted that by 1914 the Young Turks were not merely reacting as objects of real or imagined threats and provocations. They joined the Great War with alacrity and enthusiasm on the side of Imperial Germany against Russia. They hoped that victory in war would enable them to create a new homogeneous

Pan-Turkic empire stretching from Anatolia to China, rivaling in extent the old Ottoman Empire. Thus, as in the Holocaust, ideology, revolution, and world war played crucial roles in the Armenian Genocide.

The provocation thesis argues that something in the actions or the demeanor of the victims causes the perpetrator, the provoked party, to react with violence. The causal connection, though not explicit, assumes a linkage from the victim to the perpetrator, from the provocateur to the provoked. Had the Armenians behaved differently, had they acted less threateningly, the Young Turks would not have decided on genocide in 1915. By analogy, had there been fewer Jewish Communists, or bankers, or department store owners, or journalists, or beggars there would have been no Holocaust. To argue against this point of view does not at all imply that the victim is always a pure scapegoat whose motives and actions need never to be taken into account. It is to suggest that the motives, perceptions, constructions, and actions both of the attackers and their targets, as well as the circumstances under which they interact, must be examined for a complete explanation.

It is ironic that explanations for the Holocaust that stress the role of ideology tend to neglect the social forces and the structural conditions that allow ideological intentions to be translated into actions, while explanations for the Armenian Genocide emphasize social and historical forces while underplaying ideology. In the case of the Armenian Genocide, the ideology of the perpetrators is said to play no role. Their actions were completely determined by social forces like the self-determination of minorities, and historical circumstances like war. In dealing with the complex issues of the origins of genocide, one needs to keep in mind both Marx's injunction that human beings make history but not under conditions of their own choosing, as well as Isaiah Berlin's caveat that without ideas social forces remain blind and undirected.

The Modern State

A number of scholars who have attempted to formulate general explanations for genocide have singled out the modern state and society as the primary villains and perpetrators of that crime. Thus, for example, Kuper in his pioneering work has noted that it is the modern state's successful claim to a sovereign monopoly of force over a culturally plural and stratified territorial society that creates a potential for genocide, and prevents international organizations like the United Nations from acting on behalf of its victims. [25] And Roger W. Smith, citing Camus, stigmatized the twentieth century as "an age of politically sanctioned mass murder, of collective, premeditated death intended to serve the ends of the state."[26] This has been a sentiment echoed as well in the writings of Irving Louis Horowitz and others.[27] Since it is not the case, however, that every government has decided on a policy of genocide, the problem boils down to specifying the conditions under which some states commit that crime. One influential answer has been that only "totalitarian" states are capable of genocide; another suggestion has been that only states and societies under stress and in crisis commit genocide.

Totalitarianism and Genocide

A major point of Hannah Arendt's classic study was that totalitarian states, unlike other regimes, were not prepared to commit themselves to limited goals like territorial sovereignty, national integration, and economic development. Such states had transnational if not transcendent aspirations derived from their worldviews emphasizing Social Darwinism and "the Law of Nature," on the one hand, and class revolution and "the Law of History," on the other hand. Totalitarian states were in danger of pursuing the chimera of permanent war, global conquest, and genocide in that neither racial perfection nor the ultimate victory of the proletariat were attainable without world conquest and the destruction of defeated races and classes. "The Law of Nature or the Law of History, if properly executed is expected to produce mankind as its product; and this expectation lies behind the claim to global rule of all totalitarian movements."[28] In Arendt's analysis the logic of the totalitarian state led it beyond global conquest to permanent revolution and permanent genocide. As "Nature" generated new and more adaptable "races," and as "History" produced new and more productive classes, those who stood for the old order had to be subverted and ultimately destroyed. The totalitarian view of nature and social change implied no resting point and no permanent political order. It also implied permanent terror and genocide against all races and classes that were "fetters," to use a Marxist expression, on Nature and History. According to Arendt, therefore, totalitarian states obeyed what she called "the law of killing" or, in our terms, of "total genocide": "The law of killing by which totalitarian movements seize and exercise power would remain a law of movement even if they never succeeded in making all of humanity subject to their rule."[29] It cannot be denied that such nightmarish impulses toward a policy of permanent mass murder were present in the Nazi and Stalinist regimes, and that they may be active still in some revolutionary movements like the Khmer Rouge. Indeed, this was a major discovery of Arendt's work.

Thus it may be noted that, even as the Nazis were contemplating the extermination of European Jewry, they were formulating plans for the subjugation of Slavic "races" and the elimination of their leadership classes. Had they succeeded in the conquest of Russia, according to their racialist views, they would have had to continue in their quest for global domination. Having exterminated the Jews and enslaved the Slavs, they would have had to invent new categories of "unfit-to-live" and "slave races." Indeed, keeping in mind that Nazi mass killings commenced with a so-called "euthanasia" program targeting non-Jewish Germans, there was nothing in the Nazi worldview that spared potential categories of Germans themselves from such a program of destruction.[30]

Despite some objections, the concept of totalitarianism has been widely influential in the historiography and social science of the West since the Second World War. In this study the comparison of the Armenian Genocide and the Holocaust does not rest on that concept because it is too limited in scope: if only totalitarian regimes were capable of genocide, then either the Ottoman regime headed by the Committee of Union and Progress was totalitarian or it was incapable of true genocide. Since the CUP was not totalitarian in the sense of the Nazis or the Stalinists, and it did commit that crime, totalitarianism is not a useful concept for a comparative study of genocide.

Instead, without denying their historical reality, one might suggest that totalitarian systems themselves may be viewed as extreme variations on contemporary revolutionary regimes.[31] Two important differences between such regimes and other revolutionary governments are the scope of their ideology and ambitions, and their access to means of communication, persuasion, coercion, and control provided by modern industrial society. The scope of the ambitions of totalitarian revolutionaries like the Nazis and the Stalinists transcend the nation-state to include mankind as a whole, unlike, for example, the Young Turks who limited their operations to the Ottoman Empire and to Turkic peoples. Moreover, their enhanced capacity for coercion and control allow totalitarian revolutionaries to penetrate society more thoroughly than before and to impose their worldviews and their paranoid projections in a manner unimagined by revolutionaries in preindustrial societies like the Ottoman Young Turks or the French Jacobins.

In this section we called attention to the conditions under which modern states commit genocide, and we examined the suggestion that only totalitarian regimes commit that crime. Since other nontotalitarian governments are also quite capable of genocide, we questioned the utility of totalitarianism as a concept for our comparative purposes. Instead, we proposed that totalitarianism be subsumed under a broader notion of "revolutionary regime." Given this broader conception, we can compare the Ottoman Empire that gave rise to the Committee of Union and Progress to the Germany that engendered the Nazis and try to relate each to genocide. Since both the CUP and the Nazis were able to come to power in revolutionary situations, the broader implications is that genocide is related to revolution.

States and Societies in Crisis

It is apparent that genocide, in the sense that it becomes a policy of the state, does not take place under ordinary circumstances but under conditions of crisis for state and stress for society. This is a point that has been emphasized in the works of Fein and Harff on the one hand, and Mazian and Staub on the other.[32]

In the introduction to her work on the Holocaust, Fein compared some of the conditions leading to the Final Solution to those causing the Armenian Genocide. Among these she singled out "[an] elite that adapts a new political formula to justify the nation's domination and/or expansion, idealizing the singular rights of the dominant group, rises to power."[33] Such a new political formula, she suggested, was "most likely to be chosen by leaders of a state in which there is low underlying solidarity between major groups and a lack of correspondence between borders of the state and regions of settlement of the dominant nationality, and in which the state has suffered recent defeats or declines in territorial claims."[34] In another publication she referred to "ideological genocides," which she related to "hegemonic myths identifying the victims as outside the sanctioned universe of obligation."[35] Among the circumstances making for the institutionalization of such myths she singled out revolutionary or totalitarian regimes.

Similarly, in setting out an etiology of genocide, among a variety of factors Harff identified "national upheaval." Indeed, her conception of "national upheaval" comes very close to this study's notion of "revolution" as a structural precondition for genocide.

> National upheaval is an abrupt change in the political community, caused, for example, by the formation of a state through violent conflict, when national boundaries are reformed, or after a war is lost. Thus, lost wars and the resultant battered national pride sometimes lead to genocide against groups perceived as enemies.[36]

15

Mazian, a sociologist, attempted to adapt Neil Smelser's theory of collective behavior to an analysis of the Armenian Genocide and the Holocaust. She identified six factors that lead to genocide: (1) "creation of outsiders," (2) "internal strife," (3) "powerful leadership with territorial ambitions forming a monolithic and exclusionary party," (4) "destructive use of communication," (5) "organization of destruction," and (6) "failure of multidimensional levels of social control." *Why Genocide?* made an important point when it stressed that collective behavior like genocide follows a sequence of events that make the outcome cumulatively more likely (value-added approach).

Staub, a psychologist, elaborated a frustration-aggression theory of genocide that he applied to the Holocaust, the Armenian Genocide, and to other cases. Genocide and other forms of group violence are a function of "difficult life conditions," which can include economic problems, war, rapid changes in technology, social institutions, values, and ways of life. Such difficult life conditions can be experienced as a threat to a person's well-being and to his or her self-concept and values. Since difficult life conditions often cannot be changed directly, some people respond by scapegoating and harming others. The aggressive responses that are the result of difficult life conditions are themselves mediated by personal, cultural, and situational factors that help to determine their form and intensity. Staub's work is especially interesting in its discussion of the psychological and cultural intervening variables that link historically produced frustration to the aggression of genocide.

As will be seen, this study is indebted especially to the works of Fein and others who emphasize the crises and stresses of state and society as preconditions for genocide, but it also departs from their work in two main ways. First, it tries to relate revolution not to a large class of genocides but, on the contrary, to a small set of what we have called "total domestic genocides." This subset is small—including at most four or five cases—but important in that it contains the Armenian Genocide, the Holocaust, the extermination of the Gypsies, the destruction of the Kulaks, and the "autogenocide" of Cambodia. Second, it relates total domestic genocide specifically to revolution and not to other structural crises of the state or of modern society. Factors such as low underlying social solidarity, the activities of diasporas living outside of the boundaries of the state, defeats in wars, national upheavals, "internal strife," and "difficult life conditions" may be suggestive for other kinds of violence and genocide, but they do not link up as closely with total domestic genocide as does revolution.

Given the complexity of the problem, general explanations for genocide simply may not exist. By limiting our study to a comparative analysis of the Armenian Genocide and the Holocaust, and limiting the problem to an explanation of total domestic genocide, some tentative propositions may be suggested. This will be discussed in the next section and in more detail in the Conclusion (Chaps. 8 and 9).

A Conceptual Framework

Assuming that genocide is a product of a public policy process, a causal analysis or etiology of genocide ought to be able to address four questions that might be asked of any public policy.

1. What were the motives, perceptions, and ideology of the perpetrators that led them to decide on genocide?

2. What were the domestic and international conditions that allowed movements having the potential to commit genocide to seize state power?

3. What was the situation and the behavior of the victims that made them especially vulnerable to attack by the state?

4. What were the domestic and international conditions that facilitated the implementation of genocide?

The comparison of Armenian and Jewish history in the Ottoman Empire and Germany, respectively, that will be discussed more fully later in the book suggests some of the following answers:

1. Both the Committee of Union and Progress and the Nazis were revolutionary vanguards that were motivated by ideologies of revolutionary transformation.

2. Both movements came to power during a revolutionary interregnum after the fall of an old regime.

3. Both Armenians and Jews were ethnoreligious communities that had occupied a low or pariah status in traditional society, and both had experienced rapid progress and social mobilization in the modern world.[37]

4. Both genocides followed revolutions and wars.

Revolution and Genocide

As will be seen again in Chapter 9 with some variation similar observations can be made with respect to the destruction of the Kulaks by the Stalinist regime and to the "autogenocide" in Cambodia. There are other similarities as well as significant differences among these cases that will be discussed in the study below. For the moment, however, it may be suggested that:

1. Revolutions created the conditions for genocidal movements to come to power.

2. Revolutions made possible the imposition of radical ideologies and new orders that legitimated genocide.

3. The social mobilization of low status or despised groups helped to make them targets of genocide.

4. Revolutions leading to wars facilitated the implementation of genocide as a policy of the state.

From this brief list it can be seen that a major theme of this study is the link between genocide and revolution. This can be put in the form of a proposition: *Total domestic genocides like the Armenian Genocide and the Holocaust, including the extermination of the Gypsies, and by extension the destruction of the Kulaks and the Cambodian "autogenocide" were the products of revolutions. This does not imply that all revolutions lead to genocide, nor that all genocides are caused by revolutions.*

This proposition will be discussed more fully in Chapter 9. Here, for the sake of orientation, a brief indication of why it may be true is suggested.

Revolutions destroy not only the institutions and power of the old regime, they also undermine the legitimacy of the state and place in question the political identity of the community itself. Revolutions, therefore, provide the structural opportunities for ideological vanguards to come to power and to impose their views on society.

Revolutionary governments, like the Young Turks and the Nazis, that come to power after the breakdown of old regimes want to impose their ideology on society, but they also need to create a new order that will support the revolutionary state. It is not enough for the revolutionaries to have seized the buildings and offices of the old regime. They desperately need support from society at large, but that is often an inchoate mass itself looking for leadership. The revolutionary regime soon comes to understand that it cannot simply wait for support to bubble up from below. It must be mobilized and shaped.

In order both to implement its vision of a new society and to mobilize support, a revolutionary regime needs to construct a new system of legitimation and to redefine the identity of the political community as the "people," the "nation," the "class," or the "race." This collectivity is then labeled, perceived, and treated by the regime as the authentic political community.

The new authentic political community is that subset of the territorial state's inhabitants who are expected to fulfill the ideological vision of the revolutionary regime and to support the postrevolutionary state. By the same token there exist members of the old order who were either opposed to the revolution or whose identities cannot be made to fit into the new postrevolutionary political community. These others are likely to be excluded from the new political community and declared as "enemies of the revolution." It is just such "enemies," that is, those excluded from the postrevolutionary community, who may become victims of repression and even genocide.

There are two more conditions that may lead from exclusion to repression and make genocide more likely. These are war and the prerevolutionary identity of the excluded groups or collectivities. War itself, however, is intimately related to revolution.

War and Genocide

A revolutionary regime at its founding looks not only toward reshaping domestic society in its image but also to improving the state's international situation. Indeed, as may be seen from the French, Russian, Chinese, Turkish, and German revolutions, a major reason for the onset of the revolution was the inability of the old regime to deal with international pressures. This suggests that revolutionary regimes create international tensions that may lead to war.

There are at least three ways in which revolutionary war is closely linked to genocide:

1. War gives rise to feelings of vulnerability and/or exultation. Such feelings engender or intensify the fear that the state's internal enemies, those that earlier have been labeled as the "enemies of the revolution," are part of an insidious plot with the regime's international foes to undo the revolution or even to destroy the state and the political community itself. Such fears appeared in all of the major revolutions, including the Turkish and the German.

2. War increases the autonomy of the state from internal social forces, including public opinion and its moral constraints.

3. War closes off other policy options of dealing with internal "enemies," such as expulsion, assimilation, or segregation. The first option may not be feasible in the midst of war, while the second and third may take too long or may not be advantageous in a wartime situation.

It follows, therefore, that three conditions, all linked to revolution, cumulatively increase the danger of total domestic genocide: (1) the labeling by the state of certain collectivities as "enemies of the revolution," (2) the perception by the state in wartime that the groups labeled as "enemies of the revolution" are part of a domestic and international plot to destroy the state and the legitimate political community, (3) the sense that other options of dealing with internal enemies in wartime have been closed off and that the only remaining choice is destruction.

"Problem Communities" and Genocide

What are the collectivities that are likely to be identified, in the first instance, as not belonging to the legitimate political community? It would seem that communal groups that had been traditionally despised but had experienced rapid progress in the modern period were especially prone to victimization by revolutionary regimes. This is especially a danger when the revolution leads to war. Thus were Armenians and Jews said to pose a problem and were likely to be labeled as "enemies of the revolution" for whom "final solutions" had to be devised.

Armenians and Jews became a "problem" and raised a "question" because in the prerevolutionary old order they occupied low or even pariah statuses, while experiencing rapid social, economic, cultural, and even political progress and mobilization in the modern period that some historians have called a renaissance. The social mobilization or progress of despised groups created a "problem" for at least three reasons. First, they began to compete successfully with members of the dominant community for scarce goods, such as university positions, commercial endeavors, political office, and, in the Armenian case, even land. Second, in still hierarchical societies, such competition engendered not only resentment but also a sense of moral outrage in the dominant group. The majority felt that a valued traditional order was being challenged not only by external forces but by domestic upstarts and parvenus. Such sentiments were at the core of nineteenth-century conservative and *Volkisch* thought, not only in Germany but throughout Europe, and constituted one of the motives behind the repressions of the Armenians in 1894–96 by the regime of Sultan Abdul Hamid II. Third, the social mobilization of groups like the Jews, who opted for assimilation instead of separation or territorial autonomy, created a crisis in European and German society among those who still viewed Jews as "despicable" pariahs. After emancipation Jews might have believed that they had become "Germans of Mosaic persuasion" by attaining middle-class status and internalizing German norms and values, but for many Germans and Europeans imbued with the negative stereotype of the "Jew," such integration was seen as something to be feared and resisted. Indeed, since assimilation of minorities was valued both by liberal and socialist thought, Germans and Europeans who resisted Jewish assimilation found in racial antisemitism an ideology that helped them to struggle against Jewish progress and assimilation.

It will be contended in Chapters 2, 3, and 4 that in the old regime states of Imperial Germany and the Ottoman Empire, preceding the German and Turkish revolutions, such "problem" communities may have suffered discrimination, repression, and even pogroms, but not total genocide. That policy could be implemented only by later revolutionary regimes. Therefore, this study does not argue that social progress of despised minorities is equally as important a factor as revolution in the production of genocide. It does suggest that the progress of despised minorities may be an important intervening variable between the antecedent revolutionary seizure of power and the genocidal outcome.

Clearly, it is not the case that every revolution leads to genocide, or that every genocide in history has occurred because of revolution. It is likely, however, as this work tries to show, that in the modern world domestic total genocides have mainly been launched by revolutionary states seeking to transform society in their image. In addition to the Armenian Genocide and the Holocaust—from which this hypothesis is derived—the three other examples that may be cited as confirming instances are the extermination of the Gypsies by the Nazis, the destruction of the Kulaks by the Stalinists, and the "autogenocide" by the Khmer Rouge.

In Chapter 9 we shall turn to destruction of the Kulaks and the class genocide in Cambodia as illustrative and confirming examples. The extermination of the Gypsies has not been used as a point of comparison to the Holocaust, because—with significant differences—both instances were a product of Nazi racialist ideology and German revolutionary circumstances. For a credible comparison, one needs cases that are independent of each other in the manner that the Armenian Genocide was independent of events in Nazi Germany.[38]

Other writers have labeled these as "ideological genocides," stressing the motives of the perpetrators.[39] This essay does not mean to neglect ideology in an explanation of total genocide. However, it does emphasize revolution as a structural and historical setting—a necessary but not sufficient condition—making it possible for ideologically motivated

21

vanguards actually to implement their ideas, including those favoring genocide.

The explanatory framework suggested makes no claims to being deterministic or predictive. It emphasizes the ideology of the perpetrators, and includes the exigencies of their organizations, the status and behavior of the victims, and the role of the state. But it treats these dimensions as intervening variables which raise the probability that a revolution may lead to genocide. In this manner revolutions are viewed as antecedent variables, and the pattern briefly outlined above, derived from a comparison of the Holocaust with the Armenian Genocide, seeks to provide the beginnings of an explanatory framework for understanding the origins of modern or total domestic genocide. It should also be noted that this is a conceptual framework of limited scope. It does not claim to explain all massacres and genocides, only those that will be defined as total and domestic in the sense that has been indicated above and will be discussed more fully below.

Since it has been claimed that total domestic genocide like the Armenian Genocide and the Holocaust are related to revolutions, we need to explain what is meant by "genocide" and "revolution."

A Definition of Genocide

In 1944, while Jews, Gypsies, Poles, Russians, and others were being systematically exterminated and massacred by the Nazis, the eminent jurist Raphael Lemkin found that he needed a word to define the destruction. To remedy this situation he coined the term "genocide," by which he meant "a coordinated plan of different actions aiming at the destruction of essential foundations of the life of the national groups, with the aim of annihilating the groups themselves."[40] By destruction he meant to include not only the biological aspects of a group but its social, economic, cultural, and political institutions as well. In 1948 the United Nations formulated its own definition of genocide, relying on Lemkin's version but also significantly departing from it.

Lemkin's definitions of genocide and those of the UN have been by far the most influential, having been taken up by writers like Kuper and Bauer.[41] It would take us too far afield to discuss the many implications and ambiguities concerning these definitions. Here we have set ourselves a simpler task: we need a definition suitable to a comparative study of genocide, without straying too far from Lemkin's and the UN's formulations.

The UN Definition of Genocide

According to the widely accepted UN definition formulated in 1948, genocide means actions "committed with intent to destroy in whole or in part a national, ethnic, racial, or religious group as such."[42] For the purposes of this essay the UN definition is both too broad and too narrow. It is too broad in that it fails to make a sharp distinction between what it calls "genocide-in-part" and "genocide-in-whole," and it is too narrow because it limits the victims of genocide to communal groups and by implication excludes other collectivities such as social classes.[43]

For analytical purposes the UN definition does not discriminate sharply enough among a pogrom, or the massacre of part of a group, a policy of state-sponsored killing whose aim is the repression of a group, and the extermination or total destruction of a collectivity. Thus, the UN definition of genocide has been applied to such varied instances as the communal massacres committed in India during partition, the colonial atrocities in Algeria, the partial genocide of the Hutu in Burundi, the destruction of the Communist party and its followers in Indonesia, the massacres and mass starvation of the Ibos of Biafra, the killings and atrocities perpetrated by the Idi Amin regime in Uganda, the communal massacres in Lebanon and Sri Lanka, and, most recently, the gassing of Kurds in Iraq.[44] Still, one hesitates to equate these actions with the Armenian Genocide, the Holocaust, and the "autogenocide" of Cambodia. These latter cases, as will be discussed, were instances of planned and total destruction of a collectivity by the state. Indeed, as has already been suggested, their origins can be found in revolutions that differ in significant ways from the causes of massacres, atrocities, and partial genocides.

The UN definition of genocide is too narrow for at least two reasons. First, it limits its definition to the killing of a group (or to acts that would prevent its biological perpetuation), and unlike Raphael Lemkin who coined the term "genocide," it neglects policies of cultural, social, economic, and political destruction. Second, as Kuper has effectively argued, the UN definition is too narrow because it leaves out massacres of classes and other collectivities or social categories that are not necessarily ethnic or communal groups. This was done apparently for political reasons, in order to mollify certain powers, and not on moral or theoretical grounds.[45] Thus the UN definition might not be applicable to the destruction of the Kulaks and the mass starvation of the Ukrainian peasants during the collectivization period under Stalin, where it is estimated that millions perished by government fiat. Nor without amendment could it be extended to the destruction of the Cambodian upper and middle classes who were for the most part ethnically identical to their Khmer Rouge killers. [46]

A Definition of Genocide Proposed

One rationale of definitions is to subsume things that are similar and to discriminate these from objects or events that differ in essential ways. Definitions need not be written in stone, and, depending on what is to be compared, they may be altered as long as their terms of reference are clear and explicit. A good test of the utility of definitions is their ability to generate insights about the phenomena that they address. One can formulate definitions as one pleases, but these are of no interest unless they lead to credible insights and propositions. The definition of genocide formulated here should be useful in shedding some light on the events themselves.

A definition of genocide is needed that will be both inclusive and restrictive, since the major task of our study will be to compare the Holocaust to the Armenian Genocide and to distinguish these from other instances of massacre and genocide. It needs to be inclusive enough to subsume both of these events, and others like them, in order to allow for comparison and analysis. By the same token it needs to be restrictive enough to exclude instances of violence which are not in essence equivalent to the Holocaust and the Armenian Genocide. Here it needs to be made clear what is meant by "destruction" and the nature of the "group" that is singled out for victimization.

Referring to the distinction that Lemkin made between the biological and the social destruction of a group, it may be noted that the Holocaust was an instance of a policy that attempted the total biological extermination of a human group from the world and the destruction of its social identity in all its facets. This implies, following Bauer, that the Holocaust was an instance of a policy of destruction that lay at the extreme of three continua: (1) the dimension of killing, from none to total extermination; (2) the dimension of the destruction of identity, including all or some of its political, social, economic, and cultural aspects; and (3) the dimension of its geographical and political scope, including the world as a whole or a part of the world such as a country or a region. [47] These three dimensions are especially useful for definitional and comparative purposes and will be relied upon in the definitions below to distinguish between "massacre," "partial genocide," "total genocide," and the "Holocaust."

Having indicated that policies of genocide can be located on three dimensions, the problem arises: How to define the groups that are destroyed? A definition based on Lemkin and the United Nations would be limited to ethnic or communal groups alone. Following the broader approach of Kuper it would include social classes and political groups, and following the still broader conception of Chalk and Jonassohn it would include any group or category defined by the state or other perpetrators. [48] Thus, for example, the Kulaks were destroyed by the Stalin regime not because they were a communal group but because they were a social class deemed a threat to the state. Similarly, the Communists in Indonesia were slaughtered in 1965 as a political not a communal group. Should these be included or left out of a definition of genocide?

Following Kuper this study includes the planned destruction of social classes, like the Kulaks or the "compradore bourgeoisie" in Cambodia, because these mass murders were fundamentally equivalent to the destruction of communal groups like the Jews, the Armenians, and the Gypsies. In both instances people were killed not because of what they did or did not do but principally because of their membership in a social collectivity or category. Though social theory distinguishes between classes and communal groups, in practice, in some societies, the class origins of individuals have been regarded as being immutable in the manner of ethnic or religious affiliations. The genocide of a class included not only the active participants but often their families as well, and it implied not only the killing of members of the group but its destruction as a social collectivity. [49]

The inclusion of political groups as victims of total genocide is more problematic. For example, should one consider as examples of total genocide the destruction of political groups, as occurred in Indonesia in 1965 and Argentina in the early 1970s? Here one needs to distinguish between the juridical and moral condemnation of the destruction of groups and the theoretical understanding of genocide. Clearly, political groups, unlike communal groups and classes, are less "basic" to the social structure. Indeed, political groups are "secondary" and not "primary" in that they are composed of members who belong to classes and communal groups, whereas members of communal groups and classes do not necessarily belong to political groups. Thus the killing of members of political factions—unless it leads to the destruction of classes and communal groups—need not be based on a person's social background and need not involve his or her family. That kind of violence has been called "politicide" and can be classified as a form of partial genocide in a broad definition; nevertheless, the difference between "politicide" and the Armenian Genocide and the Holocaust also needs to be kept in mind.[50] The latter two cases were instances of total genocide in the sense that not only members of political groups were killed but all persons including the families of members were destined for destruction.

In sum, the definitions proposed below rely on (1) the UN's distinction between genocide-in-whole and genocide-in-part; (2) Lemkin's distinction between the biological or physical annihilation of a group and the destruction of its social, cultural, political, and economic institutions; (3) Kuper's and Chalk and Jonassohn's inclusion of a wide spectrum of collectivities and human categories, in addition to communal groups, as victims of genocide. In sum, *genocide* is defined here as *a public policy mainly carried out by the state whose intent is the destruction in whole or in part of a social collectivity or category, usually a communal group, a class, or a political faction.* From this, the following definitions may be derived. It may also be noted that the progression from massacre to Holocaust forms a scale of genocide.[51]

1. The term "massacre" or "pogrom" will be defined as a mass-murder, often implicating the state, whose intent is to kill (or allow to be killed) some members of a collectivity or category, usually a communal group, class, or political faction while for the most part leaving its social, cultural, economic and political institutions unchanged.

2. "Partial genocide" will be defined as a public policy whose intent is to kill a large proportion of a collectivity or category and to undermine its status and political power, while stopping at extermination and leaving its cultural institutions largely unchanged.

3. "Total genocide" will mean a public policy whose intent is either a) the extermination of a collectivity or category usually a communal group or class, or b) the killing of a large fraction of a collectivity or a category including the families of its members, and the destruction of its social and cultural identity in most or all of its aspects.[52]

4. "The Holocaust," or "Shoah," or "Final Solution" will mean a specific historical instance of total genocide practiced by the Nazis whose intent was to exterminate the Jewish people from the face of the earth and to obliterate their identity in all its dimensions.[53]

Massacre and Partial Genocide

Though in practice it is not always easy to distinguish between massacre or pogrom (the two terms are used interchangeably here) and what I have called partial genocide, they differ on two dimensions of proportion of group members killed and extent of group identity destroyed. The term *massacre* implies a much smaller fraction of a group killed and less of a group's identity destroyed than does *genocide*. For example, in 1953 in Kano, a city in Northern Nigeria, fewer than 100 Ibos were killed due to communal riots instigated by local politicians. In 1966, however, some 10,000 Ibos were massacred in Northern Nigeria, and the Ibo population fled or was driven out of the region.[54]

This study refers to the second mass murder as a partial genocide because, though it did not intend nor succeed in destroying the Ibos as a group—thus it was not a total genocide—it drastically affected their political identity and relative social status in the area. Indeed, following the mass murders of 1966, the Ibos recognized that their position in Northern Nigeria had been irrevocably undermined. They seceded and formed Biafra. By way of contrast, the events in 1953 did not have such an effect. After the riots Ibo "strangers" returned to the Sabon Garis (strangers' quarters) of the north, their lives and statuses largely unchanged.

Partial and Total Genocide

Unlike the instances of state-sponsored massacres or partial genocides, in cases of total genocide like the Holocaust, the Armenian Genocide of 1915, and the destruction of the Romany (Gypsies) by the Nazis, the state carried out a policy whose intent was to destroy not some but all of the targeted communal group. This destruction could make use of two kinds of policies: (*a*) the extermination of the members of the group, or (*b*) the killing of a large fraction of its membership together with the obliteration of its identity. In either case, the group so targeted would be eliminated from the social structure and culture and would cease to be a factor affecting the state or society.

The distinction between partial and total genocide rests on both the physical and cultural dimensions of group destruction. If *total genocide* implies either (*a*) the extermination of a group, or (*b*) the mass murder of a large fraction of its members together with the destruction of its cultural and social identity, then *partial genocide* is less drastic. It stops short

27

of intending the total extermination of the members of the group, and, though it may affect the identity of a group in some dimensions, it does not attempt to destroy completely its cultural and social identity in all of its aspects. Partial genocide means to use mass murder in order to coerce and to alter the identity or the politics of a group, not to destroy it. Politicide may be seen as an instance of partial genocide. In contrast, total genocide means to do away with a group entirely, including the families of members of political parties. Thus, for example, Nazi policies of partial genocide toward Poles and Russians in the occupied territories utilized mass murder against whole segments of these populations and attempted to alter drastically their identities, but they stopped short of extermination and the destruction of identity. These measures of total genocide were reserved for the Jews and the Gypsies alone.[55]

As already suggested above, the genocides of Jews, Armenians, and Gypsies, ethnoreligious and racial groups, bear a greater similarity to the attempted destructions of whole socioeconomic classes such as the Kulaks under Stalin and the urban Cambodians under Pol Pot than they do to the more limited massacres and partial genocides of Poles and Russians. The attempted total genocides of Armenians, Jews, and Gypsies were not mass murders designed to terrorize a civilian population, or to turn it into a mass of helots, or to intimidate an upwardly mobile or recalcitrant ethnic group, or to repress a political movement. These were instances of revolutionary violence meant to transform the social structure by physically and socially eliminating a communal group or class from society. This is why we wish to discriminate them from massacre and partial genocide and to refer to them as "total genocide."

Total genocides like the Armenian Genocide and the Holocaust, where they do not annihilate everyone, in practice destroy a larger proportion of a group than massacres or partial genocides. It should be noted, however, that the prefixes "partial" and "total" as attached to the term "genocide" may be misleading if they imply that more people in absolute numbers perished due to "total" genocide, or that their fate was necessarily more cruel than those who were killed in "partial" genocides. Quite the contrary: because massacres and partial genocides have been more frequent occurrences, it is safe to say that in the twentieth century fewer people have been killed due to total than due to the sum of all partial genocides. For example, we know that the Nazis killed more non-Gypsies by way of massacre and partial genocide than they killed Gypsies by way of total genocide.

The distinction between "partial" and "total," therefore, does not lie in absolute numbers killed. It lies in the killers' intent to destroy a communal group or class, thereby eliminating it from state and society. Indeed, from the perspective of the victim it makes very little difference whether he or she is being tortured and killed in a "massacre," a "partial," or a "total" genocide. From the perspective of group survival, however, it of course does make a difference whether the killers are intent on annihilating a group or destroying some parts of it.

"The Holocaust"

The Holocaust may be distinguished from other instances of total genocide in representing the extreme of physical annihilation, cultural destruction, and global scope. Whereas total genocide implies the destruction of a communal group in its physical and cultural aspects, it leaves open the possibility that some members of the group might save their lives by abandoning their identity. Thus, in the Armenian total genocide, some people were able to survive by converting to Islam. This was not possible in the Holocaust which meant to kill everyone defined as "Jews," even those who had converted and even those who did not consider themselves to be Jews.[56] Hence, while the Holocaust lies at the extreme of the two dimensions of physical and cultural destruction, it also lies at the extreme of the third dimension of global scope.

As far as its racism and antisemitism was concerned, Nazi ideology did not recognize national or imperial boundaries. It was a form of Manicheanism that divided the world into the good Aryans and the evil Jews. The destruction of the Jews was a twisted crusade against an imaginary evil. Jews had to be killed not only in Germany or in the occupied areas of the Third Reich, they had to be annihilated throughout the world so that it might be redeemed.[57] In a word, Nazism was not only a political ideology, it was a theodicy whose scope was global.

Not even the Stalinists or the Khmer Rouges were motivated by such extraordinary delusions, and as we shall see in Chapter 5, the Young Turks, impelled by Pan-Turkism and nationalism, wanted to eliminate the Armenians as a factor in the Ottoman and the Pan-Turkish empires of their dreams. They did not pursue them to the ends of the earth. In each other case the scope of the revolutionary movement's murderous policies was more restrictive than that of the Nazis. Thus there are features of the Holocaust that it shares with policies of partial and total genocide; there are other elements that it shares in common only with total genocides, and there are elements that are uniquely its own.

It bears repeating that the destruction of the Gypsies also followed

29

from Nazi racialist policies. In that sense it can be said that a holocaust was perpetrated against the Gypsies as well. But in this study, following contemporary usage, the "Holocaust" will be reserved only for the attempted annihilation of the Jewish people by the Nazis.

According to the definitions proposed here, therefore, the Holocaust may be classified with other instances of violence and the destruction of human groups that include massacres and partial genocides. The latter, however, should not be lumped together with the Holocaust or the Armenian Genocide as instances of total genocide. Some researchers are quite justified in including the Holocaust and the Armenian Genocide in their empirical studies of partial genocides, but they would be mistaken to try to use cases of violence, massacre, and partial genocide alone to try to explain the origins of the Holocaust or the Armenian Genocide. As we have seen, these latter two events included other significant factors without which total genocide cannot be explained.

In contrast to studies of massacres and partial genocides, therefore, this study explores the origins of policies of destruction that seek to kill all or most of the members of a communal group or class, and to obliterate its identity in all of its aspects from the very same society that is governed by the state that organizes the violence. We call such policies "total domestic genocide" in order to differentiate them from other mass murders. This definition allows us to compare the Holocaust to other instances like the Armenian Genocide and to differentiate these instances from partial genocides and massacres. [58]

A Definition of Revolution

Our understanding of revolution has been strongly influenced by Skocpol's important essay. [59] There, social revolutions are defined as rapid and basic transformations in society's political and social structures that are carried out in part by class-based uprisings from below. [60] The implication is that social revolutions differ from political revolutions, rebellions, and revolts in that they entail fundamental transformations both of the political order and the social structure, whereas political revolutions and rebellions may leave the social structure unchanged.

Though this distinction between social and political revolutions is suggestive, the stipulation that social revolutions entail the participation of lower classes is needlessly restrictive. Beyond that, it may be suggested that the structural perspective, though essential for an understanding of the causes of revolutions, neglects cultural and ideological facets that have important implications for their outcomes.

Skocpol's discussion of the causes of the French, Russian, and Chinese revolutions emphasizes the role of class movements from below, but neglects ethnic, religious, and linguistic groups, that is, communal groups, recruited on the basis of ascription in each of these social revolutions. Such a structural schema cannot provide a role for Armenians and other ethnic minorities in the Turkish revolution. Indeed, the important role that national and other minorities played in the Russian revolution is hardly mentioned. Moreover, though lower classes, especially peasantries, played a significant role in the French, Russian, and Chinese revolutions, under other circumstances, as happened in Germany, middle and upper classes can also be radicalized. Finally, in the discussion of the outcomes of revolutions, the structural perspective stresses the situational exigencies facing revolutionaries in power, but it underestimates the role that ideology and culture have for the formulation of policies. This is an important point, since in the present study genocide is viewed as a kind of policy that may be an outcome of revolution.

A Definition of Revolution Proposed

A structural perspective is essential to an analysis of revolution, but it neglects at least four cultural and ideological factors that are especially important for the outcomes of revolutions and an understanding of genocide. These are (1) the worldview, or the ideology of the revolutionaries; (2) the political creed of their followers; (3) the political myth, or formula of society at large; and (4) the political identity of persons living within the boundaries of the territorial state. Each of these terms has a host of meanings and connotations. For greater conceptual clarity in this context, we shall use these terms as follows. [61]

"Political ideology" refers to an individual's or a group's more or less coherent and consistent set of beliefs about the origin, identity, functioning, and purpose of the political world, including society, the state, and the interstate system. Such beliefs are akin to philosophical and scientific theories of politics, but they differ from these in that political ideologies suggest actions in the real world, and they cannot be readily falsifiable by rational or empirical proof. Usually leaders of revolutionary regimes or political movements have a more elaborated ideology than followers whose actions, among other things, are governed by a simplified version of the ideology—an "operational code"—which we shall call a "political creed."

A political myth or formula refers to a set of beliefs widely held by members of a political community concerning the state's origins, identity, functions, and purpose. A political myth like the "divine rights of kings," "the scientific nature of Marxism-Leninism," "the biological superiority of Aryans," or the "consent of the governed" can serve as a major instrument for legitimating the state. A political myth, however, may be in conflict with the reigning ideology of the state, a situation prevalent throughout Eastern Europe in the reign of Communist states. Revolutionary situations enable ideological vanguards to create a new political myth more in keeping with their ideological preferences.

Modern states claim to rest on the consent of the governed, that is, the "people," the "race," the "nation," or the "class," but these identities are not primordial givens nor are they equally shared by all members of a territorial state. On the contrary, following a revolution a regime in power attempts to redefine society's political myth and its identity in line with the regime's ideology. It often proceeds to label a subset of the persons living in a territorial state as the "people," etc., to mobilize their support, while relegating others to the status of "minorities," or "enemies of the revolution."

The definition of revolution that is proposed here is as follows: *A social revolution is a fundamental transformation, usually carried out by violence, in society's political, economic, and social structures and cultural values and beliefs, including its reigning ideology, political myth, and identity.* A political revolution entails primarily a transformation in the polity's structure and political culture, including its reigning ideology, political myth, and identity, while a social revolution implies transformations in all of the order of society including the polity, the economy, the social structure, and the culture.

Causes and Outcomes of Revolutions

This study envisions the process of revolution as commencing with the gradual or rapid collapse of an old regime and old order, followed by a revolutionary interregnum that can last for years. During the interregnum various factions and vanguards vie for power. Once a revolutionary vanguard has attained power and established the authority and legitimacy of its regime, the revolution is over.

The causes of modern social revolutions are linked to the spread of capitalism and the modern state on a world scale. Old regimes that are "situated in disadvantaged positions within international arenas," in the sense of being militarily backward or politically dependent, are especially vulnerable.[62] As to the outcomes of revolutions, it may be asserted that, to the extent the revolutionary regime becomes autonomous of social forces, its policies are likely to be influenced by the ideology of its leaders. [63] Thus to understand the outcomes of revolution—including especially genocide—volitional, ideological, and cultural factors need to be added in order to supplement structural variables.

Having suggested that genocide may be related to revolution and having defined these terms, in the following chapters we shall be ready to discuss more fully the relationship between genocide and revolution. It has been noted earlier, however, that the attempt to compare the Holocaust to the Armenian Genocide may lead to controversy. Indeed, some scholars have asserted that the Holocaust is a unique and, therefore, an incomparable event, a claim that calls the aims of this essay into question. Before proceeding with the rest of this study, therefore, a word needs to be said about the uniqueness and comparability of the Holocaust.

On the Uniqueness of the Holocaust

As has been noted, comparisons of the Holocaust to other instances of genocide, including the Armenian Genocide, may lead to controversy. The "comparativist" perspective I share with other writers welcomes such comparisons. For the most part comparativists are aware of the extraordinary aspects of the Holocaust, but they wish to refer to it as a standard against which other instances of genocide might be measured and condemned. In this view the Holocaust may include some unique elements, but these should not prohibit its comparison to other instances of genocide or mass murder. From another perspective, however—here called "particularist"—the Holocaust cannot be subsumed under a category of "genocide" because it is a unique and essentially incomparable event. [64] Thus before comparing the Holocaust to the Armenian Genocide, or indeed to any other mass murder, one needs to discuss, even if briefly, the particularist position.

The Particularist Perspective

The particularist position contends that to include the Holocaust of the European Jews among other instances of massacre and genocide is to deflect its moral impact and to confuse its meaning. For the particularists the Holocaust was unique because it is fundamentally unexplainable and because the intentions of the Nazis were unprecedented. Thus, for example, Jacob Katz, the respected Israeli social historian, remarked:

> For Auschwitz and Treblinka there was no earlier historical analogy
> and there was no philosophical, or for that matter theological, frame
> of mind that could possibly integrate them into any system of

thought. The Holocaust was an absolute *novum* lacking accountability in any rational terms at the disposal of the generation that experienced it . . . [For] the generation that lived through it, [the Holocaust] can only be characterized as a trauma, a wounding experience beyond the reach of intellectual conceptualization. [65]

And Saul Friedländer, the Israeli historian and writer, himself a survivor, asked a crucial question: "Are we dealing with a phenomenon comparable with some other historical event, or are we facing something unique not only within any traditional historical context, but even within Nazism itself?" [66] Friedländer answered his own question by noting that the murder of the Jews by the Nazis could not be compared to any other phenomenon nor subsumed under any previous category. [67]

The particularists maintain that the Holocaust was unique, not only because so many millions perished and so large a percentage of the Jewish population was destroyed but because the intentions of the perpetrators, the Nazis, were extraordinary. Never before nor since has a political or religious movement made one of its primary aims the annihilation of a people from the face of the earth. Such a project was unprecedented in its motives, scope, and methods of execution.

Thus Dawidowicz observed:

> The murder of the 6 million Jews stands apart from the deaths of the other millions, not because of any distinctive fate that the individual victims endured, but because of the differentiative intent of the murderers and the unique effect of the murders. [68]

In a similar vein Friedländer wrote:

> It was the absolutely uncompromising aspect of the exterminatory drive against the Jews, as well as the frantic extirpation of any elements actually or supposedly linked to the Jews or to the "Jewish spirit," that is, the identification of the Jews as absolute evil, which fundamentally distinguished the anti-Jewish actions of the Nazis from their attitude toward another group. [69]

And, one might add, of the Holocaust from other cases of genocide.

The particularist stance need not be driven simply by emotion. Nor does it need to be a vehicle for ethnocentric values. It insists on the uniqueness of the Holocaust because of the extraordinary intentions and projects of the Nazis. And it fears that careless comparisons of the Holocaust to other instances of violence will diminish its moral force as an example and warning of radical evil in the world.

It is apparent that both the comparativist and particularist positions have merit, but when carried to extremes both may be logically and morally flawed. A possible flaw in the comparativist position is to imply that comparison is the same as equality. To say that *A* can be compared to *B* does not imply that *A* equals *B*. When one commits this error by equating the Holocaust with less drastic events, one runs the moral danger of hyperbole and of trivializing and relativizing radical evil. By the same token, a possible flaw in the particularist position is to hold that uniqueness implies incomparability. Indeed, all historical events are both unique and comparable. To hold that the Holocaust cannot be compared implies that it cannot be thought about, and that it has no important lessons for other peoples who in the past have been or in the future may be in mortal danger. These points bear further discussion.

A Critique of the Comparativist Position

On closer examination, the comparativist position masks at least two quite contradictory impulses. The first is to refer to the Holocaust as an archetype, a warning sign, and a moral standard that might be used to alert other peoples of mortal danger or to condemn other mass murders by noting how closely these approximate the extremes of the Holocaust. The second is to set up a tendentious equivalence between an instance of violence and the Holocaust in order either to indulge in hyperbole or to attempt to mitigate and relativize the evil of the Holocaust itself.

Since, at least in the West, the Holocaust has become a standard by which to measure genocide and radical evil, people like Sartre who were outraged by the brutalities of the Vietnam war compared that war to the Holocaust and implied equality in order to condemn American actions.[70] This is hyperbole in the service of antiwar propaganda. Indeed, this is a practice that has been indulged in even by survivors of the Holocaust like former Prime Minister Begin when he compared Yassir Arafat to Hitler, implying that the PLO is the equivalent of the Nazis. There is moral danger to hyperbole: if indeed the bombings of Vietnam were like the gas chambers at Auschwitz, and if Arafat is like Hitler, then Auschwitz was no worse than the bombings in Vietnam, and Hitler was no worse than Arafat. It is hard to believe that either Sartre or former Prime Minister Begin would have agreed to the logical and moral implications of their positions.

This is trivialization, but comparison can also be used to relativize the evil of the Holocaust. The contemporary conflict among West German historians, the *Historikerstreit*, ably summarized by Charles S. Maier, is a case in point.[71] Thus when some West German historians have argued that the Holocaust is comparable in some ways to the Stalinist destruction of the Kulaks, they were not necessarily wrong. The two were mass murders on a vast scale, and they did eliminate collectivities from their respective societies. However, the issue is, on the one hand, equating the two events without drawing historical distinctions, and, on the other hand, intending to draw the horror from the Holocaust by relativizing its evil. Some of the historians cited by Maier seem to find extenuating circumstances for the Nazis, and they argue that, because others were also culpable of genocide, the Nazis were not absolutely evil but only relatively so.

As noted above, failure to stress some of the unique features of the Holocaust, especially its Manichean theodicy and its global scope, is to blur important historical differences. The Nazis fought a phantom "Jewish spirit" in a manner unparalleled in the destruction of the Kulaks or any other group. Moreover, the Stalinists did not intend to pursue the last Kulak to the ends of the earth, but the Nazis did intend and did attempt to exterminate all Jews wherever they could. Thus to argue that the Holocaust was equal to the destruction of the Kulaks is mistaken. But the moral issue is equally important: the fact that the Young Turks, or the Stalinists, or the Khmer Rouge committed genocide does not in any way mitigate the crimes of the Nazis and those Europeans who supported them. What it does is to alert us to the possibility that the crime of genocide can be perpetrated by others besides Germans and Europeans. If that, too, is relativization, so be it.

A Critique of the Particularist Position

There are, indeed, no examples in history wherein a political movement has set as one of its main goals the extermination of a people and of its "spirit" from the face of the earth. While agreeing with some of the premises of the particularist perspective, however, I find its conclusions misleading: an event like the Holocaust may be unique, but that does not imply that it is incomparable or that it is unique in all dimensions. The French revolution may be unique in many ways, but it is clearly comparable to other revolutions like the American and the Russian. Thus the particularist insistence on uniqueness can lead to conclusions that are overly restrictive. From the perspective of a careful comparative history, the particularist position may be especially misleading because it may reduce the causes of the Holocaust to the motives or intentions of the

Nazis. In doing so, it neglects other nonideological, structural dimensions of comparison and analysis.

To understand a criminal event like the Holocaust it is crucial to distinguish between the intentions, including the ideology and worldview of the human beings who did the killing, and the structural conditions under which the murders were perpetrated. Both are crucial to an understanding of the Holocaust or any other genocide. Though the intentions of one group of killers may have been different from another, the possibility, nevertheless, remains that the structural conditions that allowed murderous intentions to be actualized in genocidal behavior were comparable and instructive. Besides the motives of the perpetrators, an etiology of genocide must address those factors that helped the killers to seize power and those that facilitated the implementation of their murderous policies. This distinction between intentions and other causal conditions will be discussed more fully below, but it is a recurring theme throughout this book.

On closer examination, it turns out that some studies, while insisting on the uniqueness and incomparability of the Holocaust, do in fact compare it to the other events. They do not compare the Holocaust to other instances of genocide, but implicitly or explicitly they compare it to other catastrophes in Jewish history. They find its "roots" in the persecutions and calumnies of the early Church fathers, in the many expulsions from various parts of Christian Europe, and in former massacres like those carried out by Chmielnitski in the seventeenth century. From this perspective the Holocaust is perceived as the apotheosis of Christian Europe's millennial persecution of the Jews.

This view will be examined in more detail in Chapters 3 and 4. Here one might note that, in the middle of the nineteenth century, no one could have predicted the Holocaust and least of all that it would be initiated in Germany by Germans. Quite to the contrary, most Jews and liberal Germans would have predicted that Jews would successfuly assimilate to German society and become Germans of "Mosaic persuasion." Though modern antisemitism was becoming a force in Imperial Germany, by and large it played a minor political role. Indeed, by 1912, before the Great War, antisemitic parties that had never been able to get more than a few percentage points of the vote experienced a steep decline. Thus, before the war and before the collapse of the old regime, there was no inkling that a Holocaust was possible, at least not in Germany.

Admittedly ancient stereotypes of Jews as pariahs were active in Germany and elsewhere, and such images played a crucial role in the Holocaust. Without the right historical conditions, however, traditional and modern anti-Jewish and antisemitic sentiments could not be translated into state policy. This essay will argue in Chapters 4, 6, and 7 that the Holocaust was not the preordained culmination of Jewish history in Europe, and that it was unlikely without the destruction of Imperial Germany and the revolutionary interregnum that followed.

Implicit objections to the comparability of the Holocaust have been registered, not only by some studies of Jewish and German history but also by some works on the Ottoman Empire (see Chap. 5). Such histories object to comparing the destruction of the Armenian community—which they refuse to call a "genocide"—to the Holocaust. As already indicated, these works present the destruction of the Armenians as stemming not from the intentions of the Young Turks—in the manner that the Holocaust derived from the ideology of the Nazis—but from the provocative behavior of the Armenians themselves.

This argument will be taken up in detail in Chapters 5, 8, and 9. No doubt the ideology of the Young Turks differed from that of the Nazis, and it goes without saying that the conditions prevailing in Turkey between 1908 and 1923 were not equivalent to those in Germany between 1918 and 1945. Nevertheless, whatever one wishes to call the Armenian Genocide, it can certainly be compared on ideological and structural dimensions to the Holocaust.

Like the comparativist position when carried to extremes, the particularist argument, which insists on the incomparability of the Holocaust, runs a moral danger. The moral danger is insensitivity to the suffering of others and blindness to warning signs of genocides to come. If, indeed, the Holocaust was totally and absolutely unique and incomparable on any dimension, then one must conclude that the suffering of its victims was distinctive from the suffering of others, and other victims have less of a claim to a respectful hearing and a just verdict from the court of history. Moreover, if the Holocaust is incomparable, then it also follows that studying its origins has nothing to teach us about the causes of other genocides in the past or about the possibilities of genocides in the future. The implication of both of these views is that one can learn nothing from the Holocaust that might be of use for the contemporary world and that the only valid stance is horror before its perpetrators and grief for its victims.

It seems to me that the genius of Jewish history does not lie in its claims to a unique victimization but in its commitment to transmit Jewish learning, memory, and identify from generation to generation and in its eternal hope to mend the world. It is precisely because I feel the injunction to remember Jewish history and to improve things that I have tried to learn lessons from the Holocaust which might be of use to others.

The aims of this book are to avoid the extremes of universalism and particularism and to focus on a careful comparative history that will demonstrate both the significant similarities and crucial differences between the cases compared. This study was launched in the belief that one, indeed, can learn something from a comparative analysis of the Holocaust and the Armenian Genocide, and that one should try to enlarge one's scope of empathy to include all victims of genocide. In this modest way I hope to contribute to the understanding of genocides in the past and to their prevention in the future.

Plan of Study

This introductory chapter noted that the purpose of our study is to compare the Armenian Genocide to the Holocaust and to identify some of the conditions that lead to total domestic genocides. It suggested that some of these conditions may be found in revolutionary transformations of states and societies. Since it was claimed that total domestic genocide was related to revolution, this Introduction defines and discusses these concepts as well as the uniqueness of the Holocaust.

The first part of this study, Chapters 2, 3, and 4, will discuss the situation of Armenians and Jews of the Ottoman Empire and Imperial Germany, respectively. It will explain why total domestic genocide did not, indeed, could not take place in these prerevolutionary situations. The second part, Chapters 5, 6, and 7 will try to demonstrate that the Armenian Genocide and the Holocaust were products of the Turkish and German revolutions.

Having defined total domestic genocide and revolution in the Introduction, in the Conclusion (Chaps. 8 and 9) the main thesis will be reviewed and elaborated. Chapter 8 will sum up the similarities and differences between the Armenian Genocide and the Holocaust. Chapter 9 will elaborate the theoretical relation between revolution and genocide and will cite other cases besides the Armenian Genocide and the Holocaust. Two of these cases, the destruction of the Kulaks and the Cambodian "autogenocide," will be used to confirm the relation between revolution and genocide, while other instances will be cited and discussed as apparent exceptions to the general pattern.

PART ONE

Armenians and Jews under the Old Regimes in the Ottoman Empire and Imperial Germany

Even before the genocide of 1915 and the Holocaust, both Armenians and Jews occupied problematic positions in the Ottoman Empire and Imperial Germany, respectively. Armenians were the victims of major massacres in 1894–96, while by the end of the nineteenth century Jews began to experience organized political antisemitism that threatened to undo their emancipation. In passing, it should be noted that antisemitism was not confined to Germany alone but was a European-wide phenomenon. An important question arises, therefore, as to the connection between these earlier forms of violence and discrimination and the later genocides.

Part One will contend that, although massacre and discrimination occurred under the old regimes, total genocide as a policy of the state became a serious option only after both the Ottoman Empire and Imperial Germany were swept away by revolution. In order to grasp why it was that Armenians and Jews were targeted for genocide during the Turkish and German revolutions, however, it is crucial to understand their situation in the prerevolutionary period.

Here two observations are in order. First, in the traditional, pre-nineteenth century, or premodern era, both Armenians and Jews were ethnoreligious communities occupying low or even pariah statuses in their respective systems of social stratification. Second, with the spread of capitalism and modernization and with the opening up of new avenues of participation in the nineteenth and early twentieth centuries, both minorities experienced rapid rates of progress and social mobilization. As has already been noted in Chapter 1, both factors tended to generate resentment and even violence on the part of the wider societies.

From the accepted Christian point of view, which was still wide-

41

spread in nineteenth- and twentieth-century Europe, the Jews were despised as deicides and usurers. At best they were to be tolerated as a witness people, not included as equals in the new national-states or deferred to as members of an economic and social middle and upper class. As to the Armenians, according to Islam and the *Shariah*, the law that governs Muslim behavior, they were to be tolerated as a religious community so long as they made no claims to be the equals of Muslims. Capitalism and modernity helped to undermine such traditional arrangements; nevertheless, neither Central and Eastern Europe nor the Ottoman Empire succeeded in creating social structures and cultures that allowed for the legitimate progress of despised minorities.

There are other similarities as well as significant differences in the pregenocidal situations of Armenians and Jews. Nevertheless, the question arises, Might the social mobilization of despised groups by itself account for genocide? Indeed, such an explanation would fit the provocation thesis. The argument might go something like this: because Armenians and Jews were able to rise swiftly in still traditional societies, they evoked widespread resentment, even violence, that ultimately led to genocide. This would suggest that so long as minorities accepted their lowly status, refrained from challenging their rulers, and did not upset the sensibilities of majorities, they would remain safe and unharmed. The further implication is that powerlessness, poverty, and humility are a small price to pay for life itself. This is a proposition that will be examined and rejected below. All explanations of genocide that neglect the ideology, perceptions, and power of the perpetrators are necessarily incomplete. This is why in Part Two I turn to the perpetrators themselves for a more complete explanation of genocide.

Chapter 2 will relate the Armenian massacres of 1894–96 to the social mobilization of Armenians in the Ottoman Empire; while Chapters 3 and 4 will connect the rise of European antisemitism to the rapid progress of the Jews in the modern period. It will be pointed out that in neither case could social mobilization alone account for the genocides that followed. Terrible as they were, the massacres of 1894–96 were still not the total genocide of 1915. And although murderous antisemites plied their trade in the nineteenth as well as the twentieth centuries, it was only after the German revolution that they acquired the power to put their fantasies into practice. Part Two will turn to the revolutionary transformations of the Ottoman Empire and Germany, respectively. There it will be pointed out that under revolutionary conditions despised minorities that experienced progress were indeed in danger of genocide.

T W O

Armenians in the Ottoman Empire:
The Massacres of 1894–1896[1]

I have been informed at the Porte in answer to an inquiry, that Armenians at Talori, in the Vilayet of Bitlis, have risen, and that in order to quell the revolt a small number of troops are being sent to the scene.

> Sir Philip Currie to the Earl of Kimberley
> Constantinople, 31 August 1894[2]

During the period 1894–96, some twenty years before the genocide of 1915, tens of thousands of Armenians were massacred in the Ottoman Empire ruled by Sultan Abdul Hamid II. This suggests that even before the genocide the existence of Armenians in the Ottoman Empire was both problematic and tenuous. The questions raised by this chapter are, What caused the massacres and what was their relation to the later genocide?

A number of prominent historians contend that the massacres were the understandable result of Armenian provocations, especially those of the revolutionary parties. In response to this provocation thesis, the suggestion will be made that it is impossible to account for the policy of any regime without taking its ideology, motives, and perceptions into account. And these cannot simply be reduced to a response to "provocations."

It will be proposed that the Armenian massacres were either initiated or allowed to take their course because the regime of Sultan Abdul Hamid II wanted to preserve the Ottoman Empire and the old order based on Muslim law and tradition. He feared nineteenth-century Armenian social and political mobilization—some have called it a renaissance—and to abort it he was willing to use force, including massacre.

43

Nonetheless, as has been suggested in Chapter 1, massacre is not the same thing as genocide.

Chapter 5 will show that although some of the same factors that precipitated the massacres also led to the genocide, the latter instance of violence was qualitatively different. In the first instance the regime of Abdul Hamid II used massacre against the Armenians not to destroy the community but to restore an old order; in the later genocide the regime of the Committee of Union and Progress used genocide to eliminate the Armenians from the Turkish social structure. This suggests that under the old regime there were limits to the extent of violence against component communities of the Ottoman Empire and that these limits were breached by the Turkish revolution.

Chapter 2 is divided into five sections. The first one briefly discusses the massacres; the second addresses the provocation thesis. The third section suggests that the massacres were an attempt by the regime to preserve an old order. Here the situation of the Armenians in the Ottoman Empire is briefly described. The fourth section raises the question, If the regime wanted to use force against the Armenians, why did it choose massacre and not some other means? The last section concludes with a brief discussion contrasting the massacres of 1894–96 to the genocide of 1915.

The Massacres

The massacres of 1894–96 began in August in Sassoun, a community in the *vilayet*, or province of Bitlis; here Armenian peasants, possibly encouraged by agitators, resisted the depredations of Muslim Kurdish pastoralists and were set upon by regular troops and Hamidiye regiments.[3]

A most telling source for details of the Sassoun massacres is the correspondence between Sir Philip Currie, the then British ambassador to the Sublime Porte—the Ottoman court—and his vice-consul, C. M. Hallward, who was dispatched to the area to investigate allegations of massacre.

In Hallward's final report, he indicated that "the attention of the Government appears to have been drawn towards that district by one Damadian, an Armenian Catholic from Constantinople who was engaged in political agitation among the Sassunis."[4] He had been captured in 1893 and later pardoned in Constantinople. "I do not believe that the agitation amounted to much, or had much effect on the villagers,"[5] continued Hallward. Shortly after Damadian's capture, however, the fate of the Sassoun Armenians was sealed.[6]

In the summer of 1894, after an attack by tribal Kurds was repulsed by armed Armenian villagers, Hamidiye regiments, as well as regular troops from the Bitlis and Moush garrisons joined by reinforcements from the Fourth Army Corps, were sent in, and massacre ensued. "The operation lasted some twenty-three days, from the 18th of August to the 10th of September."[7] Though he had heard higher estimates, Hallward suggested a figure of 8,000 killed.

Were the massacres a disproportionate response to Armenian insurrection?

> There was no insurrection, as was reported in Constantinople; the villagers simply took up arms to defend themselves against the Kurds. The statement made to me by an official here of their having killed soldiers and Zaptiches, I found after careful inquiry to be false. Before arriving in Moush, I naturally supposed that something of the sort must have occurred to call for such a display of military force, but neither the Mutesarif nor the Military Commandant with whom I spoke on the subject hinted at anything of the sort, nor did I learn elsewhere that the Armenians had been guilty of any act of rebellion against the Government.[8]

The massacre at Sassoun was followed by a brief period when European powers protested the treatment of the Armenians, leading the Porte to appoint a commission of inquiry that met from 24 January 1895 to 21 July 1895 in Moush. The commission, however, refused to hear Armenian testimony and stated in its terms of reference that it should inquire "into the criminal proceedings of the Armenian brigands."[9] The vali of Moush, who had called in the troops in the first place, as well as Zeki Pasha, the commandant of the Fourth Army Corps, were decorated for their participation in the massacres while the mutessarif of Moush, who had protested, was dismissed.[10]

In protest, the British, French, and Russian consular delegates themselves traveled to Sassoun to hear evidence. Following testimony from the consular delegates, the European powers exerted pressure on the Porte to institute reforms that had been agreed upon in the treaties of San Stefano and Berlin in 1878 but which had never been implemented.

The Massacres Spread

The reforms upon which the Europeans insisted were to go into effect in October 1895, but this was precluded by the launching of widespread massacres of Armenians throughout the Ottoman Empire. These are the phenomena that concern us here. The occasion for violence was a procession organized in Constantinople on 30 September 1895 by the Hnchakist party, an Armenian nationalist organization.[11] The ostensible aims of this party in organizing the procession was to present the grand vizier with a petition, but its real goals were to add emphasis to the demands of the European powers and to dramatize the plight of the Armenians. The procession was set upon, and hundreds of Armenians were killed. Soon after, massacre became widespread throughout the empire but especially in the six vilayets of Erzerum, Bitlis, Van, Harpout, Sivas, and Diarbekir, where reforms had been slated to go into effect. Commencing at Ak-Hissar and Trebizond on 3 and 4 October, massacres were perpetrated at fifteen locations in the month of October, at twenty locations in November, in five locations in December, and ceased briefly after an outbreak at Biredjik on 1 January 1896.[12]

Then on 24 August 1896 another revolutionary Armenian party, the Dashnaktsutiun, seized the Imperial Ottoman Bank in Constantinople to protest the massacres and apparently to prompt external intervention. Though the protest succeeded in dramatizing the Armenian situation, and the revolutionaries were allowed to escape, their action was followed by the wholesale massacre of Armenians in Constantinople, where it is estimated that six thousand perished.[13] As to European succor, one scholar has noted, "European intervention unsustained by force added to the tragedy of the Armenians."[14]

Although this is not the place for detailed controversy pertaining to population statistics, it should be clear that those writers who seek to underestimate the extent of death and damage will underestimate the size of the victimized population before the violence and overestimate the number of survivors; while, conversly, writers wishing to exaggerate the carnage will reverse that procedure. This caveat will serve in good stead not only here but also in Chapter 5, when I turn to the genocide.

The reader should therefore be cautioned by Roderic H. Davison's warning: "There are no trustworthy figures on the population of the empire. Reasonably accurate statistical methods have not existed in Turkey until very recent years under the republic."[15] Under the circumstances, given the problem of amassing reliable data, it should be no surprise that there is wide variation in the numbers of people reported to have been killed and in the estimation of material damage. Louise Nalbandian[16] estimates that between 50,000 and 300,000 Armenians were massacred; Richard G. Hovannisian[17] suggests that the number may vary between 100,000 and 200,000, and Johannes Lepsius[18] cites a figure of some 88,000. The Shaws do not cite overall figures, but they do believe that the estimate of 20,000 killed following the events at Sassoun to be a great exaggeration.[19] Using Davison's figures, the population of the Ottoman Empire in 1876, when Abdul Hamid came to power, was 38,493,000, of whom Ottoman Turks constituted 13,500,000 or 35 percent, and the Armenians 2,500,000 or 6.5 percent. If one assumes a low figure of 50,000 dead and a high figure of 300,000 dead, between 2 percent and 12 percent of the Armenian population was killed during the massacres.[20]

The Initiation of the Massacres

According to Lepsius, the massacres were initiated by the Porte, that is, the regime of Sultan Abdul Hamid II from Constantinople. He notes that "the Armenian massacres were nothing but an administrative measure, which was ordered by the central government in the name of the Sultan, and was executed with only too great willingness by the provincial officials."[21] Indeed, Lepsius suggests that variation from place to place depended only on how quickly violence could be prepared.[22] Another source, the British vice-consul G. H. Fitzmaurice, who was chief dragoman of the British Embassy and was sent to the provinces to investigate, reports that the massacres were centrally initiated and made legitimate on political and religious grounds.

Writing of orders that had come down from the Porte after the demonstration of Constantinople, Fitzmaurice noted:

> The Mussulmans here and elsewhere interpreted them as the Sovereign's wish that they should put into execution the prescription of the "Sheri" [Shariah or Islamic law], and proceeded to take the lives and property of the rebellious Armenian "rayahs" [reaya or subjects]. The demonstration at Constantinople was represented by the officials as an attempt by the Armenians to storm the Sublime Porte; rumours reached here of massacres of Armenians by their [sic] co-religionists in other towns in Anatolia; they were told that the Armenians were attacking mosques and using dynamite, while word came from their Mussulman brethren in towns where massacres had

occurred inciting them to do their duty by Islam. The government, too, began to serve out arms and cartridges to the Zaptiehs and other guards, and had the Armenian quarter patrolled.

I should add that the telegraphic news of acceptance of reforms was interpreted to the Mussulmans as the granting of autonomy to the Armenians, an interpretation which must have come from the government officials, and which had a disastrous effect on Moslem feeling towards Armenians.[23]

According to Lepsius, the civil and military authorities had different but complementary roles to play in the massacres. The military authorities were in charge of distributing weapons to Kurdish and Circassian irregulars as well as to those of the Muslim population who were still in need of them. In terms of direct participation, the army was mostly called to assist the Hamidiye regiments when and if there was Armenian resistance, as occurred at Sassoun, Gurun, Diarbekir, and Zeitoun. "In one or two places just before the massacres, the authorities removed garrisons whose relations with the Christian population were suspected of being too friendly."[24] The civil authorities, on the other hand, had the difficult double task of preparing the Muslim population for massacre while at the same time convincing the targeted groups that no violence was about to take place, so as to prevent resistance and thus maximize the extent of the slaughter.[25]

Lepsius suggests that some of the motivation of local Muslims derived from the active encouragement of authorities, the legitimation of violence in the name of the sultan and of religion, the opportunity for plunder, and the absence of external fetters or fear of resistance. Another point worth mentioning is one raised by the Shaws. They suggest that the lead in the massacres was taken by Muslim refugees who themselves had fled violence at the hands of Christians, most notably the Russians.[26]

This is an important point because, as the Shaws point out, "millions" of Muslim refugees were resettled not just anywhere in the Ottoman Empire but precisely in the vilayets where the majority of Armenians lived. To the intentions implied by Lepsius and Fitzmaurice, one might, therefore, add the motives of revenge and displaced aggression.[27] This too is a point that will be picked up again in the discussion of the genocide in Chapter 5.

At odds with the Lepsius-Fitzmaurice interpretation, the Shaws' explanation as to the role of the sultan is somewhat ambiguous. They seem to make two arguments: (1) that if the sultan had a hand in the massacres, it was as a result of the provocations of the Armenian revolutionary parties, but they also raise another possibility: (2) that the massacres were mass uprisings of Muslim peasants against the Armenians. These two views are not mutually exclusive. The massacres may have commenced as popular uprisings as, for example, at Sassoun (though we have Hallward's testimony to the contrary), and the sultan may have then placed himself at the head of such an uprising and, indeed, may have encouraged it. In that case, we are still left with the question of the motive for his role, that is, why would he have encouraged the massacres? But in any event, for a full explanation we need more information about the Muslim peasantry and pastoralists at the time of the massacres. This, unfortunately, the Shaws leave out.

Leaving the sultan and the government out of the explanation is possible but not credible. It assumes that the Ottoman regime played no role in the massive violence that lasted for two years, occurred in forty-one locations (some of them hundreds of miles apart), and in which tens of thousands of Ottomans participated either as perpetrators or victims. Had the Ottoman regime been extraordinarily weak and incompetent, one might yet want to argue that the process of massacre spread by a kind of diffusion, but that is not at all the picture of the regime that the Shaws themselves paint. To the contrary, they argue forcefully that the administration of Abdul Hamid was competent and extremely well informed.[28] We are, however, left with a last possibility—that the massacres were initiated and spread by others but that the sultan decided to stay aloof. This still begs the question why he or his regime would decide to stay aloof from the massacre of one of his millets. And so we return to the role of the sultan and his regime. This brings us back full circle to the Shaws' first implication, namely, that the sultan was provoked by the activities of the Armenian revolutionary parties.

Massacre as Reaction to Provocation

As noted, the Shaws in their influential work of 1977 suggest that the massacres were a reaction to Armenian provocation. Their picture is that of a strict but beneficent Ottoman order sorely tested by the vagaries and insubordination of the Armenian millet and by the revolutionary activities of the nationalist parties. According to them, these parties pursued a kind of "the-worst-the-better" strategy. They hoped that, by provoking the sultan into mass reprisals against the Armenians, they could elicit intervention by the European powers and thus bring about the liberation of Armenia. Thus the Shaws noted that in the period 1890–93, terrorism and counterterrorism went on for three years with the government acting sternly, albeit sometimes harshly to keep order. The Hunchaks were, however, denied the kind of harsh reprisals that they really needed to make their case in Europe. They then organized a major coup at Sasun . . . the strongest area of Armenian population, where there were many marauding tribesmen who had caused trouble to the cultivators in the past.[29]

Further, the Shaws claim that the Hnchakists intended to create "a Socialist Armenian Republic presumably in the six Anatolian provinces from which all Muslims would be driven out or simply killed."[30] Beyond the fact that there is no confirming evidence for this opinion in the writings of other historians, the Shaws make this assertion without any citations or qualifying remarks. What is left is a clear intention to place the blame for the massacres on the Hnchakist and Dashnak parties, and beyond them on the Armenians themselves.

Armenian Revolutionary Parties

In the nineteenth and early twentieth centuries, three Armenian revolutionary parties were active in the Ottoman and Russian Empires. These were the Armenakan party, the Hnchakist party, and the Dashnaktsutiun. All three parties were nationalist, favoring a lesser or greater degree of autonomy or self-determination. The Hnchakist party, in particular, had a socialist orientation, indicating the growth influence of Russian revolutionary thought and activity.[31]

Given the available evidence, it is not possible to assess precisely the extent of support and influence of these parties, and it is therefore difficult to judge with precision whether they were or were not a threat and a provocation to the Ottoman regime. The impression one gets, however, is that the influence of these parties was limited. Van was the place where the Armenakan party was most influential, but it seems to have declined after the massacres. It is possible that the Hnchakist party was influential in the Sassoun area, but any power it might have had also declined after the massacres and gave way to the more popular Dashnaktsutiun. As to the extent of Hunchak support, Nalbandian notes dryly: "The opponents of the Hunchaks were not willing to see a large part of their nation destroyed in order that the Hunchaks attain a dubious political goal."[32] To this Hovannisian adds that the views of the Hunchaks were assessed by most Armenian leaders as "impracticable and utopian."[33]

Although Sarkis Atamian argues that the Dashnaktsutiun was widely popular,[34] Davison, writing of a somewhat later time, suggests that "the peasant mass was not very vocal. Higher classes of Ottoman Armenians wished rather for a regenerated and orderly Turkey and thought that Autonomy would be possible only within Turkey and not under Russian domination."[35]

Assessment of the Provocation Thesis

The provocation thesis falls short of being a credible explanation for the massacres because it neither convincingly demonstrates that the revolutionary parties were a serious threat nor does it address itself to the question of why they were seen as a threat. If they were viewed by the government as a threat, the question arises as to the perceptions and motives of the Porte itself, a question the provocation thesis does not raise. There are other problems with the argument as well. It does not explain why the reaction was so heavily incommensurate to the supposed provocations. It does not explain why some of the most serious reprisals were taken against upper-class Armenians in Constantinople and Trebizond who had opposed the revolutionary parties.[36] And it does not explain why some massacres of Armenians, preceding the 1894–96 period, occurred prior to the formation of such parties. In all, as proposed in Chapter 1 and discussed again in Chapter 5, the provocation thesis rests on a simple action-reaction model of human events without making either action or reaction credible.

Perhaps without meaning to, the Shaws themselves point to a more tenable explanation. They note that at the time of the supposed provocations "the mass of Ottoman Armenians remained loyal subjects, but the deeds of the few who did not left a feeling of mistrust."[37] This statement completely undermines the provocation thesis, for if it is the case that the mass of Armenians was loyal, where are we to place the blame—on "the deeds of the few," or on those who were left with "a feeling of mistrust"? We suggest that the feeling of mistrust of the Ottoman regime is at least as important a source of explanation as the deeds of some of the Hnchakists and Dashnaks.

Finally, it is of interest that a provocation thesis need not ipso facto derive from a desire to defend the Ottoman regime. Johannes Lepsius, as we have seen, no defender of Ottoman rule during the massacres, suggests an explanation that also rests on a theory of provocation, albeit not the provocations of the Armenians but those of the Great Powers. It should be noted that Lepsius's thesis, published in 1897, is presented in opposition to the notion, popular at the time, that the massacres were due to a religious conflict, that they were a form of religious persecution.

> What are the Armenian massacres then? A conflict of race? No, for during the centuries Turks have managed to get on more or less well with their Armenian subjects. A national rising? No, for the Armenian population in Armenia neither knows, nor wishes to know, anything of the political propaganda of certain agitators who in London, Paris, or Constantinople form revolutionary clubs and issue political pamphlets. A persecution of the Christians? Not simply this, for there was no immediate provocation. Then what do the Armenian horrors mean? Without any question their origin was purely political, or to state it more exactly, they were an administrative measure. [38]

To his argument that the massacres may have taken the form of a religious persecution but were not caused by religious motives, he may have added the observation that the Greeks, who were after all Christians, were for the most part not harmed during the massacres of the Armenians. Further, to say that the massacres were due to an administrative measure begs the question of why such a measure was taken. Lepsius addresses himself to this question in a later passage:

> For years the instruments of destruction appointed by the government had been working silently and unnoticed, when suddenly the Porte saw itself forced by threatened Armenian reforms to hasten the process, and even at the risk of a general rising in Europe, determined at one stroke to annihilate the Armenian nation, and to sweep away that hated Christianity which was always awakening the sympathy of Europe. [39]

It is hard to make out what were the "instruments of destruction" and why they worked for years "silently and unnoticed," but the second part of the explanation does have an empirical reference. If we may phrase it differently, Lepsius suggests that the Armenian massacres were provoked by the demands for reforms made by the Great Powers. He does not develop this argument further, nor does he draw the conclusion that the Shaws do, namely, that the Ottoman regime was not to blame for the violence. Nevertheless, without an examination of the perceptions and motives of the regime, even his argument can be used to shift responsibility from those who made the decision to use violence onto to those who were said to have provoked it. Our goal is not to blame the Ottoman regime and the sultan, but it is clearly not possible to examine or explain the massacres without taking them into consideration.

The Massacres and the Preservation of the Old Order

The following discussion attempts to move beyond the provocation thesis to the beliefs, motives, and perceptions of the sultan and his regime that might have affected their actions, including their decisions concerning the Armenians. It seeks to establish that the sultan's actions were shaped by the context against which he viewed the Armenians, by his beliefs and ideology, and by the activities of the Armenians themselves.

The term *context*, as used here, does not mean "general historical background as might be understood by a student of the Ottoman Empire"; rather it means "the situation as might have been experienced by the sultan and his regime." This is an important distinction because it draws the study away from the general history of Armenian-Ottoman relations while concentrating on that portion of history that may have been known to Abdul Hamid himself. In particular, two aspects of this history seem to be significant: (1) Armenian history in the nineteenth century unfolded against a background wherein other millets and nationalities of the empire were agitating, some with notable success, for self-determination and even secession. Often they were aided in such endeavors by the great powers who used minority demands for self-determination as pretexts for intervention in the affairs of the Ottoman state. (2) The majority of Ottoman-Armenians lived in Eastern Anatolia close to the border with Russia at a time when that traditional enemy loomed ever more powerful and threatening.

As to the sultan's ideology and beliefs, we maintain with other historians that Abdul Hamid was a deeply conservative if not reactionary head of state who wanted to preserve his empire even at the cost of severe repression. This readiness to use violence for the sake of the unity of the empire may have been one of the factors leading him to initiate or tolerate massacre against recalcitrant minorities like the Armenians. [40]

Concerning the behavior of the Armenians, not only the emergence of the revolutionary parties but the flowering of the Armenian millet—some have called it a renaissance—may have had unintended consequences. The very success of the Armenians gave this Christian minority the appearance that it was challenging a traditional and hierarchical, Muslim and imperial, religious and political order.

Context

Millet and Nationality

A useful beginning for a discussion of the context in which Abdul Hamid perceived the Armenians is the millet system and its challenge by the nationality problems of the nineteenth century.

The religious communities of the Ottoman Empire were called *millets*, and each had well-defined status, duties, and obligations. The Muslim community was governed by Islam and the *Shariah*, or Islamic law, but *dhimmi* communities of Jews and Christians, though assigned a status lower than that of the majority, were themselves protected by this law and by long usage.[41]

The root of the attitude toward the *dhimmi* millets goes back to the Prophet, who was acquainted with five religions: Judaism, Christianity, Sabianism, Zoroastrianism, and the various polytheistic cults of Arabia. The peoples of Scripture—the *dhimma*—were singled out by Mohammed in contrast to the polytheists. Jews and Christians were not to be slain or enslaved, as long as they did not rise and take up arms against Muslim authority. Having once been conquered, the *dhimma* were allowed, under special conditions, to practice their religion as before.

Treatment of the millets in the Ottoman Empire varied over the years according to beliefs prevalent in the main orthodox branches of Islam, according to whether they were Jews or Christians, Orthodox or Armenian, and according to whether the empire was expanding or contracting, conquering or being conquered. Despite all these variations certain constants remained. Millets were given a great deal of local autonomy. This derived not only from the corporate nature of the empire but also from the Sacred Law itself, which regulated Muslim behavior and the relationship of *dhimmi* to Muslim. The *Shariah* did not claim to regulate behavior within the *dhimmi* community. Under the millet system, behavior within each community was governed by ecclesiastical authorities, rabbis or patriarchs, and these functionaries were themselves responsible to the sultan for discipline within their flocks. Despite their local autonomy, millets were responsible for a *cyzia*, or tax, and their members were excluded from military service. Both of these features were viewed as emblematic of *dhimmi* inferiority.

Until the nineteenth century, the two main Christian millets were the Greek Orthodox and the Armenian. The Orthodox, both because of its size and of its special relations dating back to the *devsirme* conscription, had great influence.[42] It consisted of the Greeks, Serbs, Bulgarians, Rumanians, and the inhabitants of Southern Albania. Significantly, these national differences carried no particular meaning for the Ottoman government, not, that is, until the nineteenth century when nationalism began to foster new political identities. "To the Ottomans, these various groups were part of the *Rummilleti*, and since *Rum* also denoted Greek, they tended all to be regarded more or less as Greeks."[43]

As to the Armenians, "the precedent set by Mehmed the Conqueror of organizing the various communities of Dhimmis [sic] into recognized millets was not followed by his successors. They simply maintained the three original millets and classified all their non-Orthodox Christian subjects as Armenians."[44] The Armenian patriarch's authority extended over such incompatibles as Catholics, Nestorians, and Jacobites. It was not until the nineteenth century that non-Apostolic Armenian groups like the Catholics and the Protestants were granted millet rights of their own.

It has been claimed that religious communities, millets, found a great deal of autonomy if not tolerance in the Ottoman Empire. Especially some dissenting Christian sects like the Nestorians preferred the relative autonomy and tolerance of the millet system to the intolerance and persecutions of Greek Orthodox Christianity. Indeed, Hovannisian notes that the millet system with all its limitations and inequalities "proved workable and beneficial for the Armenians."[45]

One needs to view Ottoman tolerance toward minorities in some perspective: it was tolerant compared to the Christian world, and it was certainly more tolerant than the regime headed by the Committee of Union and Progress that replaced it in 1908. A distinction, however, should be made between the Ottoman theory of tolerance and the actual experience of Armenian peasants living in the eastern vilayets or provinces. Here the relatively defenseless Armenian may have been allowed to practice his religion, but his life and property became increasingly less secure as, in the nineteenth century, the plateau became populated by Turkish and Kurdish pastoral groups.[46]

The process whereby Armenian security was undermined in Anatolia can be traced back to the sixteenth century. The conquest of Arab lands incorporated large Muslim populations, making the Empire more Orthodox, practicing a stricter form of Sunni Islam, and becoming less dependent on the Greek millet for manpower. Both of these developments made for a decreased level of tolerance of all minorities, which was reduced still more as the empire began to lose territory to Christian powers. *Dhimmis* once thought to be innocuous were increasingly viewed as in league with the foreign enemy.[47] Beyond the vagaries of rise and fall, however, there did remain certain constants: though the conditions of life for the *dhimmi* millets remained insecure, the Ottoman state *as state* did not begin to persecute them, especially the Armenians, until the latter part of the nineteenth century.

Official Ottoman tolerance and devolution of power, however, had a price. This was the explicit agreement that *dhimmis* were never to consider themselves the equals of Muslims. The Ottoman state considered Muslim superiority to be both just and natural, and the necessary if not sufficient condition for its continued tolerance of inferior minorities.

> Christians . . . were inevitably considered second-class citizens in the light of religious revelation—as well as by reason of the plain fact that they had been conquered by the Ottomans. This whole Moslem outlook was often summed up in the common terms, Gavur (or Kafir), which meant unbeliever or "infidel" with emotional and quite uncomplimentary overtones.[48]

Reform and Repression: The Reign of Abdul Hamid II

It would take us too far afield to recapitulate the fascinating and important work of other historians who have described the decay of the millet system and the rise of the nationality problem in the Ottoman Empire of the nineteenth century. Here we can touch only on some of the highlights that may have been pertinent to Abdul Hamid and his regime and that provided the context against which they perceived the Armenians.

When the sultan came to power in 1876, the empire had already experienced more than a century of dissolution and dismemberment. Not only was it subjected to the military and economic pressures of the Great Powers, but it also found itself trying to stem the tide of nationalism and self-determination among its own nationalities and millets.[49] Notably, in 1829 Greece had become independent, and after the treaty of San Stefano in March of 1878, Romania, Serbia, Montenegro, and Bulgaria either became autonomous regions or independent states. In each of these instances one or another of the Great Powers had a hand in fostering the autonomy or self-determination of minorities in the Ottoman Empire.

It should be noted that prior to Abdul Hamid's reign the empire had tried limited reforms as a policy to maintain unity. Beginning roughly in 1856 with the proclamation of the *Hatt-i Hümayun*, an imperial edict, the Ottoman regime attempted to satisfy the demands for equality and self-determination of the various peoples under its rule by granting greater autonomy and legal rights to *dhimmis*. It is significant that the reform movement failed to promote unity and that Abdul Hamid came to power in part as a reaction to its failure.

Although he came to power at the crest of the *Tanzimat*, or period of the reform movement, within a short time Abdul Hamid shelved the reform constitution and had Midhat Pasha, the grand vizier most associated with that liberal document, assassinated.[50]

> I made a mistake when I wished to imitate my father, Abdulmecit, who sought to reform by persuasion and by liberal institutions. I shall follow in the footsteps of my grandfather, Sultan Mahmut. Like him, I now understand that it is only by force that one can move the people with whose protection God has entrusted me.[51]

As the Shaws note, instead of reform Abdul Hamid "developed a structure of personal control that, with the centralized system of administration created by Tanzimat, made possible a far more extensive and complete autocracy than anything ever achieved by the greatest of the Sultans."[52] And Midhat Pasha remarked: "Everything that had been accomplished in the way of reform or high politics during the time of his father and his predecessors he considered to be misfortunes for the dynasty and the Empire."[53]

On the other hand, it is well not to overdo the contrast between the reign of Abdul Hamid and the Tanzimat reform period. Though this is not the place for a full discussion of Tanzimat, there are two important points that should be stressed about its intentions and about its effects, especially as these pertained to the Armenians. First, though Tanzimat, notably as expressed in the *Hatt-i Hümayun*, was ostensibly a movement toward equality, at bottom it was a reform meant to preserve the empire. And second, the equality proclaimed for the millets was hardly put into practice. In all, the failure to institutionalize the Tanzimat reforms revealed the incapacity of a traditional order, the millet system in particular, to deal with the disintegration of empire and the emergence of the nationality problem.[54]

In brief, the sultan may have become wary of the Armenians, seeing them against a backdrop of disloyal millets, seceding nationalities, and Great Power pressures. His suspicions may have been reinforced by the geographical location of the Armenians on the Russian border. Indeed, it was very dangerous for the Armenians to be straddling the Russo-Turkish border in a period of war, when the Ottoman Empire was contracting and the Russian expanding.

Between Empires

Hovannisian estimates that, out of a population of 4,700,000 in Russian Transcaucasia in 1886, there were 940,000 Armenians, or 20 percent. By 1917, the Armenian population had grown to 1,783,000, but the area as a whole had also expanded to 7,500,000, leaving the fraction of Armenians, at 24 percent, nearly unchanged. In Erevan and Kars, disputed border provinces under sometimes Ottoman sometimes Russian rule, however, there were 669,000 Armenians or 60 percent, and 119,000 or 30 percent, respectively. Throughout the period 1877–1917 there was something of a population transfer, with Muslims fleeing Russia and Armenians fleeing the Ottoman Empire:

> In 1878 three-fourths of the inhabitants of the Kars oblast were Moslem, but in the following two years approximately seventy-five thousand of them sought refuge within the Ottoman Empire. Their abandoned lands were repopulated by Russian religious dissenters and Turkish dissenters who continued to filter across the border. [55]

Had relations between the Ottomans and the Russians been peaceful, it is possible that the Armenians on its border would not have been viewed with alarm by the Porte. As we know, however, relations between the two great empires of the area were anything but harmonious, and it is in this context that Armenians in the eastern vilayets came to be seen as harboring pro-Russian sympathies. And, indeed, this mistrust was not totally unfounded. Russian Armenians led by Armenian generals in the Russian forces had fought with valor against the Ottomans, especially in the Russo-Turkish war of 1877–78; the Great Powers used the Armenian question as a pretext to force concessions from the Porte, and the Hnchakist and Dashnaktsutiun parties were either influenced by or had their origins in Russia. It takes no great empathy, therefore, to understand why the sultan may have been wary of the Armenian millet. That he fostered massacre in 1894–96, and that his successors, as can be noted in Chapter 5, perpetrated genocide is another matter altogether.

Ideology

Restoration and Massacre

Abdul Hamid's attitudes and intentions concerning the massacres may be gauged from a letter sent by the sultan to Sir Philip Currie, the British ambassador, in which he explains why harsh measures had to be taken at Sassoun, the scene of the first massacre in August 1894. To Sir Philip's allegations that "shocking atrocities were said to have been committed and the number killed is said to have reached several thousands,"[56] the sultan replied as follows:

> His majesty states that he is well aware of your Excellency's friendly disposition towards himself and the Empire; and he does not for a moment imagine that in bringing these matters to his notice Your Excellency wishes to raise the Armenian Question. . . .
>
> His Majesty continues by stating that just as in other countries there are Nihilists, Socialists, and Anarchists, endeavouring to obtain from the Government concessions and privileges which it is impossible to grant them, and just in the same manner steps had to be taken against them, so it is with the Armenians who for their own purposes invent these stories against the Government, and finding that they receive encouragement from British officials, are emboldened to proceed to open acts of rebellion, which the Government is perfectly justified in suppressing by every means in its power. . . .
>
> His Majesty says that your Excellency will remember that the Bulgarians, [sic] concocted the same stories against the Government, and proceeded just as the Armenians do, and that the British Government extended a certain protection to the Bulgarians, who have now been formed into separate provinces. This cannot possibly, however, happen in the case of the Armenians. *The Armenian population is spread over a large extent of the country and in no place are they a majority. Their expectations, therefore, can never be realized, and all the exaggerated stories of oppression and persecution, got up with the object of exciting European sympathy to enable them to obtain an impossible end, should not be relied upon. . . .* [emphasis added].

Naturally the Ottoman government was bound to take strong measures to put down sedition, and when people were found with arms in ther hands resisting the authorities, it was only natural that the Government should mete out to them summary punishment. Only a short time ago in Italy, the Italians put down disorder with a strong hand. England herself had, in India, resorted to the strongest measures to stamp out rebellion, and even in Egypt, England had put down disorder with a high hand. *His Imperial Majesty treated the Armenians with justice and moderation, and as long as they behaved properly, all toleration would be shown to them* [emphasis added], but he had given orders that when they took to revolt or to brigandage the authorities were to deal with the Armenians as they deal with the authorities. . . .

His Majesty had read the account which your excellency had given him with horror and sorrow. His Majesty had had no knowledge of these facts, and yesterday morning, when he read the report, he immediately instructed the Minister of the Interior to make inquiries and cause a telegram to be sent to Zeki Pasha, Commandant of the Fourth Corps d'Armée, instructing him to report at once.[57]

The letter fails to mention that this same "Zeki Pasha, Commandant of the Fourth Corps d'Armée," had been decorated for his "bravery" at Sassoun.

We have quoted the sultan at length in order to show his relative sophistication pertaining to world affairs, his resentment of British pretensions to moral superiority, and above all his views on the Armenians. As regards the Armenians, we see that the Bulgarian secession "into a separate province" agitates him, and he imputes to the Armenians the same desires for secession and independence that had motivated the Bulgarians: "This cannot possibly, however, happen in the case of the Armenians. . . . Their expectations . . . can never be realized."

Beyond wanting to preserve the unity of the empire and imputing to Armenians secessionist intentions which he was willing to repress by force, possibly even by massacre, Abdul Hamid, as many historians have pointed out, wanted to guard the old order and to revitalize Islam. It is not unreasonable, therefore, to assume that he wanted to preserve the millet system and its orderings as well. Here again Armenians challenged his most sacred values.

Thus Ismail Kemal Bey, who had served under the liberal Midhat Pasha and was well situated to understand the sultan's perspective, wrote that the bulk of the Muslim population gave the sultan no cause for alarm, but it was a different matter with the Christians, who frequented the foreign educational establishments in the country, who traveled and carried on constant relations with Europe and America, and he felt powerless to stay their evolution. In the Sultan's mind, the Armenians, spread as they were all over the Empire and in close relationship with their Muslim neighbors, whom they resembled in manner and customs, and whose language they spoke, were the only people in the Empire who might propagate liberal—and from this point— pernicious ideas. The same Armenians who had been considered useful to the state by former liberal statesmen, he now regarded as highly dangerous and for the same reasons. [58]

If he felt powerless to stay their evolution, what indeed might be the sultan's reaction and that of the Ottoman ruling class who believed in the millet system and the subservient status of *dhimmis*, to discover that the structure of the millets was crumbling and that *dhimmis*, especially Armenians, had experienced a social, economic, and cultural renaissance that was altering the relative status between them and their Ottoman superiors?

It may be suggested that the reaction of the sultan would be to attempt to restore the previous traditional equilibrium by destroying the gains in status of the Armenian millet. One of the policies that would be available to him would be the use of force, including massacre. What needs to be shown is that Armenians during the reign of Abdul Hamid II did in fact rise in status, that their status was seen to rise to the point where they could challenge a traditional, hierarchical, and valued rank ordering among Muslims and *dhimmis*, and that massacre was a preferred response to their many challenges.

The Armenian Renaissance

There is consensus among writers, even among those not sympathetic to Armenian claims, that in the nineteenth century the Armenian community experienced a sudden flowering in culture, a development in its economic standing, and a new assertiveness in politics to an extent that some have called it a renaissance.

The Armenian people, subjected for centuries to foreign domination, experienced a cultural and political renaissance during the eighteenth and especially the nineteenth centuries. The growth of national consciousness was manifested in literary movements, in the

establishment of hundreds of schools . . . throughout the Ottoman
and Russian empires, and in the emergence of societies striving for
Armenian self-administration. The focus of concern was the great
Armenian plateau in eastern Anatolia. On this land the Armenian
nation had taken form in the first millennium before the Christian
era. It was there that Armenian kings had reigned and a distinctive
native culture had developed.[59]

The Armenian renaissance had cultural, economic, and political
features. As to cultural activity, in the late eighteenth and early nineteenth centuries there occurred a marked advance in Armenian literacy,
an increased development of the press, and a flowering of a literature in
the vernacular. Until 1790 Armenians had been allowed only to educate
seminarians and to build seminaries. Under the rule of Selim III, however,
they were permitted to form community schools, and these multiplied
rapidly, first in Istabul and later in the interior. By 1830 a school for girls
was established and a number of secondary schools as well.[60]

As for the press, by the middle of the nineteenth century two outstanding Armenian journals were founded in Istanbul and one in Moscow,
indicating among other things that there was a growing reading public
capable of and interested in consuming news pertinent to Armenian life.
The three papers were the *Massis*, the *Ardzvi Vaspurakan*, and the *Huisissa-*
pile.[61] The *Ardzvi Vaspurakan* is of special interest because it was published
by Bishop Mekertitch Khirimian (1820–1907), known popularly as Khirimian Hairig, who combined both religious and early nationalist leadership in one person. In 1858 he moved his paper from Istanbul to Van, in
the Armenian heartland, a significant development in that it indicates
that the Armenian reading public was not limited to Istanbul but had
appeared as well in the eastern vilayets.

As to economic activity, several writers point out that in the nineteenth century Armenians became quite active in trade, banking, and
industry, and the *Amira*, a wealthy Armenian merchant class, was in the
forefront of early Ottoman economic development.[62]

As to political activity, we know that figures like Odian Efendi and
Artin Dadian Efendi were active at the highest levels of the reform movement and that Armenians were active as well in the ranks of the revolutionary parties. The Armenian renaissance, in all of its dimensions, not
only may have appeared to threaten the unity of the state but may also
have confronted the ideology and practice of Muslim superiority and
Armenian inferiority.

The Perspective of the Sultan

One need not agree with observers like Edwin Pears who argue that the sultan had an irrational hatred for Armenians to see that from his perspective the Armenians represented an intolerable challenge. Nor, however, must one then side with writers like the Shaws who contend that the Porte's view was fully justified by the intentions and activities of the Armenians themselves. There is a third alternative that may be suggested: given the disintegration of empire due to Great Power pressures and minority secessions, and given the location of the Armenians on the border with Russia, their contacts with the European powers, and especially their renaissance at a time of trouble for the Ottoman Empire, the ground or context against which they had once been viewed shifted, and what had once been perceived as a loyal and useful millet came to be seen as insurrectionary and provocative.

The alteration of perceptions on the part of the Porte need not have had anything to do with the intentions or even the actions of the Armenians. The conservative ideology of the sultan, however, was a most important predisposing and magnifying factor. Not only did he want to maintain the integrity of the empire, he thought he could do it by reinvigorating Islam and by restoring the old order—that is, the millet system with the Muslims on the top and the Christians on the bottom—and he felt that he could affect these changes by the use of force. In this interpretation, if restoration was a means toward unification, force, including massacre, was a means toward restoration.

Returning briefly to the role of the Armenian revolutionary parties, their role in the perceived provocation did not stem from their feckless activities and improbable manifestos but from the wider context in which the Armenian millet was viewed as leaving its preassigned place and challenging the traditional order of the Ottoman Empire. An observer of the period comes close to my own interpretation:

> When I say that the Armenian massacres were caused by the revolutionists, I tell the truth, and a very important one, but it is not the whole truth. It would be more correct to say that the presence of the revolutionists gave occasion and excuse for the massacres. That the Turks were looking for an excuse, no one can doubt who has traversed that country.[63]

For the Armenians or for writers who understand the Armenian situation and outlook, the revolutionary parties did not represent a real threat to the Porte, and the Porte's reaction was totally disproportionate to the actual level of provocation. Viewed from the vantage point of the Porte, however, given the context of the times, these parties represented an intolerable danger. This is a far cry, of course, from arguing that the Armenians were somehow responsible for their own massacres. It is one thing to begin to understand the motives and perceptions of the perpetrators, and quite another to blame the victims for what went on in the minds of their killers.

Force and Massacre

To this point is has been suggested that the massacres were prompted not only by the supposed provocations of the Armenian revolutionary parties but also by the ideology of the sultan and his regime, by the shifting context of Armenian-Ottoman relations, including Great Power pressures on behalf of the Armenians, and by the unintended consequences of the Armenian renaissance. The question, however, remains, Why did the sultan choose or accede to massacre when he could have used policies short of mass murder? For example, he could have used legal repression and police powers to cut down or even to destroy the parties. Or, conversely, he might have sided with the liberal reforms and opted for genuine egalitarian pluralism. Given his reactionary perspective, the hierarchical structure of Ottoman society, and the many challenges of the Armenian renaissance, however, the sultan may have found massacre to be the most useful and desirable policy option.

Police repression as such could be directed effectively against individuals or parties, but it could not be used to prevent the renaissance of a major communal group. For renaissance implies a whole population on the move in the economic, cultural, social, and political spheres. To abort such a broad-based social mobilization, what is needed is a broad-based policy designed to prevent change not only in one sphere of human progress but in all of them. Consider what massacre accomplished: it "thinned out" or reduced the Armenian population; it seriously harmed its economic base; it humiliated, where it had not destroyed, its leadership; and it demonstrated in no uncertain terms that the Muslim segment and the Ottoman state had sufficient power to repress any challenge from *dhimmis*.

To argue from the advantageous results of a policy to the intentions of policymakers is not necessarily to fall into the *post hoc, ergo propter hoc* fallacy. What is needed is indication that the regime itself recognized in advance the results that a policy of massacre might produce.

In the case of the sultan, the evidence is not conclusive, but it is suggestive. First, massacre was not a new policy in the area. Massacre had been used against Christians before, most notably in Bulgaria, and it had been used against Armenians even before the period of 1894–96. The regime may have been well aware of the destructive and repressive aspects of massacre before that time. Further, Muslims, too, had been the victims of massacre, notably in Crete and in the Balkans, and it has been said that many of the Muslim refugees who had experienced Cossack violence in the Crimea had been settled in the eastern vilayets among the Armenians. Thus Muslims too knew from firsthand experience the effects of massacre, and among those seeking revenge it might have been a popular measure. And as a last point, massacre may also have been attractive to the regime because it was a subterfuge. In permitting local authorities and peasants to participate in repressing Armenians, massacre could achieve the desired results without clearly implicating the central government. At a time when the regime was hard-pressed by European powers and was afraid of external intervention, this may have been by no means the least of the attractive features of this policy.

It should be noted, however, that the sultan had before him a policy alternative that would have avoided massacre. He might simply have continued the policies of his predecessors by institutionalizing the reform constitution for which Midhat Pasha and other Ottomans, including Armenians, had labored so long and so diligently. As it turned out, in the long run the sultan failed in any event to stem the forces of disintegration. Ironically, though he likely also would have failed had he followed the liberal reformers—nationalism was probably unstoppable—it is possible that no massacres of Armenians would have occurred.

This is an attractive argument, but it neglects a basic contradiction. The sultan and indeed the Ottoman Empire as a whole could not, at one and the same time, accommodate both the Armenian renaissance, with its implications of equality, and the millet system, with its implications of hierarchy and Muslim superiority. Something had to give. Either the Armenians had to be prevented from becoming the equals of Muslims, or the ideology, political myth, and practice of Muslim superiority had to be scrapped and replaced by a genuine egalitarian pluralism, one that might even have permitted self-determination. As has been seen, the sultan was not prepared to move in the direction of authentic equality and liberty.

Conclusion

We started this chapter by raising two questions: (1) What caused the Armenian massacres? (2) Why did they not evolve into a total domestic genocide like that of 1915 or the Holocaust? The first question has been addressed in the main body of this chapter, but some of the factors identified, such as the perceptions and ideology of the sultan, the alleged connections between the Armenians and the Russians, the enemies of the Ottoman regime, and the social mobilization of the Armenian millet may be restated in general terms as lessons that might apply to other cases of massacre. The second question cannot be fully answered until we discuss the genocide of 1915 in Chapter 5, but a provisional discussion is suggested below.

Lessons of the Massacres

There are at least three lessons derived from the violence of 1894–96 that might apply to other instances of massacre or partial genocide.

1. A communal group may appear to a regime as threatening enough to massacre, not only because of what that group intends to do or does, but also because of the ideology of those who feel threatened by it or because of changes in the context in which it is being perceived.

2. No matter how small or inoffensive it really is, a communal group may appear as threatening enough to massacre if it appears that it is in league with the enemies of the ruling regime.

3. In culturally plural societies undergoing the rigors of rapid change, upwardly mobile communal groups are likely to generate intergroup tensions. The more steep and rapid a group's ascent—from alien or pariah to elite status—the sharper the reaction against it. In instances where traditional elites are losing their grip on power or have already lost it, the rapid rise of low-status communal groups can lead to violence, including massacre.

The first proposition is so elementary that it is restated here only because it is so often forgotten. As against the provocation thesis, which argued that the Armenians themselves were responsible for the massacres, a principal design of this chapter has been to show that the stance of the perpetrator, how he views a threatening situation, must also be taken into account. Here Abdul Hamid imputing to Armenians the same motives that he had found among the Bulgars and other secessionist minorities is a case in point.

The second proposition is a generalization drawn from the apparent threat that the geopolitical situation of the Armenians posed to the Porte. Though there are other communal groups straddling borders in various parts of the world, the notable threat derives not just from the geographical location but from an alleged connection between the group and an external enemy of the state. Preceding the First World War, Ottoman rulers assumed that Armenians were in league with the empire's external enemies, above all Russia. Following Pearl Harbor, many Americans were convinced that Japanese Americans were in league with Japan. Though Japanese Americans were not massacred like the Armenians, the general principle that minorities who may have ethnic or other links to the enemies of the state are in danger of repression holds for both instances.

As to the third proposition, it is seldom when the wretched of the earth are most wretched that they suffer massacre. To the contrary, it is when they become upwardly mobile, begin to improve their economic, social, cultural, and political situations that they are most likely to be the subjects of massacre. "Negroes" were most likely to be lynched after, not before, Reconstruction. Pogroms in the Russian pale coincided with Jewish advance and increased in the latter part of the nineteenth century as the Jews began to leave the ghettos in increasing numbers. Anti-Ibo riots in Northern Nigeria, preceding Biafra by some twenty-five years, occurred with increasing severity in the urban enclaves. These riots coincided with the period of Ibo ascent, when this once despised communal group began successfully to compete with local traders and to challenge local politicians. As for the present study, it is striking that the Armenian massacres of 1894–96 occurred not when Armenian peasants lived out an isolated, backward, and obscure existence in the eastern vilayets but when they experienced a renaissance.

In the examples cited under the third proposition, the ruling elites suffered a period of disintegration and decline, and society was challenged by forces it lacked the capacity to assimilate. Massacre was used or acceded to by the regime in order to restore a traditional and hierarchical order, one that seemed to be intolerably threatened by the improved fortunes of groups that in other times had occupied a low, despised, or pariah status.

As a corollary to the third proposition, it may be suggested that the state may find massacre to be an especially advantageous policy to employ in repressing upwardly mobile communal groups. Other forms of repression may be too broad, too narrow, or too difficult to execute, as the case may be. Thus genocide may be too broad an option because it eliminates a communal group from the social structure when the goal may be only to halt its progress or to reduce its status. Conversely, police repression may be too narrow an option. The arrest of leaders and the destruction of political parties may not serve to slow the progress of a communal group in the economic, cultural, social, and political spheres. Forced emigration as has been used by Vietnam and Cuba in recent years may not be a possibility because it may create unmanageable international tensions. There are other measures like assimilation or conversion, which may not be feasible if a majority rejects incorporating a minority or if a minority insists on a separate identity. Finally, one needs to stress, when a state ceases to view the progress of a despised minority as a "problem," it may then cease to consider massacre as a "solution."

In Chapter 3 it will be seen that Jews in Imperial Germany, who were another despised group thought to be inferior, also experienced a sharp reaction to their emancipation and progress. This reaction did not take the form of massacres but of an antisemitic movement that attempted to stem their assimilation and integration into German society. The *Kaiserreich* cannot be equated, however, to the regime of Sultan Abdul Hamid. Imperial Germany was a powerful and widely legitimate state whose elites had broad ambitions but could not be said to be disintegrating. Moreover, the institutional context was also quite different, allowing for political parties and representation in a parliament. As will be seen in Chapter 4, the structure of the state directed Jew-hatred into the direction of political party activity and ideological pronouncements that were missing in the Ottoman context.

The Massacres and Total Genocide

When we shall turn to the Armenian Genocide and to the Holocaust we shall see that some of the same elements that entered into the massacres of 1894–96 were also present in those two instances of total genocide. Given revolution and war, Armenians and Jews were perceived as deadly threats to the Turkish and German states; Armenians and Jews were said to be in league with the enemies of Turkey and Germany, respectively; Armenian and Jewish social mobilization were viewed as illegitimate in Turkey and Germany, though by 1908 and 1918 both states paid lip service to the values of equality. And yet, the massacres of 1894–96 were not a total domestic genocide. [64]

Sultan Abdul Hamid II had no intention of exterminating the Armenians or destroying the Armenian millet as such. Indeed, it may be noted that once the massacres were over,

> relations between Muslims and Armenians in the empire for the most part returned to normal. Armenian officials again were appointed to high positions in the bureaucracy, and Armenian merchants and cultivators resumed their activities. But the terrible events had taken their toll. The harmony that had prevailed for centuries was gone. [65]

Though the massacres poisoned relations between Muslims and Armenians and may be viewed as a prelude to the genocide, the Armenian community survived the violence as a component millet of the Ottoman Empire. [66]

Why did the massacres—terrible as they were—not lead to a total genocide of the Armenians? Such a hypothetical question necessarily leads to speculative responses, but these may be instructive for the discussion of total genocide that will follow later. One possibility, of course, was that the Porte was constrained by external forces, especially the fear of the Great Powers, but that is not the main point.

The main reason total genocide was not perpetrated by the Ottoman regime in 1894–96 was its commitment to Islam, to the millet system, and to restoring the old order. Abdul Hamid was not a revolutionary. He was a reactionary conservative who opposed radical transformations of state and society. Indeed, to commit genocide by destroying the Armenian millet would have been a radical departure from the sultan's ideology, and it would have undermined Islam and the millet system as myths of legitimation linking the Ottoman state to Ottoman society.

The Porte was able to go along with or to help perpetrate massacre, but it was not willing to go so far as to destroy the Armenian millet. In contrast, as we shall see, by 1915 the Young Turks had no such scruples. They were revolutionaries who wanted to destroy the old order, including the millet system, and to replace it with one based on Turkish nationalism. When the time came, for the sake of a homogeneous national state and a Pan-Turkish empire, they did not hesitate to annihilate the Armenian community.

THREE

Jews in Imperial Germany: Antisemitism and the Upwardly Mobile Pariahs

The Jews are our misfortune.

Heinrich von Treitschke[1]

Since the Jew is a misfortune for the people
This makes it very easy for the people
To recognize a Jew. For this neither
A birth certificate nor external
　　characteristics are necessary—
All these can be deceptive—it is only
　　necessary to ask:
Is that man a misfortune for us? Then
He is a Jew.

Bertolt Brecht[2]

　　　　Like the Armenians in the nineteenth-century Ottoman Empire, Jews in imperial Germany underwent an extraordinary renaissance in social, economic, political, and cultural spheres; unlike the Armenians they did not suffer a massacre, but they did experience a sharp antisemitic reaction that at first threatened to undo their emancipation and social mobilization. In the context of Imperial Germany, antisemitism took the form of political party agitation and organization. It is significant, however, that antisemitic political parties in Imperial Germany were a failure. Though they began with a flourish, by the end of the century they had not accomplished what they had set out to do, and by 1912—on the eve of the Great War—they seemed to have been a passing phase in German development.

70

These observations raise at least three questions: (1) What was the connection between Jewish status, social mobilization, and antisemitism in Europe and in Imperial Germany? (2) Why did the antisemitic movement fail in its political goals in Imperial Germany? (3) What are the lessons of its failure for the later success of the Nazis and the implementation of the Holocaust? In the present chapter we shall deal mainly with the first and in the following chapters with the second and the third questions. Before starting to address these questions, however, it is important for us to distinguish among anti-Judaism, Jew-hatred, and antisemitism.[3]

Anti-Judaism refers to a religious antagonism, *adversus Judaeos*, which can be traced to the earliest texts of the Christian church, including the Gospels. It is an antagonism that stemmed from the Church's attempt to supplant Judaism as a popular religion and to appropriate its holy texts, including the Hebrew Scriptures. Anti-Judaism took the form of denouncing Judaism as a spent religion that had been superceded by Christianity and Jews as wicked killers of Christ who were too blind and stubborn to see the truth that might save them. Implicit in anti-Judaism was the notion that Jews had a providential role to play in the world and that their conversion was crucial to Christianity itself. Indeed, their conversion would validate Christianity's claim to being the one true faith. Though it formed some of the basis for Jew-hatred and later antisemitism, Christian anti-Judaism always held out the possibility that Jews might save themselves by conversion.

The preaching of anti-Judaism over many centuries in Christian Europe, but especially following the Crusades, led to the spread of Jew-hatred, a popular and stereotyped antagonism to Jews as people and to Judaism as a faith. By the Middle Ages, it is possible to identify a system of religious and popular beliefs as well as everyday practices, which demonized the Jews and relegated them to a pariah status in Europe.

Although later generations of Jews were emancipated and given equal rights in various European countries, their status as a former pariah clung to them. Moreover, though prejudice on religious grounds alone also declined in Europe, as did organized religion, anti-Judaism remained as a potential powerful resource of arguments, images, and stereotypes for movements that opposed the Jews and sought validation and legitimation in the Christian tradition.

Following the Industrial and French Revolutions and the unsettling effects of capitalism and the modern state, antisemitism became a new and qualitatively different addition to Europe's history of antagonism to

71

the Jews. Antisemitism was an ideology, expressed in a contemporary political movement, that was bitterly opposed to Jewish emancipation, progress, and assimilation. In attempting to justify this opposition, anti-semites argued that the Jews were radically non-European, a separate tribe or race, and the cause of the major dislocations of the modern world including its economic cycles, revolutions, and wars. The antisemites warned that these dislocations were part of a Jewish world conspiracy that aimed to Judaize and control the world. Though antisemitism was never as elaborate an intellectual construction and ideology as Marxism or liberalism, and its political parties failed in their mission in the nine-teenth century, it succeeded only too well in the period following the First World War.

While an ideology can never be reduced to the social forces it ex-presses and to the historical conditions in which it is formulated, it may be suggested that modern antisemitism developed in a climate of increas-ing Jew-hatred that was itself a product of the pariah status of the Jews in Christian Europe, of their rapid social mobilization in the postemanci-pation period, and of the deep-seated opposition that various groups and classes harbored, not only against the Jews but against those forces in the modern world that had made Jewish emancipation, progress, and assimi-lation possible in the first place.

Thus modern antisemitism, while it centered on the Jews, always included others among its enemies. In Germany these were the Liberals, the Socialists, and later the Communists. Some antisemites, who looked beyond the programmatic positions of their adversaries to the social and economic forces making for emancipation, turned against the modern world itself. There developed a reciprocal attraction between those who hated the Jews and those who despaired of the modern world. Those who hated the Jews came to hate the modern world for making it possible for the Jews to advance and to assimilate to European society, and those who hated the modern world came to view the Jews as emblematic of everything they hated. [4]

The more steep the ascent of the Jewish "pariahs," the more rapid their social mobilization, acculturation, and assimilation, and the weaker the liberal and socialist forces that might have come to the Jews' defense, the more widespread was popular Jew-hatred and the more likely was the appearance of a political movement expressing antisemitic ideology and advocating political, social, economic, and cultural measures against Jews.

It should be pointed out in passing that similar forces had been arrayed against the Armenians in the Ottoman Empire. There too a minority that had started out by being despised on religious grounds came to be feared for its progress and its connections to threatening social forces including modernity, and, in the Armenian case, the Great Powers. The striking difference, however, was that in the Ottoman Empire political parties and ideologies with a specifically anti-Armenian animus never did appear.

The violence that developed under Sultan Abdul Hamid was not linked to a contemporary ideology that identified the Armenians as the agents of the world's ills. Ideology did play an important role once the sultan's regime was swept aside by the Young Turks. But here again it was not a specifically anti-Armenian ideology that led to the genocide of 1915–23. Rather, as we shall see, anti-Armenian policies were devised as a result of the Young Turks' commitment to Turkish nationalism from which Armenians had been excluded. These points will be discussed more fully in Chapter 5.

In the following discussion we shall try to establish the following four points: (1) starting with the fourth century but especially after the Crusades, Jewish status was severely degraded until Jews became a pariah caste in Christendom; (2) with the rise of the modern national state and the spread of capitalism, however, Jews became emancipated legally, and they experienced unprecedented social and economic mobilization; (3) these circumstances led to the spread of Jew-hatred and the rise of antisemitic movements that rejected Jewish emancipation, mobilization, and assimilation; (4) the spread and politicization of antisemitism depended in part on the views of the state and on its leading social forces. The last two points will be touched upon in this chapter and discussed more thoroughly in Chapters 4 and 6.

The Jewish Pariah

Hannah Arendt has remarked that it is a fallacy to assume that modern antisemitism can be directly derived from anti-Judaism, the ancient tradition of Christian animosity toward the Jews.

> Antisemitism, a secular nineteenth century ideology . . . and religious Jew-hatred, inspired by the mutually hostile antagonism of two conflicting creeds, are obviously not the same; and even the extent to which the former derives its arguments and emotional ap-

73

peals from the latter is open to question. The notion of an unbroken continuity of persecutions, expulsions, and massacres from the end of the Roman Empire to the Middle Ages, the modern era, and down to our own time, frequently embellished by the idea that modern antisemitism is no more than a secularized version of popular mediaeval superstitions, is no less fallacious (though of course less mischievous) than the corresponding antisemitic notion of a Jewish secret society that has ruled, or aspired to rule, the world since antiquity.[5]

Arendt is not alone in holding this view. Other respected scholars like Schorsch support her position, while others like Tal point out that the worst kind of antisemitism was propagated not by believing Christians but by publicists and agitators who themselves had broken with the Christian tradition and had become not only anti-Jewish but anti-Christian as well.[6]

Although modern antisemitism and Nazism cannot easily be reduced to traditional Christian anti-Judaism, it would be going to the other extreme to argue that there is no connection between the two. Indeed, to draw an analogy, as does Arendt, between a history of persecutions based on a Christian religious tradition and a fabrication of Jewish world domination is to confound reality with illusion. Unlike the paranoid fantasy of a Jewish conspiracy to dominate the world, there is a verifiable history of Christian-inspired discrimination, expulsion, and massacre, and it may not be a fallacy to link that experience with modern antisemitism.

By the same token, the observation that antisemites themselves can be anti-Christian does not imply that Christianity cannot be a basis of antisemitism. A person exposed to Christian anti-Judaism may wind up hating both Judaism and Christianity. One's animus toward Christianity does not, however, absolve Christian teachings from the responsibility of implanting in him or her hatred for Jews.

The Jewish people arrived at the threshold of the modern world—the world of capitalism and the national state—with a heavy burden that had been thrust on their backs as early as the fourth century of the Christian era when Emperor Constantine had converted to Christianity and had joined the force of Rome to the anti-Jewish animus of the Christian Church. This burden was their pariah status in Christendom. Though by itself it cannot explain the rise of modern antisemitism or Nazism, with-

out it these latter phenomena are incomprehensible. Modern antisemitism, in the first instance, can be seen as a reaction to the emancipation,
mobilization, and assimilation of the Jews viewed as pariahs. This, of
course, raises the question about the nature and origin of the pariah status of Jews in the context of European and German society.

Following Weber a pariah people may be defined as a communal
group whose social, economic, and political autonomy is strictly limited
while it has to endure social, economic, and political discrimination in
the larger society.[7] It is a group that is largely prohibited from commen-
sality and intermarriage and is legally and forcefully segregated in its own
residential neighborhood or ghettos. Finally, it is a group that is forced
to endure the burdens of a derogatory stereotype and public image that,
while having little to do with the reality of the group's beliefs and practices, reflects the fears and negative identity of the dominant forces in
the larger society.[8] Besides the Jews in preemancipation Europe, the Untouchables or *Harijans* of India and the "Negroes" of the United States in
the segregated South may be cited as examples.

Parenthetically, it should be noted that a major difference between
the Hindu Untouchables and the Jews, one neglected by Weber, was the
former's self-understanding and internalizing of the pariah status.
Though in the modern world this may be changing, the lower castes or
jatis of the Hindu tradition believed in the Hindu worldview that had
ascribed to them their status, which they hoped through the process of
metempsychosis to escape in time. Similarly, African-Americans in the
segregated South were in danger of internalizing their lowly status—
something that the civil rights and Black Power movements recognized
and struggled against. In contrast, traditional Jews did not accept the
Christian definition of the Jewish fate.

In the preemancipation period, though suffering discrimination,
Jews never considered themselves to be pariahs. Quite to the contrary,
they believed they were chosen for a special task, to be a "light-unto-the-
nations" in exile, and that their powerlessness and homelessness continued to have providential significance within the Jewish self-
understanding. For the most part, therefore, believing, traditional Jews
failed to internalize the negative image that was current in all Christian
societies. It was largely in the modern postemancipation period when
Jews tried to assimilate or acculturate to the larger society that they became vulnerable to self-hatred.[9]

Following the important work of the Catholic theologian Rosemary

Radford Reuther, it is possible to make the case that the pariah status of the Jews and hence their victimization was to a crucial extent forged from a tradition of Christian anti-Judaism. [10] This tradition rested on three principal Christian beliefs concerning the Jews: (1) Christianity had superceded or displaced Judaism as the one true faith; (2) the Jews were deicides; (3) nevertheless, they were to be preserved as a "witness people."

Historically, these three beliefs came to be embodied in Roman and Church law and later in folk and popular culture. While the practical consequences of such views were only sporadically felt in the early years of Christendom, Jewish status became deeply degraded during and after the Crusades and the Black Death. Jews were segregated, expelled, and sometimes massacred in the countries of Christian Europe.

It would be a mistake, however, to reduce the history of Jews in Europe to a story of victimization alone. Baron and Biale have cogently argued that such a lachrymose view of Jewish history blinds us to the fact that to a large extent the Jews themselves desired to live separate and autonomous lives from Christians. [11] Moreover, points out Baron, even during the Middle Ages, said to be so inhospitable to Jews, the Jewish people experienced long periods of relative security and prosperity in various parts of Europe, especially Poland.

Such incisive arguments notwithstanding, temporary Jewish autonomy, security, and even prosperity do not belie the fact that, from the perspective of the Church and of their Christian neighbors, Jews had become members of a despised and hated caste. They seldom had rights of residence, and they lived out their lives at the sufferance of their Christian neighbors and rulers. [12] It is telling that to this day Shylock's defense of his own humanity still strikes us with dramatic and tragic impact.

Adversus Judaeos

Ruether suggests that by the time of the Church Fathers (second to fifth century C.E.), the hermeneutic tradition of Christianity had elaborated two sides: christology, the contemplation and glorification of Christ as the Messiah and the son of God; and *Adversus Judaeos*, the theological denunciation and condemnation of Judaism and the Jews. This second side she calls "the left hand of christology" and proposes that it is not an accidental but an essential aspect of the Christian worldview. [13]

Ruether argues that much of the synoptic conception as well as the writings of Paul—despite his continuing to view the Jews as the people of the first covenant—as, for example, in Thessalonians 2:14–16, is anti-

Jewish, in that it accuses Jews of deicide and of murdering their own prophets. She also contends that "the anti-Judaic tradition in Christianity grew as a negative and alienated expression of a need to legitimate its revelation in Jewish terms."[14] From this perspective the Church could not feel fully validated until the Jews (that is, their rabbis and teachers) admitted the truth of the Christian vision and the falseness of their own doctrines.

> The "wrath upon the Jews," poured out by Christianity, represents this ever unsatisfied need of the Church to prove that it has the true content of the Jewish scriptures by finally making "the Jews . . . admit" that this is the true interpretation. Until Jewish religious tradition itself accepts this as the "real meaning" of its own scriptures, "the Jews" must be kept in the status of the "enemies of God."[15]

In essence, Christianity and Judaism began to conceive of each other as mutually exclusive by making a claim to the same sacred texts and the same tradition but giving these radically different interpretations. If Jesus was the Messiah then the rabbinic tradition was wrong, and if the rabbinic tradition was right then Jesus could not be the Messiah. By its very existence each religion was a living disproof of the other. Judaism viewed Christianity as a species of false messianism and excommunicated those Jews who professed that Jesus was the Christ. By the same token, Christianity sought to disprove the validity of Judaism and presented itself as having superceded it as the one true faith.[16] In the process of trying to displace Judaism, the early Church formulated a body of doctrine, including the accusation of deicide that as a consequence degraded and stigmatized the Jewish people as Christ-killers.

Thus, for example, in Ruether's view Christian anti-Judaism does not stem from the accusation of deicide, but to the contrary the accusation of deicide is a product of Christian anti-Judaism. This anti-Judaism itself had roots in early Christianity's desire to appropriate the Jewish Scriptures for itself and to have its message validated by a conversion of the Jews.

Since, according to Christianity, the Jews were deicides and the Church had superceded the synagogue—indeed all of Israel—as the true vehicle of God's love and His holy covenant, it followed that, far from being the "Chosen People" the Jews had become much inferior to Christians. The themes of deicide, supersession, and the degradation of Jewish status are expressed pungently and pointedly in the following quote from St. John Chrysostom (344–407 C.E.), an early Church Father.

It is because you killed Christ. It is because you stretched out your hand against the Lord. It is because you shed the precious blood, that there is now no restoration, no mercy anymore and no defense. Long ago your audacity was directed against [God's] servants, against Moses, Isaiah and Jeremiah. If there was wickedness then, as yet the worst of all crimes had not been dared. But now you have eclipsed everything in the past and through your madness against Christ, you have committed the ultimate transgression. This is why you are being punished worse now than in the past . . . if this were not the case God would not have turned his back on you so completely. . . . But if it appears that he has utterly abandoned you, it is evident from this anger and abandonment that He is showing even to the most shameless that the One who was murdered was not a common lawbreaker, but was the very lawgiver Himself, and the Cause, present among us, of innumerable blessings. Thus you who have sinned against Him are in a state of dishonor and disgrace, while we who worship Him, though we once were less honored than any of you [that is, as gentile pagans], are now established through the grace of God in a more respected position. [17]

The saint was writing in Antioch at a time when the Jewish community, though a minority, was active and powerful. It had attracted a number of judaizing Christians who were drawn to various aspects of the Jewish liturgy and tradition. This helps to explain his somewhat overheated rhetoric—he was not only lambasting the Jews but was trying to discourage his flock from straying back into the synagogue.

The views of St. Chrysostom and other Church Fathers like Origen (184–253 C.E.) were relatively innocuous as long as Christians had limited political and juridical power and could not translate their antipathy toward Jews into law and practice. With Constantine (approx. 288–337 C.E.) that changed. A once small, despised, and persecuted sect that had broken with Judaism, Christians became the heirs of the Roman Empire and formulators of its laws. The *Adversus Judaeos* polemic infused Roman law and later became assimilated into the folk and popular culture of Christendom. Thereafter, Christians may have tolerated the contemporary Jews whom they knew, but in their churches they were taught to abhor the "Jews" of scripture. Once the real Jews came to be viewed as the liturgical "Jews" of Christian faith and polemic, they became an object of hatred and violence.

The early Church construction of Jews as deicides and as blind to the truth of the Scriptures had some portentous implications for the future of anti-Judaism. [18] It led to the creation of a bifurcated stereotype of Christianity and Judaism where the latter, to borrow a term from ego-psychology, became a negative identity of the former. [19]

> Eventually all the dichotomies of salvation between spirit and flesh, light and darkness, truth and falsehood, grace and damnation, life and death, trust and self-righteousness, were projected on the opposition between Church and Synagogue until the Jewish people became the embodiment of all that is unredeemed, perverse, stubborn, evil, and demonic in the world. [20]

Thus it was that the anti-Judaic tradition of Christian Europe got its start.

The Witness People

Having stigmatized the Jews as deicides and having staked out her claim as the one true faith, the Church had to reconcile her views with the Jews' continued existence in exile. The Church arrived at a brilliant synthesis, based on the teachings of St. Augustine, that was to help determine the fate and status of Jews until the Holocaust.

In the writings of St. Augustine (354–430 C.E.), who was a contemporary of St. Chrysostom, there is an ambivalence toward the Jews. [21] On the one hand, he accepts that part of the Pauline doctrine that continues to view the Jews as the people of the first covenant, on the other hand he accuses them of the crucifixion.

> The Jews held Him; the Jews insulted Him, the Jews bound Him, they crowned Him with thorns . . . they hung Him upon a tree, they pierced Him with a lance. [22]

Augustine resolved his ambivalence and that of the Church by formulating a doctrine that would at one and the same time continue Pauline tolerance, keep the accusation of deicide, and demonstrate that Jewish suffering in exile was still providential in terms of a Christian eschatology. According to this formulation, Jews were to be a witness people, *testes iniquitatis* and *veritatis nostrae*. Their continued existence in exile was to testify both to the evil of the crucifixion and to the truth of the Church. Implicit in this conception was the view that Jews had to be tolerated and not exterminated, but their toleration hinged on their living in a debased and pariah status in exile. Thus according to Ruether,

> Judaism was to exist until the end of time, but as an empty religion that had lost its elect status and inner spiritual power. It was to continue to exist in a pariah status in history, both to testify to the

present election of the Church and to witness the final triumph of
the Church. . . . The Church felt called upon to enforce this status
of reprobation in the form of social "misery," but the "final solution"
could not be executed by men, but lay in the hands of God at the
time of the final eschatological drama.[23]

The *Adversus Judaeos* doctrine of the Church Fathers came very close to
advocating the destruction of the Jews, but the theory of the witness
people helped to preserve them as living relics in Christendom.

The Jews did not immediately become pariahs nor did they always
live in a degraded status in Christendom, but the force of Christian doctrine was always there potentially both to degrade and to preserve them.
As Trachtenberg and Poliakov have shown, especially after the Crusades
and the Black Death, Jews had become the untouchables of Europe,
whose very presence was fearsome, disgusting, and contagious.[24]

It is beyond the scope of this study to document how the theological doctrines of *Adversus Judaeos* and the witness-people were translated
into a corpus of laws which affected popular attitudes that led to the
creation of the status of the Jewish pariah. The best one can do is to
highlight a few events in the evolution of Jewish status under Roman law,
during the Middle Ages following the crusades, and during the modern
period following emancipation.

Under Roman Law

Until the Crusades there was a fairly wide gap in Christendom between the legal status of Jews and their actual or practical existence. It
was one thing for the State and the Church to formulate discriminatory
and degrading laws, it was something else again to enforce them. Thus
before the Crusades popular attitudes and official practice lagged behind
imperial and canonical law in implementing disabilities. In the wake of
the popular passions aroused by the Crusades, however, popular attitudes
and practices marched ahead of Church doctrine, so much so that often
the Church had to bridle the fervor of the mob before it massacred the
Jews.

Following Constantine, the statutes of the Roman empire, which
officially had become Christian, were formulated and promulgated in the
Theodossian Code.[25] As Flannery had remarked, the code is not entirely
anti-Jewish, though the chapters pertaining to the Jews were largely devoted to circumscribing and demoting their status.[26] Indeed, the potency
of the doctrine of the witness-people was demonstrated by the existence
of statutes meant to protect the Jews.

Thus for a time, under the Code, Judaism remained a *religio licita* and did not become a prohibited sect in the manner of some pagan rites (CT 16-8-9). It was permitted to excommunicate its members (CT 16-8-8). Initially its clergy and its patriarch were to be afforded customary privileges (CT 16-8-13, 16-8-15). From these statutes it followed that Jews were not to be molested (CT 16-10-24), their sabbaths were not to be disturbed, and their synagogues were not to be violated. These then were some of the tolerant features of the Theodossian Code that reflected the view of the Jews as a witness-people whose continued existence was deemed to be providential in the light of Christian doctrine. On the other hand, that conception implied that Jews were to live out their existence in a degraded and inferior status, and the code made sure to institutionalize that part of the doctrine as well.

At the same time that that were not allowed to reconvert their own apostates (CT 16-8-28), Jews were forbidden to proselytize, and conversions to Judaism were declared invalid (CT 16-8-1, 7 and 16-7-3). They were not allowed to circumsize slaves or to own Christian slaves (CT 3-1-5).[27] They were not permitted to beautify old or to construct new synagogues without permission. In 415 C.E. Nasi Gamaliel VI was stripped of his office as patriarch for having built a synagogue without authorization. With his passing, the office of Nasi or Patriarch was abolished, depriving the Jewish community of the Roman Empire of an important voice in its affairs. Other legislation known as *privilegia odiosa* further diminished Jewish status.[28] This barred Jews from the army and from the imperial administration and, under penalty of death, prohibited intermarriage between Jews and Christians.

As early as the fifth century, such discriminatory statutes and the attitudes that they implied encouraged violence against Jewish communities. This could be derived from the "continual need in imperial law to legislate against vandalism, synagogue burning, or confiscation, interference with Jewish celebration of the Sabbath or other religious observances, and even pogroms."[29]

In this period ancient centers of Judaism in the diaspora that had existed for hundreds of years were destroyed and the Jews massacred or expelled. Most notably, anti-Jewish violence engulfed Alexandria in 414 C.E. and Antioch in 610 C.E.

In 534 C.E. the emperor Justinian abolished the principle that Judaism was a *religio locita*, in effect placing the legal status of the Jewish community at the whim of the emperor and later Christian kings. Thus was Jewish status undermined in law and practice during the imperial period.

At the same time, however, Jewish status had not yet sunk to that of pariahs. Jews were still farmers, artisans, and traders. They were still able to defend themselves physically, and they were able to travel and live in most places of the empire. If anything their status and economic position was, by and large, higher than that of the slaves and peasants still laboring on the latifundia and estates of the Christian kings and nobles. After the Crusades, however, the Jewish image was increasingly demonized, Jews were forcibly segregated, disarmed, and relegated to economic tasks distasteful to the gentile society.

The Crusades and the Middle Ages

Between the eleventh and the thirteenth centuries, hundreds of Jewish communities were destroyed, and thousands of Jews were massacred by the Crusaders on their way to Jerusalem. It is ironic and tragic that the Church, which had done so much to isolate and stigmatize the Jewish community, thereby creating some of the essential conditions for the massacres, had to condemn violence against the Jews in order to prevent a total debacle.

Over the next two centuries, in the wake of the first Crusade in 1096, Jewish status declined precipitously, and the Jewish community became relegated to a pariah caste in Christendom. These developments were due in large part to the undermining of the Church's Augustinian tolerance and to the emergence of popular Jew-hatred or Judeophobia.

Jeremy Cohen has argued that there were two principal reasons why the Church's Augustinian tolerance was undermined in this period.[30] First, the Church became more politically active and ambitious and sought to create a unified Christendom under her aegis. Second, it became apparent to the Church even before the Crusades that rabbinic or Talmudic Judaism was a departure from the Augustinian conception of traditional biblical Judaism. To many churchmen, especially those concerned with enforcing Christian orthodoxy over a newly militant Christendom, Talmudic Judaism was perceived as a departure from the implicit Augustinian agreement in which Jews were to perform the function of a "witness people" testifying to the divinity of Jesus.

Thus at a time when the Church became increasingly more militant and eager to establish her claims to political power, she became increasingly less tolerant of all ideological opposition and heterodoxy and sought to eradicate all elements that would not fit her notions of Christian unity. Her attitude to Jews also became far less tolerant since Jews had implicitly departed from the Augustinian compact and apparently were not playing their assigned role in the Great Chain of Being. The Church's increased militancy and decreased tolerance could only give a spur to popular Jew-hatred or Judeophobia which manifested itself violently during the Crusades. [31]

Gavin I. Langmuir has suggested that the great massacres of 1096 mark the appearance of a militant Jew-hatred in Christendom that "defied both ecclesiastical and secular prohibitions." [32] According to him, Christian Jew-hatred was based not only on anti-Judaism but also on the irrational projection unto the Jews of Christian doubts about the validity of their own faith. Those classes of Christians who were most eager to squelch their doubts or prove their militancy while setting out on the Crusades were also most likely to persecute or massacre Jews whom they viewed as the quintessential unbelievers and internal enemies. Thus popular Judeophobia which was aggravated by the excitement of the Crusades was given implicit permission by a newly militant Church seeking ideological uniformity and temporal power.

In the popular mind, Jews became more despised and feared—"and if you wrong us, shall we not revenge?" asks Shylock—precisely because they had been murdered. Not the murderers but their surviving victims were blamed. As Poliakov has noted:

> [Massacres have] as their principal effect a recrudescence of hostility toward the Jews . . . the killers in general only hate their victims more; the simple witnesses decide that there must be a reason for the killing; finally the profiteers, the pillagers, and looters great and small, fear the return of those who have escaped. [33]

Following the crusades the Church formulated a set of canonical statutes that in effect forcefully segregated and further degraded Jews. In the past Jews had lived in their own compact neighborhoods both for reasons of religion and ethnic solidarity. The notion that Jews had to live segregated lives—usually in the most decrepit areas of the towns—and were prohibited from living among Christians first appeared in the Third Lateran Council (1179). Measures were passed in the Fourth Lateran Council (1215) and further elaborated in the Council of Basel (1434) that required the Jews to wear distinctive clothes, a conical hat, a "Jew badge," and a yellow circle symbolic of their betraying Christ for gold. In 1555 Pope Paul IV, in his bull *Cum nimis absurdum*, put into effect statutes segregating the Jews and compelled them to live in their own ghetto (a term borowed from Venetian practice) on the left bank of the Tiber. The practice spread, and throughout many parts of Europe Jews came to be immured behind ghetto walls—a condition that they endured until the nineteenth century and that was renewed by the Nazis.

With the notable exception of Poland, where Jews found a sanctuary between the thirteenth and twentieth centuries, in much of the rest of Europe their situation was tenuous indeed. Living behind ghetto walls at the sufferance of the lord or king whose property they had become, prohibited from owning land, excluded from the guilds, their economic lives narrowed to peddling and usury, subject to expulsion or worse, "[b]y the end of the Middle Ages Western Jewry was ruined."[34] In the minds of their Christian neighbors, "the image of the Jew deteriorated . . . to that of a deformed monster, with horns, tail, cloven hoofs, and sulfuric odor to betray his fundamentally diabolic character."[35] Powerless, segregated, circumscribed to despised occupations, stigmatized and demonized, the Western European Jew had become a pariah in practice as well as in theory.

Despite its inequality and bigotry, as Baron and Biale have shown, the medieval world had a place for the Jews. The social structure of that world was corporate and hierarchical, and the Jews had a place in it as a despised but often protected pariah caste—a witness people—whose location in the economic stratification system could be found somewhere between the peasants and the burghers. With the rise of the modern national state and the emergence of the capitalist economy, the medieval system of estates and corporate bodies disintegrated and with it the separate status of the Jews.

Jewish Emancipation and Mobilization

Following the Enlightment and the French Revolution, Jewish civil and legal status changed dramatically in Western Europe. Jews became emancipated in France in 1791 and legally at least the equals of their compatriots. By 1848 it seemed to many Jews and sympathetic Christians alike that the "eternal Jewish problem" was well on its way to being resolved. In the liberal revolutions of the period, Jews played a small but significant role. Out of 230 Prussian casualties in the revolution, twenty were Jews.[36] Five Jews were members of the Frankfurt Assembly while Gabriel Riesser (1806–63), a Jew, was a vice-president.

By 1871 they were emancipated in Germany and in all of the German states.[37] So rapid and extensive was their progress that Graetz referred to it as a renaissance. The Jewish renaissance was stimulated by rapid increases in their rates of migration from east to west and from less developed to more developed areas of the globe, by urbanization, education, commercialization, and political participation.[38] It was a renaissance that would flower most profusely in Germany where Jews contributed to the general culture in a manner unsurpassed since the Golden Era of Spain.

Emancipation and capitalism opened up unprecedented opportunities for Jews to assert themselves in politics and economics. Their newly found freedom and social status was not, however, reflected as easily in the cultural sphere and in the attitudes and stereotypes of their Christian neighbors. To the stereotypes of the Jewish pariah and Christ killer, which had by no means been destroyed by the Enlightment and by emancipation, was added the new image of the Jew as parvenu—the despised and unwanted outsider who tries to become a member and even a master by wielding his economic and political resources. This post-emancipation antipathy to Jews, based as much on social, economic, and political as on religious factors, and often taking the form of racism, created some of the conditions for the rise of antisemitic political parties and ideologies. Jewish emancipation and social mobilization, together with the previously established pariah status, were necessary conditions for the rise of modern antisemitism.

Migration and Urbanization

At the start of the nineteenth century there were some 2.5 million Jews in the world including 100,000 in Germany. Following a period of rapid population growth, by the 1930s there were some 16 million Jews, most living in Eastern Europe, and with some one-half million in Germany. With regard to the Jews, the period of European history preceding the Holocaust can be characterized as an era of migration from Eastern Europe to Western Europe and the United States, and from less industrialized and commercialized regions to more developed areas of the world.

Thus between 1881 and 1933 some 4 million Jews migrated from Russia and Eastern Europe toward the west. This represented a shift in proportions of the world Jewish population. Before the migration, Russia and Eastern Europe constituted some 75 percent of the Jewish population, while the United States, Latin America, and Australia contained some 3.5 percent. At the end of the period the proportion of the Eastern European Jewish population had shrunk to 46 percent while the United States, Latin America, and Australia came to represent approximately 30 percent. Throughout this period the proportion of the Jewish population of Western and Central Europe remained about the same, 13.5 percent.[39]

This last figure masks the fact that thousands of Jews also emigrated from Western and Central Europe to the Americas and were replaced by migrants from Russia and Eastern Europe.

In 1870 some 20 percent of Jews lived in developed countries; by 1900 that proportion had increased to 24.5 percent, and by 1933 it had soared to 48.1 percent. Beyond that, most European Jews, whenever they could, migrated to the more developed areas of their various countries, especially the capital city. [40]

As the infrastructure of communication and transportation networks associated with modernization were put in place in Western European countries, such areas urbanized, and a migration of people from the country to the city began. But as Ruppin has noted, "This movement, although a universal concomitant of modern industrial development, set in earlier and stronger in the case of the Jews." [41]

He points out that by 1925 "[n]early one-half of world-Jewry lived in large towns, nearly one-fourth in cities, and nearly one eighth in New York city alone. This concentration in cities or metropolitan towns has not been reached by any other nation." [42]

In a few cases a majority of Jews of a country lived in the capital city. Thus, in 1921, 92 percent of Danish Jews lived in Copenhagen; in 1926, 70 percent of French Jews lived in Paris; in 1923, 67.3 percent of Austrian Jews lived in Vienna; and in 1926, 66.6 percent of English Jews lived in London. [43]

In 1816, out of a total population of 197,717 Germans living in Berlin, there were 3,373 Jews; by 1849 there were 412,154 Germans of whom 9,595 were Jews, an increase of a 108 percent and 185 percent, respectively. By 1895 there was a total population of 1,677,304 Berliners of whom 86,152 were Jews. Thus in the forty-six years between 1849 and 1895 the total population of Berlin grew by 307 percent while the Jewish population alone increased by 798 percent. [44] Moreover, though the concentration of Jews in Berlin never reached the levels of Copenhagen or Paris, in 1925 out of a population of 564,379 German Jews, some 172,672 or 30.6 percent lived in Berlin. [45] In sum, both in terms of rate and concentration, the processes of urbanization that had affected world Jewry were also transforming German Jews. These processes were part of a larger package that included education and occupational change as well.

Education

Up to the seventeenth century there were very few Europeans—mostly gentry and nobility—who had become literate. Because it was a necessary skill for the study of Talmud and the pursuit of commerce, however, literacy was much more common among Jews than non-Jews.

In the modern period Jewish children were taught in both Jewish and non-Jewish schools. There were three types of Jewish schools: *chayders* and *yeshivot* taught mostly traditional subjects in Yiddish and some Hebrew; Jewish elementary and secondary schools included secular subjects taught in Yiddish and Hebrew; other elementary and secondary schools taught secular subjects in the vernacular, but some of the time was also devoted to the study of Jewish subjects. It should be noted that, as late as 1886, 37.4 percent of Jewish children still attended Jewish communal schools, not Prussian public schools.[46] The trend, however, was unmistakably away from Jewish education to public, secular, state-directed education and away from Yiddish or Hebrew to German as the language of instruction.

Within a generation or two after the establishment of state-supported schools in Germany, most Jewish children not only attended but many excelled in them and continued on to secondary education at a rate that far exceeded their non-Jewish neighbors. For example, in 1921, 60.5 percent of Jewish children in Prussia went on to secondary schools while only 9.7 percent of non-Jewish children did so.[47] In Berlin in 1929 the figures were 48.6 percent and 23.7 percent, respectively. These figures no doubt reflect the higher urbanization of the Jewish population, its greater ability and desire to pay for higher education, and its stronger emphasis on education as a value. Such ratios also may show that population's eagerness to acquire *Bildung*, the cultural requisite for assimilation into German culture.[48] The irony may be, as has been suggested, that the more educated and assimilated the Jews became, the more threatening they appeared to certain sectors of German and European society that had not ceased to view them as pariahs. By the nineteenth century they were becoming educated and mobilized pariahs—more dangerous than ever.

This desire for secular education and culture among European Jews can be seen with particular force in the rate of Jewish attendance at universities (see table 3.1, below). It should be noted that in all countries the percentage of Jewish students was far greater than the percentage of the Jewish population. This suggests a number of points pertaining to Jewish social mobilization and antisemitism.

To the extent that university education is a scarce good and a measure of modernization and social mobilization, this ratio suggests that Jews were proportionately more able to attain it and were more highly mobilized than the population as a whole. Where the Jewish population was relatively small and the country at large relatively developed and prosperous, the high rate of Jewish university education and social mobilization need not have stimulated a reaction. On the other hand, where the Jewish population was relatively large, as in Poland, and the country underdeveloped, one might suspect that the relative success of Jews in the modern sector could have produced communal resentment. [49] Nevertheless, to relate the political movement and ideology of antisemitism to Jewish social mobilization and communal competition alone is a serious mistake and verges on a provocation thesis of antisemitism.

This last point can best be seen in table 3.1 from a comparison of the percentage of Jews in the population as a whole and Jewish attendance at universities in Germany and Poland, respectively. In Germany, Jews represented .92 percent of the whole population and 3.4 percent of the university student body. The figures for Poland were significantly greater—10.2 percent and 19.3 percent. In terms of communal weight and competition, Jews represented more of a challenge in Poland than in Germany, yet it was in the latter country that an elaborated antisemitic movement and ideology first took hold.

Consider another example: in countries like the United States where Jewish progress was by and large perceived as being legitimate, an overrepresentation of Jewish students may have led to discrimination and quotas but need not have triggered political antisemitism. [50] That the same ratio did spur such antisemitism in nineteenth- and twentieth-

TABLE 3.1 Attendance of Jewish and Non-Jewish Students at Universities and Postsecondary Schools by Country

Country or City	Year	Total Students	Jewish Students	% Jewish Students	% Jewish Pop.
Germany	1929	87,353	2,970	3.4	.92
Poland	1929	45,135	8,711	19.3	10.20
United States	1918	152,959	14,837	9.7	3.03
Czechoslovakia	1927	16,648	2,414	14.5	2.59
Hungary	1930	12,857	1,350	10.5	5.83
Latvia	1930	8,552	744	8.7	4.83
Lithuania	1926	2,408	756	31.4	7.66
Soviet Russia	1926	153,890	23,699	15.4	2.61
Vienna	1928	11,160	2,377	21.3	10.65

Note.—This table was derived from table 21 in Ruppin, 313.

century Germany and elsewhere suggests that antisemitism as an ideology and the antisemitic political movement were produced by factors other than communal competition alone. Communal competition no doubt stimulated antipathy to Jews in Germany and other areas of Europe, but by itself it was not sufficient to create an ideology and a political movement that claimed that the modern world was controlled by a nefarious conspiracy of Jews whose emancipation should be revoked.

Occupation

It is striking that in the nineteenth century, at a time when most non-Jews in Germany were still occupied in agriculture, some 78 percent of Jews were classified as earning their living in commerce, industry, and the professions.[51] By 1907 most Jews in Germany were working squarely in the modern industrial-commercial sector, while nearly half of their non-Jewish compatriots were still part of a rural-agricultural world dominated by traditional values.

This pattern was seized upon both by antisemites, on the one hand, and by Socialist and Zionist reformers, on the other hand, to argue that the Jewish occupational structure was somehow abnormal.[52] In order to move the discussion away from invidious comparisons to historical analysis, there are at least three points to be made about this pattern. First, Jews were more likely to be part of the commercial-industrial-capitalist sector than non-Jews because during and after the Middle Ages discrimination barred them from being farmers and artisans. Second, although Jews were more closely tied into the capitalist sector, they were not all middle class. Indeed, in Eastern Europe there was a large segment of the Jewish population that was working class, unemployed, or making its living in very marginal occupations. And third, it shoul be pointed out that, far from being "abnormal," the Jewish occupational structure presaged changes that would later characterize the rest of modern industrial society. It was not the Jews who came to resemble the non-Jews in their occupational structure, it was the non-Jews who eventually caught up with the Jews in leaving agricultural pursuits and crafts for modern commerce and industry.

Medieval restrictions barring Jews from owning land and pursuing occupations other than commerce have been discussed and documented extensively. When with the rise of the early bourgeoisie even trade was circumscribed, Jewish economic life in much of Western Europe collapsed, and Jews were shoved to the margins of society where for the most part they became petty traders and peddlers.[53] With emancipation and the rise of modern capitalism, however, Jews once more entered the main stream of commerce and industry.

Richarz points out that prior to emancipation in Germany about 80 percent of Jews were small shopkeepers, peddlers, domestic servants, and beggars. Some 2 percent belonged to the "protected" elite of the *Schutzjuden*, a class of wholesale merchants, bankers, and court Jews whose dealings were mainly with the princes and with other Christians. [54] By 1861, while only 2 percent of non-Jews were engaged in trade in Prussia, 58 percent of Jews were merchants; this implies that 20 percent of all German merchants were Jews. [55] With the tremendous expansion of German industry between 1850 and 1871, Jews moved rapidly into capitalist enterprises, especially the fledgling textile industry. [56] Their progress was so rapid that "by the middle of the nineteenth century, half of all the known entrepreneurs in Berlin were Jews." [57]

Adapting rapidly to capitalism and free enterprise and rising swiftly with the general improvement of economic conditions in Germany, most Jews in the nineteenth century were able to join the economic version of the middle class within one or two generations after emancipation. Writing about his village of Walldorf in Thuringen, where about 500 Jews had lived, the one-time textile manufacturer Faibel Siegel later reminisced:

> At one time there were quite a number of poor Jews in the community, who received small gifts of money, flour, and other items, but this slowly changed for the better. Conditions improved considerably, because of emigration to North America and greater freedom of movement for Jews in trade and industry. Towards the end of the 1860's hardly any paupers were left. Those who still knew the last remnants of those earlier times must acknowledge that a transformation took place before their very eyes, which the new generation could not even imagine. [58]

Not all Jews had made it. Even in Germany in the middle of the nineteenth century, 9 percent of Jews were domestic servants, and 8 percent were beggars. In Eastern Europe, Poland and Russia in particular, few Jews had attained middle-class status. Although there, too, most Jews were engaged in commerce, including petty and even marginal trade, there was a large Jewish industrial working class, with some 39.2 percent of Jews belonging to a proletariat. [59] Thus the impression of a rapid embourgeoisement of Jewish society in Germany should not be generalized to all European Jews.

The whole question of the normality of development hinges on what standard one chooses to define what is normal. If the normal pattern of economic development is defined as the creation of a class structure emphasizing a large rural-based peasantry, a smaller middle class, and a yet smaller upper class and nobility, then Jewish development in the nineteenth and twentieth centuries was distinctly abnormal. On the other hand, if the norm is borrowed from the pattern of developed or modern contemporary societies such as the United States, Great Britain, and West Germany, then the Jewish pattern was normal, and indeed it was ahead of its day.

Like later more advanced societies, German Jews in particular were largely urban, highly literate, with a large university-educated middle class, and concentrated mainly in commercial and industrial occupations rather than in the agricultural sector. The paradox of Jewish development was that in a brief span of time one of the most traditional of peoples, stigmatized as a pariah group by the larger society, had become modern in its socioeconomic profile.

Beyond that, to the extent that one can speak of modern values and modernism, cultural trends that are often associated with socioeconomic development, many German or culturally German Jews embraced the modern world and contributed disproportionately to its emergent culture. In this connection one thinks of Marx, Freud, Mahler, Einstein, Kafka, Wittgenstein, and Buber and the thousands of other German and Austrian Jews who made striking contributions to world and Jewish culture.[60] They and the Jewish people from whom they issued—sometimes in opposition—were not always admired or appreciated for their talents. Indeed, often emotions of envy, resentment, and fear were stirred by the Jewish renaissance. This was also part of the backdrop to the emergence of modern antisemitism.

Of course, the modern Jewish renaissance does not imply that every Jew was a great success or that Jews experienced a flowering of culture in every country at the same time. If the Jewish renaissance can be dated to the beginning and middle of the nineteenth century in France and Germany, it appears that similar levels of economic development, urbanization, education, and political participation did not occur in Poland and Galicia—where the majority of Eastern European Jews lived—until after World War I.[61]

Moreover, the renaissance of the Jews did not necessarily mean a revival of Judaism or that Jews themselves were untroubled by the extraordinary changes they were experiencing. As can be seen from the vitality of Jewish liberalism, socialism, and Zionism, the social mobilization of the Jewish community led to a flowering of Jewish secular culture and to the participation of Jews in European politics. At the same time social mobilization and the desire to be done with exclusion led to rapid rates of assimilation and even rejection of Jewish identity. Both of these tendencies, paradoxically, had the same roots and often worked themselves out in the same family, even in the same person. [62] The tragedy for many assimilated European Jews was that at the same time as they saw themselves as having left the ghetto and moved beyond Judaism, they were perceived by Jew-haters and antisemites as Jewish pariahs in modern dress.

Jew-Hatred and Antisemitism

In the discussion above it was suggested that antisemitism as a political movement articulating an ideology centering on the Jews was directly related to the Jews' pariah status and to their emancipation and rapid social mobilization in the context of the modern world, and inversly related to the strength of liberal and socialist forces that were defenders of Jewish rights. The last point will become clearer in the next chapter. Here I wish to touch on the first two points: Why should the progress of a former pariah group like the Jews have generated Jew-hatred and provided some of the conditions for the rise of antisemitism?

Three main reasons may be suggested: (1) in part the antisemitic movement was a defensive reaction of certain groups and classes that were in conflict with Jewish progress; (2) even those groups and classes like the peasantry that were not directly in conflict with Jewish competitors tended to blame Jews for the dislocations of the capitalist system and the modern state; and (3) the advance, social progress, and assimilation of a despised pariah group like the Jews in a still largely hierarchical and traditional society like Germany created moral outrage that a traditional order had been violated and the fear that assimilation would lead to the pollution and domination of the majority by the scorned minority. In the German case this was expressed as fear of "Judaization." [63] Indeed, it was this irrational fear of contagion and domination by Jews that underlay what has come to be known as "racialist" antisemitism. [64]

Communal Competition

As was noted in Chapters 1 and 2, communal competition is a form of class conflict that pits one communal group against another for the scarce rewards of wealth, power, and status. As can be seen in Chapter 2, when the Armenians experienced a renaissance in the socioeconomic and cultural spheres in the nineteenth century, the sultan and the Ottoman Muslims reacted with resentment. When the Ibos of Nigeria successfully started to mobilize and to compete with Yorubas and Hausas for scarce jobs, overcrowded markets, and rare elite positions, not surprisingly their very success led to anti-Ibo feeling in places where there had been no such thing in the past. Similarly, when Jews in Germany, Poland, and other European countries successfully began to compete with their Christian neighbors for scarce admissions to universities or in the commercial and industrial sector, it might be expected that their competition bred antagonism. This resentment sometimes took the form of intensifying the Jewish stereotype and calling for protectionist measures against Jewish advancement. In that sense communalism played a distinct role in fomenting anti-Jewish feeling.

It has been suggested above that in Poland, where Jews made up close to 10 percent of the population and up to one-third of the population of Warsaw, this kind of communalism may have accounted for some of the anti-Jewish sentiment in the interwar period.[65] The problem arises, however, with using communalism alone to explain antisemitism in countries like Germany. Despite their social mobilization, in Germany Jews constituted less than 1 percent of the total population and a small fraction of the bourgeoisie. Although they may have been relatively more successful than their Christian neighbors, in absolute terms—except in some selected spheres such as textiles—they could not play a dominant economic or social role even if they had wished to do so. As remarked above, though communal competition may have been a component of Jew-hatred, by itself it cannot explain the rise of the antisemitic movement.

Opposition to Capitalism and the Modern World

In trying to explain antisemitism in a context where Jews constituted only a small fraction of the population and of the bourgeoisie, Marxist writers like Bebel, Kautsky, Bernstein, and Marx himself argued that resentment of the Jews was an epiphenomenon, a by-product, of a wider and far more serious opposition to capitalism and modernity.[66] "Doomed" classes like the *Mittelstand* and the peasantry blamed the Jews for the dislocations of capitalism and the bourgeois state because they did not know any better.[67] They did not understand that their real enemy was not the Jewish capitalist but capitalism itself.

To the extent that Conservative antisemites like Pastor Stoecker focused on Jews as the cause of social and economic dislocation, they were mystifiers and opportunists, and the workers who were taken in by this kind of rabble rousing were fools. [68] Indeed, Socialists called antisemitism "the socialism of fools." If the victims of capitalism and the modern era had really understood what was happening to them, argued the Socialists, they would have turned away from antisemitism toward socialism. Ironically, certain Marxists, both in Germany and Russia, including some Jewish Marxists, saw antisemitism as a "progressive" force because, they argued, it was a harbinger of true Socialist consciousness in the working class. Both kinds of Marxists dismissed antisemitism as having any long-term consequences, however, because it was bound to give way to a clearer understanding of real social forces and true interests.

We shall return to these points again in Chapter 4. In the meantime it might be noted that it was not much comfort to the peasants and the *Mittelstand* to be told that they were "doomed" classes, and it certainly did not wean them away from antisemitism. On the contrary, it was not mere stupidity that led *Mittelstand* and peasant leaders to blame the Jews for the dislocations of the modern world. They realized that by attacking the Jews they were also targeting those capitalist and liberal forces that had made Jewish progress possible while causing hardships for their followers. The Jews were a handy stick with which to beat their political opponents because Jewish progress of any kind was viewed as illegitimate, and any social or political forces that made it possible for Jews to advance ipso facto discredited their own positions.

Indeed, far from disappearing and yielding to socialism, antisemitism as an ideology both resisted and interpreted the modern world and thus had extraordinary staying power. Racialist antisemitism and the postulate of the Jewish conspiracy to dominate the world came to challenge Marxism and liberalism themselves as popular theories of social transformation and political legitimation.

Jew-hatred stemming from communal competition and as a reaction to capitalism or modernity are not mutually exclusive conceptions. One opposes Jewish progress because it is in conflict with one's own, and one rationalizes one's position by claiming that Jewish advancement destroys tradition and creates a hateful modern world. By the same token one opposes Jewish progress because it is emblematic of those forces of modernity like capitalism and the liberal state that one hates. The problem with both these views, however, is that they beg a very important question: Why the Jews?

If the Polish student or the German petty bourgeois had been in competition with Jews only, one might come to the conclusion that his resentment of Jews was caused by communal competition in a context of capitalist insecurity. Jews, however, were not the only competitors, nor did they in Germany constitute the bulk or the most powerful segment of the capitalist class. If the *Mittelstand* and the peasantry found themselves threatened by capitalism, why did these groups pick on the Jewish capitalist and not on the Bavarian, Hessian, Prussian, or Catholic capitalist? For many, like Marr, Glagau, Böckel, Fritsch, Dühring, Liebermann von Sonnenberg, Ahlwardt, and Stoecker in Germany, Drumont in France, later the Endecja party in Poland, and others, Jewish success was deeply offensive because it was Jewish.

What accounts for the felt illegitimacy of Jewish success? Why was it that, when Jews tried to shed their pariah status in the modern world, they emerged not as free and equal citizens of the states where their emancipation and renaissance had taken place but as frightening interlopers and parvenus—illegitimate claimants to status and membership? The point is that, despite their outward emancipation, Jews were not able to shed their pariah status which had become deeply embedded as part of the "cultural code" of modern Europe.[69] Indeed, their progress was not only illegitimate but it tainted the very forces of capitalism and liberalism that had made it possible.

Judaization

Beyond the antagonism produced by competition and the dislocations of social change, there was another element agitating antisemites. This was the fear that Jewish emancipation and social mobilization would lead to the "Judaization" of culture and the domination of society by the Jews. Indeed, as Aschheim has noted, antisemites dreaded that Jewish emancipation and mobilization would lead not to the assimilation of Jews to German culture but to the reverse: German culture would become Judaized.

> That the notion of *Verjudung* achieved its greatest popularity and plausibility in the postemancipation period is not surprising. The full myth of a "Judaized" society was dependent upon the perception that Jews had access to the levers of power, a state of affairs that had been facilitated by the abolition of previous disabilities. . . . This myth was essentially one of social and ideological contagion. Not Jewish purification but German pollution and powerlessness, it held, was the outcome of emancipation.[70]

The myth of a society that has become Judaized and dominated by the Jews recurs throughout the antisemitic literature of Imperial Germany. Thus, for example, Wilhelm Marr, an early antisemite, who, it is said, coined the term "antisemitism," contended that the Jewish problem should not be considered from a religious or denominational-confessional point of view but from a political, social, and ultimately racial perspective.[71]

According to Marr the problem arose not because Jews were weak and persecuted but because they were powerful. Indeed, they were the most powerful force in modern Europe. It was they who succeeded in the contemporary capitalist era, and it was this feat that was going to allow them to triumph over real Germans. "Without striking a blow, in fact, politically persecuted throughout the centuries, Jewry today has become the sociopolitical dictator of Germany."[72] Marr claimed that such an antagonist could not be defeated because he had superior racial qualities. It is significant that his pamphlet, *The Victory of Jewry over Germany*, first published in 1879, went through twelve editions in that year alone.

In 1879 also Marr founded the League of Antisemites (*Antisemiten-Liga*), the first antisemitic party in Imperial Germany. Its stated purpose was to prevent the "Judaization" of Germany.

> The purpose of the association formed under the name of "League of Anti-Semites" is to bring together non-Jewish Germans of all denominations, all parties and all walks of life into a common, fervent union which will strive, by setting aside all special interests and all political differences, and with the greatest energy, earnestness and industry, towards the one aim of saving our German fatherland from complete *Judaisation* [sic, and my italic] and to make life tolerable there for the descendants of the original inhabitants.[73]

The fear of "Judaization" discussed by Aschheim and others cannot be separated from the preemancipation status of the Jew as pariah. Indeed, it was the fear that Jewish assimilation would not turn Jews into Germans but Germans into Jewish pariahs that helps to explain the link between antisemitism and racism.

> Amazingly, the stubbornness and endurance of the Semites have led them in the course of the nineteenth century to the position of preeminence in the society of the West. In fact, in Germany it is not Jewry that has merged into Germandom but Germandom that has merged into Jewry.[74]

Pariahs and Racists

No doubt emancipation and success in the economic and social spheres transformed Jewish identity and helped to destroy some of the more egregious stereotypes of the Jewish pariah that were prevalent throughout European society. While Jewish mobilization may have had a salutary effect on some Christians, others were shocked and appalled by the changes. For many non-Jews—even those who had ceased to be believing Christians—the stigma of traditional Jewish status hung on. It was not their renaissance as such that was so offensive to some Jew-haters, it was that emancipation and mobilization made it possible for Jews to claim membership in the wider society and nation. Such claims were both illegitimate and menacing because pariahs could not and should not be equal. Their demands for equality and inclusion undermined the old order and the new, often fragile, national identity. According to the antisemites, Jewish assimilation and integration threatened to pollute culture and to dominate society. It was especially this fear of contamination and domination by Jews, of becoming pariahs themselves, that was so abhorrent to the antisemites. [75]

Even as Jews had changed and were trying to abandon their corporate status by acculturating and integrating into German society, so had non-Jews changed. Modern Europeans had become citizens, participating in the national politics of the newly minted states and in the emergent class systems open to talent and money. Gone were the estates and corporate groups of the Middle Ages that had kept Christians and Jews apart and shielded Christians from those they viewed as fearsome pariahs. After emancipation the question then arose, Did Jews have a place in the new national community and the evolving class structure? For many Europeans the answer was affirmative, but for others it was not. [76] For antisemites Jews were ineluctably separate and unassimilable—their pariah status made them so. It was impossible to include Jews as Germans in German society because Jews were the radical opposites of Germans, they were the anti-Germans, the embodiments of all that was in the negative identity of the Germans. For Germans to mix with Jews would be to become the "Other." That Jews were successful in the modern world only compounded the problem.

Indeed, it is only by keeping the stigmatized or pariah status of Jews in mind that one can begin to understand the appeals of racism. Thus antisemites were most opposed not to the traditional *shtetl* Jew whom they simply despised, they were most fearful of the upwardly mobile, modern, assimilating Jew who had left his place behind and was threatening the antisemite's sense of propriety, order, and purity. Unlike other conceptions of Jews, including the traditional Christian one that allowed for conversion and therefore integration, racial theory by conceptualizing the Jew as "biologically" or intrinsically alien guaranteed his apartness and inferiority forever.

Thus Karl Eugen Dühring, who wrote some of the early works of racial antisemitism, remarked in his tract of 1881:

> A Jewish question would still exist, even if every Jew were to turn his back on his religion and join one of our major churches. Yes, I maintain that in that case, the struggle between us and the Jews would make itself felt as ever more urgent. . . . It is precisely the baptized Jews who infiltrate furthest, unhindered in all sectors of society and political life.[77]

Conclusion

As discussed earlier, Ruether and others have suggested that the stereotype of the Jewish pariah was largely a creation of the Christian teaching of contempt for Judaism and a by-product of Christian persecutions. By the same token, Christian anti-Judaism has such a long and bloody history that some writers have implied that this factor alone causes and sustains modern antisemitism. Antisemitism viewed simply as anti-Judaism parading in modern clothes is so compelling a view that a word needs to be said about it.

If Christianity were the only culprit in modern antisemitism, then one might expect that the more Christian the country, the more antisemitic it would be. But that was not the case, and modern antisemitism seemed to vary independently of the strength of Christian institutions in modern Europe. Otherwise, a strongly Christian country like Italy should have been more antisemitic than Germany, and the relative weakness of antisemitism in Britain would have to be explained by reference to the weakness of her Christian institutions. Clearly, neither is a tenable position. Furthermore, if antisemitism can be explained by reference to Christianity alone, how are we to account for the rise of modern antisemitism, which appeared in the most vicious guise—that of racism—precisely at a time when Christian institutions and beliefs were themselves on the defensive and had lost much of their luster and dynamism when compared with the Middle Ages? The proposition that anti-Judaism was the sole or primary cause of modern antisemitism will not stand up to critical inquiry; it is less easy, however, to dismiss the results of a Christian past that had stigmatized the Jews as pariahs.

This does not mean that Christian teachings of anti-Judaism have lost their capacity to promote and to rationalize antisemitism. Indeed, when in the recent documentary film, *Shoah*, its director Claude Lanzmann asked a group of Polish peasants, who had witnessed the effects of the Final Solution near Chelmno, to explain why such things had happened to the Jews, the answer he received was formulated in a manner that St. Chrysostom would have easily recognized. Thus a peasant told Lanzmann that he had heard the following story told to him by a "friend":

> The Jews were gathered in a square. The rabbi asked an SS man: "Can I talk to them?" The SS man said yes. So the rabbi said that around two thousand years ago the Jews condemned the innocent Christ to death. And when they did that, they cried out: "Let his blood fall on our heads and on our sons' heads." Then the rabbi told them: "Perhaps the time has come for that, so let us do nothing, let us go, let us do as we're asked."[78]

Here one sees in its stunning simplicity how an ancient theological condemnation is used as an intellectual and moral framework for dealing with the Holocaust. Its function is to rationalize the horror by distancing oneself from the events and by blaming the victims for their own murders. From this perspective the SS were simply the instruments of God's will. It should, of course, be noted that Polish peasants were not alone in such views. The irony and tragedy in this whole episode—a point that Lanzmann does not bring out—is that in terms of civilians killed by the Nazis, next to the Jews and the Russians, it was the Poles who suffered most gravely during the period of the Holocaust.[79]

In conclusion, it might be noted that the fateful tragedy of the Jews in the modern European world obscures a historical irony: as long as the Church held sway over the state and the masses, Jews were preserved as a moral lesson, a living relic, a tableau testifying to the crucifixion of Christ and to the misery meted out to those who rejected Him. When the Church lost her political authority in the modern world, she lost her power to preserve the Jews. The Jewish pariah that she had done so much to create was handed over to the tender mercies of the national state and the newly conscious peoples on which the state increasingly rested its legitimacy. These now debated the proposition that the Jews deserved or could become members of the newly formed societies and nationalities.

Not infrequently voices were heard that would deny to the Jews the membership they sought.

Thus the emancipation and mobilization of the Jews, in states and societies newly opened to talent, not only failed to stem hatred, but, indeed, they promoted it. By encouraging the Jews to integrate into a society that rejected them—without at the same time helping them to cast off their pariah image—Jewish emancipation and social mobilization assured the rise not only of a new kind of Jew-hatred, but of an antisemitism that would be formulated in racialist and biological terms. No longer religion but the specter of race mixing kept Jew and non-Jew apart; meanwhile, Jews trying to enter the body politic were increasingly likened to vermin, germ, and cancerous growth—all metaphors for insinuation, infiltration, decay, perceived as products of Jewish assimilation that an influential portion of the Gentile world rejected. Such were the roots of modern political antisemitism.

Antisemitism as an organized movement articulating its ideology of Jewish pollution and control could not translate its objectives—which at the minimum included the abolition of Jewish emancipation—without state power. As discussed in Chapter 1, however, power and the structure of the state are crucial dimensions often overlooked in discussions of antisemitism and of its consequences for the Holocaust. In Chapters 4 and 6 we shall examine the political shape that this new antisemitism took within the state and party system of Imperial Germany. Since in the first instance it started out as a minority political movement, it had to find allies among those parties and social forces that were not primarily motivated by a fear and hatred of the Jews. As will be seen, this the antisemites failed to achieve under the auspices of Imperial Germany, but they succeeded only too well under the Weimar Republic when that regime was swept away by revolutionary forces.

F O U R

The Failure of the Antisemitic Parties in Imperial Germany

Anti-Semitism which by its very nature can appeal only to the basest drives and instincts of a backward stratum of society, expresses the moral depravity of the groups that accept it. It is a comfort [to know] that in Germany it will never have a chance to exert a decisive influence upon the life of state and society.

August Bebel[1]

Soon after the unification of Germany in 1871, especially after the crash of 1873, there arose an antisemitic movement that took the form of political party activity. For nearly twenty years the antisemitic political parties, led by men like Adolf Stoecker (1835–1909), Max Liebermann von Sonnenberg (1848–1911), Otto Böckel (1859–1923), Theodor Fritsch (1852–1933), and others threatened to undo Jewish emancipation and appeared as if they might have a major impact on the politics of the country. By the late 1890s, however, the antisemitic movement went into decline, and by 1912—on the eve of the Great War—it was clear that political antisemitism was a failure in Imperial Germany. Since only a few years later the Nazis appeared and seized power, it is of some interest to inquire why it was that in one context an antisemitic movement failed, even in its minimal goals, while in another it succeeded beyond the expectations of most contemporaries. What, if anything, was the connection between the earlier and later forms of Jew-hatred?

The thesis that will be developed in this chapter suggests that the antisemitic political parties failed in Imperial Germany because both the parliamentary and the revolutionary routes to power were blocked to their aspirations. Neither route allowed them to implement their minimal program which was the revocation of Jewish emancipation. Those that tried the parliamentary route, such as Stoecker's Christian Socials, soon discovered that antisemitism stirred up populist resentments, not only against the Jews but against the state and its elites.[2] The withdrawal of the state's support, at least in this context, assured the failure of the Christian Socials. Realizing that the parliamentary route was a mistake, other antisemitic parties began to propose that only a revolutionary transformation of state and society would lead to a solution to the Jewish question. But again, in the context of Imperial Germany, these revolutionary parties had even less chance of coming to power, and in the late 1890s both kinds of antisemitic political parties faded from view.

Chapter 6 contrasts this pattern of failure with the success of the Nazis who not only articulated an antisemitic ideology but became an effective revolutionary force in a propitiously revolutionary time. Thus, as noted in the introduction to this work, what distinguished antisemitism in Imperial Germany from that of the Nazis was not ideology alone but the absence of a revolutionary route or context without which the antisemitic parties could not come to power. Some of the antisemites in Imperial Germany made much the same indictment of Jews and Judaism as Hitler did, but without the power of the state they could do nothing about it.

Some writers take a different tack. The title of Massing's book, *Rehearsal for Destruction: A Study of Political Antisemitism in Imperial Germany*, is emblematic of their position.[3] They recognize that the antisemitic parties may have failed electorally, but, so goes one of their arguments, the earlier antisemites succeeded in transmitting their bigoted views to other parties and to important strata of the German population. In that sense nineteenth-century antisemitism was a segment in a long continuous line, stretching from the past to the future, that made Hitler inevitable. Other writers like Wehler and Bracher also argue for an essential continuity between nineteenth- and twentieth-century antisemitism. They do not stress the transmission of attitudes and cultural values but the manipulations of the German state and its elites who used antisemitism as a strategy of "negative integration" to keep themselves in power.

Though Hitler's views were no doubt shaped by earlier antisemites, and in that sense there was continuity between nineteenth- and twentieth-century antisemitism, the political contexts in which earlier and later antisemites tried to come to power and to implement their ideologies were drastically different. Imperial Germany was not conducive to revolution or to revolutionary antisemitism, while the polarization of the Weimar period enabled the Nazis to come to power.

In contrast to views emphasizing continuity, therefore, the similarity we wish to stress here is the essential discontinuity between the old regime states and the revolutionary states that came after, without for a moment equating antisemitism in Imperial Germany with the Armenian massacres of 1894–96 in the Ottoman Empire. In each case, after being tempted to crush upwardly mobile despised minorities or to use their presence as a foil against their enemies, the old regime states set limits on discrimination and persecution—neither the Ottoman regime nor Imperial Germany wished to eliminate Armenians or Jews, respectively. Indeed, in Germany the government supported Jewish emancipation to the end. When both regimes collapsed in revolutionary upheavals, however, murderous forces were unleashed that did not recognize limits and did attempt to eliminate minorities from the social structure. Thus genocide ensued.

This chapter is divided into three major sections: "The State in Imperial Germany," "The Rise and Fall of the Antisemitic Political Parties," and "Conclusion." The Conclusion will address the questions: (1) Why did the antisemitic political parties fail in Imperial Germany? (2) What was their connection to Nazism?

The State in Imperial Germany

In 1858 Frederick William IV's madness forced him to abdicate his throne to his brother William I who became king of Prussia in 1861. In September 1862 William appointed Otto von Bismarck as his minister president. Until his forced resignation in 1890, Bismarck presided over Prussia for twenty-eight years and over Imperial Germany for nineteen years. The legacy of his ideas, prejudices, alliances, and institutions had fateful consequences for Germany up to and beyond the Great War.

He was a Junker aristocrat, a Prussian, and a German in that order. His policies were designed to bolster the power and prestige of his monarch, to protect the landed aristocracy in Prussia, to insure the primacy of Prussia in the German Reich, and to maintain or expand German power in Europe and the world. At the same time as the Concert of Europe was crumbling, and Germany was industrializing and modernizing at a phenomenal rate, he pursued these many goals with energy and great ability. Crucial to his policies was a German constitutional order of his own conception.

Founded in 1871, the German empire was a federal union of

twenty-five states and one administrative territory, the Reichsland consisting of the conquered provinces of Alsace and Lorraine. At the head of the Reich stood the emperor, William I, and his chancellor, Bismarck. The legislative functions and some representative aspects of imperial government were embodied in an upper house, the *Bundesrat*, and a lower house, the *Reichstag*.

In effect, Bismarck's constitutional manipulations gave Prussian representatives veto power and control over the legislative process. Prussia was assured control over any amendment, since seventeen of the fifty-eight representatives in the *Bundesrat* were Prussians, while only fourteen votes were needed to veto any constitutional amendment. By the same token, her delegates dominated national legislation, since a bill became law when it received a majority in both houses and since Prussia could always pick up the support of at least thirteen delegates in the *Bundesrat* (Prussia needed thirty for a majority). All this worked out to Bismarck's satisfaction.

Scheming to use the suffrage against the liberal parties, whom he always mistrusted, and hoping to isolate them in a body filled with his supporters, Bismarck permitted the representatives to the *Reichstag* to be elected on the basis of universal suffrage of all male voters over twenty-five years of age. The *Reichstag* had no legal rights over the chancellor, however, and it was not allowed to interfere in military, foreign, or constitutional affairs.

Though it had powers of debate and review, and it could hold up budgetary appropriations, the German version of parliament could not form a government. That crucial power was reserved for the chancellor himself who, with the permission of the emperor, had the right to appoint ministers as he saw fit. While strictly circumscribing the powers of the *Reichstag*, Bismarck had hoped that it would be an institution that could channel nationalist and populist sentiments in support of the emperor and the Reich. [4]

Bismarck's system clearly was designed to secure Prussian supremacy in the Reich and upper-class mastery in Prussia. [5] This constitutional order was not the invention of one man alone, however, or even of a coterie of men. Its origins lay in Germany's status as a late-comer to the nation-state system, in Prussia's preponderance among the German states, and in the failure of the liberal revolution of 1848. Germany as a late-comer meant that she had to seek national unification in the teeth of opposition from the other Great Powers, especially from France. Prussia's size and might assured that German unification would come under Prussia's auspices. The failure of the revolution of 1848 excluded liberals from sharing real power in Imperial Germany and presented them with a cruel dilemma. If they wanted German unity, they had to put up with Prussian power; if they acquiesced to Prussian power, they had to learn to give their allegiance to an autocratic monarch and the Junker aristocracy that headed the army and the state. It appears, therefore, that despite the high hopes of the liberals German unification was bought at the cost of the liberty of the Germans.[6]

The Crisis of Participation

Though the Bismarckian system was a cunning device ensuring the stability and unity of the German state while protecting the privileges of the aristocracy, it could not prevent the economic and social transformation of Germany nor the political problems that this entailed. Especially after 1848 and continuing to the Great War, industrialization linked to rapid urbanization created the conditions for the rise of an industrial working class. When this class—as represented by the Social Democratic party (SPD)—attempted to participate in the politics of Imperial Germany, however, it was prevented from doing so by the Bismarckian regime that had rigged the system in order to protect the economic and political privileges of the middle classes and the landed aristocracy. Craig has noted, for example, that "the salient characteristic [of Bismarck's rule] was its social immobility."[7]

Thus, while social and economic forces were producing pressures for mass participation, the political system remained closed and unresponsive and turned to repression and manipulation in order to prevent the lower classes from sharing in political power. As a number of scholars have observed, this at bottom was the major contradiction or fault line of Imperial Germany before 1919. Here it will be referred to as the crisis of participation of the German state.[8] Indeed, some scholars suggest that it was this crisis of participation, this inability of the imperial state to deal with socioeconomic change, that led the state to encourage pathological forms of social integration, among which was antisemitism. We shall return to this thesis in the conclusion to this chapter, but first a word needs to be said about modernization and participation in Imperial Germany.

The statistics on German economic and social modernization for the period in question are indeed impressive. Following the revolution of 1848, until 1857, all indices of German industrialization shot upward.[9] The value of pig-iron production increased from 24 million marks in 1848 to 66 million in 1857, reflecting a growth rate of 175 percent. Between 1850 and 1860 the railroad network nearly doubled from 6,000 to 11,500 kilometers. By 1910 it had further expanded to nearly 60,000 kilometers, an increase of 420 percent. After the economic crisis of 1857 to 1859, German industry again resumed its march. In 1866 German smelters produced a million tons of pig iron; by 1870 the figure rose to 1.5 million, and then by 1873 it rose again to 2.2 million tons. Between 1860 and 1870 coal production increased by 114 percent to 26 million tons. Between 1850 and 1870 the volume of freight traffic as measured by tonnage per kilometer grew by a factor of 21. Indeed, the index of total industrial production between 1870 and 1914 increased by 400 percent, and by 1914 Germany's rate of capital formation was nearly double that of England. [10]

In Germany as elsewhere industrialization had some significant social and political consequences. Among the social factors were population growth, urbanization, and the increasing literacy of the urbanized population. Thus between 1800 and 1914 the population of Germany burgeoned from approximately 24,000,000 to some 67,790,000. Between 1850 and 1910 those living in cities of over 100,000 multiplied by a factor of 10, from 2.8 to 28 percent of the German population. Berlin alone swelled from a city of 200,000 in 1820 into a metropolis of over 2,000,000 by 1910. [11]

It is significant that, in addition to the higher productivity and efficiency of the agricultural sector, another factor that may have spurred industrialization was the growing literacy and skill of the German population. Already by 1830 a majority of Germans could read and write, while by 1900 the rate of illiteracy was less than 1 percent, the lowest in the world. These figures can be compared with England's, where by 1860 nearly a third of the male and more than half of the female population were still illiterate. [12]

Industrialization and urbanization had some dramatic effects on the composition of the labor force. Between 1860 and 1910, while the percentage of the population living in communities of 2,000 or less declined by some 28 percent (from approximately 68 percent to 40 percent), and the percentage of the population living in cities of 20,000 or more rose by some 25 percent (from approximately 10 percent to 35 percent), the nonagricultural labor force grew by some 23 percent (from approximately 45 percent to 68 percent). [13] A country that before unification in 1871 had been largely rural and agricultural had become on the eve of the Great War one of the world's great urban and industrial centers.

Such a profound social and economic transformation had wide-ranging consequences for the social structure. A consequence that Bismarck did not foresee was the emergence of a working class. As already noted, the aristocracy and the middle classes, though they may have been rivals who disagreed on many issues centering on equality and liberty, were agreed on maintaining Bismarck's constitutional order and excluding the working class from it. Meanwhile, propelled by industrialization and urbanization, an increasingly literate and politically aware working class grew apace and demanded participation for itself and fundamental changes in the imperial system.

Indeed, much to the alarm of Bismarck, the conservatives, and the liberal parties, the Socialists received over a half-million votes in the election of 1877 and won twelve seats in the *Reichstag*. None had predicted such a development. In reaction to this success, Bismarck introduced the notorious Socialist Law on 19 October 1878. It was a legislative measure meant to cripple the Socialists. It banned the existence of clubs and organizations that promoted Social Democratic or Communist activities. It forbade assemblies favoring social democracy, the publication of materials, and the collecting of funds. Of the forty-seven leading Socialist newspapers, forty-five were suppressed outright.[14] The police shut down Socialist clubs and arrested Socialist as well as trade union leaders. It was a measure of the vitality and resilience of the Socialists that the Socialist Law did not destroy the party or stop the workers' movement. Though in the elections of 1881 support for the Socialists declined, the party soon recovered. By 1890, the SPD polled 1,427,298 votes and received thirty-five seats in the *Reichstag*. August Bebel noted in his memoirs that it was not socialism but the anti-Socialist law that had been defeated.[15]

Bismarck's constitutional system and his ability to balance the various political and social forces were severely buffeted by the emergence of the working class and the Social Democratic movement. As Craig and others have pointed out, Bismarck could balance the liberal parties with the conservatives, the periphery with the center, Imperial Germany with Prussia, and France with Russia. He could not, however, halt industrialization and urbanization and the rise of the working class, which he could neither check with other social forces, nor co-opt, nor dominate.

With the failure of the anti-Socialist law to stem social democracy, Bismarck became increasingly disenchanted with the very constitutional system that he had created. By then he was also at odds with his new emperor over domestic and foreign policy. When in 1890 William II intervened and barred his chancellor from taking radical measures against the Reichstag, Bismarck resigned.

When the great star fell, many Germans had a chilling presentiment that their country had suffered an irreparable loss and that it would not soon again be governed with such intelligence and assurance. Time was to prove them correct, although it must be said that the mistakes of Bismarck's successors might have been less disastrous if he had not contributed to the difficulties of their task by leaving them an anachronistic political system in which he had sought—in the case of liberalism with great success—to stifle every progressive tendency. . . . At the end of his career, Bismarck had no other answer to the problems of his society but violence. His successors proved to be no more fertile in expedients than he.[16]

From the time of his resignation to the outbreak of World War I, the system that Bismarck had constructed and later repudiated and the social forces that he could not control coexisted in a tense equilibrium. On the one hand, the imperial state and its constitutional framework remained as Bismarck had left it, with the significant difference that no one of his caliber was in charge. On the other hand, the industrialization and modernization of the German economy and society with the concomitant growth of the SPD continued at a furious pace.[17]

However, one should not conclude from this brief sketch that Imperial Germany was a society on the eve of revolution. Despite the crisis of participation, the *Kaiserreich* had many strengths, not the least of which was the legitimacy of the state itself. It was, after all, the German state that had united the Germans and had defeated their principal enemies in war. Moreover, while the SPD and the working classes were dissatisfied with the pace of progress, the growing appeal of revisionist socialism helped to dampen revolutionary ardor and to adjust the labor movement to the constraints of the political system.[18] The polarization between the working class and the rest of society had much more profound consequences for the Weimar Republic, where it helped fuel the Nazi revolution, than it did for Imperial Germany.

At the same time, within the limits of Imperial Germany, the crisis of participation had important consequences for the kind of alliances that were forged by the political parties. In particular, the struggle between the state, the Conservatives, and, intermittently, the liberal parties on one side and the Socialists on the other provided the poles between which the antisemitic parties had to find their place. Though they always opposed the Socialists, it was sometimes in alliance and sometimes in opposition to the other parties that the antisemites tried to exert their influence.

The Party System and the Class Structure

On 21 March 1871, the first session of the imperial *Reichstag* formally opened at the White Gallery of the Royal Palace in Berlin. Representing some of the principal segments and strata of German society, six major parties were present. These were the Conservatives, the *Reichspartei*, the National Liberals, the Progressives, the Center, and the Social Democrats. Below, we shall briefly sketch out their major features and their views on Jews and antisemitism.

1. The Conservatives defended the economic and political interests of the Prussian landlords, aristocrats, and of the army. They stood for an ordered, hierarchical, Lutheran society. Though they opposed the liberal parties and the Catholics on most political issues, including those of individual liberty and the expansion of the franchise, at crucial moments when their economic interests were at stake the Conservatives were willing to form practical electoral alliances with these parties. However, they were hostile toward the industrial working class and the Social Democratic party, which they identified with a destructive modernity. Moreover, they feared that the Socialists might succeed in organizing the peasantry which would challenge the Conservative's power.

At first, the Junkers were willing to tolerate a limited legal emancipation of the Jews. Increasingly, however, they came to oppose Jewish equality and progress, especially as this despised minority began to climb the social ladder and as populist discontent could be safely directed against it. By the same token, however, unlike the antisemitic parties, which will be discussed below, the Conservatives, with notable exceptions, seldom made a fetish of antisemitism and did not consider the "Jewish Question" to be the central issue of their day. It was the "Social Question" and the power of the working class that preoccupied them during the period of the *Kaiserreich*.

According to Levy, the Conservatives were "demagogic" or opportunistic as against the "sincere" antisemites of the antisemitic parties. [19] They were demagogic in that they were willing to use antisemitism as a ploy. Unlike the "sincere" antisemites, however, they were not willing to launch an all-out effort to abolish Jewish emancipation nor to ally themselves firmly with the antisemitic parties. This does not imply that "demagogic" antisemitism was somehow less pernicious than the "sincere" variety. It does suggest that, unlike the antisemitic parties discussed below, the Conservatives were not a single issue movement. They had other interests, and so their attention to their anti-Jewish program was less single-minded than that of the "sincere" antisemites. It was only one of the many weapons they were willing to use in defense of their privileges.

This interpretation, it should be noted, differs from that of Massing, Bracher, and Wehler who view antisemitism in Imperial Germany as deriving from and being sustained by the ruling classes and the state.[20] Indeed, they view the Conservatives as the major proponents of antisemitism in that context. The Bracher and Wehler point of view will be briefly discussed in the Conclusion.

Massing notes that in reaction to the policies of Chancellor Caprivi (1890–94), on 8 December 1892, at the Tivoli hall in Berlin, the Conservatives explicitly introduced an antisemitic plank and declared that "we fight the multifarious and obtrusive Jewish influence that decomposes our people's life."[21] What came to be known as the Tivoli program of the Conservative party, he suggests, endowed antisemitism with a measure of respectability and legitimacy that it did not previously have.

Moreover, by February 1893, when the Agrarian League (*Bund der Landwirte*) was organized—largely by the Junker landlords themselves—the Conservatives used it as an instrument with which to mobilize the peasants around their protectionist programs and to bypass the populist antisemitic parties. By the same token, however, the Agrarian league was explicitly antisemitic and remained so well into the Weimar Republic.

It is possible to respond to this thesis by noting with Levy—a point that will be developed more fully below—that by 1912 the Conservatives dropped their appeal to antisemitism, and as far as the Agrarian League is concerned "[its] brand of anti-Semitism was to prove no less 'demagogic' than that of the Conservative party. Anti-Semitism remained firmly subordinated to the interest of agricultural policy."[22]

It might further be suggested that, in the context of Imperial Germany, the antisemitism of the Conservatives and of the Agrarian League was articulated for circumscribed electoral ends and had a limited impact. In a later situation, under the Weimar Republic, during a revolutionary interregnum, this kind of Conservative and agrarian antisemitism had far more pernicious consequences.

Despite receiving only 548,877 out of a total of 4,134,299 votes cast and fifty-seven out of 397 seats in the *Reichstag* in 1871, the true and decisive power of the Conservatives lay in the Prussian Lower House and in the *Bundesrat*. This remained true for the entire period of the Second Reich.

2. The *Reichspartei* (in Prussia it was called the Free Conservatives), like the Conservative party, represented a combination of landed interests and Haute Bourgeoisie. It differed somewhat from the Conservatives, however, in that it included Catholics and the new industrialists. Much of its support came from Silesia and the Rhineland.

Despite Bismarck's solicitude for the Prussian aristocracy, the Conservatives were always suspicious of the Chancellor and opposed him on a number of occasions. This was much less true of the backers of the *Reichspartei* whose slogan was "Fatherland above Party," and who stood behind Bismarck on most issues during his term of office.[23] Indeed, it was the *Reichspartei* that formed the core of Bismarck's alliance of "Iron and Wheat" that became the major pillar supporting the imperial state before the Great War.[24]

Ironically, the *Reichspartei* tended to analyze political events from a class perspective, like its nemesis, the Socialist party, although the *Reichspartei* held that the state should protect the property and positions of the upper classes and the capitalists. On the Jewish Question, *Die Post*, the main vehicle of the party, did at times express some biting anti-Jewish remarks. At the same time, however, leaders of the party like Carl Ferdinand von Stumm-Halberg argued that, because of their class position, Jews who were capitalists were no danger to the state and should be included in the ruling coalition.[25]

3. The National Liberals represented the union of the bulk of the Prussian Progressive party with the National Liberal party founded in Hanover in 1866 by Rudolf von Bennigsen.[26] The party represented the middle classes, especially the wealthy, the Haute Bourgeoisie, and the upper levels of the civil service that were opposed to the special privileges and prerogatives of the aristocracy. The party was in favor of the centralization of state power, laissez-faire, constitutional government, the secularization of culture, and the expansion of the franchise and social equality to the propertied classes.

In alliance with the Progressives and the *Reichspartei*, and basking in Bismarck's support, the National Liberals were able to pass various laws favoring economic centralization and industrial growth. When the National Liberals tried to step beyond the purely economic and administrative spheres, however, they found Bismarck and the aristocrats in their path.[27] Like the Conservatives, the National Liberals and the Progressives feared and fought the Social Democrats and were willing to cooperate with the government when it passed laws abrogating civil liberties or limiting the participation of the working class. The legacy of the National Liberal and the Progressive opposition to the working class proved to be one of the stumbling blocks in the way of an alliance between the Social Democratics and the liberal parties during the Weimar period.[28]

Though in principle the Liberals were in favor of Jewish emancipation and quality, some writers have noted that their tolerance and support were extended to Jews as individuals, not to Jews as a separate group.[29] Like the antisemites, the Liberals hoped that the Jews would disappear, albeit not by force or expulsion but by assimilation. Indeed, when in the 1890s the antisemitic parties were able to appeal to some of their constituencies, the right-wing National Liberals, like the Conservatives, were not above using antisemitic slogans or allying themselves with antisemitic candidates for opportunistic reasons during closely fought elections.[30] Having the support of 1,171,807 voters and 125 mandates in 1871, the National Liberals were the dominant party in the *Reichstag*. Following the crash of 1873, however, they increasingly lost their base of support to some of the antisemitic parties that appealed to the *Mittelstand* and the Protestant peasantry. Though it had several prominent leaders of Jewish origin, in the wake of the *Krach* of 1873, for nearly two decades, the party ceased putting up Jewish candidates because it feared antisemitic attacks.

4. The Progressive party was representative of the committed liberals of 1866 who had resisted Bismarck in his bid to fund the army without the authorization of parliament. Like the National Liberals, the Progressives were laissez-faire in their economic policies, but unlike them they were antistatist, antimilitarist, and more committed than their National Liberal colleagues to defending and enlarging the rights and prerogatives of the *Reichstag*.

Much of the Progressives' support, like that of the National Liberals, came from the urban center, the middle classes, and the lower-middle classes. The party was also disproportionately supported by German Jews, who saw in the Progressives a bulwark against antisemitism and a line of defense for emancipation and civil liberties.

Not subscribing to the Marxist analysis of antisemitism as the wrong-headed protest movement of declining classes, the liberals—both the Progressives and the National Liberals—perceived it as a kind of irrationality, a throwback to the dark ages, that would disappear with progress, education, and enlightenment. They believed in reason, in the

Rights of Man, in a society open to talent, and in equality before the law. This was especially true of the Progressives. In the *Reichstag* it was often the Progressives who would stand up and challenge the antisemites or the Conservatives when Jewish rights were brought into question.[31]

Especially after the depression of 1873 and the subsequent social-economic turmoil that accompanied rapid industrialization, portions of the lower-middle class turned against both liberal parties. As will be discussed below, disaffiliated and disenchanted strata of the *Mittelstand* turned to the antisemitic parties in order to register their protest against the insecure social and economic conditions in Imperial Germany. The inability of the Progressives and the National Liberals to hold on to their previous lower middle class and peasant support gravely weakened the forces of liberty in Germany. A further problem, one which they shared with the Social Democrats, was the inability of the Progressives to wrap themselves in the flag quite as effectively as the Conservatives. As the Germans became increasingly nationalistic, the Progressives became defensive about their patriotism.

In retrospect it seems tragic that in order to prove their bona fides, the Progressives had to distance themselves from the Social Democrats, even to the point, in some cases, of supporting an antisemite in a close election. As noted, from the broader perspectives of German history, the split between the Social Democrats and the liberal parties weakened the opposition to the antisemites in Imperial Germany and to the Nazis in the Weimar Republic.

5. The Catholic Center party represented the political interests of German Catholics and the Church. It stood for local and states' rights against the centralizing ambitions of Bismarck and the federal government. Though the Center's leadership favored tradition and hierarchy, it was, nevertheless, open to some social change within the tradition of Social Catholicism as formulated by Adolf Kolping and Bishop Wilhelm Emanuel von Ketteler.[32]

During the *Kulturkampf*, when Bismarck in alliance with the liberals—among whom were some prominent Jews including Lasker—attempted to curb the powers of the Church and to discriminate against Catholics, the party turned to antisemitism as a defensive measure against its enemies.[33] For the most part, however, during the imperial period and after, the Center was opposed to the opportunistic uses of antisemitism, and, together with the Progressives and the Social Democrats, it served as an obstacle to its diffusion among the Germans.[34]

6. As has been noted above, the Social Democratic party was anath-

ema to the ruling classes, including the middle classes, of Imperial Germany. In a society that was still largely hierarchical, Christian, and traditional, the SPD stood for equality, secularism, and modernity. In a Germany that was ruled by a Prussian landowning aristocracy and a military caste, the SPD favored the abolition of class privilege, and in its early years it threatened to seize power by means of a working-class revolution. It was beyond the pale for any of the other parties to ally with the "enemies of the empire," though, as has been noted, the revolutionary aspirations of the party dimmed throughout the period of the *Kaiserreich*.

The party was not especially sympathetic to the Jews, but it opposed the antisemitic parties, and unlike the liberals it had a better grasp of the dynamics of antisemitism in the context of Imperial Germany. Indeed, in the early years of German socialism, notwithstanding Lassalle's Jewish origins, some antisemitic sentiment crept into the movement. Despite inoculating socialists against political antisemitism,[35] Marxist analysis proved to be an obstacle to viewing with empathy the peculiar situation of a former pariah group that was trying with difficulty to assimilate and to change its status in German society. Jewish progress was seen as embourgeoisement, and Jewish support for the liberals was perceived as a betrayal. Socialists were not likely to oppose Jews as such, but they made no distinction between Jewish and non-Jewish elements of the middle class, and like the liberals they looked forward to the Jews' complete assimilation and, in effect, disappearance.

The Socialists' reading of antisemitism was based on a straightforward class analysis. They viewed modern political antisemitism as an expression of the socioeconomic discontent of the lower-middle class and the peasantry. They understood these two classes as being victimized by capitalism and their antisemitism as an inchoate expression of their anger. Socialists believed that with industrialization these two classes were destined to disappear, and with them antisemitism. This then led to a certain complacency not only about antisemitism but about the role and future of the *Mittelstand* and the peasantry. Thus in a report that became the official word on antisemitism to the 1893 convention of the Social Democratic party, August Bebel, one of its foremost leaders, explained:

> Anti-Semitism stems from the resentment of certain middle-class groups which find themselves oppressed by the development of capitalism and which are destined to perish economically as a result of these trends. These groups, however, misinterpret their own situa-

tion and therefore do not fight against the capitalist system but against surface phenomena which seem to hurt them most in the competitive struggle: namely Jewish exploiters.[36]

In a speech to the same convention, Bebel further elaborated by saying:

What makes the position of the Social Democratic party towards the peasants, the artisans, and small business people so difficult is the fact that as honest men the Social Democrats have to say: we have no way of saving you within the existing framework of society.[37]

And commenting on the peasantry and the *Mittelstand*, Engels exclaimed, "We have in the party no use [for them] . . . These people belong to the anti-Semites, let them go there."[38] And so they did.[39]

From this brief sketch of the major parties and classes in Imperial Germany it readily can be seen that, except for the Conservatives, who were not above using the issue of antisemitism for narrow electoral ends, none of the other major parties was in favor of abolishing Jewish emancipation. While the principal parties tended to represent some of the main strata of German society, two classes, the *Mittelstand* and the Protestant peasantry, were not well integrated into the system of party representation. Afraid of capitalism and what it was doing to their status and livelihood, they resented the more secure classes above them and the better organized working class that they considered to be below them.

Beyond being plainly wrong—the *Mittelstand* did not disappear, and the peasantry, though it declined, was still an active force well into the Third Reich—the Socialist assessment of these classes had some far-reaching practical consequences. With the major parties, including the Socialists, neglecting them, the *Mittelstand* and the peasantry, especially during hard times, became principal sources of support for the antisemitic parties that made their appearance after the depression of 1873.

The Rise and Fall of the Antisemitic Political Parties

A number of writers point to the crash of 1873 as stimulating the antisemitic movement in Imperial Germany. The *Krach* had begun with the collapse of the *Creditanstalt*, an Austrian branch of the Rothschild banking empire.[40] Although many non-Jews, including Junkers and high government officials, were involved, the Jews as a whole were blamed for the crash.

115

As noted in Chapter 3, however, the accusation of Jewish involvement in the depression of 1873 must be viewed in light of the wider resentment produced by the mobilization of the Jewish pariah in the nineteenth century. Thus antisemitic publicists like Otto Glagau and Wilhelm Marr had ready at hand images of Jews as conspiratorial, ambitious, unshakable in their solidarity, who hated Gentiles, and who were "an alien force with international connections and bent on conquest."[41] It is significant that Glagau's exposés, first printed in 1874 in the literary magazine the *Gartenlaube*, reached some 270,000 subscribers.[42]

Blaming the depression on the Jews, Glagau argued that they controlled the modern capitalist world.

> Jewry is applied Manchesterism in the extreme. It knows nothing any more but trade, and of that merely haggling and usury. It does not work but makes others work for it, it haggles and speculates with the manual and mental products of others. Its center is the stock exchange. . . . As an alien tribe it fastens itself on the German people and sucks their marrow. The social question is essentially the Jewish question; everything else is [a] swindle.[43]

Though the depression of 1873–79 gave occasion to antisemitic publicists and encouraged antisemitic attitudes, it is noteworthy that organized antisemitic political parties appeared soon after what has come to be known as Bismarck's "change of course" in national policy.

Until 1878 the chancellor had relied on a coalition with the national Liberals and the Progressives in support of a policy of free trade. With cheap imported wheat coming in from the United States, Russia, and elsewhere, however, the landed aristocracy, whose privileges Bismarck wished to defend, turned against laissez-faire toward protectionism, and the chancellor followed suit. After that date he turned away from free trade, and he shifted his alliance in the *Reichstag* to the Conservatives and the Center. It was at this point, as noted above, that he cracked down on the Socialists; moreover, while purging supporters of liberal parties from the civil service, he identified them with the enemies of the Reich. Since the liberals were closely identified with championing Jewish emancipation, an attack on the former legitimized an attack on the latter. It was in this context of economic crisis and repression against the left that there appeared the first explicitly antisemitic parties.

They were led by men such as Adolf Stoecker, Max Liebermann von Sonnenberg, Otto Böckel, Bernhard and Paul Förster, Theodor Fritsch, and others less well known. Sometimes in concert, sometimes alone, they tried to fashion a political force that would be able to influence the *Reichstag* to revoke Jewish emancipation and turn back Jewish mobilization.

Some writers like Massing suggest that racist ideology provided an important distinction between antisemites.[44] Stoecker differed from Fritsch, for example, in that the former still believed in the possibility of Jewish conversion, while the latter excluded Jews on biological grounds. Levy points out, however, that to the extent they used racialist language, all the antisemites and their parties were influenced by racism.[45] The significant difference he stresses among the antisemitic leaders is their political strategy and their assessment of the Second Reich, not their image of Jews. Here he distinguishes between "conventional" and "revolutionary" antisemites.[46]

The great majority of the antisemites were conventional in the sense that they accepted the basic political, cultural, and social framework of Imperial Germany. Men like Stoecker and Liebermann, though from time to time they may have felt indignant at Bismarck's exercise of power, admired him and were faithful servants of the kaiser. Even peasant populists like Böckel, who resented the domination of the Junker landlords and wished for a more egalitarian society, did not dream of overturning the system when they first entered electoral politics. To the contrary, especially after Böckel got himself elected to the *Reichstag* in 1887, he and most of the other antisemites were confident that by working through the institutions of the *Kaiserreich* they could implement their antisemitic policies. Later, of course, when it was apparent that he had failed, Böckel turned against the regime.[47]

In contrast, the revolutionaries, men like Bernhard Förster and Theodor Fritsch, rejected the basic political, cultural, and social framework of Imperial Germany. Although at various times they were willing to cooperate with the "conventional" antisemites, the "revolutionaries" realized that the antisemitic political parties could never get their way within the Second Reich. Their antisemitism was so radical and their disappointment in the prevailing state so deep, that they were willing to contemplate destroying it for the sake of their vision of a Germany free of Jews.

Typical of the revolutionary antisemites was Bernhard Förster, Nietzsche's brother-in-law. After some early failures of the antisemitic movement, he became convinced that all conventional political approaches were hopeless, and that the German state and society had to be refashioned from top to bottom; only then would the "Jewish Problem" find a solution. Despairing of creating the kind of society he wished, he emigrated to Paraguay and tried to establish on the La Plata river his ideal community. When in 1889 it failed, Förster committed suicide.[48]

The first explicitly antisemitic party, the League of Antisemites (*Antisemiten Liga*), was founded by Wilhelm Marr in 1879. Though it set up branches in Berlin and Hamburg, it failed soon after its inception. A more durable party that evolved into but did not start as an antisemitic association was the Christian Social Workers' party founded by Fourth Court Chaplain Adolf Stoecker in 1878. It was renamed the Christian Social party (*Christlichsoziale Partei*) in 1881. Other notable parties were the Social Reich party, (*Soziale Reichspartei*) founded by Ernst Henrici in 1880, lasting until 1882, and the German People's Alliance (*Deutscher Volksverein*), founded in 1881 by Liebermann and Paul Forster, whose brother was the ill-fated Bernhard. The German People's Alliance lasted until 1885.

In 1866 Liebermann joined Otto Böckel, the Hessian populist, in forming the German Antisemitic Alliance (*Deutsche Antisemitische Vereinigung*). By 1887, the mercurial Böckel split off, however, and by 1889 he formed his own Antisemitic People's party (*Antisemitische Volkspartei*), which by 1893 was renamed the German Reform party (*Deutsche Reformpartei*). Meanwhile, in 1889 Liebermann founded the German Social party (*Deutschsoziale Partei*). In 1894, together with Böckel's former partner, Oswald Zimmermann, Liebermann tried to unify the antisemitic movement under the aegis of the Antisemitic German Social Reform party (*Antisemitische Deutschsoziale Reform Partei*). But that unity was of short duration. By 1900 Liebermann broke with Zimmermann and reconstituted his old German Social party.

In the first few years of their existence, the antisemitic parties were limited to playing a role in Berlin and Dresden. Then, in the election of 1887, they were able to gain representation in the *Reichstag*, where they played a minor role until their near demise by 1912. The historical details of the formation, integration, and disintegration of these parties are of no concern here.[49] We are interested, however, in the reasons for their founding, the causes of their failure, and the lessons that they might provide for the rise of the Nazis. Their failure in the narrow electoral sense can be readily seen from table 4.1.

Starting with a very modest level of national support in 1887, where they received 11,496 out of 7,527,601 votes cast, entitling them to one deputy in the *Reichstag*, by 1890 the antisemitic parties more than tripled their vote and their representation. By 1893 they expanded their vote by more than a factor of 8 and gained sixteen seats. After peaking in 1898,

TABLE 4.1 The Electoral Rise and Decline of the Antisemitic Parties in Imperial Germany

Year	Votes	Percentage	Deputies
1887	11,496	0.15	1
1890	45,000	0.65	5
1893	263,861	3.40	16
1898	284,250	3.70	13
1903	244,543	2.50	11
1907	248,534	2.20	17
1912	104,538	0.86	3

Note.—This table is derived from the electoral statistics provided by Pinson, 572–73. In a private correspondence (4 January 1988), Professor Levy suggests that the high point of antisemitic support in the *Kaiserreich* may have occurred in 1893 rather than in 1898. He also counts seventeen rather than sixteen antisemitic deputies in 1907.

however, they declined, and as a percentage of the votes cast, by 1912 they were back to the levels of the early 1890s.

What accounted for the rise and fall of the antisemitic political parties? We have suggested that they rose by trying to ally themselves to the Conservatives and by appealing to the populist resentments of the *Mittelstand* and the peasantry. As the state and the ruling elites came to distrust this populism, as economic conditions improved, and as other organized pressure groups came to represent the economic interests of classes that voted for the antisemites, the antisemitic parties declined. This pattern was fairly typical of all the antisemitic parties and the careers of all the conventional antisemites. To illustrate this pattern, we shall briefly describe the political career of Court Chaplain Adolf Stoecker.[50]

Stoecker

Fourth Court Chaplain Adolf Stoecker (1835–1909) was an enthusiastic nationalist and supporter of the Imperial German state who had come to the attention of Kaiser Wilhelm I during the Franco-Prussian war. He became involved in politics in 1877 when, upon taking over the leadership of the Berlin city mission, a Lutheran charitable organization, he realized that the workers' support for the Socialist party stemmed in large part from their desperate economic situation.

Encouraged by Bismarck's attack on the Socialists and the liberal parties, Stoecker set to work organizing the Berlin working class. He hoped that at one and the same time he might improve the conditions of the working poor and wean them away from the Socialists. To this end he founded the Christian Social Workers' party (*Christlichsoziale Arbeiterpartei*) in 1878.

He started by calling public meetings where he denounced capitalism, "this system of unlimited competition, of crassest egoism," and supported some progressive legislation such as direct taxation on income and inheritance, care for the disabled, restriction on child and female labor, and prohibition of work on Sundays. [51]

He was a splendid orator and an impressive figure; nevertheless, for the most part, he was rebuffed by the working class which stuck to its party, the Social Democrats. Thus at a typical working-class mass meeting, it was decided:

> *Whereas* the consummation of the Christian Social Program would not bring about any change.
> *Be it resolved* that this meeting expects a thorough elimination of all existing political and economic restrictions solely through the Social Democratic Party, and that it is our duty to support and spread with all our strength the teachings of that party. [52]

In the three districts where the Christian Socials ran candidates in 1878, they received a mere 1,421 out of 53,718 votes cast.

Even before the debacle of 1878, Stoecker had been experimenting with blaming the "Manchesterite Jews" as the chief cause of economic misery. Then on 19 September 1879, he changed his tactics and launched a full-scale antisemitic attack in a public speech entitled "What We Demand of Modern Jewry." This speech was significant both because it set Stoecker and his party on a new and far more successful course, and because it articulated some of the major antisemitic themes that were first identified here in Chapter 3. Three of the major themes that appeared in his speeches were (1) that Judaism was a dead religion superseded by Christianity, (2) that contemporary Jews were the agents of modernity and secularism undermining Christian beliefs and German nationalism, and (3) that modern Jews in their claims to equality and assimilation were threatening to "Judaize" Germans and to dominate Germany.

Stoecker began by asserting that the Jewish problem was a "burning question" for all Germans, transcending party. Some like Marr even wrote that "the end of Germany has come." [53] For his part, Stoecker contended that the end might be averted and that Germany could rid herself of "the foreign spirit" and social "disease" that was plaguing her. He called on

Christians as well as Jews to be seriously concerned "for the rumbling of a far-off thunderstorm can already be heard."[54]

After bitterly complaining of the criticism he had suffered for his views, he launched an attack on Orthodox and Reform Judaism:

> This ossification of the Law, the Old Testament without a temple, without priests, without sacrifice, without a Messiah, is neither attractive nor dangerous to the children of the nineteenth century. It is a form of religion which is dead at its very core, a low form of revelation, an outlived spirit, still venerable but set at nought by Christ and no longer holding any truth for the present.[55]

So much for Othodoxy. Reform did not fare any better:

> It is neither Judaism nor Christianity, but a pitiful remnant of the age of enlightment. Its ideas did not originate on Jewish soil but in a wretched period of the Christian church, a period long since overcome by the church itself.[56]

What exercised him most, however, was that despite the "ossification" of Orthodoxy, and the "pitiful remnant" of Reform, contemporary Jews seemed to take pride in Judaism. Thus they

> boast that they are bearers of the loftiest religious and moral ideals for mankind and the world and that it is the mission of Jewry, now and in the future, to maintain those ideals, to develop and spread them.[57]

Having pilloried what he mistook to be religious Judaism, Stoecker exclaimed: "Here we wish to make our first request. We ask: *please be a little more modest!*"[58] He did not deny that in the past Israel had a great mission, but as to having any value as a light unto the nations in the contemporary world, "the Jews should not be told such foolishness."[59] Since they rejected Christ they had become "a dry well and a withered tree."[60]

In these passages can be discerned a repetition of the themes that first appeared in St. Chrysostom and the *Adversus Judaeos* literature. Judaism is dead. It has been superseded by Christianity. In their blindness and stubbornness religious Jews cling to a "dry well and a withered tree." Like so many of his contemporaries, Stoecker knew nothing of the rabbinical Judaism of Hillel, Maimonides, and Rashi. He had an unexamined contempt for the Talmud, the Mishna, and the Gemara, and 1,900 years of rabbinical commentaries. Like all antisemites, Stoecker did not understand religious Judaism, nor could he account for its survival, but what annoyed him even more was the changed status and behavior of contemporary Jews—many of whom were not even religious.

These he characterized as a "repulsive generation," and he blamed secular Jews for undermining all faith including Christianity.[61] It was in this context of a threatening secular modernity that he attacked the press, which he also identified with the Jews: "The truth is that modern Jewry is most certainly a power against religion; a power which bitterly fights Christianity everywhere, uproots Christian faith as well as national feeling in the people."[62]

This brought him to a denunciation of the liberal press which he took to be controlled by Jews. "It is a fact that the worst Berlin papers are in the hands of the Jews and that the Jewish element completely dominates the editorial staffs."[63] In an ironic turn, he made his second demand: "We really mean it if we address our second request to the Jewish press: *please be a little more tolerant!*"[64]

The Jews were identified with the forces of modernity and secularism that were dissolving the Christian faith, but what worried the pastor even more was that Germans were becoming "Judaized." Referring to a prophecy made as early as 1816 that Germany's splendor may perish with the Jews, Stoecker explained:

> If the Christians continue to expose themselves constantly to the influence of the Jewish spirit which deprives them of their German and Christian character this prophesy will certainly come true. But perhaps—and this is our hope—Germany's splendor will arise with new life after this period of decline. We should be indeed a nation without honor if we did not break these chains of a foreign mentality, if we really became judaized.[65]

The implicit fear expressed in this passage was that, as Jews assimilated to German society, it was not they who would become like the Germans but that the Germans would become like the Jews. Since the Jews were loathsome pariahs, believers in a dead religion or in no religion at all, there was the danger that with Jewish assimilation Germans would become "Judaized," that is, loathsome pariahs themselves.[66]

This fear was expressed even more strongly in the following passage:

> All immigrants are eventually absorbed by the people among whom they live—all save the Jews. They pit their unbroken semitic character against Teutonic nature, their rigid cult of law or their hatred

of Christianity against Christianity. We cannot condemn them for this; as long as they are Jews, they are bound to act in this way. But we must, in all candor, state the necessity of protecting ourselves against the dangers of such intermingling.[67]

As noted, the fear of Jewish mobilization and assimilation included not only the danger of becoming "Judaized" but of actually becoming dominated by the Jews.

They control the arteries of money, banking, and trade; they dominate the press and they are flooding the institutions of higher learning. . . . We are moving toward the point when public opinion will be completely dominated and labor completely exploited by the Jews. The process of disintegration is under way; nothing will stop it, unless we turn about and make the Jews turn about too. And this is where we make our third request. Modern Jewry must take part in productive work: *a little more equality please!*[68]

Keeping in mind his largely *Mittelstand* audience, among whom was a scattering of workers, the pastor then called on the Jews to become "artisans, factory workers, and peasants. We should ask nothing more of them."[69] He concluded his speech with the warning: "Either we succeed in this and Germany will rise again, or the cancer from which we suffer will spread further. In that event our whole future is threatened and the German spirit will become Judaized."[70]

The speech was greeted with great interest and enthusiasm, not as had been anticipated by the politically committed working-class audience to whom it had been addressed but by members of the lower-middle class, the *Mittelstand.* Stoecker's appeal made it possible for disgruntled clerks, shopkeepers, artisans, petty civil servants, and primary and secondary schoolteachers to express a profound resentment against their social and economic position while still affirming their loyalty to kaiser and country. In 1881 the party dropped the word "Workers" from its banner and became simply the Christian Social party. In this way Stoecker conceded that his party had failed among the working class and that most of his support now came from the lower-middle class.[71]

Though his language was racist, Stoecker still believed that conversion to Christianity was an active alternative for Jews, if they wished to shed their Jewish characteristics and become Germans. Most other antisemites of his time were not as generous.

Stoecker's Dilemma

For some thirty years, in alliance with the Conservatives and other antisemitic parties, Stoecker's Christian Socials were able to keep the issue of antisemitism alive, first in Berlin and then before the *Reichstag*. But they could never get that body or the government to support their program. Indications of where the problem lay appeared from the party's inception.

When in 1878 Bismarck turned against the liberal parties and the Socialists, the chancellor and the kaiser at first gave Stoecker their tacit approval. Though from the start Bismarck had some qualms about the pastor's rabble-rousing and his attacks on property, he viewed Stoecker as a handy stick with which to beat the liberals. On 11 June 1880, however, for the first but not the last time, Stoecker crossed the limits of his tacit understanding with the government.

On that date he publicly attacked Gerson von Bleichröder, Bismarck's personal banker and a Jew.[72] Stoecker called him a capitalist "with more money than all the clergymen taken together."[73] Protesting the pastor's speech, the banker sent a letter to the kaiser who sent it to Bismarck, who forwarded it to Robert von Puttkamer, Prussian Minister of Public Worship and Instruction. Puttkamer who was both Bismarck's brother-in-law and a friend of Stoecker delayed his response. When he finally sent a draft of a letter back to Bismarck, the chancellor did not accept it. Instead, he wrote a reply to his minister which was revealing of his views about Stoecker, antisemitism, and the Jews.

> In my opinion, the activity of Court Chaplain Stoecker remains serious even if the meetings he organizes should in the future lose their tumultuous character. The tendencies he furthers are in several points identical with those of the other Social Democrats. . . . He rouses desires that cannot be achieved. . . . With reference particularly to the Jewish question, it is an error to assume that *rich* Jews of our country exert a strong influence upon the press. It may be different in Paris. Not the moneyed Jews but political reformers among the Jews are aggressive in our press and in the parliamentary bodies. Rather the interests of wealthy Jews are tied up with the preservation of our state institutions and cannot dispense with the latter. . . . Herr Stoecker's agitation is not primarily directed against these liberal and discontented Jews. His speeches address themselves to the envy and greed of the have-nots against those who possess.[74]

This warning that the antisemites were stirring up trouble against the state itself and that the Jews were not the terrible danger that they were made out to be was sounded by Bismarck and even more by the chancellors who came after him.

It can safely be said that, although he was no friend of the Jews, Bismarck was opposed to the revocation of the Emancipation of 1869. Nor was he a friend of the antisemites when he found them stirring up popular passions. Indeed, he had broader concerns to occupy him and used now this group and now that one to get his ends. When he wanted to embarrass the liberals or to weaken the Social Democrats he did not hesitate to encourage Stoecker's brand of Christian Social antisemitism; when Stoecker attacked Bleichröder, as we have seen, the chancellor turned on the pastor.

The final parting of the ways between Bismarck and the pastor occurred after 1884 when the former reconstructed a new parliamentary coalition that included the National Liberals and the Conservatives. By 1887 he hoped that this *Kartell* would become the bulwark against social democracy. "Discretion and moderation with regard to anti-Semitism was now imperative in bringing the Conservatives and the National Liberals closer together. Stoecker's movement was an obstacle in the path of the new alliance and measures had to be taken to clear it away."[75] By 1889, with Kaiser Wilhelm II on the throne, Stoecker was made to choose between his office and his political activities. He pledged to the new Kaiser:

> Since his Majesty considers activity in the political life of Berlin, of the kind in which up to now I have been engaged, as incompatible with the office of court Chaplain, it goes without saying that I give it up while being entrusted by His Majesty with continuing in office.[76]

But the pastor was not through. In 1890 it was clear that Bismarck's strategy of relying on an alliance with the National Liberals had failed. Due to protectionist legislation supported by the *Kartell*, the cost of living rose and had dramatic consequences for the elections of 1890. The National Liberals lost fifty-seven seats and the Conservatives twenty-eight seats, while at the same time the SPD gained twenty-four and the Progressives forty-four. The forces of social democracy were once more threatening, and the chancellor wanted to crush them by force. He was dissuaded from this desperate course by the kaiser himself who forced him to resign. Bismarck left to his successors the task of resolving some of the basic contradictions in the state that he had designed, but they were not better at it than he was.

After Bismarck's resignation, Stoecker once more thought that he might regain his place in the sun. Already in 1889 an editorial in *Das Volk*, the paper of the Christian Socials, predicted his return to active politics. But Wilhelm II had no intention of sacrificing the Conservative-National Liberal alliance for the sake of the old pastor. After Stoecker had made an incendiary speech, he was forced to resign. In his memoirs the kaiser would recall that

> I often pointed out that the National Liberals were devoted to the Reich, and thus to the Kaiser, and accordingly should be welcomed as allies of the Conservatives. . . . I removed Court Chaplain Stoecker—a man who had done excellent social work in his *Mission* activities—because he had delivered a demagogic, incendiary address in South Germany against the liberals there.[77]

Having been forced to resign his office, however, did not prevent Stoecker from pursuing antisemitic politics. When in the 1890s the Conservatives sought to broaden their base and to create a more populist image, Stoecker was once more brought back and played an important role. But his dilemma and that of his party was always the same: in attacking the Jews he also attacked the liberal parties, and he stirred up populist passions against the state and the prevailing class system. This would induce the Conservatives or the kaiser or both to turn away from him, thereby leaving him isolated in the Reichstag and among the electorate. His career of trying to patch up Junker conservatism and populism with antisemitism came to its inevitable end when the Christian Socials tried to expand their appeal beyond the lower-middle class to the peasant farmers.

In siding with the peasants, the Christian Socials ran up against the very real economic and political interests of the Junker landlords. Indeed, in the 1890s, the party had attracted to its colors certain brilliant and well-meaning reformers such as Friedrich Naumann, a Protestant minister and author of the *Cathechism for Workers*. Such men and the young guard that clustered around *Das Volk*, the party paper, became increasingly more radical in their populism. Such developments did not go unnoticed in the upper reaches of the Conservative party.

By 1895 Stoecker found himself in the untenable position of having to choose between his Conservative superiors and his populist followers.

Then, on 2 December 1895 the Conservative leadership asked him to disavow the Christian Social paper. He agreed to break all relations with *Das Volk*, but he refused to denounce it on the grounds that it would give ammunition to his opponents. On 11 February 1896 he was forced to resign from the Conservative party, and he never regained his old influence. For all of his efforts on behalf of the crown and the ruling classes, Stoecker received what amounted to the back of the hand from the kaiser himself:

> Stoecker had ended as I predicted years ago. Politicians of the cloth are monstrosities (*ein Unding*). He who is a Christian is also social; the Christian Social idea is nonsensical and leads to arrogance and intolerance, both totally opposed to Christianity. The gentlemen of the cloth (*die Herren Pastoren*) should busy themselves with the souls of their flock and cultivate Christian love but they should keep out of politics which is none of their business in any case.[78]

Stoecker's dilemma was not his alone. All the antisemitic parties including those that were more radical and less dependent on the conservatives than his Christian Socials faced similar insoluble problems in the confines of Imperial Germany.

Conclusion

In the course of this chapter two questions were raised: (1) What accounted for the rise and fall of the antisemitic parties in Imperial Germany? (2) What lesson might be drawn from the history of these early predecessors for the rise of the Nazis and hence for the Holocaust? In this Conclusion these questions will be addressed. Let us begin by considering the thesis, raised earlier, that antisemitism and the rise of the antisemitic political parties can be attributed to the state itself and to its use of the techniques of "negative integration."

Negative Integration

Asserting that Imperial Germany was a "faulted society," a number of prominent contemporary German historians and sociologists have suggested that antisemitism can be viewed as a form of "social imperialism" and "negative integration."[79] In brief, their argument goes that, given Bismarck's legacy, neither the state nor the ruling classes could resolve the crisis of participation. Germany's rulers, therefore, purposely stimulated antisemitism, nationalism, and imperialism, in order to pacify the lower classes and to distract them from their authentic political and economic interests.

According to Wehler, it was Bismarck himself who had initiated this practice.

> He made use of the primeval socio-psychic opposition between "in-groups" and "out-groups" and thus stylized internal conflicts so as to lead a majority of elements "loyal to the Empire" against a minority of "enemies of the Empire". . . . The various coalition of groups loyal to the Empire were held together primarily by their enmity towards a common foe—in other words, on a negative basis. [80]

This argument notes, "The Jews as the 'progressive enemy of the Empire' became, with Bismarck's express approval, the scapegoat of German domestic politics long before the cliché of the 'Marxist Jew' gained currency."[81]

In addition to providing an etiology of antisemitism in Imperial Germany, the thesis of negative integration makes the connection to the Nazi period. In this analysis the manipulations of the Second Reich accustomed the Germans to view each other on a "friend-or-foe" basis that continued into the Third Reich.

> That one had some neighbors who were inferior became part and parcel of everyday life during the fifty years of the German Empire's existence . . . This helps to explain why the psychological barriers against physical liquidation of minorities could be broken down so quickly. . . . viewed from an historical perspective, it is possible to trace the line from the "enemies of the Empire" both to the attacks on Jewish synagogues in 1938 (*Reichskristallnacht*) as well as to the Nazi ideal of the "folk community" (*Volkesgemeinschaft*) with its necessary corollary of "parasites of the nation" which had to be exterminated. [82]

The thesis suggesting that antisemitism in Imperial Germany was a form of negative integration assumes that Germany was a faulted society suffering from a crisis of participation and that it was the state and the Conservatives who had initiated this form of scapegoating. The argument asserts, furthermore, that negative integration set the stage for Nazi policy toward the Jews.

This analysis of antisemitism in Imperial Germany and beyond has some problems. One can accept its basic premise, namely, that Imperial Germany had a crisis of political participation, without necessarily accepting the inference that antisemitism derived primarily from the tactical manipulations of the ruling classes, nor that antisemitism in the *Kaiserreich* was directly connected to the later phenomenon of Nazism. Although Bismarck himself was highly ambivalent about Jews, and for a time the Conservatives allied themselves with Pastor Stoecker's antisemitic Christian Social party, in the final analysis neither the imperial state nor the Conservatives chose to rescind Jewish emancipation as the antisemites wanted. [83]

There were at least two main reasons why the imperial regime and the parties that supported it were reluctant to play the role assigned to them by the "negative integration" thesis. In the first place, the demon they feared most was social democracy, not the Jews. No matter how they felt about them, the rulers of Imperial Germany did not consider the Jews to be a great danger to them or to the country. In the second place, Bismarck, the chancellors who followed him, and the Conservatives became alarmed that the populism stirred up by the antisemitic parties need not stop with the Jews but might spread to attack the state and the privileged groups of the Reich. For both of these reasons, the rulers of Imperial Germany came to mistrust political antisemitism and, in time, distanced themselves from the antisemitic parties.

What this analysis suggests is that antisemitism in Imperial Germany could not come to power without the aid of the state and the Conservatives, and indeed when this aid was cut off it failed. By the same token, it is apparent that antisemitism was not a product of "social imperialism," "negative integration," and elite manipulation alone. It had other sources, as we have seen, in the pariah status of Jews in Christian Europe, in the resentment caused by Jewish mobilization and assimilation, and in the populism of the *Mittelstand* and the peasantry. [84]

Why Did they Fail?

What then accounts for the failure of the antisemitic political parties in Imperial Germany, and what lessons might be drawn from it for the Nazi period? Referring back to Stoecker, we have already noted that his was a conventional antisemitism in that it accepted the basic framework of state and society. Indeed, with the tacit acquiescence of Bismarck and the kaiser, he had launched his political career in 1878 in order to preserve the state, the ruling classes, and traditional values. As has been noted, his dilemma stemmed from the fact that his appeal had a boomerang effect: by stirring up antisemitism among the lower-middle class and later the peasantry, he unintentionally mobilized these groups against the very ruling circles he had hoped to defend. This phenomenon was not lost either on the state in the persons of Bismarck, later chancellors, and the kaiser himself. In time, both the state and the Conservatives distanced themselves from the pastor.

Other antisemites like Otto Böckel, the Hessian peasant leader mentioned above, found the state in Imperial Germany to be an obstacle to their ambitions but for different reasons. Though he did not enter politics with the approval of Bismarck and the kaiser, and, indeed, his slogan "Against Junkers and Jews" was far from Stoecker and Liebermann, Böckel's populist appeal to the Hessian peasantry also faded. He could get himself elected to the *Reichstag*, but once there he discovered—as did his admirers—that he had no power. In order to wield influence he had to enter into coalitions with other parties, but none of the major parties, including the Conservatives, would have him. Indeed, the other antisemites had to be careful that by associating with him they not be tarred with the epithet "enemies of the Empire." Thus, for most of his parliamentary career, Böckel was powerless either to punish the Jews or to improve the economic conditions of his peasant clients. When in the 1890s the economy began to improve, and peasant associations rose and addressed themselves to the specific economic needs of that class, his popularity waned.[85]

Finally, as has been noted, there were the "revolutionary" antisemites like Bernhard Förster, Theodor Fritsch, and Heinrich Class.[86] They played a marginal role even in the antisemitic politics of Imperial Germany. Truly they had come before their time. They were right in rejecting the parliamentary path which in the long run turned into a dead end for the antisemitic parties, but except for propaganda and education they had no credible alternative in that context.

Indeed, how could it be otherwise? Imperial Germany was a great power that had unified the Germans and had defeated their enemies in battle. The state and its officers had widespread support and legitimacy. For all of the problems of the *Kaiserreich*, including its chronic crisis of participation, revolutionary parties whether Marxist or antisemitic had very little chance of overturning the state and transforming society. This situation was diametrically opposed to that of the Weimar Republic and the Nazis. Thus on both counts, claims that negative integration gave rise to the antisemitic movement in imperial Germany and that it had some direct or even indirect connection to Nazism must be treated with some caution.

In Imperial Germany antisemitism as a political strategy was self-limiting. In large measure, this derived from the very purpose and structure of the Bismarckian state. It was a system that was designed to preserve the empire and the aristocracy by limiting popular participation. To the extent that the antisemitic political parties tried to expand political participation, however, they often inadvertently challenged the edifice of the Bismarckian regime and class structure. This was the limit that the antisemitic political parties in Imperial Germany could not cross, and that is why they failed.

Having analyzed their failure, next we need to turn to the even more significant question as to the connection between the antisemitic political parties of Imperial Germany and the Nazis. Were these parties a dead end for antisemitism or an omen of bad times to come?

The Connection to Nazism

There is no doubt that especially in the pronouncements and manifestos of the antisemites and their parties in Imperial Germany there are obvious parallels to the Nazis. In each manifestation of antisemitism one can find the same calls for the abolition of Jewish emancipation, for the segregation of Jews, and, even in some instances, for their extermination.[87] Moreover, it was in the nineteenth century that antisemites first identified Jews as a racial category intrinsically alien to the Germans and furthered the view that Jews control the modern world. Nevertheless, the failure of the antisemitic parties in Imperial Germany poses a problem for the thesis that a simple continuity exists between the movements preceding the Great War and the Nazis. Does not the abject failure of these parties and the rousing success of the Nazis call into question their similarities or at least the conditions under which they sought to rise to power?

In an important article, challenging what has been the main thrust of this chapter, Volkov suggested that the failure of the antisemitic political parties in Imperial Germany was not a good measure of the spread of popular antisemitism as an ideology or as a "cultural code."[88] She advanced the thesis that in Imperial Germany, in part because of the agitation of the antisemitic parties, the public came to be polarized between those who accepted the modern industrial world and expressed this support by championing Jewish emancipation and those who rejected this modernity and articulated their resentment in the language of antisemitism.

> Wilhelminian society underwent a process of cultural polarisation. While internal divisions and controversies over principles and tactics continued to preoccupy the activists, two main blocks of ideas,

two clusters of words, two sets of norms and values, in short—two
cultures were formed. These were often symbolised and denoted by
two concepts: antisemitism and emancipation.[89]

Like France split between the Dreyfusards and the anti-
Dreyfusards, Imperial Germany came to be divided between the eman-
cipationists and the antisemites. The implication here is that, in spite of
the failure of the antisemitic parties, antisemitism as a "cultural system"
and as an ideology diffused ever more widely throughout German society. Thus, indeed, when the Nazis came along, the Germans were ready
for them, and the antisemitic parties had helped to prepare the way.

Though some form of polarization between those favoring and
those rejecting the modern world may have occurred in the *Kaiserreich*,
the decline of the antisemitic political parties would suggest that, at least
before the Great War, the antisemites were losing the struggle. More to
the point, however, it seems that not only did parliamentary antisemitism
decline before the Great War but Jew-hatred as a prejudice and antisemitism as a compelling ideology did so as well. Since, as far as we know,
there were no public opinion surveys taken in this period, one must rely
on indirect evidence for the wider decline of Jew-hatred and antisemitism.

Thus, for example, while in 1892, in its Tivoli program, the Conservative party included an antisemitic plank, by 1911 its handbook substantially played down antisemitism. Indeed, it condemned the antisemitic parties for "excesses and rowdyism" that had "inhibited the process
of Jewish assimilation [and] had even promoted an unwanted Jewish solidarity."[90]

By the 1913 party congress, the Conservatives refrained from discussing the issue at all, and in the Prussian state elections of the same
year they stopped using their customary antisemitic arguments and slogans against their opponents. Levy remarked that "no single fact provides
such convincing evidence of the failure of parliamentary anti-Semitism
in the empire as the behavior of the opportunistic Conservatives in
1913."[91] Indeed, the Conservatives' decision not to use antisemitism by
1913 may be used as an indication both of their opportunism and of the
decline of that ideology preceding the Great War.

A second piece of evidence is provided by the Hessian Peasant Alliance, Böckel's populist stronghold. By 1904 it muted its antisemitism
and *Volkisch* ideology in favor of stressing the peasantry's economic inter-

ests. Levy notes that "among Hessenland peasants, the commitment to finding a solution to the Jewish question had lost all force."[92]

A third piece of evidence for the general decline in antisemitism is suggested by the activities of the liberal parties. The Progressives always had been in the forefront of the fight against antisemitism, but from 1911 on they were increasingly joined by the National Liberals. At this time the National Liberals drew away from their former flirtations with anti-semitism. They adopted a more principled stand on the issue, while at the same time they became more aggressive in recruiting among the peasantry and the *Mittelstand*—two groups, as we have seen, that had been a major source of support for the antisemitic parties.

Finally, at Stoecker's death in 1909 there were seven representatives of Jewish origin in the *Reichstag*—nearly half as many as the antisemitic parties combined—and the number grew still higher in the years before World War I. Such evidence of the decline of prejudice preceding the Great War may not be conclusive, but it does question the view that, despite the failures of the antisemitic parties, antisemitism spread and helped to polarize Imperial Germany.

Even if the spread of cultural antisemitism and Jew-hatred can be assumed to have taken place before the Great War, however, it is still significant that in Imperial Germany these trends could not translate their goals into political action. The state and the political system in the Second Reich were an obstacle to the realization of the political aspirations of a growing antisemitic cultural movement. This implies that, without a revolutionary transformation, antisemitism would have been confined to matters of culture and prevented from having an impact on social and political reality.

It may be proposed that Volkov's thesis fits better the period of the revolutionary interregnum following the war and the establishment of the Weimar Republic than it does the *Kaiserreich*. What started out as a contentious division among Germans in the earlier period became an unbridgeable gap in the later era. In Imperial Germany, major disagreements may have centered on issues of modernization, the rise of the working class, imperialism, and the emancipation of the Jews; during the Weimar period, however, these issues persisted but were joined and cumulated with a cleavage centering on the authority and legitimacy of the state itself. It was then that Germans became polarized, and a revolutionary antisemitic party seized power.

Volkov's suggestive thesis does not resolve the problems raised by the failure of the antisemitic parties and by the Levy study charting that decline. Levy himself views the very failure of the conventional anti-semites, men like Stoecker, Liebermann, and even Böckel, as opening up the field to revolutionaries like Fritsch and Class who were the true fore-runners of and living links to the Nazis. But in the context of Imperial Germany these rightwing revolutionaries could do nothing.

Thus Levy noted that in 1912 "Fritsch stood ready to pick up the pieces." He organized the *Reichshammerbund*, a select band influenced by his ideas that was dedicated not only to antisemitism but to "the abolition of the *Reichstag*, the removal of the Kaiser, and the need for strong powers in the hands of a leader, a constitutional dictator."[93]

Meanwhile, Heinrich Class of the Pan-German League, writing under a pseudonym, published his *If I Were the Kaiser*. The novelty of the book stemmed less from its racialist antisemitism than from its attack on the state.

> The *Reichstag*, elected by Jewish capital and grown unrepresentative of the educated and propertied elite, had to be brought to heel. This *Reichsreform* could be accomplished either by a coup d'etat or a suc-cessful war, certainly not by parliamentary politics or, in all likeli-hood, by the kaiser's timid government.[94]

Fritsch's and Class's were certainly revolutionary aspirations that would never have been articulated by the more conventional antisemites who respected the state and the kaiser, but what were the implications of such radical views? If anything, in the context of Imperial Germany, the revolutionaries were even greater failures than the conventional anti-semites.

Commenting on Fritsch, Levy remarked that "his plans seemed too bizarre to take seriously."[95] Even the more respectable Class had scarcely more success with his program of *Reichsreform*:

> The German Conservatives, *Reichspartei*, *Verein Deutscher Studenten*, and big businessmen regarded these demands as unrealistic, immoder-ate, impossible, and something out of a fairytale.[96]

Though the revolutionary antisemites appeared before the First World War and shared with the Nazis a hatred for a state that would protect the Jews, their links to the later movement were tenuous in the extreme. They were a fringe of a fringe group. Alone they were power-less, and the right in imperial Germany, their only ticket to power, had no use for them.

In 1914 the German right, despite all its grumbling, still had ways of defending vital interests—a government at its beck and call, a reliable military force to keep the "social peace," or even the possibility of a short, successful war with conquests enough to buy off all those demanding democratic changes.[97]

Before the Great War, the German right did not need antisemitism, conventional or revolutionary, to stay in power or to expand power; that was the real reason for the failure of the antisemitic parties and revolutionary movements in Imperial Germany. After the war was another matter. "By 1918 all these options had disappeared in war and revolution. Much of the German right thereupon lent itself, with some hesitation to a violent antisemitic movement."[98]

To put it simply: without a revolution the antisemitic revolutionaries were impotent. Here we see again that the context of Imperial Germany was unsuitable for an antisemitic movement and even less so for a revolutionary antisemitic movement to succeed. We will show in Chapter 6 that because a revolutionary situation did emerge during the Weimar period, a revolutionary antisemitic movement found the right conditions for taking power and implementing its policies. This occurred not only because antisemitism as an ideology had spread more widely—a debatable point—or because revolutionary antisemites appeared on the scene but because lacking widespread legitimacy and incapable of resolving major crises the Weimar Regime collapsed, allowing the Nazis to come to power.

With this we come to the end of our analysis of Armenians and Jews in the old regime states of the Ottoman Empire and of Imperial Germany, respectively. In Part One (Chaps. 2, 3, and 4) of this study we saw that, despite discrimination and even widespread violence against them, Armenians and Jews did not—could not—suffer total genocide. In both states these minorities had a role to play, and their existence was in some measure protected by the state itself. In Part Two (Chaps. 5, 6, and 7) we shall see that, after these states were swept away by revolutionary upheavals that led to major wars, the situation changed drastically and total genocide ensued.

Armenians and Jews under Revolutionary Regimes in the Ottoman Empire and Germany

Before their destruction, Armenians and Jews were ethnoreligious communal groups that had existed as minorities in the Muslim Ottoman Empire and Christian Europe, respectively, although Armenian communities could also be found in Europe and Jewish communities in the Muslim world. Until the late eighteenth and early nineteenth centuries both groups had been treated as distinct inferior corporate groups that were tolerated as long as they made no claims to equality. Following the French Revolution, however, Jewish status in Europe shifted from corporate separation and segregation to legal, if not actual, emancipation. By 1871 Jews were emancipated in Imperial Germany and were allowed far more political and economic liberty than heretofore. Similarly, in the nineteenth century, the Ottoman Empire launched itself on a process of internal reform that was meant to include some measure of equality for the diverse communities, including the Armenians.

For various reasons, including their new political and economic opportunities, Jews and Armenians experienced rapid economic progress and social mobilization in the nineteenth century. Such changes were not welcomed by large sections of the larger societies which viewed the progress of traditionally despised religious minorities as a challenge to their socioeconomic positions and their worldview. It was seen in Chapters 2, 3, and 4 that the massacres of 1894–96 against the Armenians under the regime of Sultan Abdul Hamid II and the rise of the modern antisemitic movement in Germany and elsewhere may be viewed in part as reactions to the progress of these two traditionally scorned and excluded minorities.

But continued scorn and exclusion and even massive violence against a minority are not the same as genocide. For the perpetrators to embark on a policy of total domestic genocide they need an ideology that targets a group and justifies their drastic actions, and they require the political power to put their policies into effect. Both conditions, ideology and power, are more likely to appear in revolutionary situations, especially in revolutions that lead to war or occur under the threat of international war. Chapters 5, 6, and 7 will try to demonstrate that it was the revolutionary situations following the fall of the Ottoman Empire, on the one hand, and of Imperial Germany, on the other, that provided the conditions that made genocide possible in each case. The two revolutionary movements that initiated and to a large part carried out the Armenian Genocide and the Holocaust were, respectively, the Committee of Union and Progress (CUP), also known as the "Young Turks," and the Nazis.

The CUP came to power in 1908, following the inability of the regime of Sultan Abdul Hamid II to repulse the pressures of the Great Powers, and the demands for self-determination made by the many minorities of the Ottoman Empire. At first the CUP was unsure how to proceed with its newfound power. The committee experimented with institutionalizing the liberal Ottoman constitution of 1876, but its liberal Ottoman phase proved to be a failure. It could not prevent military defeat abroad, nor the disintegrative demands and activities of minorities at home.

When by 1912 the CUP had lost control over nearly half of the Ottoman Empire's former territory, its leaders abandoned liberal Ottomanism and turned to a narrow chauvinistic and xenophobic Turkish nationalism, one of whose variations was Pan-Turkism. Talaat, the minister of interior, Enver, the minister of war, and especially Gökalp, "the father of Turkish nationalism," became intent on creating a new empire stretching from the Caucasus to the center of Asia that would be dominated by Turks and from which minorities would be excluded or relegated to having nominal rights.

This change of course from Ottomanism and Islam toward Turkic nationalism indicated a profound transformation of identity for the Turks. It also had serious implications for the Armenians. They ceased being regarded in Muslim terms as one of the legitimate *millets*, ethno-religious communities, of the empire and came to be viewed as a rival nationality. Indeed, from this perspective the Armenians were more dangerous than any other group, including the Greeks, because they were a nationality that laid claims to Anatolia, the heartland of the newly discovered "Turkey." It was significant, as well, from the perspective of the

Young Turks, that Armenian communities straddled the border between Turkey and Russia, the Ottoman Empire's traditional enemy.

When the First World War broke out, some members of the CUP, most notably Enver, led Turkey into an alliance with Germany against Russia. His aim and those of other radical Pan-Turkists was to create a new homogeneous Turkish empire rivaling in extent the Ottoman Empire itself. The CUP's decision to join Germany against Russia was fateful for the Armenians. Viewed as a separate nation occupying the heartland of Turkey and siding with Russia in the war, the Armenians were accused of being a mortal threat. It was in this context of exclusion and war that the CUP made a decision to destroy the Armenians as a viable national community in Turkey and the Pan-Turkic empire. Thus a revolutionary transformation of ideology and identity for the majority had dangerous implications for the minority. As will be discussed in Chapter 5, the Turkish nationalist revolution, as initiated by the Young Turks, set the stage for the genocide of the Armenians during the Great War. A similar, though by no means equivalent, march of events occurred in Germany.

Commencing with the inability of Imperial Germany to adapt itself to the rise of the working class and to find a niche in the international arena, the German state experienced defeat in the First World War, a failed revolution from the left, inflation, depression, and the collapse of the democratic Weimar Republic. It was this sequence of events, starting with the fall of Imperial Germany—what can be called a revolutionary interregnum—that enabled the Nazis to come to power.

As is well known, the Nazis were led by a charismatic leadership that was profoundly if not pathologically antisemitic. Unlike the CUP, they formulated their worldview not as a result of crises while in power but even before Hitler had become chancellor of Germany. It cannot be said, however, that they attained power because of their antisemitism. It is likely, as will be discussed in Chapter 6, that their appeal to a radicalized middle class and their superior organization made it possible to maneuver into a favorable position for seizing power once Weimar collapsed.

It is fair to point out, however, that Nazi antisemitism was no secret. It did not prove to be an obstacle to Nazi electoral victories, and, indeed, it may have been useful in the climb to power, demonstrating that *Völkisch* ideology and antagonism to Jews were widespread in Germany. Popular Jew-hatred was no less lethal under the circumstances, because antagonism toward the Jews manifested itself largely as indifference when the persecutions started.

139

Just as the CUP took a radical turn by 1912, the Nazis ousted the moderates of the Weimar Republic in 1933, and both regimes represented the radical phases of their revolutions. Once in power, the Nazis drastically attempted to recast Germany as an Aryan nation from which the Jews would be completely excluded. Indeed, their nebulous conception of "Aryan" took on concrete meaning mostly when it was defined as "Non-Jewish." In the period of the Third Reich, in order to be included in the charmed circle of the Aryans and not to be thrust out into the living hell of the Jews, the Germans scrambled to prove to each other and to themselves how "Non-Jewish" they really were. This accounts in large part for the growing radicalization of anti-Jewish policies under the Nazi regime. In the context of the Second World War, especially with their attack on Russia, which they took to be the seat of the "World Jewish Conspiracy," the Nazis launched the Final Solution.

The revolutionary vanguards that came to power in the Ottoman Empire and Germany did so at a time of revolutionary crises for their states and societies. Upon seizing the reins of government, both movements were intent on transforming the political community in light of a new vision concerning the state, society, and, in the case of the Nazis, man himself. The revolutionaries believed that this transformation would usher in a new era where a more perfect and powerful state would rule over a more coherent and united nation or race.

Having seized power, both revolutionary movements propelled their nation toward world war, expecting to transform radically the international system to their benefit. In the midst of war, the views of the Young Turks and the Nazis became drastically radicalized, and the Armenians and Jews, in the Ottoman Empire and the Third Reich, respectively, were accused of being part of an international plot against the Turks and the Aryans. This plot then became the ideological excuse for the destruction of each minority. Thus was revolution linked to genocide.

FIVE

The Turkish Revolution and the Armenian Genocide[1]

In Turkey . . . in 1915 . . . the deportations were deliberately conducted with a brutality that was calculated to take the maximum toll of lives *en route*. This was the CUP's crime; and my study of it left an impression on my mind that was not effaced by the still more cold-blooded genocide, on a far larger scale, that was committed during the Second World War by the Nazis.

Arnold Toynbee[2]

I am a soldier [the nation] is my commander
I obey without question all its orders
With closed eyes I carry out my duty.

Ziya Gökalp[3]

The decline of the Ottoman Empire accelerated throughout the nineteenth century. During this period it was caught between the jaws of Great Power military pressure from abroad and the demand for self-determination of newly conscious national minorities from within. In response to Great Power pressures, the various sultans attempted to play the great game of international balance of power politics, while at the same time they tried to modernize the empire, especially its armed forces, in a manner that would strengthen their hand and preserve Muslim and Ottoman identity. In response to the minorities the sultans vacillated between, on the one hand, reforms that at least nominally extended equality and some measure of self-administration, and, on the other hand, policies of repression, including wide-scale massacre.

141

By the end of the century the empire's apparent incapacity to deal with the Great Powers and the minorities helped to precipitate the coup of 23 July 1908 against Sultan Abdul Hamid. This coup initiated a series of events that brought the Young Turks to power and propelled the empire along a path of nationalist revolution, war, and genocide. In the period between the Great War and the founding of the Turkish Republic in 1923, well over a million Armenians were killed by mass shootings, massacres, deportations, and induced starvation. Despite individual survivors, at the end of this period the Armenian community was destroyed as a viable collectivity in Anatolia. Significantly, its destruction was so intended by the Committee of Union and Progress (CUP) that had come to power in the revolution of 1908. This policy of mass destruction was the first total domestic genocide of the twentieth century and provides the subject of this chapter.

Why did it happen? One explanation traces the origins of the genocide to the provocative behavior of the Armenians themselves—or at least to their revolutionary parties. But as already indicated in Chapter 1, this response, what earlier we called the "provocation" thesis, is inadequate, not least because it neglects the independent motivations of the perpetrators themselves. The explanation advanced in this chapter finds the primary causes of the genocide in the revolutionary situation following the events of 1908 and in the Pan-Turkish ideology of the CUP.

Many studies of the Young Turks and the CUP, which led the revolution of 1908 against Sultan Abdul Hamid and which controlled the Ottoman Empire from 1908 to 1918, would agree with Davison's judgment that although the revolution failed in the short run, "in the long run, it not only transmitted to the future the progress made in the preceding hundred years, but also contributed to the institutional, ideological, and social development that underlay the emergence of the modern Turkish nation and Turkish republic."[4] Since this chapter is not concerned with the salutary effects that the Young Turks might have had on Turkish progress but with their effects on the Armenians, it can be said without hesitation that the Young Turk regime, especially in its later phases, was an unmitigated disaster for the Armenian people.[5] Significantly, it was the Committee of Union and Progress, headed by Talaat Pasha, minister of interior, and Enver Pasha, minister of war, that was responsible for the deportations leading to the genocide.

The Turkish revolution destroyed Ottomanism and Pan-Islam, two conceptions of state and society that would have permitted Armenians to continue to exist as a separate community of the Ottoman Empire and replaced these with the political myth of Turkish nationalism. The new political and social construction of "Turk" excluded all minorities, but especially the Armenians from the new dispensation. When the Great War broke out and the Ottoman Empire joined Germany against Russia, the excluded Armenians came to be viewed as internal enemies, threatening the continued existence of Turkey, and for that reason they had to be destroyed.

This chapter is divided into four sections. The first briefly synthesizes some of the evidence pertaining to the Armenian genocide; the second touches on some of the trials of the perpetrators following World War I; the third critically and in more detail than in Chapter 1 examines the "provocation thesis"; and the fourth briefly relates the growing radicalization of the Committee of Union and Progress, which led it on a path of nationalism, war, and genocide, to the crises attending the Turkish revolution.

The Genocide

So many years after the events, a detailed recapitulation of the genocide remains to be written, and the best source in a Western language is still Toynbee.[6] As has been noted, however, a sharp controversy concerning the motives of the actors, the extent of the destruction, and the actual course of events still exists.[7] Within this limited space, it is impossible to resolve all such quarrels, some of which are tendentious in the extreme. The best that can be done here is to make note of the controversy and steer the reader to accounts that differ from mine. The next sections, however, which deal with the motives of the perpetrators, take up the controversy directly.

Massacres and Deportations

The killings started in the spring of 1915 with the deportation of the total Armenian population from the *vilayets* or provinces of the east to the Syrian desert at Aleppo in the south. Portents of what was to come, however, became apparent by February 1915, when Armenian troops serving with the Ottoman forces were disarmed, demobilized, and grouped into labor battalions. Concurrently, the Armenian civilian population was also disarmed, with each community required to produce a specified number of weapons. The search for weapons became an occasion for destroying the local leadership; when community leaders were

143

unable to produce the officially required number, they were arrested for secretly stashing arms; when they did come up with the required number, they were arrested for conspiring against the government.

The deportations were coordinated between Talaat Pasha's Ministry of the Interior, which was in charge of the civilian population, and Enver Pasha's Ministry of War, which was in charge of the disarmed labor battalions. On 8 April 1915, when the deportations commenced from Zeitun and other population centers, the Armenian labor battalions were rounded up by troops of the regular army and summarily massacred.[8] On 24 April 1915, by order of the Ministry of the Interior, thousands of Armenian community leaders were arrested. In Istanbul hundreds of such notables were imprisoned; later most were executed.[9] To this day the Armenian Genocide is commemorated on 24 April by Armenians and others throughout the world.

After Armenian troops had been massacred, the deportations started with killing the able-bodied men and deporting the remainder. Toynbee summarizes the process as follows:

> On a certain date in whatever town or village it might be . . . the public crier went through the streets announcing that every male Armenian must present himself forthwith at the Government Building. In some cases the warning was given by the soldiery or gendarmerie slaughtering every male Armenian they encountered in the streets . . . but usually a summons to the Government Building was the preliminary stage. The men presented themselves in their working clothes. . . . When they arrived, they were thrown without explanation into prison, kept there a day or two, and then marched out of the town in batches, roped man to man, along some southerly or southeasterly road. They were starting, they were told, on a long journey—to Mosul or perhaps to Baghdad. . . . But they had not long to ponder over their plight, for they were halted and massacred at the first lonely place on the road. The same process was applied to those other Armenian men . . . who had been imprisoned during the winter months on the charge of conspiracy or concealment of arms. . . . This was the civil authorities' part.[10]

Except for Bitlis, Moush, and Sassoun, where the total population was marked out for extermination by the army, presumably because these population centers were close to Van, the women, children, and the surviving men in other areas were deported. As columns of defenseless Armenians were marched through towns and villages they would be set upon again and again, sometimes by brigands but more often by Turkish or Kurdish villagers.[11] Some, if not most, of the massacres were organized by Enver's "Special Organization" (*Teshkilat-i Makhsusiye*).

Indeed, as early as 5 August 1914 Enver had ordered the setting up of the "Special Organization," which was to be a supervisory and administrative organ of the CUP. Led by Dr. Nazim and Dr. Behaeddin Shakir, the Special Organization's first duties included espionage and sabotage and the infiltrating and turning of populations on the border, as in the Caucasus and Iran, to the Ottoman side. Later it had a major role in the deportations and the ensuing massacres.[12]

For the purposes of the deportations and mass killings, the Special Organization formed cadres from among convicted criminals who were released for their duties by the Ministries of Interior and Justice.[13] A captain in the Ottoman War Office's Intelligence Department noted after the war:

> The criminal gangs who were released from the prisons, after a week's training at the War College's training grounds, were sent off to the Caucasian front as the brigands of the Special Organization, perpetrating the worst crimes against the Armenians. . . . The Ittihadists intended to destroy the Armenians, and thereby to do away with the Question of the Eastern Provinces.[14]

Meanwhile, the gendarmerie from the Ministry of the Interior, which was ostensibly there to "protect" the deportees, far from discouraging such attacks joined in the violence.[15]

With the deserts beyond Aleppo as their final destination, Toynbee draws the following pattern in the timing of the deportations:

> The months of April and May were assigned to the clearance of Cilicia; June and July were reserved for the east; the western centres along the railway were given their turn in August and September; and at the same time the process was extended, for completeness' sake to the outlying Armenian communities in the extreme southeast. It was a deliberate, systematic attempt to eradicate the Armenian population throughout the Ottoman Empire, and it has certainly met with a large measure of success.[16]

Extent of the Destruction

An extensive massacre or genocide always leads to controversy over the number of victims. Those who would deny it tend to minimize the number; those who would affirm it may tend to overestimate the casualties. Clearly, no precise measures can be cited. To gauge the extent of the destruction, Toynbee estimates the predeportation population, the number who escaped the massacres, and the number who perished. Subtracting the second from the first number gives him an estimate of the third.

If one takes the Armenian patriarchate figures as a bench mark, the mid–nineteenth-century Armenian population in the Ottoman Empire was 2.5 million. Presumably due both to emigration and massacre, it declined to 2.1 million by 1914, prior to the genocide. Toynbee, however, is more conservative. Suggesting that the patriarchate figures may be inflated, he averages these with the Ottoman census figures, which claimed that the Armenian population of the day was 1.1 million. This gives him a predeportation figure of 1.6 million (the average of 2.1 and 1.1)[17]

He estimates that some 600,000 Armenians escaped the deportations. Among these were 182,000 who fled as refugees into the Russian Caucasus, and 4,200 who fled into Egypt. Significantly, he points out that the Armenian populations of Smyrna and Constantinople were not deported, and, nominally at least, Armenian Catholics, Protestants, and converts to Islam also were not deported. But "[i]t is impossible to estimate the numbers in these categories . . . for the conduct of the authorities in respect of them was quite erratic."[18]

Combining the predeportation figure with the figure of those who escaped gives Toynbee a figure of 1 million Armenians who were deported.[19] Of these, he estimates some 50 percent perished due to massacre or other causes.

> A large combined convoy, for instance, of exiles from Mamouret-ul-Aziz and Sivas, set out from Malatia 18,000 strong and numbered 301 at Viran Shehr, 150 at Aleppo. In this case, however, the wastage appears to have been exceptional. We have one similar instance of a convoy from Harpout which was reduced on the way to Aleppo from 5,000 to 213, a loss of 96 percent; but in general the wastage seems to fluctuate, with a wide oscillation on either side of 50 percent.[20]

This should give Toynbee a figure of some 500,000 who perished, but this he revises upward and suggests a final estimate of 600,000.

> We can sum up this statistical enquiry by saying that, as far as our defective information carries us, about an equal number of Armenians in Turkey seem to have escaped, to have perished, and to have survived deportation in 1915; and we shall not be far wrong, if, in round numbers, we estimate each of these categories at 600,000.[21]

146

Toynbee's description and analysis stop with the winter of 1915 and the spring of 1916, by which time the bulk of the Armenian population had been killed or deported. As valuable as it is, this work cannot take into account what subsequently happened to the deportees in 1916, nor can it take into account the Armenians who were deported from some of the major urban areas after 1916. For this period the report of Aram Andonian is crucial. His translator summarizes Andonian's findings as follows:

> Three great massacres took place after 1916. . . . Men, women, and children from Constantinople and the surrounding district, from the Anatolian railway line and Cilicia, were driven into the desert, where they met people from the six Armenian provinces and from the shores of the Black Sea, but this latter contingent consisted only of women, girls and boys of seven and under, as every male over seven had been slaughtered. All these were the victims of the three massacres. The first massacres was that of Res-ul-Ain, in which 70,000 people were killed; the second took place at Intilli, where there were 50,000 people assembled, most of them working on a tunnel of the Baghdad Railway; and the third, which was the most fearful of all, at Der Zor, where Zia Bey slaughtered nearly 200,000 Armenians. . . . These figures only given the numbers of people killed by massacre. If we add to their numbers the victims of misery, sickness and hunger, especially in Res-ul-Ain and Der Zor, the number of Armenians who were slain or died in the desert will exceed a million.[22]

Leaving out further killings of Armenians such as occurred in the Caucasus in 1918 and in Smyrna in 1922, after the conclusion of World War I and after the demise of the CUP, an estimate of close to 1 million people killed results. This amounts to nearly half of the Armenian population, according to the patriarchate figures, and more than half according to Toynbee's estimate for the initial population. The figure of about 1 million killed is independently arrived at by Johannes Lepsius.[23]

Responsibility for the Destruction

Unlike the massacres of 1894–96, discussed in Chapter 3, where the connection between Sultan Abdul Hamid II and the violence had to be constructed on persuasive but nonetheless circumstantial evidence, in the case of the deportations the orders were clearly given by the CUP headed by Talaat and Enver. Indeed, when Henry Morgenthau, the

American ambassador, in trying diplomatically to intercede on behalf of the Armenians, attempted to distinguish the massacres and mass death attending the deportations from the real intentions of the CUP, he was rebuffed by no less a figure than Enver Pasha:

> In another talk with Enver I began by suggesting that the Central Government was probably not to blame for the massacres. I thought this would not be displeasing to him.
>
> "Of course, I know that the Cabinet would never order such terrible things as have taken place," I said. "You and Talaat and the rest of the Committee can hardly be held responsible. Undoubtedly your subordinates have gone much further than you have ever intended. I realize that it is not always easy to control your underlings."
>
> Enver straightened up at once. I saw that my remarks, far from smoothing the way to a quiet and friendly discussion, had greatly offended him. I had intimated that things could happen in Turkey for which he and his associates were not responsible.
>
> "You are greatly mistaken," he said. "We have this country absolutely under our control. I have no desire to shift the blame on to our underlings and I am entirely willing to accept the responsibility myself for everything that has taken place. The Cabinet itself has ordered the deportations. I am convinced that we are completely justified in doing this owing to the hostile attitude of the Armenians toward the Ottoman Government, but we are the real rulers of Turkey, and no underling would dare proceed in a matter of this kind without our orders.[24]

The reports of Toynbee, Morgenthau, and Lepsius are absolutely crucial to ascertain the intentions of the perpetrators and to apportion responsibility for the genocide. The validity of their testimony is further reinforced, moreover, by the trial record of the courts-martial that were handed down against the perpetrators by Ottoman courts after the First World War.

The Trials of the Perpetrators

As news of the Armenian Genocide leaked out to the world, the Entente powers on 24 May 1915 warned the Ottoman authorities, "In view of these new crimes of Turkey against humanity and civilization . . . the Allied governments announce publicly . . . that they will hold personally responsible . . . all members of the Ottoman government and those of their agents who are implicated in such massacres."[25] Following the armistice of World War I, the acting government of the Ottoman Empire led by Sultan Mehmet VI Vahideddin and his Grand Vezir Damad Ferid called for trials of the perpetrators to be held in Ottoman courts. Ironically, the Turkish domestic trials were able to take place while the international trials promised by the Allies with such fanfare during the war never got off the ground.

The International Trials

The Ottoman Empire signed the Armistice on 30 October 1918. In January 1919, the Preliminary Peace Conference in Paris established a Commission on Responsibilities and Sanctions, chaired by U.S. Secretary of State Lansing. The commission was charged with examining the practices of the Central Powers and their allies, including the Ottoman Empire, that had conducted "barbarous and illegitimate methods of warfare . . . [including] offenses against the laws and customs of war and the principles of humanity."[26]

Following the commission's efforts, several articles in the Peace Treaty of Sèvres, signed on 10 August 1920, called for the trial and punishment of those who had been implicated in the genocide. Article 230 of the treaty called on Turkey

> to hand over to the Allied Powers the persons whose surrender may
> be required by the latter as being responsible for the massacres com-
> mitted during the continuance of the state of war on territory which
> formed part of the Turkish Empire on August 1, 1914.[27]

The Treaty of Sèvres, therefore, provided for an international adjudication for war crimes and might have set a precedent for Nuremberg; unfortunately, the international trials were never held. A series of circumstances, especially the rise of Turkish national forces led by Mustafa Kemal and intrigues among the Allies themselves, undermined the international trials.[28] Moreover, at the end of hostilities on 1–2 November 1918, seven of the most prominent leaders of the CUP, including Talaat, Enver, and Jemal made their escape from Istanbul aboard a German vessel. From a judicial point of view, however, all was not yet lost.

There was a series of domestic courts-martial that, although failing to punish the guilty, left an invaluable record, adding further documentation of the genocide. Their significance derives not only from the additional detail describing the killings but from their provenance. The trial records consisted of evidence brought forward by the postwar Ottoman regime against personnel who had served the CUP. In that sense it supplements evidence left behind by survivors, consular officials, missionaries, and historians with testimony provided by Ottoman authorities themselves.

The Domestic Courts-Martial

The Ottoman authorities and public who called for trials of those responsible for the genocide did so from mixed motives. On the one hand, they hoped that if they themselves initiated the proceedings they and their country would be less harshly treated at the Peace Conference. Furthermore, the Sultan and his Grand Vezir, Damad Ferid, who came to power after the war, were no friends of the CUP nor were they admirers of Turkish nationalism. They were joined by others in politics and the press who had been victimized by the Young Turks and now demanded speedy trials against the perpetrators. Last, there were Ottomans, including Turks, who were appalled by the crimes that had been committed in their country's name. [29]

The evidence for the trials was collected by a parliamentary committee and the Administration's Inquiry Commission which came into being on 23 November 1918. The commission had broad powers, including those of subpoena, search, seizure, arrest, and detention. Much of its evidence was in the form of orders issued by the CUP or the Special Organization that had been transmitted by telegraph. In addition, the commission gathered evidence by interrogating suspects. By January 1919, the Inquiry Commission had files on 130 suspects, most of these high officials in the former government or in the CUP. [30] As noted, the principal perpetrators like Talaat and Enver had by then already escaped.

After some preliminaries, the statutes of the final court-martial were formulated on 8 March 1919. The "principal task of this Tribunal [was to inquire into charges of] massacres and unlawful, personal profiteering." [31] The presiding judge ordered the trials to be held in public: "In order to demonstrate the intent of the Court to conduct the trials impartially and in a spirit of lofty justice." [32]

Though, of course, the term "genocide" was not used, the principal indictment against the CUP and its leaders was "the massacre and destruction of the Armenians." [33] It also included the CUP's role in orchestrating Turkey's disastrous entrance into the Great War. In bringing forward his charges the prosecutor singled out especially the CUP's Central Committee, General Assembly, and "two provincial control groups headed by Responsible Secretaries and Inspectors." [34] Also included were the Ministry of Defense, in particular the Special Organization, and the Ministry of the Interior. The leaders of the CUP were accused of formulating a plan of "extermination" which was to be implemented by Responsible Secretaries.[35]

The indictment also raised the issue of intent and prompted two rationalizations, which were later used by the defense. The first was military necessity: the Armenians had to be deported and eliminated because they were a threat to the Empire's security. The second was justified punishment: the Armenians were treacherous and had to be punished for their disloyalty. Both rationalizations, it will be recalled, also appear in various forms as part of the "provocation thesis" of some historical accounts, and both were dismissed by the prosecution.

The indictment charged that the deportations and ensuing massacres were "neither a measure of military necessity, nor a punitive, disciplinary act."[36] The Armenians were deported not only from areas of military conflict but from all corners of the Empire, and there had been no incident provoked by the Armenians justifying the measures that had been taken against them.[37] On the contrary, charged the indictment, the Armenians were destroyed as part of a "centrally directed plan"[38] to solve "the Eastern question [sic]."[39]

The indictment made use of a detailed affidavit submitted by General Vehib of the Third Army's command zone, which operated in the six vilayets where most of the massacres had taken place. In part, this is what General Vehib stated:

> The massacre and plunder of the Armenians and the plunder and pillage of their goods were the results of decisions reached by Ittihad's Central Committee. . . . The atrocities were carried out under a program that was determined upon and involved a definite case of premeditation.[40]

The defense, led by Professor C. Arif of the Istanbul Law University, did rely on the provocation thesis and argued among other things that the massacres were incidental to the deportations. Dadrian sums up the court's position as follows:

> Even if it is granted that the massacres were incidental to the deportation, the Court noted that massacre was still murder, a separate and distinct state act. Only if new evidence established that the massacres were not intended but were merely inevitable results attending the fulfillment of official duties, would the Court consider the argument. The Court found, however, that the available evi-

dence demonstrated that the massacres were part of policies and decisions arrived at by the defendants, not as Ministers conducting official work, but as members of a secret, conspiratorial association.[41]

The court submitted its verdict on 5 July 1919. It found the defendants guilty both of attempting to destroy the Armenians and of driving Turkey into war. "The fact" of the premeditated and organized massacres of the Armenians "had been proven and verified by the Court Martial."[42] It sentenced the principal leaders of the CUP and the architects of the Armenian Genocide to death in absentia. This included Talaat, Enver, Jemal, and Dr. Nazim. Other defendants were given fifteen years at hard labor. "The ex-Ministers of Post and Commerce were acquitted."[43]

As Dadrian points out, however, the sentences of the court were never carried out because by then a government in Ankara parallel to that of the sultan in Istanbul had acquired broad legitimacy, and the Kemalists rejected the verdict of the court. Moreover, in Istanbul itself cells of the previous CUP regime continued to operate, helping to subvert the intent of the sultan's government.[44]

But whether or not sentences against the principal perpetrators were carried out by the Ottoman courts-martial is immaterial to the argument presented here. The courts-martial demonstrate that Turkish authorities once did exist with the integrity not to deny but to face up to the truth of the Armenian Genocide.

The Provocation Thesis

In his later works, such as *The Western Question in Greece and Turkey* and *Acquaintances*, Toynbee was to repudiate some of his own denunciations of the Young Turk regime, especially as these suggested that Islamic civilization was more likely to produce atrocities than Christendom.[45] Nevertheless, it is striking that more than fifty years after his original report on the deportations, Toynbee assessed these as an instance of genocide, comparable if not equal to the Nazi Holocaust.

> In Turkey . . . in 1915 . . . the deportations were deliberately conducted with a brutality that was calculated to take the maximum toll of lives *en route*. This was the CUP's crime; and my study of it left an impression on my mind that was not effaced by the still more cold-blooded genocide, on a far larger scale, that was committed during the Second World War by the Nazis.[46]

Adding further shading to the picture, no sooner had the Armenian population been physically removed or liquidated and replaced by Turks or Kurds than all symbolic, cultural traces of the former inhabitants like churches and place names were destroyed and eradicated. It was as if the Committee of Union and Progress had wanted to obliterate even the memory of Armenian existence. In contemporary Turkey, as Michael Arlen remarked, "The Armenian connection" has been erased "as though by an act of will."[47] It is not only the extent of the destruction it is this "act of will," this desire to wipe the slate clean, to eliminate Armenians from the social structure and culture of Turkey, that convinces us that genocide was perpetrated. The question is, "Why?"

Earlier, in the Introduction, we pointed out that a number of historical accounts derive the Armenian Genocide from the supposed provocative behavior of the Armenians themselves. Here we wish to examine the provocation thesis in greater detail, both to refute it and to sketch out more fully the situation of the Armenians at the time of the genocide. Having accomplished both purposes, we shall then go on to a discussion of the role and intentions of the CUP in the genocide.

Bernard Lewis's statement of the provocation thesis is most succinct and influential. We have chosen to focus on his explanation because it both attempts to be fair and is part of what has become a classic study of the history of modern Turkey. Other explanations that rely on the provocation thesis may be more verbose and more strongly felt, but they are not more convincing.

Referring to the rise of Armenian nationalism in the latter half of the nineteenth century, Lewis points out:

> For the Turks, the Armenian movement was the deadliest of all threats. From the conquered lands of the Serbs, Bulgars, Albanians, and Greeks, they could however reluctantly, withdraw, abandoning distant provinces and bringing the Imperial frontier nearer home. But the Armenians, stretching across Turkey-in-Asia from the Caucasian frontier to the Mediterranean coast, lay in the very heart of the Turkish homeland—and to renounce the lands would have meant not the truncation, but the dissolution of the Turkish state. Turkish and Armenian villages, inextricably mixed, had for centuries lived in neighbourly association. Now a desperate struggle between them began—a struggle between two nations for the possession of a single homeland, that ended with the terrible holocaust of 1915, when a million and a half Armenians perished.[48]

153

In this account the matter of the Armenian Genocide seems to be a clear-cut case of two nationalisms in conflict. Armenians were a Christian national minority living, unfortunately for them, on both sides of the Turkish-Russian border. Like the other minorities of the Ottoman Empire, they came to be caught up in the nationalism of the nineteenth and early twentieth centuries. Hence, like the Serbs, Bulgars, Albanians, and Greeks they desired self-determination and wanted to secede. Whereas the secession of the former nationalities might have been a blow to the power and prestige of the Ottoman state, the secession of Armenia would spell its demise, for the Armenians lived in the very heartland of Turkey. Lewis is appalled that once friendly relations between Armenians and Turks deteriorated into massacres and genocide. Indeed, he refers to the Armenian Genocide as a "holocaust" in clear allusion to the Final Solution, and he cites a figure of a million-and-a-half dead, which one presumes includes all those Armenians who perished between 1915 and 1923. The problem with this analysis, as with other provocation theories, does not lie in its insensitivity to the moral issues but in the too easy analogy that is made between Turkish and Armenian nationalism, between the views of the perpetrators and those of the victims. Thus paradoxically it calls for a historical treatment of the genocide while ignoring Armenian history and Armenian intentions.

A Struggle between Two Nations

Let us consider the assumptions of the provocation thesis one at a time: to say that there were two nations locked in a desperate struggle for the possession of a single homeland without adding qualifying remarks is to impute a level of equality of force and self-consciousness that is unwarranted by any evidence. Clearly, without knowing more about the situation, one would be under the impression that the Armenians, like the Turks, were in possession of a government, of an army, or of some other centralizing, directing agency representing a monopoly of legitimate force. One would also expect them to be armed and in some ways powerful. The truth of the matter is that the Armenians were not united under a single agency, even under a single political party, and they certainly did not have any army or police force either to conquer the Turks or to defend themselves.

Beyond an assumption of equality of power, the "two-nations-same-land" argument assumes that Armenian national sentiment was somehow symmetric or equivalent to Turkish nationalism. That Turkish nationalism was a real force by the time of the revolution of 1908 is documented

in the *Emergence of Modern Turkey*. This work stresses that Turkish nationalism as yet had not found its proper boundaries in the manner of Kemal
Ataturk, but it existed in the manner of Ziya Gökalp, and it had broken
with Islam and Ottomanism. To imply that a parallel evolution or
transformation of identity and ideology had occurred for the Armenians
as well, however, is to beg some important questions: What was Armenian nationalism? How did it differ from fealty to the millet system?
What boundaries and powers did it claim for itself? And how did it
differ from other nationalisms, including Turkish, in the disintegrating
Ottoman Empire?

Finally, the idea that "for the Turks the Armenian movement was
the deadliest of all threats" is highly ambiguous. Does this mean that the
Turks *perceived* the Armenians to be a deadly threat? Or is it that they were
in fact a deadly threat? If the first is meant, there is no disagreement.
Talaat and Enver themselves have clearly stated that they feared the Armenians as a deadly threat to the integrity of Turkey. Indeed, given the
drastic situation of the Young Turks, where the secession of minorities
was joined to military defeat on a large scale, one might assume that their
perceptions and judgments were not clear. The question remains, however, Did their fear of the Armenians rise out of the actions and capabili-
ties of the Armenians themselves, or out of other sources including the
Young Turks' own desperate situation and their newfound faith in Turkish
nationalism?

The Armenian "Threat"

In raising the question of the Armenian threat—Were the Armenians the threat that the Young Turks thought they were?—it is important
to make clear what time and which Armenians one is talking about. Distinctions need to be drawn among the periods 1896–1908, 1909–15, and
1915–23. Moreover, differences need to be pointed out between the bulk
of the Armenian population living as peasant farmers in Anatolia, and
revolutionary parties and bands of irregulars that claimed to speak or act
on behalf of the larger population.

Following the massacres of 1894–96, which were discussed in
Chapter 2, two Armenian political parties, the Hnchackist and the Dashnaktsutiun, joined the broad coalition of Ottoman forces that opposed
the regime of Sultan Abdul Hamid. Moreover, they were in league with
the liberal wing of the Young Turks when that movement took power in
1908. Neither the Armenian population as a whole nor any of its parties
was a threat or even perceived to be a threat in 1908 when the revolution

first broke out. Quite the contrary, Armenians took great satisfaction in the victory of the army and its CUP-affiliated commanders, as well they might. The downfall of the hated sultan and the restoration of the constitution of 1876 were everything and more the Armenian parties, like the Dashnaks, had hoped for.

The Armenian revolutionary parties' long years of active participation in the liberal wing of the Young Turk movement had finally borne fruit, and Lewis himself writes of the enthusiasm of the hour:

> The long night of Hamidean despotism was over: the dawn of freedom had come. The Constitution had once again been proclaimed and elections ordered. Turks and Armenians embraced in the streets. [49]

And on 4 August Sir Gerard Lowther, the British ambassador, reported:

> An extraordinary event took place yesterday in the Armenian cemetery at Shishli, where the victims of the massacres in 1895 and 1896 were buried. A procession of Armenians and Turks numbering several thousand proceeded thither and prayers were offered by the priests of both religions over the dead. [50]

One assumes, therefore, that in 1908 Armenians as a whole and Dashnaks in particular were neither "a deadly threat" to the Young Turks and the Ottoman Empire, nor were they viewed as such. What intervened that might have turned them into a threat or that might have made them seem to be one?

Following the euphoria of 1908, relations between Armenians and the Young Turk regime began to deteriorate. Though it is questionable that the government should be blamed for the Adana massacres of 1909, where it is estimated that 15,000–20,000 Armenians perished at the hands of troops loyal to the old sultan, these atrocities, the increasing harshness of the CUP regime, and the continuing insecurity of Armenian peasants in the face of Kurdish violence undermined Armenian trust. As one of the more careful scholars of the period has noted:

> Armenian disillusionment sprang from the massacres of 1909, the so-called "Cilician Vespers," in Lesser Armenia for which the Young Turks must bear a goodly share of responsibility. More lasting troubles came with Kurd depredations in Greater Armenia. . . . Wandering Kurds or *Muhajirs* had seized the lands of many Armenians who had been massacred or had fled in 1895. When some of the refugees returned in 1908, the Kurds would not restore the

lands. . . . From 1909 on there was what the French vice-consul in Van described as real war between the two peoples.[51]

The Armenian response was to ask for greater autonomy in internal matters and for greater government protection against Kurdish depredations. The precariousness of the Armenian situation was noted by Russia, which in 1912 once more reopened the Armenian Question. Since Britain and Russia had come to terms in 1907 by concluding an Eastern settlement, Russia once more felt the temptation to expand her influence over the Ottoman Empire. Here she found some support among the Armenian leadership in the National Assembly, which wanted to use Russia as leverage against the CUP. Russian moves were checked by Hans von Wangenheim, the German ambassador, but by 8 February 1914 an accord was reached between the powers and the CUP that called for the appointment of European inspectors-general in the eastern vilayets. Their duties were to oversee intercommunal relations.[52]

One can only imagine the sense of humiliation and rage felt by the Turkish nationalists at this proposed interference. Nevertheless, even at this late date, it cannot be said that there ensued a "struggle between two nations." For the Armenians were not struggling to destroy the Ottoman Empire or the Turks, nor were they even attempting to secede or to join Russia. As Davison notes: "The peasant mass was not very vocal. Higher classes of Ottoman Armenians wished rather for a regenerated and orderly Turkey and thought that autonomy would be possible only within Turkey and not under Russian domination."[53] Turning to the Dashnaks, easily the leading Armenian party, which by 1907 claimed a membership of 165,000, Davison writes: "Their program was essentially one of reform within the Ottoman Empire. They did not believe that Russian occupation would bring them more freedom."[54] On the contrary, continues Davison, they did believe that "a complete separation of Armenians from Turkey was ethnographically and geographically impossible."[55] As late as 1913, when the CUP had become more authoritarian and intolerant, "on the whole Dashanksoutium [sic] seems not yet to have favored separatism or Russian occupation but to have pursued a policy of waiting and pressure for reform and autonomy."[56]

What about Armenian reactions at the start of the Great War? If there had been a mass uprising against the Turks, this might have justified, if not genocide, then at least some extraordinary measures to protect the security of Ottoman forces on the Eastern front. But no such uprising occurred. Certainly there were Armenian troops in the Russian armies, some of which were led by Armenian commanders, and there were Armenian irregulars who were also active in the area. Furthermore, in the wake of the genocide there may have been instances of reprisals taken against Muslims in the war zone. [57] But these activities were not commensurate with a conclusion that the Armenian population as a whole needed to be deported and exterminated and the Armenian community destroyed in Turkey.

Ahmed Emin, a prominent Turkish historian of the period, could not help but frame the issue quite clearly, despite efforts to be apologetic for the CUP's behavior:

> The deportations taken as a whole, were meant to be only a temporary military measure. But for certain influential Turkish politicians they meant the extermination of the Armenian minority in Turkey with the idea of bringing about racial homogeneity in Asia Minor. [58]

According to Emin, the thought process of "certain influential politicians" went like this:

> A dense Armenian population, in the Eastern Provinces, has proved to be a danger to the very existence of Turkey. We are acting as instruments to remove this danger. We know that successful or not successful, we shall be universally despised and condemned. Only in a very distant future can our personal sacrifice for the national cause hope to be recognized. [59]

Writing in the late 1920s, Emin ironically had his "influential politicians" anticipate the thought processes of Heinrich Himmler. He was less than candid, however, when he failed to point out that his imaginary politicians were none other than Talaat, Enver, Shakir, and Nazim, virtual rulers of Turkey during the war. [60]

Starting with the battle of Sarikamish on 25 December 1914 in which the bravery of Armenian troops was praised by none other than Enver himself, until the start of the genocide, the great majority of the Armenian millet remained loyal to what it still conceived to be an Ottoman state. In retrospect, Enver's message of February 1915 to the Armenian bishop of Konya, in which he praised Armenian troops while already planning for their destruction, is stunning in its cold-blooded cynicism:

> I am giving you my thanks and using this opportunity to tell you that the Armenian soldiers of the Ottoman army are executing their duty in the theatre of war scrupulously, as witness my own experi-

ence. I wish you to communicate to the Armenian nation, known for its complete devotion to the imperial Ottoman government, the expression of my satisfaction and gratitude. [61]

It is safe to say, therefore, that between the revolution of 1908 and the genocide of 1915 Armenians were not a major threat to the integrity of the Ottoman Empire, but it is also true that increasingly they came to be perceived by some members of the CUP as a deadly enemy. Since the radical change in the perceptions of the Young Turks cannot be derived only from Armenian behavior, it is entirely possible that this transformation had its origins in the altered worldview and perspectives of the CUP itself. Such alterations in the worldview of the Young Turks were themselves directly related to the fate of the Turkish revolution following the coup against Sultan Abdul Hamid II and the start of the Great War. The Armenians did not realize that, through no fault of their own, the identity of the Ottoman state and its political myth of legitimation had been drastically altered by the Young Turks, and that their self-conception as a component millet of that state was no longer shared by the Pan-Turkish leadership of Turkey.

The Turkish Revolution and the Armenian Genocide

We come closer to the truth of why the Armenians were seen as a deadly threat, leading to genocide, when we move away from the intentions and alleged provocative actions of the victims and examine, on the one hand, the context of Armenian-Turkish relations and, on the other hand, the experiences and views of the perpetrators. Both the context of relations and the views of the CUP were drastically altered when between 1908 and 1915 the Young Turks were not able to stem further defeat in battle or the secession of minorities.

Throughout this period preceding the Great War, the continuing retreat of the empire from Europe to Anatolia was nothing less than a military and political disaster for the Turks, but it was a disaster that had even more serious consequences for the Armenians. Not only did the retreat isolate this minority, making it available for labeling as an "enemy of the Turkish revolution," it produced a crucial shift from Ottoman pluralism, if not liberalism, to narrow Turkish nationalism in the ideological perspective and worldview of the ruling party. When Turkey joined the Central Powers against Russia, the Armenians were labeled as potential traitors and a deadly threat against whom a deadly response seemed justified. It may be suggested that this is a better explanation for the Armenian Genocide than the provocation thesis.

Military Disaster and Nationalist Reactions

When they took power in 1908, the Young Turks were a coalition of intellectuals, many of whom lived abroad, including representatives of minorities like the Dashnaks, and military officers, especially from the Third Army stationed in Salonika. They joined together in a movement to limit the power if not to topple Sultan Abdul Hamid and to restore the constitution of 1876. Reflecting their differing origins, their aims were also divergent.

Intellectuals like Ahmed Riza and Prince Sabaheddin sought to introduce secular and Western values to enable the Ottoman Empire to modernize not only its technology, as Abdul Hamid had tried to do, but also its political, social, and cultural institutions. More than Ahmed Riza, the prince supported liberal economic and political reforms and was sympathetic to some of the minority demands for greater autonomy, if not self-determination.

In contrast, the young military officers and civil servants like Enver, Talaat, Jemal, and Mustafa Kemal, who had direct or indirect links to the army, were more pragmatically focused on the precarious military situation of the Ottoman Empire. At first they were willing to entertain all sorts of political notions, including Ottomanism and liberalism if these would work to unite and strengthen the state.

All the Young Turks hoped that having limited Sultan Abdul Hamid's power and proclaimed the constitution of 1876, they would convince the Great Powers of their progressivism and good will, thereby alleviating international political, economic, and military pressures. Unfortunately, the opposite occurred. Far from being impressed by the hopeful changes that were occurring in the Ottoman Empire, the Great Powers took the opportunity of momentary Ottoman weakness and distraction to grab more territory and to ask for more concessions. The consequences for the Turkish revolution and its outcomes were disastrous.

On 5 October 1908, some three months after the Young Turk revolution, Bulgaria proclaimed her complete independence, and, on the following day, Austria annexed Bosnia and Herzegovina, which she had occupied since 1878. Due to the rapaciousness of the Great Powers and Turkey's military weakness, the empire experienced still more extensive losses: in 1911, the Italians occupied Libya, and the next year the Balkan states effectively eliminated Turkey from Europe.

Out of a total area of approximately 1,153,000 square miles and from a population of about 24 million, by 1911 the empire had lost about

424,000 square miles and 5 million people. By 1913, when Talaat and Enver were already in power, the Ottoman government had lost control over all of its European territory, except for a strip to protect the straits of Istanbul itself. As Feroz Ahmad has noted, "The significance of these losses is difficult to exaggerate."[62] The military failures of the regime had crucial consequences for the situation of the Armenians and for the evolution of the ideology of the Young Turks.

Of profound significance for the Armenians was the fact that the loss of the European provinces, in effect, reduced the multinational and multireligious character of the Ottoman Empire. The Greeks and then the Balkan Christians had seceded, leaving the Armenians as the last of the great Christian minorities still under Ottoman rule. Moreover, the Armenians were not just any minority.

As was discussed in Chapter 2, though Armenians had experienced the full measure of Ottoman contempt for *dhimmis* and infidels—tolerance did not mean equality under the empire—they had throughout the nineteenth century undergone a process of social, economic, cultural, and political renewal and development that has been called a renaissance.[63] This social mobilization may be viewed as a contributing factor to the massacres of 1894–96. Abdul Hamid's regime initiated or tolerated the massacres in order to teach the Armenian millet a lesson, to abort its renaissance, and to preserve the old hierarchical order with the Muslims above and the Armenian *dhimmis* below.

The coming of the Young Turks with their emphasis on Turkish renewal and modernization seemed like a new opportunity to the Armenians, and they invested their energies in the new regime. Ironically and tragically for them, however, by 1912, as the Young Turks became increasingly more nationalistic, xenophobic, and intolerant, the very aptitude of the Armenians for modernization only worked to emphasize their apparent threat to the new regime. In sum, the disastrous loss of territory and population that the empire experienced between 1908 and 1912 isolated the Armenians and made them more salient and exposed than they wished to be. Meanwhile, their talent for modernization challenged Turkish and Muslim supremacy, exacerbating fears that non-Turks were a threat to the Turkish national revolution. But this was not all, even the location of the Armenians conspired to endanger their lives.

Recall that the great mass of Armenian peasants lived in Eastern Anatolia, an area claimed to be the heartland of Turkey, bordering on Russia, Turkey's traditional enemy. Across the border was a sizable Armenian population among whom there were parties that evinced irredentist sentiments. Under these circumstances even a benign regime devoted to pluralism and the rule of law might have cast an uneasy glance in the direction of the Armenians. But by 1912, certainly by 1915, the Young Turks were not particularly benign or dedicated to pluralism. They had become xenophobic integral nationalists for whom the identity and situation of the Armenians were sufficient proof of their treachery and potential threat to the continuity of the empire. This was the decisive factor in the genocide.

Indeed, had the Young Turks remained true to the ideology and political myth of Ottomanism, which made legitimate the presence of minorities among them, the isolation of the Armenians as the last great Christian minority in the empire, their aptitude for modernization, and their location in the heartland of Turkey and on the Russian border need not ipso facto have produced thereby a radical change in Armenian-Ottoman relations. But as Lewis has noted, the Young Turks themselves, partly in response to the military and political crises of 1908–12, experienced and helped to engender a radical change in identity, ideology, and political myth that replaced Ottomanism with radical nationalism.

Significantly, he begins his classic work by noting:

"The Turks are a people who speak Turkish and live in Turkey." At first glance, this does not seem to be a proposition of any striking originality, nor of any revolutionary content. Yet the introduction and propagation of this idea in Turkey, and its eventual acceptance by the Turkish people as expressing the nature of their corporate identity and statehood, has been one of the major revolutions of modern times, involving a radical and violent break with the social, cultural, and political traditions of the past. [64]

The point made here and developed so ably throughout *The Emergence of Modern Turkey* is that the heirs of the Ottoman Empire, the Young Ottomans, the Young Turks, Kemal Ataturk himself, had to preside over a major revolution in cultural identity, ideology, and political myth in order to create a modern Turkey. It is contended here that the genocide of the Armenians, the first genocide of our modern era, was at one and the same time a product of the Turkish nationalist revolution and a stage in its development.

Ottomanism and Pan-Islam

To understand the rise of Turkish nationalism and its connection to the Armenian Genocide, we need to contrast it with two ideologies, Ottomanism and Pan-Islam, that competed for the commitment of the

Young Turks, and we need to explain why these lost out. During the *Tanzimat*, the nineteenth-century reform period, when it seemed that the millet system could still be adapted to the exigencies of empire, the dominant ideology was Ottomanism, whose tenets were embodied in the reform constitution of Midhat Pasha.[65] Ottomanism had hoped to maintain the integrity of the empire by allowing greater autonomy to the minority millets and by introducing certain liberal reforms and rights that were to be used equally by all Ottomans regardless of religion or national origin. During the autocracy of Sultan Abdul Hamid, supporters of Ottomanism such as the Armenian Dashnaks and the liberal wing of the Young Turk movement had to go underground.

With the overthrow of the sultan, Ottoman pluralism and liberalism came into their own for a brief period, but their success was short-lived. Ottomanism was abandoned by some of the minorities that preferred self-determination over its proffered autonomy and protofederalism. Above all it was undermined, as has been noted, by the crushing military defeats that pared the empire down to the Anatolian core. In a sense, except for the Armenians, these defeats solved the minority problem by excising most of the minorities from the empire. But by eliminating the minorities, such defeats at the same time undermined the very raison d'être for the doctrine of Ottomanism and gave rise to two competing ideologies and political myths of legitimation, these were Pan-Islam and Turkish nationalism.

One should bear in mind that Sultan Abdul Hamid already had been unsuccessful in his attempts to preserve the empire by making appeals to Pan-Islam. After 1908, however, Pan-Islam once again came into vogue, but with the successful revolt and secession of Muslim nationalities, especially in Albania and Macedonia, the hope that Islam could serve as a basis for imperial unity was seriously undermined. Still later, it was to be dashed by the Arab revolt. As Davison has noted, "The crowning blow to Pan-Islamism was the wartime attitude of the Arabs within the Ottoman domains."[66] When the Arabs, on the side of Britain, began to attack their Turkish rulers, it became clear that "Islamic unity was a mirage, and Pan-Islam was worthless as a political doctrine."[67] Having abandoned Ottomanism and Pan-Islam by 1914, the Young Turks turned ardently toward Turkish nationalism.

Turkish Nationalism

Though it was to be Mustafa Kemal who would finally nail down the boundaries of the Turkish state, thereby defining the territorial, cultural, and political scope of Turkish nationalism, at first this ideology took the form of a rather nebulous doctrine of Pan-Turkism, sometimes called Turanism.[68] According to this ideology and political myth, passionately believed by Enver Pasha until his end, all Turkic-speaking peoples share a common culture and should be unified into a political entity. Since Turkic-speaking peoples were present as far afield as the Russian Caucasus, Central Asia, Kazan, and the Crimea, in theory Pan-Turkism aspired to an extent rivaling that of the Ottoman Empire but without that empire's vexing minority problems. In practice, Pan-Turkism had little chance of succeeding, but is primary result was to "increase a sense of Turkishness among Ottoman Turks."[69] By the same token, it was to decrease the sense that minorities like the Armenians had a right to exist in Turan, the newly invented and valued entity.

As expressed in the thought of Ziya Gökalp, "the father of Turkish nationalism," and in some of the public statements of Talaat and Enver, Turkish nationalism had close parallels to the ideology of organic or integral nationalism devised by figures like Herder and Fichte in continental Europe.[70] In its rejection of minority rights and individual liberties implicit in liberal nationalism, and in its glorification of the ascriptive and "primordial sentiments" of the majority nation, it had certain affinities to Pan-Slavism and to German *Völkisch* thought and racism as well.[71]

Classifying Turkish nationalism under the rubric of "integral nationalism" and seeing Pan-Turkism as related to "Pan" movements on the Continent, does not imply that European movements and ideologies were imported by an ideational process unrelated to the very real political and military conditions of Turkey in the latter nineteenth and early twentieth centuries. On the contrary, the coup of 1908 which started the Turkish revolution helped to undermine autocracy, but it failed to institutionalize Ottomanism or liberal nationalism. As has been seen, the string of military defeats following the revolution gave rise to a felt need for a new political myth and ideology linking state to society. This need came to be satisfied by a homegrown Turkish nationalism.

To help articulate this new ideology, Turkish intellectuals were willing to use whatever material was at hand. Indeed, in the case of Ziya Gökalp it was neither Herder nor Fichte, spokesmen for a surging German nationalism, who were influential, but Durkheim! More precisely it was Gökalp's reading of Durkheim and his adaptation of the French sociologist to the political landscape that proved to be seminal.

This analysis does not imply that Turkish nationalism was predetermined to become narrow, exclusivist, and antiliberal. When the Young

Turk revolution first took power in 1908, in addition to the integral nationalism of the CUP, which was later to succeed, another tendency existed, namely, that of liberal nationalism led by Prince Sabahaddin. Its failure to take hold along with the liberals' fall from power set the conditions for the rise of Pan-Turkism and the Armenian Genocide. Its existence however, indicates that this catastrophe was not a foregone conclusion in 1908. Had the Great Powers, even without Russia and Austria, helped Turkish democracy to establish itself, it is likely that even then the empire would have undergone grave tribulations, but the Armenian Genocide possibly could have been averted.[72]

Ziya Gökalp

To illustrate how integral nationalism came to be defined and used in the Turkish context, it may be instructive to refer to Ziya Gökalp, about whom Heyd, his intellectual biographer, has noted, "He laid in his writings the foundation of the national and modern state which was eventually established by Mustafa Kemal."[73] Beyond his intellectual influence on Talaat and Enver, Gökalp became a member of the CUP's Central Committee in 1911 and stayed there until 1918. Indeed, he was designated to investigate the conditions of minorities, especially the Armenians. Heyd notes rather cryptically, "A considerable part of his suggestions were accepted by the Party and carried out by its Government during the First World War."[74] On 21 September 1919 he was arrested together with other members of the Committee of Union and Progress. When he was placed on trial for his part in the genocide,

> Gökalp denied that there had been any massacres, explaining that the Armenians had been killed in a war between them and the Turks whom they had stabbed in the back. He admitted, however, without hesitation that he had approved of the expulsion of the Armenians. The Military Court sentenced him and his friends to be exiled from the country.[75]

In trying to assess the consequences of Gökalp's thought, Heyd notes without irony, "The Turkish Republic tried to achieve Gökalp's ideal of a homogeneous Turkish nation. The majority of the Greek population was exchanged against the Turks, and the bulk of the Armenians left Turkey gradually."[76]

According to the doctrine of integral nationalism, familiar to most students of nationalist thought by now, the primary units of historical and political action are not social and economic forces like classes, or

165

dynasties, or heroic personalities. They are nations. In all essentials unchanged from time immemorial, such nations have their origins in a dim but glorious past, a Golden Age. Since the beginning, the history of nations, and hence the history of humankind, is one of ceaseless struggle of one nation over another for power and territory, with the result that in some instances nations become militarily defeated—usually through inner corruption or treachery—wherein they run the risk of being physically eliminated. But their destruction, or rather their temporary submergence, can also be accomplished by the stifling of the national culture and the national language.

For his part Gökalp saw in the Turkish past, not in the Ottoman past, a Golden Age that predated the coming of Islam. He gloried in the military exploits of such "Turkish" conquerors as Attila, Genghis Khan, and Timur Babur. He contrasted their times with the weakness and decadence of his own times. He emphasized the national affinities among Turks and such ancient peoples as the Scythians, Sumerians, and Hittites, among whom he found the same moral qualities that distinguished the Turks from other peoples. These were "open handed hospitality, modesty, faithfulness, courage, uprightness. . . . Especially praiseworthy was their attitude to the peoples subdued by them. Strong as was their love for their own people . . . they did not oppress other nations."[77] He lamented, however, that "the sword of the Turk and likewise his pen have exalted the Arabs, Chinese, and Persians. He has created a history and a home for every people. He has deluded himself for the benefit of others."[78] In a poem, Gökalp wrote,

> We succeeded in conquering many places
> But spiritually we were conquered in all of them.[79]

According to Heyd, Gökalp defined the nation as

> a society consisting of people who speak the same language, have had the same education and are united in their religious and aesthetic ideals—in short those who have a common culture and religion.[80]

On the surface this definition is innocuous enough, but in the context of the empire's cultural pluralism it excludes Armenians as well as other minorities on the basis of religion, history, and descent from the newly realized entity, the Turkish nation. "Greeks, Armenians and Jews who lived in Turkey were Turks only in respect of citizenship but not of nationality . . . they would remain a foreign body in the national Turkish state."[81]

For Gökalp, as for all integral or organic nationalists, the nation is not merely an analytic construct; it is a basic principle of moral action. Heyd notes that "replacing the belief in God by the belief in nation," for Gökalp "nationalism had become a religion."[82] Simply put, the good without limit is the good of the nation and for its sake all is permissible.

> I am a soldier it is my commander
> I obey without question all its orders
> With closed eyes I carry out my duty.[83]

Given Gökalp's identification of the good with the good of the nation and his exclusion of Armenians from the nation, it follows that he excluded Armenians from his moral concerns. The myth of integral nationalism was quite distinct from Ottomanism, which not only accorded minorities a place in the empire but also defined certain moral and political responsibilities of the state toward them and toward all millets. They had once been a legitimate, even valued, community under the old Ottoman regime, but from the novel perspective of Turkish nationalism Armenians came to be viewed as an alien nationality. In this sense it might be said the Gökalp's formulations of Turkish nationalism excluded Armenians from Turkey and set the stage for their destruction.

Turkism and Pan-Turkism in Action

One of the principal exponents of Turkish nationalism and Pan-Turkism was Enver Pasha, the minister of war, who defined some of his major military and political objectives according to the precepts of this worldview. Indeed, Enver's choices of military campaigns were directly affected by his ideology. Thus the disastrous campaign in the Caucasus in late 1914, which was mentioned above, is "virtually inexplicable outside of [Enver's] commitment to Pan-Turkism."[84] During the war and even after, Enver did what he could to realize his nationalist commitments. Indeed, when he died fighting in Central Asia in 1922 he was in command of Basmachi forces, "and his assumption of the title of 'Emir of Turkestan' appeared to many as the realisation of the Pan-Turk ideal."[85] Significantly, Turkism and Pan-Turkism affected Turkey's entry into the Great War on the side of the Central Powers against Russia, and they helped to exclude Armenians from the moral universe of the state. Both of these effects had direct and indirect consequences for the genocide.

Indeed, it is by now widely recognized that the Ottoman Empire's entry into the First World War on the side of the Central Powers was significantly motivated by Enver's Pan-Turkism.[86] The Pan-Turkists joined the Central Powers in the expectations of carving or reclaiming a new Turkic empire out of Russian lands.[87] This is crucial for tracing the origins of the Armenian Genocide because, had the Ottoman Empire decided to stay on the sidelines in 1914 or to join the Entente, war with Russia might have been avoided.

With the Eastern frontier at peace, the Armenians would probably still have been viewed with suspicion as an alien "nation" occupying the heartland of Turkey, but their perceived threat would have been greatly diminished. Once the war started, however, it was alleged, as we have seen, that the internal enemy of the Turkish revolution was in league, indeed, had to be in league, with its principal external foe. Moreover, this same internal enemy was a major obstacle to the Pan-Turkic ideal of a homogeneous Turan stretching from Anatolia to the borders of China. Prompted by Enver himself, the CUP secretly joined the Central Powers on 2 August 1914, and Ottoman forces bombed Russian Ports on the Black Sea on 29 October 1914. The CUP, in effect, had declared war not only on the Russians but on the Armenians as well.

Some historians have argued that it was military necessity stemming from the World War that dictated the CUP's decision to deport, if not to exterminate the Armenians. They neglect to note, however, that it was after all the CUP's own decision that precipitated war between the Ottoman and the Russian Empires. These hostilities then were used to justify the deportations of the Armenians—a clearer case of self-fulfilling and self-justifying prophesy is hard to find. A well-regarded scholar of Pan-Turkism comments laconically that "the strong-handed exile [sic] of the Armenians may be partly seen as motivated by the wish to eliminate a barrier between Turkey and several Turkic groups in Russia living near the frontiers."[88] Thus what led to the deportations and the genocide was not the alleged threat of the Armenians but the Pan-Turkism of CUP leaders like Enver.

In the minds of Talaat and Enver the Armenians were viewed as aliens beyond the moral ken of the Ottoman or Turkic state. This image of the Armenians can readily be ascertained from conversations recorded by Henry J. Morgenthau, the American ambassador, when he tried to intervene on their behalf with leaders of the Young Turks. When, at the height of the deportations and the killings, Morgenthau asked Talaat why the supposedly disloyal Armenians could not be separated from those who remained loyal, the minister of the interior replied: "We have been reproached for making no distinction between the innocent Armenians and the guilty; but that was utterly impossible in view of the fact that those who were innocent today might be guilty tomorrow."[89] In an even more chilling passage that reveals Talaat's attitude, Morgenthau recalls:

> One day Talaat made what was perhaps the most astonishing request I had ever heard. The New York Life Insurance Company and the Equitable Life of New York had for years done considerable business among the Armenians. . . . "I wish," Talaat now said, "that you would get the American life insurance companies to send us a complete list of the Armenian policy holders. They are practically all dead now and have left no heirs to collect the money. It of course escheats to the State. The Government is the beneficiary now. Will you do so?"[90]

The ambassador, of course, refused. Nevertheless, this passage shows in fine detail how astonishing was the change from the traditional Muslim and Ottoman view of the Armenians as "people of the book," as the "most loyal millet," who had a vital role to play even under Sultan Abdul Hamid, to that of Talaat, in which the Armenians had become so alien that, even in death, their sole function was to be exploited for their money.

Conclusion

The Turkish revolution of 1908–23, while it redefined Ottoman Turkish identity, also had fateful consequences for Ottoman Armenians. For a transformation in the identity, ideology, and political myth of the majority group implies a change in how it views minorities. Once Ottomans became Turks, nationalists like Gökalp, Talaat, and Enver came to view Armenians in a fresh new light, not as an ancient millet but as aliens who did not belong among them. Moreover, from the perspective of Turkish nationalists, such "aliens," unlike the Greeks and the Jews and other minorities some of whom had seceded, were occupying the very heartland of Turkey, there had been nationalist stirrings among them, and in the midst of war it was said that they favored the Russian side. No wonder Turkish nationalists viewed Armenians as a "deadly threat."

The genocide of the Armenians should be understood not as a response to "Armenian provocations" but as a stage in the Turkish revolution, which as a reaction to the continuing disintegration of the empire settled on a narrow nationalism and excluded Armenians from the moral universe of the state. Once the Ottoman Empire joined the Central Powers against Russia, the CUP could use the excuse of military necessity to destroy the Armenians. As many historians have noted, the Turkish revolution initiated by the CUP was successful in creating a new Turkey, but it also came close to destroying an ancient people in the process.

S I X

The German Revolution and the Rise of the Nazi Party

There was no point of contact with the men in power [of the Weimar Republic]. For they had banished the glorious old black-white-and-red banner [of Imperial Germany] and substituted a flag in its place that meant nothing to the front fighters. What became of the memory of the dead? Their blood called to high Heaven for vengeance! Then came light in the darkness. . . . In 1923 we heard the name Adolf Hitler for the first time.

From the comments of a veteran of the Great War.[1]

"We come as enemies! Like the wolf tearing into a flock of sheep that is how we come."

Joseph Goebbels[2]

As suggested in Chapter 4, the main reason the antisemitic parties failed to come to power in Imperial Germany was opposition to them by the regime and other leading social forces, including even the conservatives. In time Imperial Germany's rulers came to fear the influence of the Jews less than the populist indignation that had been stirred up by the antisemites. By the same token, when frustrated radical antisemites like Fritsch realized that the state itself opposed them, they became revolutionary in their outlook. To solve the "Jewish Question" they were even willing to contemplate destroying the imperial state itself, but in the context of the *Kaiserreich* they could do very little about their resentments.

Imperial Germany may have had its internal and international problems, but by and large it was a powerful, popular, legitimate, and stable regime that could not be brought down by the agitation of antisemitic cranks. It was her defeat in the Great War that destroyed Imperial Germany and ushered in the German revolution, not the machinations of revolutionary malcontents.

This chapter will try to show that a revolutionary antisemitic party like the Nazis was able to come to power and to implement its radical policies precisely because, after defeat in the Great War, a revolutionary situation had developed in Germany. A moderate democratic regime that had replaced the Second Reich was too illegitimate and too divided to resist class and political party polarization, and when it fell the Nazis came to power. Thus the revolution against the Jews had its immediate origins in a political revolt against the democratic Weimar Republic.

At first the Nazis tried to come to power by force, but that route was blocked by the ambiguous role of the army. After the failed putsch of 8–9 November 1923 Hitler discovered that he could use the democratic electoral process to destroy democracy itself. It is ironic—given what came later—that antisemitism as a central core of Nazi ideology was of only marginal importance in the electoral climb of the Nazis to power. This is not to deny that antisemitism became overwhelmingly important once Hitler had become chancellor.

As in the Turkish case, discussed in Chapter 5, a radical movement was able to seize state power in Germany not only because of its ideology, organization, or leadership but also because the old regime and the moderates that for a brief period ruled in its stead were swept away by revolutionary forces. Genocide was then perpetrated in Germany, as earlier it had been in Turkey, by radicals who attempted to reconstruct state and society according to a compelling ideological vision.

The important point that needs stressing is that without the vulnerability and ultimate fall of Weimar, the Nazis would not have come to power and the Final Solution would not have become a policy of the state. Thus an analysis of the causes of the Holocaust must examine the prior conditions, especially those facilitating the Nazi electoral triumph and their snaring of power, that made the implementation of a genocidal ideology possible.

Chapter 6 is divided into five sections: "The German Revolution and the Fall of the Weimar Republic," "The Polarization of Germany and the Rise of the Nazis," "Antisemitism and Other Sources of Nazi Support," "Nazism, Fascism, and the 'Extremism of the Middle,'" and "Conclusion."

The German Revolution and the Fall of the Weimar Republic

As noted in the Introduction to this book, a social revolution entails a fundamental transformation in a society's political, economic, and social structures and cultural values and beliefs, including its reigning ideology, political myth, and identity. A political revolution leaves the social and economic structures largely unchanged while it profoundly affects the political structure, the ideology of its ruling regime, and the political myth that binds society to the state.

From this perspective, the German revolution that commenced with the fall of the *Kaiserreich* in 1918 and ended with the destruction of Nazism in 1945 did not start out as a social revolution in the manner of the French or the Russian revolutions. It began as a political revolution that destroyed the German Empire's political structure, ideology, and political myth and tried to replace it with the Weimar Republic and its system of democratic and socialist legitimation. Weimar, however, was a failure because it was never able to acquire legitimacy or to bridge the deep class divisions that had persisted and intensified since before the Great War. That failure enabled the Nazis to step in and to reshape the political structure of the state, the ideology of the ruling stratum, and the political myth of legitimation binding society to the state.

In this analysis one needs to distinguish the Nazis' coming to power from the German revolution as such.[3] The German revolution, which lasted from 1918 to 1945, included the Nazi ascent to power, while Nazi rule constituted the German revolution's radical phase.[4] The Nazis did not start the German revolution. The failed war did that, but they were able to profit from the destruction of the old regime and the failure of its democratic successor state. They created the Third Reich, a novel political structure, and they drastically tried to substitute their own conceptions centering on racism, antisemitism, and the charisma of the führer for the political myths that had once bound Germans to the imperial state and that had failed to take hold during the Weimar interlude. In the process they committed genocide on a wide scale, and they started a world war.

In sum, the German revolution commenced with the defeat and destruction of the imperial regime in the Great War and ended with the defeat of the Nazis and the rise of the two successor states following the Second World War. The revolutionary interregnum that lasted from 1918 to 1945 may be divided into two intervals. From 1918 to 1933 Germany was led by the democratic Weimar Republic, while from 1933 to 1945 she was governed by the Nazis. Both of these ill-fated regimes can be seen as moderate and radical phases of a single German revolution, and the Nazis' attainment of power in 1933 cannot be understood without the prior fall of the Weimar Republic.

The imperial regime was destroyed by experiences attending its defeat in the First World War. The Weimar Republic that replaced it, however, was itself extremely unstable. A series of domestic and international circumstances, as well as a history of intense class conflict, conspired to undermine its legitimacy, its control over the means of coercion, and its ability to deal with economic and social crises. These factors contributed to the democratic regime's collapse and the triumph of the Nazis.

Legitimacy

Born in defeat and aborted left-wing revolution—for which it was blamed—the Weimar Republic was undermined by the circumstances of its inception and by the legacy of intense class and ideological conflict deriving from Imperial Germany. Thus the "November Revolution," the armistice, and the Versailles treaties made it appear to many Germans that their new republic had been foisted on them by victorious enemies with the support of treacherous German civilian politicians. Germany, it was said, had been "stabbed in the back."[5] Meanwhile, the civil service and the army were left largely unreformed from the days of the *Kaiserreich*, while the upper and middle classes longed for the glory days of Imperial Germany. These were not propitious conditions for the survival of a democratic republic.

In the summer and early fall of 1918 German armies suffered serious reversals on the Western Front, and their allies collapsed in the East.[6] At the end of September, General Ludendorff informed his government that Germany had no choice but to sue for peace. This arrogant war hero had been, together with Hindenburg, the de facto dictator of Germany in the last year of the war. He had held out for victory when earlier a peace without annexations might have been possible. Now that defeat was imminent he turned to the civilians in his government to shoulder the responsibility for the debacle. A noted historian remarked: "Having brought Germany to the end of its resources, he left to the civilian leadership whose authority he had systematically undermined the harsh task of seeing what could be saved from the ruins."[7]

As he departed, Ludendorff urged the immediate formation of a democratic government, in the hope that constitutional reforms would impress the allies and they would deal less harshly with Germany. Stunned by such reversals of fortune, the principal democratic parties in the *Reichstag*, the SPD, the Progressives, and the Center lined up behind Prince Max von Baden, the new chancellor.

In October 1918, the *Reichstag* passed a series of laws that provided for ministerial responsibility and abolished royal command over the armed forces whose legal control was taken up by the civilian government. "This was a constitutional transformation that at any other time would have transfixed the imagination of the country."[8] Under the circumstances, however, this transfer of power to civilians initiated a period of strife and disorder that has come to be known as the "November Revolution."

The "November Revolution"—merely an episode in the larger German revolution—started with the Kiel naval mutiny on 28 October 1918. It lasted at least until 6 February 1919, when the National Assembly of the Republic met at Weimar. On 7 November King Louis of Bavaria was deposed. On 8 November the princes of the old regime were dethroned in Baden, Württemberg, Thuringia, and Saxony. Meanwhile, in Bavaria, Kurt Eisner, an Independent Socialist, a Jew, and a revolutionary, seized power and declared himself "premier." On 9 November on the advice of the German military high command, Prince Max advised Wilhelm II to abdicate, and on the same day he resigned as chancellor. On 10 November Freidrich Ebert, the leader of the Social Democrats, became the new chancellor, and on 11 November 1918 a German delegation headed by Matthias Erzberger concluded an armistice with the allies.

In the following months, the provisional government was challenged both from the left and the right. On 29 December the Independent Socialists (USPD) resigned from the government—they were not to return to the fold of the SPD until September 1922—and on 31 December the Spartakists broke from the USPD and formed the German Communist party (KPD). Led by Rosa Luxemburg and Karl Liebknecht, between 5 and 12 January the Spartakists initiated an uprising in Berlin. This rather ineffective show of revolutionary ardor, like that of Eisner in Bavaria, was crushed by the army and *Freikorps*, operating at the behest of Ebert.[9]

The chancellor was intent on keeping order until a constituent assembly could meet. He had not counted on nor commanded the brutal murder of Luxemburg and Liebknecht, but then on 15 January those two popular working-class leaders were assassinated by the army. These events further embittered relations on the left and made it impossible to unite later against the revolutionary right.

On 19 January 1919 elections for the Constituent Assembly were successfully held, and on 6 February the National Assembly met at Weimar, where Goethe lived most of his life and where Schiller's early plays were performed. This was a temporary triumph for the SPD and the rest of the Weimar coalition.[10] The electoral triumph of the democratic forces soon was dashed by the Versailles treaty and its punitive provisions that were signed into law on 28 June 1919.

To understand the Germans' perspective, one must recall that prior to the armistice they had believed that the peace settlement would follow the outline of President Wilson's fourteen points and his spirit of magnanimity toward the vanquished. Despite Wilson's objections the treaties were punitive and insulting.[11]

Germany had to give up one-eighth of her territory and nearly 10 percent of her population. She lost all of her colonies. A 100,000-man limitation was placed on her army. The Saar coal and industrial region was to be occupied and exploited by France for a period of fifteen years. Her merchant fleet was confiscated, and she had to pay 5 billion dollars in immediate reparations. In 1921 Germany discovered that she had to pay 32 billion dollars more. Adding insult to injury was Article 231, known as the "war guilt clause":

> The allied and Associated Governments affirm and Germany accepts the responsibility of Germany and her allies for causing all the loss and damage to which [they] and their nationals have been subjected as a consequence of the war imposed upon them by the aggression of Germany and her allies.[12]

Snyder remarked:

> Instead of helping to make Germany safe for democracy, the Allies burdened the fledgling Republic with the onus of war guilt. The peace treaty strengthened the reactionaries by giving them a propaganda weapon of inestimable value.[13]

In retrospect, it would have been better for Germany and the world had the civilian leaders in 1918 refused to take up the burden left for them by the army. As it turned out, however, not Ludendorff, Hindenburg, and the German general staff, but the civilians who had taken upon themselves the obloquy of suing for peace were blamed by many German nationalists for the debacle. Indeed, the defeat, the November Revolution, the armistice, the treaty of Versailles with its punitive reparations measures and its insulting language, even the new constitution came to be viewed in Germany as part of the *dolchstoss*, "the stab-in-the-back." It was this treachery at home, so it was said, that had brought Germany failure and humiliation while her army stood proud and unvanquished. "The Weimar Republic could not survive this reputation."[14]

It was apparent that the consequences of the defeat and the founding of the Weimar Republic had divided Germany into two camps, those who supported and those who opposed the new Republic. Each camp had its own version of the events that had transpired after the fall of Imperial Germany, and these were diametrically opposed to each other.

Thus Philipp Scheidemann, the Social Democratic leader who had announced the birth of the Republic and was to become its first elected chancellor, squarely placed the blame for Germany's defeat on the old regime and the military circles.

> The catastrophe we tried our best to avoid has not been spared us, because our proposals for peace by consent were rejected and we ourselves scorned and despised. The foes of an industrious people, the real foes in our midst, that have caused Germany's downfall, are silent and invisible. These were the warriors who stopped at home, promoting their demands for annexation, bitterly opposing any reform of the constitution, and especially supporting the scandalous electoral system of Prussia. These foes are, it is hoped, gone for good. The Emperor has abdicated. He and his friends have decamped. The people have triumphed over them all along the line.[15]

A contrary view was later given by General Hermann von Kuhl, who argued in his report to the *Reichstag* commission investigating the defeat that in truth the phrase "stab-in-the-back" was not totally accurate. He preferred "poisoning of the army" by pacifist, internationalist, and antimilitarist circles. He wanted to preserve the term "stab-in-the-back" for the revolution that had indeed attacked the German army.[16] And the *Neue Zuricher Zeitung* reported on 1 December 1918: "As far as the German army is concerned, the general view is summarized in these words: it was stabbed in the back by the civilian population."[17]

Hitler, of course, had his own gloss on these events: Germany was defeated by a Jewish conspiracy of which the Social Democrats and the Republic were merely a tool.

Thus the felt illegitimacy of Weimar on the part of many nationalist

Germans provided the Nazis with a major issue in their rise to power and should, therefore, be viewed as one of the main preconditions of the Holocaust. But Weimar lacked support not only from significant strata of the general public, it lacked commitment from the very people who were asked to staff its major institutions.

Shortly after Versailles, on 11 August 1919, the Weimar constitution was promulgated. Like the terms of the peace, the constitutional framework, both in the things that it left undone and in the provisions that it established, helped to undermine the legitimacy of the Republic. [18] Among the major things left undone by the Constituent Assembly and the constitution was reform of the civil service, the educational system, and the army.

In part because of the violence and chaos of November 1918, Weimar's leaders had decided to leave the civil service of the old regime, including its judges and teachers, largely untouched in order to assure order and continuity. This was perhaps an understandable but nevertheless serious mistake. The personnel that staffed Weimar's major institutions was drawn mainly from the old regime and felt no commitment to the new republic.

The civil servants were contemptuous of the Republic and disdainful of its instability. In the early days of the Republic, they voted first for the anti-Republican but conservative German National Peoples party (DNVP), and then, as the Nazis appeared on the scene, they shifted their support to the radical right. Indeed, the Protestants among them were more likely to do so than any other middle-class white-collar group. [19]

The judges in particular flaunted their contempt for the Republic. Article 54 of the constitution guaranteed their tenure, and they used it to undermine the regime they hated. "In many German court-rooms after 1918, libelous attacks upon republican ministers and defamation of the Republic and its symbols were more likely to be commended than punished." [20]

The federal penal code stipulated that anyone attempting to overthrow the Republic by force should be imprisoned for life. The judges who tried the participants of the Kapp putsch of 1920 and Hitler's attempt at a violent seizure of power in 1923 meted out nominal sentences. "Against this kind of encouragement of the Republic's enemies, the constitution gave no protection." [21]

Teachers, too, and especially professors were enemies of the Republic. They helped to infect their students with disdain for the regime and a longing for the more authoritarian past.

178

> History, government, and geography texts and anthologies of poetry not only abounded in aggressive nationalism and praise of the monarchical past but placed responsibility for all of Germany's present misfortunes at the door of foreign Powers and the republican government.[22]

Though the impact of teachers and professors was no doubt only one of many influences on the young, the educational system contributed to the undermining of Weimar and the rise of the Nazis.

No democratic state can long endure if even its civil servants, public school teachers, and members of the armed forces resent its elected officials and deny their legitimate authority to rule. As Craig has remarked with pungent effect:

> It is no exaggeration to say that [Weimar] failed in the end partly because German officers were allowed to put their epaulets back on again so quickly and because the public buildings were not burned down, along with the bureaucrats who inhabited them.[23]

By leaving the civil service, including the system of higher education of the old regime, largely untouched, the Weimar Republic allowed itself to be sabotaged from within.

From the discussion thus far we can note that the terms of the peace following the war were both too lenient and too harsh. They were too lenient in that the Allies had not invaded Germany and had not dismantled her major institutions, such as the army, the civil service, and the landed aristocracy that were unalterably opposed to democracy. They were too harsh in that the Weimar Republic—a democratic and reformist government—was saddled with the onus of defeat, war guilt, and heavy reparations. Both sets of conditions made it very difficult for a democratic government to sustain its legitimacy and to govern.

Thus the very establishment of the Weimar Republic, instead of uniting Germans under a democratic regime, had created a deep division in Germany between supporters and opponents of democracy. What made this cleavage especially dangerous for the Republic was that it coincided in large part with, and powerfully reinforced, social class and political party conflicts that, as we have seen in Chapter 4, had their origins in Imperial Germany.

The result was that the establishment of Weimar helped to polarize Germany into two camps: those classes and parties that supported and those that opposed the Republic. The opposition was itself divided into a right and a left wing. At the start, the right split into a conservative nationalist grouping and a revolutionary wing headed by the Nazis. The left was headed by the Communists. When the conservative nationalist parties began to collapse in 1930, the Nazis surged forward and positioned themselves to take power. Before turning to a discussion of how this polarization worked itself out in the electoral political arena, a word needs to be said about the class and party divisions of Weimar Germany and their origins in the Bismarck period.

Class Conflict

Recall from Chapter 4 that Bismarck's system of aristocratic domination supported by limited middle-class participation could not assimilate the social and political forces generated by Germany's extraordinarily rapid industrialization and modernization of the nineteenth century. Instead of opening up the system to the working class and its party, the SPD, Bismarck chose to stigmatize it as an "enemy of the empire." The result was that even after the Great War, the SPD and the industrial working class were viewed by many nationalists, especially those from the upper and middle classes, as un-German and certainly not as rightful heirs to the elites and the political rulers of the *Kaiserreich*.

Writing of the cleavage between the middle class and the working class apparent in German politics from the 1890s, Childers has noted:

> War and revolution would reshape the liberal and conservative parties and would permanently divide the working-class movement, but the deep social cleavage dividing the constituencies of these parties would survive both disruptions to dominate the electoral politics of the new republic. [24]

Generalizing from his case study of Northeim before the outbreak of World War II, Allen has remarked that, in prewar Germany, political, social, and cultural life were strictly divided and segregated by class. [25] The working class lived in neighborhoods separate from the middle and upper classes. Working-class men had separate jobs and drank in separate pubs; working-class women met in separate sewing circles, and their children played on separate soccer teams. Many if not most of the social and cultural activities of the working class were organized by the SPD. This was a party of class integration par excellence.

Although until the Nazis came along the middle class was not as tightly organized as was the working class; nevertheless, middle-class status was no mere census category. There were middle-class and upper-class neighborhoods, clubs, and, significantly, political and military societies, most of which were right wing and nationalist. Moreover, the middle class mistrusted the working class, and hated the SPD, failing to differentiate it from the more radical Communists. Northeim's burghers could not care less that by the 1920s the SPD had evolved into a moderate democratic working-class party that was willing to tolerate the class structure and saw revolution as a millenarian dream best delayed indefinitely.[26]

Under the conditions of Weimar the SPD had the worst of both worlds. While it appeared too radical for alliance with middle-class parties, with the exception of the German Democratic party (DDP), it was too moderate to foment a radical revolution that might have given it the power to defend itself and Germany against the Nazis. Although writing about the dilemmas of the SPD in Northeim, Allen clearly meant to implicate that party's stance in Germany as a whole.

> The SPD was not "Marxist," though it used language that made it appear to be so. Thus it was doubly encumbered, for it was unwilling to be a revolutionary party at a time when the best defense of democracy may have been social revolution, and secondly, its revolutionary tradition made it incapable of seeking or receiving the support of any but the working class. Furthermore, the SPD's defense of democracy meant, in practical terms, defense of the status quo which was identified in the minds of most Northeimers [and Germans] with national humiliation and economic ruin.[27]

Beyond that, should the SPD have "relaxed its ritualistic radicalism, the Communists were there to lure off dissidents. Thus neither Socialists nor the moderate middle class worked for a rapprochement."[28]

Similarly, Craig has remarked that the SPD's base was limited mainly to the blue-collar industries and trade unions of the Weimar economy, and that may have been its fatal flaw.

> The fatal ills of the SPD . . . were complacency and parochialism. Instead of making an effort to transform the party into one that could appeal to all classes and rally them to the defense of the Republic, its leaders acted as if they owed responsibility only to the working class.[29]

Such narrowness was to do "irreparable harm" to the party and by extension to the Republic when the Nazis came along. The revolutionaries of the right, unlike the SPD and the KPD, were able to create an umbrella catchall party that included the lower-middle classes and the peasantry.

Such problems that might have plagued the SPD did not concern the good burghers of Northeim and Germany. For them it was a party beyond the pale.

> The Socialists carried a red flag. They sang the *Internationale*. There had been laws against them in the days of Germany's glory. They were associated with the cataclysm of 1918. They represented the proletarians, the unwashed workers, the restive unemployed. They preached Marxism and class struggle. . . . One never met them socially, yet there they were in the City Hall—touchy, aggressive, demanding. [30]

In any event, the war and the circumstances of the defeat widened class divisions in postwar Germany and helped to initiate the polarization of German society that would ultimately result in the destruction of Weimar and the ascent of the Nazis to power. [31]

Although social class divisions were important, they alone did not account for Nazi success. The Nazi movement was not simply a later expression of the class struggle, and polarization did not primarily take the form of violent confrontation—though violence, including assassinations, street demonstrations, and attempted putschs was a recurring and menacing leitmotif of the era.

Radicalization, polarization, and the destruction of democracy were fueled both by class antagonisms, whose origins lay in Imperial Germany, and also by the felt illegitimacy of the Republic and the manner of its formation following the Great War. Thus both sets of cleavages—those of social class and those of political allegiance—worked in tandem to polarize German society. This polarization, though punctuated by violence, worked itself out through the electoral process that tragically was meant to express and safeguard democracy. This was the revolutionary situation that the Nazis exploited in order to come to power.

The Polarization of Germany and the Rise of the Nazis

A host of writers have written about Hitler and the rise of the Nazis to power. This is not the place to recapitulate that story. What we wish to do here is to show that the rise of the Nazis to power originated in the revolutionary situation discussed above and was channeled into an electoral path by the role that the army played in the Weimar Republic.

When one thinks of revolutionary vanguards like the Nazis, one imagines their coming to power by way of violent upheavals. The storming of the Bastille or of the Winter Palace, Fidel's guerrillas in the mountains, and the fall of Phnom Penh are the usual and indelible images of revolution that we possess. The Nazis, too, started as a revolutionary vanguard eager to seize power by means of a violent stroke, but that bit of melodrama was denied them when on 8–9 November 1923 their opera buffa putsch was suppressed.

The Nazis finally triumphed when Hitler became active again upon his release after nine months from Landsberg prison on 20 December 1924.

> He had learned *one* bitter lesson: the road to power did not lead via a putsch but via the more tedious and slow route of "legality." The defeat of democracy by pseudo-democratic means was the new course to which Hitler now devoted himself.[32]

The party that detested democracy would come to power by means of elections and of the democratic process itself. This is what Bracher has ironically but aptly called the "Legal Revolution."[33] Why the Nazis failed in the putsch of 1923 and why they took the electoral route to power can be traced directly to the role of the army in the Weimar Republic.

The Role of the Army

It will be recalled that when Ebert first became chancellor on 9 November 1918, he was concerned not only with protecting the new Republic from threats from the right but from the left as well. Squeezed between right and left, the republican leadership made fateful compromises with the army which left that body independent of civilian control and leaning in its sympathies toward the rightist forces that wanted to destroy the fragile democratic regime.

On 9 November 1918, the same day he became chancellor, Ebert received a telephone call from the new spokesman for the Supreme Command, General Wilhelm Groener. The general proposed placing the army at the disposal of the new regime. In return he asked cooperation from the government in the withdrawal of the German army from France and a promise that the Republic would combat Bolshevism. Ebert agreed to this Faustian pact.[34]

In effect, the new chancellor had consented to perpetuate an army headed by an officer corps recruited largely from the Junker aristocracy that was overwhelmingly monarchist, opposed to the Republic, or both.

At the same time he had agreed to use this army to crush his colleagues on the left. In the end, the army was not grateful to him. It did crush the left but did not support the Republic.

Neither backing the Republic nor supporting a violent seizure of power, the army's position eventually in effect forced revolutionary vanguards both of the left and right to attempt to seize power by means other than revolt or a coup d'état. In the meantime, standing on the sidelines but leaning heavily to the right, the army was a political force unto itself. It waited for an opportune moment to give its backing to a regime more to its liking than the democratic Republic for which it had scarcely disguised contempt.

Thus, as we have seen, it crushed the Spartakists' revolt of 1919, but it refused to move against the rightist Kapp putschists of 1920. The right-wing coup collapsed, not because of armed intervention by the army but because a massive general strike in Berlin left that city paralyzed and the rebels powerless. An even more revealing and significant role was played by the army in 1923 when Hitler tried to seize power by way of a putsch.

The Hitler Putsch

In September 1919 Hitler joined the DAP, the German Workers' party in Munich. By February 1920 he had reconstituted it as the National Socialist German Workers party (NSDAP), established his control over the party, and by July 1921 he had become its undisputed leader. The problem as he saw it was how to destroy the Weimar Republic and to seize power in order to implement his revolutionary visions for Germany and the world. He did not have long to wait for an opportunity.

By 1923 the Republic was in crisis. Following the government's defaulting on reparation payments, between 11 and 12 January, French and Belgian troops occupied the Ruhr. By the summer, inflation, underway since the last years of the war, had spun out of control, and on 13 August Stresemann of the German Peoples party (DVP) formed his first cabinet. When the new chancellor ordered the cessation of passive resistance to the French, mutinous rumblings were heard throughout Germany. This was the context for Hitler's abortive putsch of 8–9 November 1923.

In the summer and fall of 1923, because of right-wing threats of an imminent seizure of power, the Bavarian government declared a state of emergency and appointed Ritter von Kahr state commissioner. Unbeknown to the Bavarian premier, his commissioner was himself a right-wing plotter with ambitions to seize power. Kahr, who was in league with Hitler, was able to include in his scheme General von Lossow, the *Reich-*

swehr commander, and Hans Ritter von Seisser, head of the provincial police force. At first these four had coordinated their plans with other right-wing groups in Munich. By seizing power in Bavaria, they aimed to induce the *Reichswehr* to capture Berlin and to destroy the Republic.

When the time came to march on Berlin, the plotters hoped to get the support of General Hans von Seeckt, the commander of the army. At the time this was no mere delusion.

> Throughout the crisis months of 1923 the General was seriously considering the possibility of taking power into his own hands, openly or by disguised means. He was in touch with Kahr and, in a letter to him in November, was to express his antagonism to Social Democracy, his antipathy to the constitution, and his confident expectation that it would soon be changed. [35]

At the same time, under the chairmanship of Ebert, the Berlin government went into session. The question was the role of the *Reichswehr*. Would it support the Republic in this new emergency? When General Seeckt was asked by the president where the army stood, he replied, "[T]he *Reichswehr*, Mr. President, stands behind me." [36]

Constitutionally, Ebert was commander-in-chief, but in the last analysis Seeckt's sibylline remark implied that the army would take its marching orders from him and from no one else. In effect, this meant that the army leadership felt itself to be an independent force in the Republic, free to support the regime or not. In any event, the army decided not to join the putsch.

Earlier, Kahr had been impressed by the ruthlessness with which the army had crushed a Communist plot in Saxony and Thuringia. Then, lacking the support of Seeckt and the army, and without consulting Hitler, Kahr decided to abandon the idea of a coup. This led to the fiasco of 8–9 November 1923 when Hitler and Ludendorff, trying to stage a coup without Kahr or the army, were fired on by the police and ignominiously arrested.

The army's vacillation was due to Seeckt's irresoluteness: "[He] was the kind of man who marched bravely up to the Rubicon and then decided to go fishing." [37] By no means was this vacillation due to Seeckt's or the army's allegiance to the Republic and acceptance of its constitutional provisos. Judging from its behavior, the army was still biding its time and was not ready to support a putsch. In effect, it was building up its strength and waiting for an opportune moment to lend support to a regime in which it could believe. That regime was not the Republic as then constituted, but neither was it, at this early date, a dictatorship headed by Kahr and Hitler.

Without the backing of the army and divided into promonarchist and pro-National Socialist factions, the Hitler putsch of 1923 failed. From this debacle Hitler learned that without the active participation of the army he could not come to power by force. Another way was needed. It was then that he decided on the electoral path to power, on the "legal revolution."[38]

It goes without saying that when Hitler took the "legal" electoral path to power, he had not converted to democracy. He had abandoned the path of a direct seizure of power because at this early date the army stood in his way. This did not mean that he had ruled out violence. The SA Brown Shirts continued to intimidate opponents by force. Indeed, the presence of the SA and other right-wing paramilitary forces would have made the army hesitate even if it had decided to crush the threat from the right. Furthermore, for the Nazis, taking the electoral path was a tactical ploy. They would use the democratic electoral process to destroy democracy itself. Goebbels expressed the aim of this tactic in his usual brazen manner:

> We go into the Reichstag in order to acquire the weapons of democracy from its arsenal. We become Reichstag deputies in order to paralyze the Weimar democracy with its own assistance. . . . We come as enemies! Like the wolf tearing into the flock of sheep, that is how we come.[39]

Fortuitously for the Nazis but tragically for the Republic and the world, the democratic forces inside and outside of the *Reichstag* did not take them seriously enough. The right-wing revolutionaries, who wanted to destroy democracy and seize power, skillfully used the deep political and social cleavages of Weimar Germany as reflected in the electoral process. It is to this process that we turn next.

Elections

Despite the military defeat and the transfer of power to civilians, with some important changes, the party, class, and communal divisions of Imperial Germany carried over and were recapitulated in the Weimar Republic.[40] The main difference was that the socialist and liberal parties that had been out of power in the imperial era were in power under Weimar, and the conservative and liberal nationalists, who had ruled the roost under Bismarck and the kaiser, found themselves in the strange and unaccustomed situation of being out of power and detesting the German regime that had replaced their beloved Second Reich.

The major parties that contested for power in the Weimar Republic were the Social Democratic party (SPD), the German Democratic party (DDP), the Center, the German People's party (DVP), the German National People's party (DNVP), the Communist party (KPD), and the National Socialist Workers party, the Nazis (NSDAP). The first three parties, in large part a continuation of the SPD, Progressives, and Center of Imperial Germany, constituted what came to be known as the "Weimar Coalition." Nevertheless, even these parties, the heart of the Republic, were sometimes ambivalent about the democracy that they had created.

The next two parties, the DVP and the DNVP, harking back to the National Liberals and the Conservatives of Imperial Germany, were either ambivalent or were mainly opposed to the Republic and longed for Bismarck's Germany.[41] Until the Nazi breakthrough in the elections of September 1930, the DNVP was the core of the right-wing opposition to Weimar. In contrast to the DNVP and the SPD, and despite their obvious differences, the NSDAP and the KPD were truly revolutionary parties in that they aimed at the destruction of Weimar and the reconstruction of German society. Unlike the other parties, they were prepared to use force to attain their aims, but they were willing to consider other means—including the electoral process—to seize power. Together the two parties made up the revolutionary opposition to Weimar and did everything possible to tear it down.

From this brief description one sees that the Weimar party system reflected the deep postwar divisions of Germany that have been discussed above. On the one hand, there was the Weimar coalition that despite its other class and sectional divisions supported parliamentary democracy. On the other hand, there were a variety of parties of the left and right that were either profoundly ambivalent about the regime itself or wanted to destroy it outright. Significantly, therefore, every election that took place between 1919 and 1933 was not only about specific issues, it was also an implicit referendum on democracy and the myth of legitimation of the Republic itself.

The processes of delegitimation of the Weimar Republic, class polarization of German society, and radicalization that brought the Nazis to power can partly be traced by analyzing the careers of the major electoral blocs in the *Reichstag* elections from 1919 to 1933. This is illustrated in table 6.1 below.

TABLE 6.1 Elections to the Reichstag by Blocs, by Percentage of the Popular Vote

Date	Weimar Coalition[a]	DDP	Liberal and Conservative Nationalists	Revolutionaries		Other
				KPD	NSDAP	
1/19/1919	83.8	18.6	14.3	. . .	. . .	1.5
6/6/1920	61.4	8.3	28.8	2.1	. . .	7.5
5/4/1924	39.6	5.7	28.7	12.6	6.5	12.6
12/7/1924	45.9	6.3	30.6	9.0	3.0	11.6
5/20/1928	46.8	4.9	22.9	10.6	2.6	17.4
9/14/1930	40.1	3.8	11.5	13.1	18.3	16.6
7/31/1932	35.1	1.0	7.1	14.6	37.4	6.7
10/6/1932	33.3	.9	10.7	16.9	33.1	8.9
3/3/1933	30.8	.8	9.1	12.3	43.9	4.7

Note.—Adapted from Kopel S. Pinson, *Modern Germany* (New York: Macmillan, 1954), 574–75.
[a]Weimar Coalition = SPD (including USPD) + Center + DDP; Liberal and Conservative Nationalists = DVP + DNVP; Revolutionaries = KPD + NSDAP.

Delegitimation

Though they may have differed on other issues, the SPD (including the USPD), Center, and DDP made up the Weimar coalition that was committed to the survival of the democratic republic as such. Notwithstanding its broad support at the start—it received 83.3 percent of the vote to the Constituent Assembly of January 1919—the Weimar coalition's initial appeal was illusory. The election to the Constituent Assembly was held after the November Revolution and before the results of the Versailles Treaties were known. Germans voted for the Republic because they were tired of the November Revolution, and they feared democracy less than communism and disorder.

The vote was more a referendum on ending war and domestic disorder than on supporting specific features of the new regime. The liberal and conservative nationalists balked once Versailles was in effect, and once they realized that they would be ruled by a coalition whose senior partner was the despised SPD. They then rallied in 1920 to the two nationalist parties, the DNVP and the DVP, that had stood for God, Reich, and privilege, not necessarily in that order.

By 6 June 1920 the Weimar coalition had declined to 61.4 percent, and by 4 May 1924—the raging inflation had much to do with the result—the parties supporting the Republic received 39.6 percent of the vote. This implies that already by 1924 more than 47.8 percent of the

German electorate voted for parties like the DVP or the DNVP, which were at best ambivalent, or the Nazis and the Communists that were radically opposed to liberal democracy.

For a brief period between 1924 and 1930, the Weimar coalition experienced a mild resurgence, but after the election of September 1930—held near the start of the Great Depression—the forces of the Republic continued their decline. The apparent decline of the coalition's fortunes is a fair indicator of the delegitimation of the Republic itself, since with only slight exception support for the Weimar coalition was a measure of the backing for parliamentary democracy as such.

Class Polarization

An indirect measure of the progressive polarization by class in German society can be seen in the electoral fortunes of the middle-class parties, the DDP, the DVP, and the DNVP. What is quite apparent from table 6.1 is the rapid decline and collapse of the DDP—the only middle-class party that had unambiguously stood for Weimar democracy. Thus, in 1919, the DDP received a solid 18.6 percent of the vote. This was significant because the Democrats (DDP) were the successors of the old Progressives and staunch supporters of the Republic. They alone among the parties of the Weimar coalition might have made a claim on the allegiance of the Protestant middle class. By 1920, support for the DDP had been more than halved, and the party received a mere 8.3 percent of the vote, a bad sign for the Republic.

At the same time that the DDP was declining, the DVP and the DNVP, the parties of middle-class liberal and conservative nationalism and anti-Republicanism, were making a comeback. Together they surged from 14.7 percent to 28.8 of the vote. This suggests that already, by 1920, the German middle and upper classes had abandoned or were in the process of abandoning the Republic. The DDP declined still further in subsequent elections, nearly disappearing as a viable party after 1932.

With the failure of the DDP to reach out to the Protestant middle and upper classes, the political divisions of Imperial Germany reappeared under Weimar but in a much more intensified and dangerous form. Whereas in the *Kaiserreich*, the Protestant middle and upper classes were the principal backers of the regime, under Weimar they became among the most uncompromising foes of the new Republic. The DNVP could never bring itself to cooperate with the parties of the Weimar coalition, especially not the hated SPD.

Based on the old Conservative party, the DKP, and the right-wing of the National Liberal party, the DNVP presented itself as the core of the nationalist and right-wing opposition to Weimar. However, like the old DKP, it was limited in its appeal to the *Bauern und Beamten*, the peasants, officials, and notables, the rural and upper-class segments of German society. Despite its cultivating the stab-in-the-back legend, and despite its appeals to *Völkisch* and antisemitic clubs that proliferated in Germany after the war, the DNVP was limited in its popular attraction. Its reputation as the party of the Junkers and the upper classes prevented the DNVP from becoming a mass party strong enough to challenge first the SPD and later the Nazis.

The position of the DVP was more ambiguous and ambivalent. After 1922, under Stresemann the party did enter the republican coalition. The majority of its members, however, did so quite grudgingly— only because they supported their leader, not because they believed in the Republic.[42] Stresemann himself participated in the Weimar coalition and was one of its outstanding foreign ministers, but he did so less out of love of democracy as out of fear that if left to its own devices the SPD would become radicalized. This was the reason why he opposed an alliance with the DNVP. When Stresemann passed away in 1929, and Ernst Scholtz became its leader, the party moved inexorably to the right.[43]

Thus from 1920 until 1930 the Weimar Republic was uncertainly poised between a coalition that supported her and a group of conservative nationalist parties that were either opposed outright to the experiment in parliamentary democracy or gave it their grudging allegiance. After 1930, the opposition and ambivalence of the middle-class supporters of Weimar resolved itself by a precipitous radicalization of views and a shift of support from the conservative and liberal nationalists to the revolutionary nationalists, that is, the Nazis.

Radicalization

While the DNVP detested Weimar and the DVP would have preferred a constitutional monarchy, they had no program that would do away with socialist and liberal democracy, and their elitist leadership and views limited their appeal largely to the upper and middle classes. Indeed, at the inception of the Republic the revolutionary threat seemed to come from the left, first from the Spartakists and then from the Communists (KPD). In 1920 the Communists received 589,500 votes, representing 2.1 percent of the total, or four deputies out of 459 in the Reichstag. It was still too early for the Nazis to make their bid.

By 1924 the threat to the democratic regime was apparent both from the left and the right. The KPD received 3,693,300 votes or 12.6 percent of the total, which translated into sixty-two deputies in a Reichstag of 472 representatives. At the same time the Nazis received 1,918,300 votes, 6.5 percent of the total, or thirty-two deputies. From this brief sketch one can see that already in 1924 the two revolutionary parties that not only rejected Weimar but favored a revolutionary transformation of society received the support of 19.1 percent of the electorate. Nearly one out of five Germans who went to the polls in 1924 appeared to vote for revolution. The rest underestimated the danger or were afraid of radical change.

Between May 1924 and September 1930 the politics of the Weimar republic appeared to stabilize. The Weimar coalition of SPD, Center, and DDP continued to receive more than 40 percent of the vote, while its conservative, nationalist, and middle-class opposition could rely on 20–30 percent of the vote. Meanwhile, having apparently peaked in 1924, the revolutionary parties, the Communists and the Nazis, declined in their appeal. But in retrospect we know that this brief period of calm and recovery between the inflation and the Great Depression was misleading.

After a year of experiencing both the ravages of the Great Depression and the inability of the Republic to deal with the economic and political crisis, many Germans turned to the revolutionary alternatives, the KPD and the Nazis. In the end, it was the Nazis who triumphed. On 14 September 1930 the Nazis received 18.3 percent of the vote, and with the KPD the two revolutionary parties represented 31.4 percent of the electorate, or 184 deputies in a *Reichstag* of 577 representatives.

To a large extent it was the collapse of the middle and upper class, conservative and liberal nationalist (DNVP and DVP), alternative to Weimar that accounted for the dramatic shift in the fortunes of the Nazis. Whereas in the previous election the conservative and liberal nationalists received 22.9 percent of the vote, on 14 September 1930 they received only 11.5 percent. This was an absolute reduction of 11.4 percent and a relative reduction of 49.8 percent in the level of support. The Weimar coalition also lost support, though not at the rate of the conservative nationalists. By comparison, the Weimar coalition declined from 46.8 percent in 1928 to 40.1 percent in 1930.

One also can see the divisive role played by the KPD at this juncture in Weimar's history. Had the Communists been willing to cooperate with the Weimar coalition, even at this late date it might have been able to present a solid working class–moderate democratic front to the right. But, tragically, Weimar lacked legitimacy not only on the right but also on the left. The KPD tactically cooperated with the Nazis in destroying the democratic regime which it called "Social Fascist."[44] The unfortunate KPD slogan was "the worse the better." It suggested that, once Weimar collapsed, a revolution would ensue that would bring the Communists to power.[45] The German revolution intensified and radicalized, but ultimately it was not the German working class but the Red Army that brought the KPD to power.

But the major point is not that the conservative nationalist alternative declined more sharply than the Weimar coalition, though it did, nor is it that the Communists helped to bury Weimar, though they did. The point is that by September 1930 many Germans, especially nationalist middle-class Germans, did not see the DNVP and the DVP as viable alternatives to the Weimar Republic. Believing themselves to be in a revolutionary situation, they flocked to the party that would destroy a despised democracy, prevent Communist takeover, restore German glory, and punish Germany's enemies. That party was the Nazi NSDAP. By the election of July 1932, the Nazis received 37.4 percent of the vote. With 230 deputies they had become the largest party in the *Reichstag*.

No doubt the Great Depression and the Republic's inability to deal with it was the precipitating crisis that enabled the Nazis to come to power. Nevertheless it should be noted that other democracies besides Weimar also experienced the economic crisis without a political collapse.[46] What enabled the Great Depression to become the precipitating crisis—the rolling boulder that started the avalanche—was the deeply divided nature of German society.

The electoral process had paid off for Hitler. He could now claim that he was legitimately available to be named chancellor. Due to the machinations of conservative politicians like Franz von Papen, who thought that they could use him as a front man, on 30 January 1933 Hitler became chancellor. The Nazis were on the brink of destroying democracy and of implementing those policies that were in a short time to culminate in the Holocaust.

In this interpretation of the rise of the Nazi party, much has been made of the illegitimacy of Weimar and the deep-seated class divisions of Germany, but very little has been said about antisemitism. Yet Hitler was profoundly if not pathologically antisemitic, and the party made no secret about what it thought of the Jews. Was it not the case as some writers have suggested that it was Nazi ideology with its *Völkisch* appeals and antisemitism that played a primary role in the rise of the Nazis to power?

Antisemitism and Other Sources of Nazi Support

To understand the role antisemitism played in the Nazi seizure of power one needs to distinguish the central beliefs of the party's inner circle—principally that of Hitler and his coterie—from those of the party's other members and supporters. Although we shall examine Hitler's ideology more fully in Chapter 7, there can be no doubt that he was a fanatical, even a psychotic, antisemite. Thus antisemitism was at the very core of the belief system that kept him functioning as an apparently normal personality and drove him to seek power.[47] It was principally he who transformed the insignificant German Workers' party (DAP) into the revolutionary antisemitic NSDAP. In Hitler's mind the struggle against Weimar and world Jewry were the same thing. Other Nazi leaders who came along later "simply accepted anti-Semitism as part of the baggage of Nazism—in the bargain for other things."[48]

Beyond the importance that antisemitism may have played for Hitler himself, dating back to Imperial Germany, the antisemitic movement initiated and carried forward into the Weimar period a populist and revolutionary tradition that, unlike its Marxist counterpart, had its basis—at first insignificant—in the middle classes. Men like Marr, Bernhard Förster, Fritsch, and Class hated the *Kaiserreich* because it tolerated the Jews. The imperial regime was unwilling to repeal emancipation, and in their view it was apparently blind to the Jews' supposed bid to dominate Germany and the world.

As noted before, the antisemitic revolutionaries had no chance of coming to power under the conditions prevailing in Imperial Germany. But under Weimar those conditions changed dramatically. No longer were the revolutionary antisemites or their successors attempting to topple a legitimate regime that had broad support in the upper and middle classes. The Weimar Republic was the child of military defeat whose support came mainly from the working class and the hated SPD. This radical transformation presented the revolutionary antisemites with vistas of opportunity that their predecessors could only have imagined.

Thus the revolutionary antisemites led by Hitler created the core of the radical and intransigent opposition to Weimar on the right. To this core they were able to attract followers whose primary reasons for joining may not have been antisemitism, but who, through a process of socialization and indoctrination, became antisemites as well. "[Germans] were drawn to anti-Semitism because they were drawn to Nazism, not the other way around."[49] According to this interpretation, therefore, the

Nazis did not come to power because they rode the crest of a wave of popular antisemitism. To the contrary, the early Nazis—Hitler above all—created a revolutionary party on the right that attracted followers for many reasons, antisemitism being one of these. As will be seen in Chapter 7, however, once Hitler's followers had joined the party, antisemitism in time became their political creed as well.

This does not imply that antisemitism was incidental to the rise of a revolutionary party on the right in Germany. Without its antisemitic core a right-wing revolutionary opposition to Weimar might not have developed, or had it emerged it is unlikely that its policies would have culminated in the Final Solution. For example, in Italy a fascist party appeared under similar circumstances to those in Germany without being antisemitic. [50]

Although the principal reason for the formation of the NSDAP in Hitler's mind may have been antisemitism, its success as an electoral party did not derive mainly from its reputation as a movement that hated Jews and wanted to do them in. Its main attraction was its revolutionary opposition to Weimar and communism at a time when Germany had become polarized on the basis of class and political divisions.

In addition to being drawn to the party by a hatred for the Republic, many Germans were also attracted by its promise to transcend ordinary political and class divisions and to create a genuine German community. Here the role of Hitler's charismatic persona played an essential role. All this is said not to minimize the role of antisemitism but to place it in context as one factor—indeed, not the most important one—out of the many that drew Germans to join and to support the Nazi party.

Hatred of the Republic

Further evidence and one of the earliest sources for the view that Germans joined and supported the Nazis more out of a hatred for the Republic than out of antisemitism is the work of Abel. [51] Based on an analysis of 681 life histories of Nazis that he collected in 1932, Abel came to the conclusion that his average respondent "was strongly dissatisfied with the republican regime in Germany, but had no specific anti-Semitic bias." [52] Merkl and Gordon who reworked the data in a more precise manner were less emphatic than Abel, but they also came to the conclusion that it was not primarily antisemitism that had led the early Nazis to join the party.

Thus they both agree that out of a subsample of 440 respondents 33.3 percent gave no evidence that they were antisemitic; 14.3 indicated that their bias was limited to mild verbal projections and party clichés. Some 39.5 percent were "moderate" in their antisemitism, and the rest, 12.9 percent, were "paranoid" in that they threatened active countermeasures against Jews.[53] However one evaluates Abel's sample, it is surprising that in 1932 so few active Nazis, including members of the SA and SS, evinced a fanatic antisemitism, and that one out of three respondents did not even mention antisemitism in his autobiography.[54]

Abel noted that the most influential item of Nazi propaganda, to which nearly all of his respondents reacted with affirmation, was the attack on the state and the existing social order.[55] It was the revolutionary message with its promise to "fight to the death" against the Republic and all it represented, including "defeat" and "Marxism," that drove 69.1 percent of Abel's sample to enter politics and to join the party in the prewar years.[56]

They hated the Republic because they viewed it as betraying Imperial Germany, fomenting the November Revolution and acquiescing to the hated Versailles treaties. Thus one of Abel's respondents reported that on the ninth of November 1918, by chance, he happened to get caught in a revolutionary crowd. Being still a mere boy, he was wearing a cap with a red, white, and black cockade, the colors of the imperial regime. "I had just entered the Burgstrasse, when two men approached me tore the cap from my head and boxed my ears. The cockade was deemed sufficient provocation . . . the bitter resentment of that moment made a lasting impression on me."[57]

Another respondent who had been active in suppressing the Spartakist revolt remarked:

> All we knew was that the government was in the hands of unknown, obscure, men who could not possibly win popular support, since all their measures so far only invited further disaster. Ebert, Bauer, Muller, Noske and the rest . . . simply did not register with us, and we silently hoped for a new leader.[58]

A war veteran commented:

> There was no point of contact with the men in power. For they had banished the glorious old black-white-and-red banner and substituted a flag in its place that meant nothing to the front fighters. What became of the memory of the dead? Their blood called to high Heaven for vengeance! Then came light in the darkness. . . . In 1923 we heard the name Adolf Hitler for the first time.[59]

Positive Aspects of the Nazi Appeal

These early Nazis were not only repelled by the political and social order and attracted to the party because it seemed to be the most uncompromising and radical force against the hated Republic, they were drawn to it for other reasons as well. Among these, according to Abel, were the call to national unity that transcended class, the authoritarian structure of the party and the flight from individual responsibility and freedom that it promised, love for Hitler as the führer, and the relative classlessness and openness to talent that characterized Nazi recruitment and promotion policies. This last feature of the party goes a long way in explaining why it was more popular and successful than its competitors on the antidemocratic, nationalist, and antisemitic right.

Gemeinschaft and unity were a major source of the ideological appeal of the Nazis. Thus a respondent commented:

> Seldom was our people united and great. But whenever it was strongly united it was unconquerable. This then is the secret of our idea, and in it lies the power of National Socialism: Unity is the goal of our leader, who wants to make the people strong, so it can be powerful again. [60]

Many respondents were shocked by the pluralism and the openness of Weimar democracy and they hoped for a strong leader. Thus a Nazi high school teacher wrote,

> Around 1923, I reached the conclusion that no party, but a single man alone could save Germany. This opinion was shared by others, for when the cornerstone of a monument was laid in my hometown, the following lines were inscribed on it: "Descendants who read these words, know ye that we eagerly await the coming of the man whose strong hand may restore order." [61]

Hitler's charisma and the love he evoked cannot be overestimated.

We, oldtime National Socialists, did not join the S.A. for reasons of self-interest. Our feelings led us to Hitler. There was a tremendous surge in our hearts, something that said: "Hitler, you are our man. You speak as a soldier of the front; you know the grind, you have yourself been a working man. You have lain in the mud, even as we—no big shot, but an unknown soldier. You have given your whole being, all your warm heart, to German manhood, for the well-being of Germany rather than your personal advancement or self-seeking. For your innermost being will not do otherwise." No one who has ever looked Hitler in the eye and heard him speak can ever break away from him.[62]

Why the Nazis and Not Some Other Opposition Parties?

The main reasons why other parties and organizations on the right like DNVP, the *Stahlhelm*, the *Thule Gesellschaft*, or the *Schutz-und-Trutzbund* could not compete with the Nazis was their hidebound and caste-ridden organizations. The Nazis were innovative and open to talent. They had the reputation of taking in dynamic people wherever they could find them, even among the lower classes, and giving them positions of responsibility.[63]

In a society deeply divided by class, indeed polarized by it, Nazi classlessness was a matter of principle. A party that made its appeals on the basis of German nationalism and which explicitly denounced upper-class arrogance and lower-class resentment had its advantages. This explains, as Hamilton and Childers have shown, that although the party had far wider support among the middle and upper classes, it also found backing in the working class, and by 1930 it had become a genuine mass party. This was the kind of broad appeal that middle-class parties like the conservative DNVP simply could not duplicate.[64]

Thus, for example, one of Abel's respondents who had first joined the DNVP but later switched to the Nazis reported: "After some good work at the outset, the spirit of caste and class came more and more to the fore of the German National Party. I did not find there the thing I had sought. The gentlemen were ready enough to be Germans and nationalists, but they lacked the courage for socialism."[65] Another respondent who had joined the *Wehrwolf*, a nationalist youth group, as a young man reported that "the power of class prejudice was inescapably evident."[66] He cited this as one of the reasons for leaving the youth group and later joining the Nazis where presumably such class prejudice was absent.

Abel remarked that the bogus synthesis of nationalism and socialism concocted by the Nazis was a public relations trick of the first magnitude, a "stroke of genius."[67] It was a synthesis that

> [g]ave to the Hitler movement the broadest possible basis of appeal to the German public, which was composed, for the most part of nationalists who for social reasons refused to identify themselves with the privilege—seeking conservative party, and of socialists who for national reasons were opposed to the international doctrines of the Marxists.[68]

One of Abel's Nazis, a former veteran, explained that in the party he saw an "uncompromising will to stamp out the class struggle, snobberies of caste, and party hatreds. The movement bore the true message of socialism to the German workingman."[69]

Thus in the Abel study as reworked by Merkl and Gordon one finds further confirmation for the thesis that the principal appeals of Nazism, especially in its electoral phase, were not based on antisemitism. This is an important point because it demonstrates that historical and structural factors, above all the collapse of Imperial Germany and the revolutionary interregnum that followed it, must be included alongside ideology in any etiology of the Holocaust.

Nazism was a reaction to parliamentary democracy, which it found profoundly illegitimate, and to the deep social and political cleavages of German society following industrialization in the nineteenth century and defeat in the Great War. In that sense it resembled fascism, which was a European-wide phenomenon in the interwar period. What distinguished Nazis from other fascists was their racism and fanatical antisemitism.

Nazism, Fascism, and the "Extremism of the Middle"

Our interpretation of the rise of Nazism has been heavily influenced by Bracher. As such it differs in some of its emphases from a classic explanation of Lipset and from those of other writers like Linz who subsume the Nazi movement under fascism.[70] It might help to understand the explanation offered here by comparing it briefly to those of Lipset and Linz.

In his earlier study Lipset interpreted National Socialism as a variation of fascism, and he traced the rise of fascist movements to middle-class extremism likely to occur "in countries characterized by both large-scale capitalism and a powerful labor movement."[71] He characterized fascism as the "extremism of the middle."[72]

In this view the middle and lower-middle classes—the small entrepreneurs, the small farmers, the civil servants, and the professionals—are seen as having once stood for liberal principles of personal freedom and occupations open to talent, in opposition to European societies still dominated by feudalism and aristocratic privilege. Politically this manifested itself in a commitment to parliamentary democracy and opposition to autocracy. Once European societies had emerged from feudalism into capitalism, however, and had been transformed by industrialization, the middle classes began to experience "stratification strains."[73]

As European societies industrialized, both powerful big business interests and organized working classes arose. The developments of later capitalism challenged the status positions, economic interests, and political power of the old middle classes and made them question their earlier commitment to parliamentary democracy and modernity.[74] These then were some of the historical and structural preconditions of populist and fascist movements that found their social bases mostly in the middle classes.

> These movements answer some of the same needs as the more conventional liberal parties; they are an outlet for the stratification strains of the middle class in a mature industrial order. But while liberalism attempts to cope with the problems by legitimate social changes and "reforms" . . . fascism and populism propose to solve the problems by taking over the state and running it in a way which will restore the old middle classes' economic security and high standing in society, and at the same time reduce the power and status of big capital and big labor.[75]

In this interpretation Lipset differed from a standard Marxist explanation, which views fascism as a crisis of monopoly capitalism and imperialism.[76] He suggested that neither big business nor the old aristocracy were particularly attracted to Nazism until late in the game when the Nazis had become a major party and it was opportune to do so.

Thus in an analysis of electoral support for the NSDAP in the Weimar period, 1928–33, he pointed with special emphasis to the virtual collapse of the DDP, the DVP, and the *Wirtschaftspartei*. These were the classic middle-class and liberal parties. The ratio of their 1928 vote to the second 1932 vote was .21 while that of the SPD for example was .69, the conservative DNVP was .60, and the Nazis was 12.77! Such figures may suggest that it was the relative weakness of the liberal parties and the propensity of the middle classes to be attracted to fascist movements that explained the rise of the Nazis.

In this interpretation it was the extremist middle that supported the Nazis. The organized working class was opposed, but then the aristocratic upper class was also an enemy of Nazism. The first wanted to establish socialism, and the second yearned to restore the monarchy. According to Lipset, therefore, the supporters of the conservative upper-class DNVP should either not have supported the Nazis, or not have gone over to them as quickly as the supporters of the middle-class liberal parties.[77] On closer analysis, however, it would seem that the distinction between the rate of defections from the DNVP, the DVP, and the DDP is a spurious one. By the 1930s both the conservative nationalist and the liberal parties were losing members to the Nazis, though the aristocratic core may have clung to the DNVP somewhat longer.[78]

It may be suggested that viewing Nazism as an instance of the "extremism of the middle," as Lipset did, placed too much stress on the social bases of the Nazi movement and too little on the political crisis of Weimar and the political history of the German party system. Much of the opposition to the Weimar Republic derived from the manner in which it was founded. The feeling that the Republic lacked legitimacy, that it was not truly German, was not limited to the middle class. It was shared quite intensely by aristocratic and upper-class supporters of the DNVP and even, for example, by former veterans whose social background may have been working class but who thought that Germany had been betrayed by the democratic republic.[79]

As noted above and discussed in Chapter 4, the history of the German party system as it emerged under Bismarck was characterized by a deep political division between the SPD, on the one hand, and the liberal and conservative parties, on the other. There was a tradition of antagonism between these parties that transcended class conflict. For the middle and upper classes, liberals and conservatives, the SPD was beyond the pale. It was an enemy of the empire and of Germany. To have that party become the principal partner in a postwar coalition that ruled Germany and to have to submit to it was simply intolerable.

As Hamilton and Childers note, upper-class conservatives and even sections of the working class were attracted to the Nazis, not on socioeconomic grounds alone but on political grounds. Indeed, for some sectors of the population the political reasons might have outweighed the socioeconomic ones for supporting the Nazis. "Better a revolution from the right than Weimar democracy," seems to have been a feeling that transcended class and affected even the upper crust of the DNVP and lower sections of the working class.

Thus the Nazis were not simply an expression of middle class or lower-middle-class alienation. Like other fascist movements they were relative latecomers to the electoral party scene, and for that reason alone they had to make cross-class appeals to be successful.[80] But more significantly, they were a revolutionary party whose basic aim was the destruction of what was felt to be an illegitimate democratic regime. For that task they were eager to enlist anyone who would help. As it turned out, they found a more enthusiastic response among the Protestant middle class than among other sections and segments of society, but their appeal was not limited to that class alone.[81]

Keeping in mind the above discussion, one may agree in large part with Linz's assessment of Nazism as a fascist movement that had important parallels to other such movements in parts of post–World War I Europe.

> Fascism was the novel response to the crisis—profound or temporary—of the pre-war social structure and party system and to the emergence of new institutional arrangements as a result of war and post-war dislocations. It would be particularly acute in defeated nations . . . and those countries where the crisis led to unsuccessful revolutionary attempts. Fascism would be a counterrevolutionary response led by a revolutionary elite . . . we could define fascism as a party of revolutionaries linked with the middle classes of city and/or countryside.[82]

Our one qualification to this assessment would be to characterize Nazism as a revolutionary movement in its own right, rather than simply a counterrevolutionary response to a failed revolution on the left. It was revolutionary both because it came to power in the wake of revolutionary forces and, as will be discussed more fully in Chapter 7, because its imperialism and antisemitism propelled it in the direction of world conquest and genocide.

Conclusion

The structural and historical conditions that made it possible for the Nazis to reach power and later to implement the Final Solution were the deeply riven and polarized nature of the German political system and class structure. This portentous split in the Weimar period had its origins in Germany's defeat following the Great War and in the class and party cleavages of Bismarck's Imperial Germany.

As noted in Chapter 4, when Bismarck realized that his creation, the imperial system protecting the German elite, could not encompass and subdue the working class nor accommodate the SPD, he turned against the workers' party and stigmatized it as an "enemy of the Empire." The liberals, who since 1866 had willingly compromised with Prussian power in order to ensure German unification, followed suit. They, too, treated the working class and the SPD as pariahs and beyond the ken of normal political discourse. Unlike the English working class, for example, that found support and room for inclusion both in the Tory and

Liberal parties, the German working class was excluded by the German Conservatives, the National Liberals, and the Progressives.

In response, and especially after its banishment in 1878, the SPD became increasingly centered on the working class alone and saw itself at war with the rest of German society. Though in time, and especially with the emergence of revisionism, the party muted its Marxist message and came to accept democratic procedure, its rhetoric and symbolism continued to be revolutionary and threatening to the middle and upper classes. This was the situation even before Weimar.

The Weimar Republic was the child of defeat and a failed uprising from the left, which has been misleadingly called the "German revolution." This, however, was but an episode in a longer process of revolutionary transformation that culminated in the rise and fall of Nazism. For the middle and upper classes, and indeed for all Germans who did not side with the SPD, parliamentary democracy was viewed as an illegitimate creation of their international and domestic enemies. Thus after the Great War the aversion of many Germans to the working class and to the SPD was both intensified and transferred to the government itself.

By 1919 half of Germany hated the other half and detested the Republic which had replaced their beloved *Kaiserreich*. When the Great Depression descended, Germany began to polarize along its class and political axes. It was this polarization, not antisemitism, that was the major legacy of the Bismarck era and the defeat following the Great War. It was their ability to exploit the revolutionary interregnum of the interwar period that allowed the Nazis to come to power.

Though at first they tried to come to power by means of a violent putsch, the Nazis discovered that their way was blocked by the army. It was when they set out on the path of "legal revolution" via elections that their efforts met with unexpected success. By the time of the Depression they were viewed by many Germans as the party that would destroy the hated Weimar Republic and bridge the political and class cleavages dividing German society. It was on this basis that the Nazis found widespread support especially among the upper and middle classes, but even sections of the working class were not immune to their appeals.

We have suggested that antisemitism played a minor role in convincing Germans to join or to vote for the Nazi party, but this does not imply that antisemitism played a marginal role in the phenomenon of Nazism. Fear and hatred of Jews based on the theory of the world-Jewish-conspiracy was at the core of Nazi ideology and had at least a twofold impact.

Dating back to Imperial Germany, popular antisemitism allowed for the expression and organization of revolutionary antisemitism. This enabled Hitler to transform the DAP into the revolutionary NSDAP whose core beliefs were antisemitic. All this could be done without outraging German public opinion which was mainly ambivalent and mute on the Jewish question. While popular Jew-hatred alone did not bring the Nazis to power, those Germans who supported and voted for the NSDAP— even if it was not primarily out of Jew-hatred—helped to install a radical antisemitic party, headed by a pathological antisemite, at the head of Germany.

Some writers argue that even during the war years most Germans were not swayed by the Nazi version of antisemitism.[83] Their sin, it has been said, was one of omission rather than of commission: they were largely indifferent to the fate of their Jewish neighbors. However, "indifference" may be an unfortunate term if it implies that Germans had no views about the Jewish question.

Indifference can also be a by-product of division of views, of an ambivalence about the Jews and what to do about them. It may be suggested that antipathy to Jews was widely spread throughout Germany, but antisemitism as a theory of how the world worked, that is, as an ideology, was limited to a small coterie whose most passionate exponent was Hitler himself. When antisemites captured power and began to implement their policies, the anti-Judaism and Jew-hatred of most Germans prevented them from protesting. Thus, for genocide to have taken place, it was not necessary that most Germans be antisemites in the sense of believing Nazi ideology. It was enough for most non-Jews to dislike the Jews, to judge them as not being truly German, in order for the Nazis to carry out their murderous plans in the name of Germany.

Once the Nazis had reached power they could set their sights on two principal policies. These were the substitution of racialism and antisemitism for liberalism and socialism as myths of legitimation binding Germany to the Third Reich, and the conquest of a new German Empire, especially in the East. The implementation of these two policies implied, first implicitly and then with greater clarity, a third policy, namely, the "Final Solution to the Jewish Question." Thus what commenced as a domestic revolution against the Jews culminated—using Dawidowicz's pregnant phrase—in a world war against them.[84] Such were some of the structural and ideological origins of the Holocaust.

SEVEN

The Revolution and
the War against the Jews

A person is to be regarded as non-Aryan if he is descended
from non-Aryan, especially Jewish, parents or grandparents. . . . If Aryan descent is doubtful, an opinion must be obtained from the expert on racial research attached to the
Reich Ministry of the Interior.[1]

Then for the first time we became aware that our language
lacks words to express this offense, the demolition of a man.
Primo Levi.[2]

In Chapter 6 we discussed how the revolutionary polarization of
Weimar Germany enabled the Nazis to ascend to state power. In this
chapter our attention will shift to the issue of how this power was converted into an anti-Jewish policy that culminated in the Final Solution.
Throughout this chapter we shall be guided by the insight that the Nazis
were a revolutionary regime, and that their ideology as well as their policies—including the Final Solution—were dynamically related to the
exigencies of a revolutionary situation.

As noted in the Introduction, genocide like other public policies is
a product both of the intentions of the perpetrators and the structural
conditions enabling intentions to be translated into policy. The intentions of the perpetrators may be inferred in part from their ideologies,
while the structural conditions making for total domestic genocide may
be derived from the revolutionary situation occurring between the fall of
an old regime and the institutionalization of a new one.

Revolutions may create conditions for total domestic genocide by destroying the old regime's system of legitimation, the political myth linking state to society. When a revolutionary vanguard comes to power after the fall of an old regime, it must create a new system of legitimation and thereby reconstitute the political community. In doing so, the revolutionaries are likely to exclude certain groups and classes, labeling them as "enemies of the revolution," and it is these collectivities that are in danger of repression. The probability that repression may turn to genocide increases substantially when (1) the revolution leads to war, transforming the "enemies of the revolution" into "a deadly plot against state and society"; (2) the excluded communities included poorly integrated "problem" groups under the old regime; and (3) other options for eliminating "the deadly plot" are seen as impossible or too costly to implement.

Thus it was seen in Chapter 5 that after the fall of the old regime of Sultan Abdul Hamid there existed a revolutionary situation in the Ottoman Empire which brought to power the Young Turks and destroyed Pan-Islam, the political myth of the old regime. Between 1908 and 1912, the Young Turks tried to substitute a new system of legitimation based on Ottomanism and an inclusive Ottoman identity, but that also failed after the drastic military defeats of the period. After the failure of Pan-Islam and Ottomanism, the radicals of the Committee of Union and Progress turned to a narrow xenophobic Turkish nationalism and Pan-Turkism. They took the opportunity of the Great War both to attack Russia and to destroy the Armenians whom they perceived as constituting a "mortal threat."

As indicated in the introduction to Part Two of this book, a similar but not equivalent march of events occurred in Germany. Imperial Germany was defeated in war, and the institutions of political legitimation that had sustained the *Kaiserreich* were destroyed. The Weimar Republic that followed in the old regime's wake was unsuccessful in gaining support for itself, though Communist, Socialist, liberal-democratic, and even conservative alternatives presented themselves. After some years of instability and intensifying polarization between the champions and the enemies of a democratic republic, her enemies emerged victorious.

When the Nazis came to power in 1933 they had a unique opportunity to institutionalize a new system of legitimation and to reconstitute the German political community. They also aspired to create a new German empire in the East that would rival the British empire and to undo the humiliation of the Great War. Their opportunities to come to power and act on their wishes had been created for them by Germany's revolutionary instability following the fall of the *Kaiserreich* and the polarization of Weimar. Guided by their ideology of racialist antisemitism they set to their task with a vengeful energy. Ostensibly, they wanted to create a Third Reich that would last a thousand years and would base itself on the authentic political community of the "Aryans."

The Nazis were guided by a political myth that included elements of racialism, antisemitism, imperialism, and millenarianism. According to this view, a uniquely good and gifted biological collectivity called the "Aryans" were destined to rule the earth for a thousand years, but they were opposed in this venture by a singularly wicked race called the "Jews." By manipulating political and economic power, the Jews dominated the Aryans in Germany. Moreover, by controlling Bolshevik Russia the Jewish world conspiracy was preventing the Aryans from expanding eastward and achieving the requisite *Lebensraum* (living space) and empire that would assure their well-being.

It followed that German identity and the German political community needed to be radically transformed by including the Aryans and excluding the Jews. By the same token, the Jewish world conspiracy and Bolshevik Russia needed to be defeated in order that the Aryans might thrive. Thus was the ideology of Nazi racial antisemitism and imperialism tailored to the domestic and international aims of a revolutionary regime. Once the Nazis came to power, this tale, as it became ever more widely believed, especially as the political creed of the Nazi party and its offshoots, went a long way toward establishing some of the necessary conditions for the Final Solution. Hitler may not have come to power because of antisemitism alone, but it was antisemitism which was the guiding ideology once the Nazis were the overlords of the Third Reich.

But who were the "Aryans" upon which so much depended? Except for nebulous linguistic and racialist theories, they turned out to be none other than those German burghers, and others, who happened not to be Jewish. Indeed, the Nazis used the exclusion and ultimately the destruction of those whom they labeled as "the enemies of the revolution" to reconstitute the authentic political community and to create an empire. This does not necessarily imply, as some intentionalist arguments would have it, that when they first came to power the Nazis intended to exterminate the Jews and that they had a plan for doing so. It does suggest, however, that once antisemitism became the regime's political creed a process of radicalization set in which culminated in the Final Solution.

Thus antisemitism was no mere *folie* of Hitler's nor was the Final Solution a sideshow of the Third Reich. Racialism and genocide were the very essence of that system.

A regime's articulation of a new political myth is not the same as its formulation and implementation of a public policy. To analyze how a revolutionary vanguard in power comes to formulate and act on its public policies, it is important to specify not only its ideological intent and the political myth that it tries to institutionalize but also the means it uses and the domestic and international contexts shaping its actions. In most instances, ideological intent must compromise with its policy environment, in others it can overcome obstacles, and in a few situations the environment itself facilitates the formulation of uncompromising and radical solutions.

Some of the contextual factors that intervened between a generalized conception of Nazi ideology as formulated by Hitler and the Final Solution as implemented by the regime were (1) the requisites of a revolutionary party's consolidating power in the domestic and international arenas; (2) German preparation for imperialist war, and that war itself; and (3) the exigencies of ruling over conquered populations. From this brief list it can be seen that the Final Solution, like the Armenian Genocide before it, was a public policy whose aims and means were derived in part from ideological principles and in part from the structural requisites of consolidating power and conducting a world war.

This chapter will trace the crooked path that led from the seizure of power by a movement articulating Hitler's political creed of racialist antisemitism to the regime's implementation of the Final Solution.

Nazi Ideology

Like nationalism and Pan-Turkism for the Young Turks, millenarian racialist antisemitism provided the Nazis with a conceptual framework with which to understand their time and to fight their battles. This was a revolutionary doctrine which (1) identified the Aryans as the legitimate political community for the Nazi regime; (2) targeted the Jews as the principal domestic and international enemy of the Nazi state and Aryan society; and (3) formulated domestic and international goals, chief among these making Germany *judenrein* and creating a new racial empire. This would entail the destruction of the Soviet Union, which was in effect also the seat of the world Jewish conspiracy. Thus a domestic program set the stage for a radical foreign policy: first a revolution against the Jews in Germany and then a war against them in Russia. Nazi ideology was articulated in Hitler's worldview, principally set down in *Mein Kampf*, and in the political creed of his followers.

Hitler's Worldview

Hitler turned antisemitism into an effective political doctrine in a revolutionary period. It was noted in Chapters 3 and 4 that antisemitism as a political doctrine preceded Hitler. Publicists like Marr, Glagau, Dühring, Stoecker, Förster, and Fritsch in Germany, and Lueger and Schönerer in Austria articulated the doctrine that Jewish emancipation and assimilation were a grave danger. Most antisemites with few exceptions made the argument on racial grounds, and some like Fritsch and Class in Germany and Schönerer in Austria become revolutionaries against their respective imperial regimes. They concluded that only by way of a revolutionary transformation of state and society could the Jews be turned back and the Judaization of Germans be prevented. But it was Hitler who seized the moment of a revolutionary situation, creating out of racialist antisemitism the creed that would guide his regime's followers and lead to the Final Solution.

The Aryans: The Legitimate Political Community

Fundamental to Hitler's racialist antisemitic worldview was the notion that the human races were akin to animal species, that "nature" proscribes racial mixing, that the Aryans—so long as they remain pure—are the natural aristocracy of mankind, and that the Jews, because of their lust for power and drive to mix the races are the ineluctable enemy of the natural and moral order. According to the führer, should racial crossing occur—as the Jews desire—"[Nature's] whole work of higher breeding, over perhaps hundreds of thousands of years, might be ruined in one blow. . . . To bring about such a development is, then, nothing else but to sin against the will of the eternal creator."[3]

Among the human races, there is only one, the white, blond, and blue-eyed Aryans who are the creators of culture and civilization.

> All the human culture, all the results of art, science, and technology that we see before us today, are almost exclusively the creative product of the Aryan . . . [He] alone was the founder of all higher humanity, therefore representing the prototype of all that we understand by the word "man."[4]

History is characterized by a Darwinian struggle among the races of mankind for *Lebensraum* (living space) and domination. In the past, Aryans were able to conquer inferior races and turn them to their own uses, but in time they made the tragic mistake of breeding with those whom they had conquered, thereby polluting their own blood and reducing their own powers.

> After a thousand years and more, the last visible trace of the former master people is often seen in the lighter skin color which its blood left behind in the subjugated race, and in a petrified culture which it had originally created. For, once the actual and spiritual conqueror lost himself in the blood of the subjected people, the fuel for the torch of human progress was lost![5]

Thus it is of supreme importance that the remaining Aryans be aware of their *Rassenwert* (racial value) or *Blutwert* (blood value), and that they keep themselves from mixing with other races so that they might fulfill their destiny as the master race—the race that creates civilization and is destined to rule the world.[6]

From this analysis, it follows that the main task of the racialist state is not to represent the "people" or to maintain "law and order" in the manner of the decadent bourgeois liberal system, but to collect, preserve, and guard Aryan racial stock—"the most precious treasure for our future"—so that it might be able to fulfill its destiny in a master race.[7]

> *The German Reich as a state must embrace all Germans and has the task, not only of assembling and preserving the most valuable stocks of basic racial elements in this people, but slowly and surely raising them to a dominant position.*[8]

Hence it is the Aryans for whom the state exists and from whom it draws its legitimacy. All other segments of society are either expendable or enemies of the Aryan state.

Of supreme danger to the Aryans and hence to mankind are notions such as "brotherhood," "internationalism," "pacifism," "democracy," "parliamentarism," and "Marxism." All these creeds when they lead to action ultimately undermine the purity and power of the Aryans. Thus "brotherhood," "internationalism," and "Marxism" imply the equality of human beings and suggest that Aryans might safely interbreed with lower races; "pacifism" suggests that history is not about struggle and the victory of the stronger Aryans over the others; and "democracy" and "parliamentarism" work against the racialist conception which asserts that even among the Aryans there are those who are superior and should lead and those who are inferior and should follow. For the aristocracy of race, democracy, and parliamentarism substitute the mediocrity of mere numbers, thereby again weakening the potency and resolve of the Aryans.[9]

The Jews: The Enemies of the Aryans and of Mankind

Fundamental to Hitler's worldview was the racial antisemite's conception of the Jews as the eternal enemies of the Aryans.

> The mightiest counterpart to the Aryan is represented by the Jew. In hardly any people in the world is the instinct of self-preservation developed more strongly. . . . What people . . . has gone through greater upheavals than this one—and nevertheless issued from the mightiest catastrophes of mankind unchanged? What an infinitely tough will to live and preserve the species speaks from these facts.[10]

According to Hitler, the Jews are the eternal enemies of the Aryans because, at one and the same time, not having a land of their own, and yet being conscious of their separateness as a race, they manage to dominate other people. Indeed, they utilize the slogans of internationalism, pacifism, parliamentarism, democracy, and especially communism to undermine the resolve of the host nations and races, especially the Aryans. In this manner—like a bacillus invading a living body—they pursue their conquest.

> [The Jew's] ultimate goal is the denationalization, the promiscuous bastardization of other peoples, the lowering of the racial level of the highest peoples as well as the domination of this racial mishmash through the extirpation of the folkish intelligentsia and its replacement by the members of its own people.[11]

In the Nazi worldview, Jews were stigmatized by the use of two principal metaphors. They were, on the one hand, the masters of the world, the authors of *The Protocols of the Elders of Zion*, agents of a world Jewish conspiracy that controlled the thoughts and actions of Germany's bourgeois and Communist adversaries.[12] On the other hand, they were less than nothing. They were vermin, rodents, bacteria infecting Germany from within. Both metaphors—Jews viewed as manipulators of external enemies and as agents of internal decay and disease—represented them as the deadly and ineluctable enemy that needed to be destroyed so that Germany and the Aryans might live.

Thus, Jäckel noted that, according to Hitler,

[t]he revolution of 1918 and the entire Weimar Republic were Jewish; Marxism and the Soviet "dictatorship of blood" were Jewish; and, of course, high finance (*Börsenkapital*) were Jewish; the political parties of the left were "mercenaries of Jewry"; and finally democracy, parliaments, majority rule, and the League of Nations were all Jewish as well.[13]

Writing about the antisemitic passages in *Mein Kampf*, Jäckel was struck by what he called "a very peculiar vocabulary" derived from the realms of zoology and parasitology. Thus, according to Hitler,

The Jew is a maggot in a rotting corpse; he is a plague worse than the Black Death of former times; a germ carrier of the worst sort; mankind's eternal germ of disunion; the drone which insinuates its way into the rest of mankind; the spider that slowly sucks the people's blood out of its pores; the pack of rats fighting bloodily among themselves; the parasite in the body of other peoples; the typical parasite; a sponger who, like a harmful bacillus, continues to spread; the eternal bloodsucker; the people's parasite; the people's vampire.[14]

Jäckel notes ominously that the use of Hitler's language suggests the methods of the Jew's extermination.

Lebensraum and Empire

Hitler's racism dovetailed with his foreign policy. According to him human history was characterized by a Darwinian selection of the fittest races. In order for the Aryans to thrive they needed both to preserve their racial purity and to attain *Lebensraum*—living space, especially in the East. Bolshevik Russia, the seat of the world Jewish conspiracy that threatened Aryan racial purity and German independence, stood in the way of Aryan expansion. Hence a war against Russia was inevitable. As usual in his pronouncements, Hitler projected his most aggressive intentions onto his imagined enemies, the Jews.

It would be a catastrophic mistake, warned Hitler, for the Germans to assume that with the triumph of Nazism the danger of Communist revolution was over in Germany. The Jews had triumphed in Russia and were using communism (Bolshevism) as an instrument of world conquest.

[The] striving of the Jewish people for world domination, [is] a process which is just as natural as the urge of the Anglo-Saxon to seize the domination of the earth. . . . *In Russian Bolshevism we must see the attempt undertaken by the Jews in the twentieth century to achieve world domination. . . .* Germany is today the next great war aim of Bolshevism. [15]

Indeed, the war against Russia would be a holy war—a struggle of the forces of light against darkness—after which the Aryans would rule the world for a thousand years. Surprisingly, it was a holy war that the Aryans were assured of winning because, although the Jews can destroy civilization, they cannot create or defend it. Once the Jews came to rule Russia, she was ready for conquest by the Aryans. [16]

> By handing Russia to Bolshevism, it robbed the Russian nation of that intelligentsia which previously brought about and guaranteed its existence as a state. . . . *It has been replaced by the Jew* [my italics]. Impossible as it is for the Russian by himself to shake off the yoke of the Jew by his own resources, it is equally impossible for the Jew to maintain the mighty empire forever. He himself is no element of organisation, but a ferment of decomposition. . . . And the end of Jewish rule in Russia will also be the end of Russia as a state. We have been chosen by Fate as witnesses of a catastrophe which will be the mightiest confirmation of the soundness of the folkish theory. [17]

The role of Hitler's worldview, especially as it came to be formulated into a revolutionary doctrine steering domestic and foreign policy, can hardly be denied. There were other factors, however, that linked the timing of the Final Solution to the attack on Russia.

The Nazi Creed and Political Myth

As discussed in Chapter 6, when Hitler came to power on 30 January 1933 his main source of support was the mass of Germans who had turned their back on communism, socialism, liberalism, and even German conservatism. The failed war, Weimar's lack of legitimacy, and the economic crises preceding the Nazis' ascent to power created a revolutionary situation in which no ideology or political myth except a xenophobic nationalism had widespread support. At first it was Hitler's charisma, "The Hitler Myth," not his antisemitism, which served as the main legitimating link between the Third Reich and the German people. [18] At the same time it is true that widespread anti-Jewish sentiments and stereotypes existed in German society.

Initially, Hitler's ideology appealed mainly to a select group of Germans, especially the party activists and the SS, and elements in the state bureaucracy. Although they may have joined the party and the SS for reasons other than antisemitism, in time they became indoctrinated with the elements of the Nazi creed. It is not contended that every Nazi had read *Mein Kampf* assiduously and had memorized its lessons, though no doubt some did; nevertheless, Hitler's ideological "mission" as expressed in his writings and speeches became an ever deepening source of fundamental beliefs that tied him to his followers in the party, the SS, and the bureaucracies of the state. At first his charisma, but then increasingly his beliefs, especially his antisemitic ideology, became the basis of the Nazi party's political creed. Antisemitism was also to provide—albeit less successfully—the basis of the myth of legitimation that was to bind the German people to the Nazi state.

The Political Creed

As far as the regime was concerned antisemitism as a political creed became even more important after the Nazis seized power than before. Kershaw puts it this way:

> [It is] important to distinguish between Hitler's image as portrayed to and perceived by the mass of the population, in which anti-Semitism was no more than a subsidiary component of the "Führer Myth," and his image as viewed from within the Nazi Movement and sections of the State bureaucracy, where his "mission" to destroy the Jews functioned as a symbolic motivating force for the Party and SS, and an activating and legitimating agent for government initiatives to "force the pace" in finding a "radical solution" to the "Jewish Question."[19]

The führer's beliefs which constituted his ideological "mission" can be summarized in four points. It may be assumed that these made up the political creed of his followers.

> 1) The Aryans of Germany are the best and most gifted race on earth and form the basis of the legitimate political community; 2) In the past they had been victimized by a Jewish conspiracy to rule the world; 3) In the present the Jews are again threatening Germany by means of controlling Russia and manipulating the communist movement; 4) Only the Nazis led by the führer could save the Aryan Germans and destroy the Jewish threat.

For the Nazi true believer, or careerist who wanted to pass himself or herself off as an "idealist," the Aryan Germans became the authentic political community and the Jews its enemies. To prove one's idealism and commitment to the regime, it was necessary to demonstrate that one's "blood line" was not "polluted" by Jewish ancestors and that one was willing to go to any length to solve the "Jewish Question." Indeed, how better to demonstrate one's commitment to the regime than by the fanaticism with which one viewed the Jewish question and the radical means one was willing to use in its solution.

The internalization of the antisemitic political creed among Nazi followers of the regime led to a competition among institutional spheres and among individuals within organizations to design and to act on ever more radical measures against the Jews. Very early in the Nazi regime there were calls from below for mass murder. Indeed, even before *Kristall-nacht*, Hitler and the Nazi leadership had to take care that their followers not get out of hand by starting massacres against the Jews at an inopportune time. This potential for radicalization from below must be seen as one of the major reasons for the implementation of the Final Solution.

The Political Myth

A major problem confronting the regime was that at first the majority of Germans did not quite think this way. Most admired Hitler, many adored him as their savior. They disliked the Jews and were indifferent to their fate, but they had a hard time thinking of themselves as "Aryans" and of the Jews as the principal cause of all the world's evil.[20]

Though Hitler and his followers made good use of their leader's charismatic image as the *führer* from whom all authority ultimately derived, they were concerned with building a state that would survive him. To institutionalize their rule it was important that the führer's antisemitic racialist ideology become not only the political creed of his followers but also the political myth of legitimation linking state to society. They needed to create an authentic Aryan political community, a novel political culture, and a political myth that would support the Nazi state for many years to come.

The elements of the Nazi creed were drummed into the Germans by public spectacles, the party, the press, films like *Der ewige Jude* (The Eternal Jew) the educational system, especially the *Hitler Jugend* youth groups, and even some churches.[21] To a greater or lesser extent an increasing number of Germans came to view these elements as axiomatic. Indeed, they formed what came to be the core of Nazi culture.[22] Fundamental to the Nazi political myth was the widely shared belief that the Jews were the enemies of the Germans and that they had to be excluded from the political order.

This does not imply that every German was a Nazi or even that every Nazi was in favor of the Final Solution. In the short run, however, the regime did not need mass approbation for a policy of genocide to carry out the Final Solution. What it needed was support for the regime and a lack of organized opposition to its policies. This it got in full measure from the German people, who were either ignorant of the mass murder of the Jews, indifferent to their fate, or approving of their exclusion, if not their extermination. Moreover, those few Germans who actually opposed the regime and its genocidal policies were kept in line by state terror. Meantime, the German people were expected enthusiastically to support the regime and to think of themselves as a master race of "Aryans" and the Jews as their eternal enemies.

The Final Solution

After the Nazis came to power in 1933, there began a process of radicalization leading to the Final Solution that worked itself out in reciprocal expectations from the top down and initiatives from the bottom up of the Nazi hierarchy. Hitler and his cronies wanted to create a new Aryan nation from which Jews would be excluded, and they wanted to create an empire that would pit Germany against Russia. Since according to their worldview the world Jewish conspiracy controlled Russia, an invasion of that country would entail a genocidal war against Jewry. Both Hitler and his underlings came to share this vision. Thus, even without formulating it explicitly from the start, the moment that the Nazis seized power and intended to invade Russia, the Final Solution became an active possibility.

The Machinery of Destruction

The machinery of destruction that arrived at the Final Solution was not manned or propelled by the führer alone but by the Germans and later even non-Germans from every walk of life who believed in him and were eager to implement his programs. Moreover, as Hilberg and Arendt have pointed out, the regime did not need fanatics to make it work.[23] Ordinary Germans out of a sense of loyalty to the regime or out of a desire to do their jobs and obey their superiors would do as well. Both types staffed the machinery of destruction. Once the mandate to "solve the Jewish question" was given it was only a matter of time before ambitious, efficient, and innovative bureaucrats and managers at every level of the German institutional system—those who were true believers and those who were careerists—devised creative ways to solve the "Jewish Problem."

As Hilberg first described it, the machinery of destruction was assembled from four major institutional spheres of the German state and society.[24] These were the civil service, especially the Ministry of Interior, the army, industry, and the party, especially the SS which was put in charge of the final killing process.[25] These organizations did not at all times contribute equally to the formulation and implementation of policies dealing with Jews, including the Final Solution. At different stages, with varying enthusiasm and resources, each sphere played its role. Thus, for example, the civil service played a more important role in the prewar period when the Jews needed to be defined and expropriated, while the army and the SS played the central role during the war when millions of Jews were first captured by the invading *Wehrmacht* and then killed by the SS.

> The civil service infused the other hierarchies with its sure-footed planning and bureaucratic thoroughness. From the army the machinery of destruction acquired its military precision, discipline, and callousness. Industry's influence was felt in the great emphasis upon accounting, penny-saving, and salvage, as well as in the factory-like efficiency of the killing centers. Finally, the party contributed to the entire apparatus an "idealism," a sense of "mission," and a notion of "history-making." Thus the four bureaucracies were merged not only in action but in their thinking.[26]

As the Nazi regime solidified its power it became increasingly free to implement its revolutionary creed. This does not imply that it could do as it wished. There were domestic and international obstacles in the regime's way, and much of its behavior can be understood as a sequence of attempts to attain ideologically inspired goals while destroying, subverting, or compromising with real world obstacles.

The Three Stages of Nazi Policy

As will be seen, the manner of dealing with the "Jewish problem" was dependent on its domestic and international contexts. Different policies had to be devised depending on whether the Nazis had crystallized their power at home and whether Germany was at war. Indeed, it was the war—especially the attack on Russia—that proved to be the watershed that led to extermination. Depending on domestic and international factors, therefore, the transformation and radicalization of German policies toward the Jews can be seen as passing through three stages. Within each stage there were varying policy goals emphasized by different institutional spheres leading to distinctive though overlapping practices. The three stages were: (1) the prewar stage (1933–39), (2) the interim stage (1939–41), and the stage of the Final Solution or extermination (1941–45).

In the first stage (1933–39) the bureaucracy defined certain persons as Jews. These were then excluded from the social and institutional life of Germany. Their property was seized, and wherever possible they were expelled from the country. Reinhard Heydrich, Himmler's assistant in the execution of the Final Solution, was later to formulate these aims as "a) Forcing the Jews out of the various areas of life of the German people, [and] b) forcing the Jews out of the living space of the German people."[27]

In the second stage (1939–41) there was some vacillation in the aims of the bureaucracy of destruction. What to do with the Jews in the conquered territories? Resettle them in Madagascar? On a reservation in the Lublin district? Let them starve to death in the ghettos? Exterminate them? In the meantime, in the wake of the German armies, Jews were being randomly killed and terrorized. They were deported from the countryside and concentrated and immured behind ghetto walls.

In the third and last stage (1941–45), coinciding with the war against Russia, the decision to exterminate the Jews was made and implemented. First, *Einsatzgruppen*, special units whose goal was simply to massacre Russian Jews and other undesirables, were sent along in the wake of the conquering German armies. Soon after, as the genocide was extended to all Jews in Europe and even beyond, and the killing process required greater efficiency and secrecy, death camps were built.

Each step of German policy toward the Jews was not necessarily intended or planned in detail from the start of Nazi rule. Nevertheless, the stages of German policy leading to the Final Solution, were dependent on each other, and there was some overlap from stage to stage and from phase to phase within each stage. In sum, the three stages of Nazi policy toward the Jews spelled the ever-growing radicalization of Nazi policy and marked the regime's ever expanding power to solve "the Jewish Problem" as it wished. A process that began with defining Jews terminated with annihilating them.

First Stage (1933–39)

From its inception in the nineteenth century the antisemitic movement in Germany wished to undo Jewish emancipation and progress. As seen in Chapter 4, this aim was denied the antisemites in Imperial Germany, and while Weimar lasted Jews experienced unprecedented liberty.

With Hitler coming to power on 30 January 1933, the antisemitic movement at last began to realize its hopes. The Nuremberg laws, promulgated in 1935, abolished Jewish emancipation and curtailed Jewish participation in German political, social, economic, and cultural life. German Jews had become aliens in their own country.

When the Nazis came to power, however, they had other policy goals on their minds besides solving the Jewish question. Among these were (1) the consolidation of power, (2) the destruction of their enemies, (3) the construction of a loyal political community of Aryans, (4) the overcoming of the economic crisis, and (5) the mobilization of Germany for world war. Some of these goals, such as the destruction of their domestic enemies and the construction of a loyal political community of Aryans, were viewed as inextricably linked to their struggle against the Jews; others, such as rearmament and the solving of the economic crisis, were viewed as independent of their struggle against the Jews, and even antithetical to it. This helps to explain in part why, in the period 1933–39, anti-Jewish policy was inconsistent and lacked the radical nature of the later periods. [28]

Meanwhile, German non-Jews had to prove their "Aryan" identity to the state as well. Thus, by dividing Germans into "Jews" and "Aryans," the Nazi revolution initiated the process of reconstituting the German polity according to its own myths and its own image. Only "Aryans" could be true Germans, and the legitimacy of Hitler as the führer and the German state rested on this new definition of what constituted the "people."

Definition and Exclusion

Before the Nazis could exclude the Jews and reconstitute and reintegrate German political society on the basis of their conception of race, they had to abolish all political opposition. To give himself and his movement the semblance of legality and order that so appealed to the German people, Hitler decided to continue with his strategy of the "legal revolution." To that end he scheduled new elections on 5 March 1933.

In preparation for these elections, and so that he might be able to crush remaining political opposition to Nazism, Hitler initiated the Nazi assault on German civil liberties. He asked President Hindenburg to issue an order under Article 48 giving the Ministry of the Interior and the police the right to suppress meetings and publications deemed to endanger public security. Fortuitously, on 27 February 1933 the Reichstag was torched by Marinus van der Lubbe, a pyromaniacal Dutch Communist. The next day Hindenburg gave his new chancellor the right to proclaim emergency measures. Freedom of speech and of assembly were suspended, and the privacy of the mails, the telegram, and the telephone was nullified.

Then on 5 March the NSDAP received 44 percent of the vote—strikingly still not a majority—and formed a ruling coalition with the DNVP. Its share of the vote would have been lower still, except that by then the Communist KPD had been banned and the Storm Troopers were given free rein to intimidate voters. Hitler was now in a position to use democratic procedures to undo parliamentary democracy. He demanded an Enabling Act from the *Reichstag* that would permit him to rule without recourse to the constitution or the parliament. At first the Socialists and the Center balked. Then on 23 March the Center caved in. By a vote of 441 to ninety-four, the Social Democrats resisting to the end, the Reichstag voted to give Hitler absolute and unprecedented powers.

By July 1933 the NSDAP was the only authorized political formation in Germany. The other parties had been banned or destroyed or, like the Center, had voted themselves out of existence. As Dawidowicz has noted: "The Enabling Act provided Hitler with the legal authority for dictatorship."[29] And Bracher remarked ironically:

> Wasn't it a good thing—so state the files of many a high official of that time—that the irresistible revolution was carried out in so legal a fashion? It was therefore only logical to do everything in one's power to assure this legal revolution every technical and administrative success.[30]

In this manner German officialdom first helped in the destruction of parliamentary democracy and later—though the same officials may no longer have been in office—the state bureaucracy cooperated in everything the regime asked of it, including the Final Solution.

The abrogation of civil liberties and the destruction of political parties were paralleled by the construction of an apparatus of state repression and terror. On 20 March 1933 Dachau, a concentration camp which remained a permanent fixture during the Third Reich, opened its gates outside of Munich. Ten days later thousands of political prisoners were incarcerated in Prussia alone. These measures were meant to intimidate all Germans, not only Jews. Though it may have been Hitler's principal obsession at this early date, the Jewish problem had not yet become the primary focus of Nazi policy. Indeed, compared to what was to happen later, the first measures were relatively mild.

The Nazis initiated *Gleichschaltung*—the policy that sought the integration and coordination of Nazi state and society and the Aryanization of the Germans. It is in this context that on 7 April 1933 the first specifically anti-Jewish laws were promulgated.[31] Thus, according to "The Law for the Restoration of the Professional Civil Service,"

> Civil servants who are not of Aryan descent are to be retired . . . if they are honorary officials, they are to be dismissed from official status.[32]

After 7 April 1933 Jews were excluded from the bar, from posts of lay assessor, juror, commercial judge, patent lawyer, panel physician in state social insurance institutions, and dentist and dental technician associated with those institutions.

> Minister for Science, Art, and Public Education (Rust) to Professor Martin Buber . . . . Based on Section 3 of the Law for the Restoration of the Civil Service of April 7, 1933 [*sic*] I hereby deprive you of your tenure at the University of Frankfurt am Main.[33]

On 25 April the "Law against the Overcrowding of German Schools and Institutions of Higher Learning" was promulgated. On 6 May honorary professors, lecturers, and notaries who happened to be Jewish were dismissed from public institutions. On 29 September with the establishment of the Reich Chamber of Culture, Jews were fired and excluded from enterprises pertaining to the arts, theater, and motion pictures. On 4 October they were prohibited from being journalists or active in the press.

Thus by October 1933, notes Dawidowicz, "With German thoroughness, the laws had seen to it that the Jews were dismissed from all positions in public life—government, professions, and all of Germany's social, educational, and cultural institutions."[34] Their place was taken by "Aryans," who may have felt somewhat sheepish at taking over someone else's livelihood but who kept their reservations to themselves. In this manner, in 1933, the Nazis began the project of reshaping the German political community by including the "Aryan" and excluding the "Jew."

The year 1934 was one of the periods of lull punctuating the stages and phases of Nazi policy toward Jews. On 30 June 1934 Ernst Röhm and approximately 200 SA (*Sturmabteilung*) leaders were murdered in what came to be known as the "Night of the Long Knives." This spelled the destruction of the SA and the emergence of the SS as the NSDAP's major instrument of defense and repression. On 2 August Hindenburg died, and Hitler merged the office of chancellor and president, becoming simply the führer. On 13 January 1935 the Saar rejoined Germany in a plebiscite. Hitler was consolidating his power at home and freeing Germany from the constraints of the Versailles settlements. By then he was already preparing for war. "[He] had been able in the course of two years to free himself from the restraints of the European security system while at the same time proceeding with the policy of *Gleichschaltung* and the arms build-up that were the necessary prerequisites for his future plans."[35]

The Nuremberg Laws

It is significant that the freer and more powerful they felt from domestic and international interference, the tighter did the Nazis apply the screws of policy to the Jews. In 1935 the struggle to remake the German political community by scapegoating the Jews resumed in a more intensified manner. Sifting Jews from positions in public life was but a first step. It was also necessary to revoke their citizenship and to segregate them as much as possible from social and sexual intercourse with "Aryan" Germans. To this end a series of edicts were promulgated that have come to be known as the "Nuremberg Laws." It was in that ancient medieval city, while the party held one of its massive, menacing, and garish congresses, as earlier documented in the Leni Riefenstahl film *Triumph of the Will*, that the next set of anti-Jewish measures was initiated.[36]

On 15 September 1935 "The Reich Citizenship Law" was promulgated. Article 2, Paragraph 1 read: "A Reich citizen is only that subject of German kindred blood who proves by his conduct that he is willing and suited loyally to serve the German people and Reich."[37] Thus, in a few sentences—because they were not of "kindred blood"—Jews were denied full German citizenship and their emancipation was revoked.[38] Marr, Fritsch, Dühring, and all the other antisemites of Imperial Germany would have rejoiced in the day.

Preceding the Third Reich, Jewish Germans had not only been full citizens of the state (as status denied them by the Reich Citizen Law), they had also been members of German society. Although in retrospect German-Jewish acculturation and assimilation were not without problems and humiliations, most German Jews had felt German, many had intermarried, and most had successfully assimilated to German society.[39] It was the task of the "Law for the Protection of German Blood and German Honor," divided into seven articles and codified on 15 September

1935 at Nuremberg to reverse the process of Jewish assimilation and integration and to safeguard the "purity" of Aryan blood.

> Imbued with the insight that the purity of German blood is prerequisite for the continued existence of the German people and inspired by the inflexible will to ensure the existence of the German nation for all times, the Reichstag has unanimously adopted the following law, which is hereby promulgated:
>
> ARTICLE 1
>
> 1) Marriages between Jews and subjects of German or kindred blood are forbidden . . .
>
> ARTICLE 2
>
> Extramarital intercourse between Jews and subjects of German or kindred blood is forbidden . . . [40]

As führer and Reich chancellor, Hitler signed this law himself. "The Nuremberg laws completed the disenfranchisement of the Jews of Germany."[41]

In all, during the Third Reich, some 400 laws were passed that established the pseudojuridical basis for the reversal of Jewish emancipation and integration and helped to sever Jews from German and later from European society. The important point about such laws was not only that they were formulated but that they were assiduously and even enthusiastically obeyed by German civil servants and bureaucrats at all levels of German society. Indeed, some surprising Germans enforced Nazi laws in their own domains of jurisdiction.

On 3 November, 1933, there appeared the following announcement in the *Freiburger Studentenzeitung:*

> AWARDS OF FINANCIAL SUPPORT TO STUDENTS IN
> BADEN COLLEGES.
>
> Students who during the last few years have fought for the national revolution in the SA, SS or other armed formations are entitled, upon submission of a certificate signed by their superiors, to special consideration in the award of financial support (tuition, remission, stipends, etc.). On the other hand no awards may henceforth be given to Jewish or Marxist students. Jewish students in accordance with this regulation are students of non-Aryan descent within the meaning of paragraph 3 of the Law for the Restoration of the Civil Service . . .
>
> The Rector [Martin Heidegger][42]

If Heidegger, one of the most renowned German philosophers of his generation became a Nazi and obeyed Nazi laws, was it not reasonable to expect that his students and many other Germans would do the same?

Anti-Jewish Legislation and the Aryanization of German Society

Though anti-Jewish laws had an enormous effect on German Jews, they had nearly as powerful an impact on non-Jewish Germans. Once the Nuremberg laws were formulated, it was not only incumbent on every Jew to stop regarding himself or herself as a German, but also on every "Aryan" to prove that he or she was not a Jew. When applying for party membership or a government job everyone had to submit seven documents to the authorities to verify that he or she was an "Aryan"—his own baptismal certificate and the baptismal certificates of his two parents and his four grandparents. In the case of the SS one had to prove that one was free of Jewish ancestry for five generations. A new profession of licensed "family researchers" (*Familienforscher*) appeared to assist applicants. [43] The effect was to alienate non-Jewish Germans from their Jewish countrymen and countrywomen and to reify or to make real in its consequences the new identity of the "Aryan" forged by Nazi ideology. Hannah Arendt commented as follows:

> The Nazis placed the Jewish issue at the center of their propaganda in the sense that antisemitism was no longer a question of opinions about people different from the majority, or a concern of national politics, but the intimate concern of every individual in his personal existence; no one could be a member whose "family tree" was not in order, and the higher the rank in the Nazi hierarchy, the farther back the family tree had to be traced. [44]

Thus a major by-product of the definition and exclusion of the Jews from German society and polity, which was also the first stage of the revolution against the Jews, was the reification of the category of the "Aryan." Precisely because the Nuremberg laws excluded the Jews they were a powerful mechanism for recasting Germans as "Aryans" and for helping to legitimate and institutionalize the Nazi regime during the revolutionary interregnum. By the same token, once the Nuremberg laws had been put into effect and Jewish emancipation revoked, the Jews became vulnerable to more radical measures. In this manner the Nazis adopted antisemitism to revolutionary exigencies, but their very success—the creation of the Aryan as a counterpoint to the Jew, for example—helped to further intensify anti-Jewish policies. As we shall see below, this dialectic continued until the Nazi revolution had run its course and the Jews were gone.

Sterilization and "Euthanasia"

Antisemitism leading to the creation of the Aryan community was articulated in general racialist categories. Thus Hitler had implied in *Mein Kampf* that if the Aryans were to thrive they had to be separated not only from the Jews, as was discussed above, but from racially and biologically "impaired" Germans as well. [45] Hence a significant and ominous development deriving from Nazi racialism was the sterilization and "euthanasia" killing programs, which in the first instance were applied to "hereditarily" ill and mentally deficient Jews and non-Jews alike. It should be noted, of course, that Nazi genetics were primitive in the extreme, and what they defined as a hereditary disease need not have had any basis in genetic science at all.

Thus, on 22 June 1933, a few months after Hitler had come to power, Wilhelm Frick, the minister of the interior, promulgated a sterilization law which was supposed to avert the danger of *Volkstod*—the death of the nation or race. Among the "hereditarily" sick who were targeted were some 200,000 mentally deficient patients, 80,000 schizophrenics, 20,000 manic depressives, 60,000 epileptics, 600 suffering from Huntington's chorea, 4,000 with hereditary blindness, 16,000 with hereditary deafness, 20,000 with grave bodily malformation, and 10,000 hereditary alcoholics. In all, some 410,000 people were singled out, of which between 200,000 and 350,000 actually were sterilized. [46]

In the spring of 1939, with Hitler's active encouragement, a bureaucracy of administrators and doctors was formed to institute a "eugenics" killing program whose first aim was to destroy mentally deficient and physically deformed children. Between 1939 and 1944 thousands of such children were killed. [47] By July 1939—a few months before the war—again at the prompting of the führer, another organization was formed to deal with killing deficient or deformed adults. It started to operate out of Hitler's chancellery at Tiergartenstrasse 4—hence its code name T-4. [48]

Patients who had been selected for destruction were transferred from their hospitals to transit facilities where they were observed, and then to one of six "euthanasia" installations or killing centers where they were gassed. After some experimenting with various procedures, T-4 discovered that bottled pure carbon monoxide could do the job. This was distributed by an SS physician, Dr. August Becker, who was on loan from Himmler to the "euthanasia" killing centers. In 1941, when the gassing procedure was adapted to genocide, it was discovered that cyanide gas, whose German trade name was "Zyklon B," worked even better.[49] In all, some 80,000–100,000 people were murdered, before German public opinion brought the program to a halt.[50]

Three important points need to be made about the sterilization and "euthanasia" programs. (1) These demonstrate the depths of the Nazis' commitment to racialism. They may have been racists because they were antisemites, but racists they certainly were. Given their racist ideology, and their need to reconstitute the political community after they came to power, they turned not only to antisemitism but to racial selection to carve out their precious and "healthy" Aryans. (2) In many cases the Nazis were sensitive to German public opinion and feared alienating it. It is significant that the very voices that had been raised against the "euthanasia" program never uttered a word about the victimization of the other "races" who were destined for destruction.[51] (3) The T-4 program, as will be noted again below, anticipated the Final Solution. By the spring of 1941 most of its personnel and some of its facilities were directly transferred to the death camps in Poland. Here we see the direct application of the revolutionary myth and creed both to the creation of the Aryan community and to the destruction of the Jewish people.

Expropriation and Expulsion

With the Nuremberg laws Jews had lost their German citizenship and had been barred from public service and public office. Although by then German Jews were beginning to emigrate, thousands remained in the Fatherland.[52] Indeed, there were still some Jews active at the highest levels of the German economy. From the Nazi perspective, this was intolerable. The simplest thing would be to expropriate Jewish property and to expel Jews from Germany, but such measures had to wait for propitious circumstances. Expropriation could not take place in the midst of economic depression because it might risk the recovery, and mass expulsion could not take place in the midst of delicate international negotiations, when the Hitler regime was trying to lull the democracies into a sense of false security. Circumstances improved considerably with the *Anschluss* (annexation) and the Munich agreements. It was then that the apparent error of the *Kristallnacht* pogrom could be righted and used to continue the "legal" or bureaucratic revolution against the Jews.

When they first came to power the Nazis tried to close down the larger Jewish-owned department stores like Tietz and Wertheim in Berlin, but they found that their measures hurt the economy when it was still recovering from the depression. For the same reason, banking firms like Mendelssohn, Bleichröder, Arnhold, and others were left alone until a more promising period. That came in 1938 with the *Anschluss*, Munich, and *Kristallnacht*.

On 13 March 1938 German armies marched into Vienna, and the *Anschluss* with Austria was forged. A few months later, on 29 September 1938 the Munich conference was held. At Munich, Chamberlain and Daladier acceded to Germany's occupation of one-third of Czechoslovakia, including its most productive industrial area. Such easy and dramatic victories in the international arena signaled both the weakness of the Allies and strengthened the grip of the Nazis on Germany. As Craig has noted: "One of the most ominous products of the Munich settlement was that it reinforced the Führer's reputation for infallibility."[53] Munich accelerated the drift toward world war and created the conditions for the further intensification of anti-Jewish policies.

By 1938, especially after Munich, the Nazi regime felt itself to be much more secure at home and ready to carry out Hitler's plans for war. While the situation in 1938 was not propitious enough to conduct pogroms and massacres, it was favorable to an intensification of the policies against the Jews. The opportunity to radicalize anti-Jewish Nazi policy presented itself when on 7 November 1938 Hershl Grynzpan, a distraught Jewish youth, assassinated Ernst vom Rath, the Third Secretary of the German embassy in Paris.

In an apparent bid to increase and add luster to his power in the party, on 9 November Goebbels seized the opportunity of the assassination to call for a widespread Jewish pogrom.[54] This has come to be known as *Kristallnacht*, or the night of broken glass, for the thousands of windows and storefronts smashed during the excesses. Some 100 Jews were killed, thousands of businesses were looted and destroyed, and some thirty thousand Jewish men were incarcerated in concentration camps.[55] Goebbels, however, had overreacted. He had committed a tactical blunder. The Aryan Germans may have been ready for more radical measures against the Jews, but they were not prepared for disorder and violence in the streets.

Kristallnacht was a failure and an embarrassment. It was condemned by a majority of German non-Jews. The reaction from abroad was also unfavorable, and it helped to intensify the anti-German economic boycott.[56] Indeed, even Hitler—ever sensitive to German public opinion and intent on a "legal" facade for his revolution—disapproved, finding a pogrom too unsystematic and emotional a method for dealing with the "Jewish Problem." Pogroms only dissipated the energy of the *Volk*.[57]

Goebbels's ambition to become a major player on the "Jewish Question" stalled. Pogroms like *Kristallnacht* would not recur in Germany. Nevertheless, the excesses of 9 November accelerated the pseudolegal repression of the state and the party against the Jews. In the first instance the destruction occasioned by the pogrom was used as a pretext for their expropriation.

Thus, on 12 November 1938, during a conference called to survey the damage of *Kristallnacht*, Göring announced that he had instructions from the führer that "we must arrive at a unified and overall approach to the Jewish question and to bring it to a solution one way or the other."[58] For a start it was decided to Aryanize the German economy: "Kick out the Jews from the economy and turn them into debtors and recipients of welfare allowances."[59] On the same day, Heydrich, head of the RSHA, the Reich Security Main Office, commented: "With all the extrusion of the Jews from the economy, in the end we are always left with the basic problem, that the Jews should leave Germany."[60] To speed things along Heydrich suggested the establishment of a Central Jew-Emigration Office (*Judenauswanderugszentrale*) like the one that had been established in Austria and run by Adolf Eichmann after the *Anschluss*.[61]

Following *Kristallnacht*, expropriation and expulsion became the order of the day. The Jewish community had to pay the Nazis an indemnity of 1 billion Reichsmarks (about 400 million dollars) for the death of vom Rath and to turn over insurance benefits of some 250 million Reichsmarks. Most of the 40,000 Jewish-owned businesses still operating in 1938 were "Aryanized." The chief beneficiaries of the expropriation were giant business enterprises like I. G. Farben which, for example, took control of the Austrian Pulverfabrik Skoda-Werke-Wetzler A. G.[62]

In conjunction with the expropriation, a sustained effort was undertaken to expel Jews from the Third Reich. Of the approximately 700,000 Jews left in Germany and Austria in 1938, about half had been expelled or had emigrated before the outbreak of the war in 1939.[63] In the light of future developments, those who were expelled or had the funds and visas to emigrate were the lucky ones. (If, that is, they did not later become trapped by invading German troops.) A short time later expulsion ceased to be a Nazi policy and was replaced by extermination.

As to expropriation, it continued to be a major feature of Nazi policies toward the Jews until the very end. Indeed, confiscation of Jewish property proceeded even after their owners had perished. As Hilberg bitterly remarked,

> The Jews were deprived of their professions, their enterprises, their financial reserves, their wages, their claims upon food and shelter, and, finally their last personal belongings, down to underwear, gold teeth, and women's hair.[64]

Before the war, the policy of expulsion was limited by the restrained willingness of other countries to shelter Jewish refugees, and by the British White Paper in Palestine that restricted Jewish immigration to the one spot on earth where Jews might have been welcomed. With the outbreak of the war, fleeing refugees were quickly overtaken by invading German armies, and millions of Jews became captives of a triumphant Reich. It was to these millions who could neither flee nor be expelled that the next stages of the Holocaust applied.

The Second Stage (1939–41)

On 23 August 1939 the Nazi-Soviet pact was ratified with secret protocols providing for the partition of Poland. On the same day Britain signed a treaty guaranteeing Poland's independence. At 6:30 A.M. on 1 September 1939 Germany invaded Poland, and two days later Britain and France declared war on Germany, as they had warned they would do were Poland attacked. Such were the last few scenes leading to the debacle of the Second World War. It led to the carnage of approximately 35–50 million lives. Millions perished as military and civilian casualties of war, but other millions were deliberately murdered as victims of a policy of partial and total genocide, both domestic and foreign, for which the war provided an occasion, a justification, and a cover.

Poland became partitioned again. Twenty-one years after her independence following World War I, the Russians seized her eastern and the Germans her western and central territories. On 28 September in trade for Lithuania, the Russians withdrew from mainly Polish-speaking areas under their occupation and ceded them to the Germans. As a result of the invasion and the partition, out of approximately 30 million Polish Christians and 3.3 million Polish Jews, the Nazis exercised power over approximately 22 million Poles and 2 million Polish Jews. On 30 January 1939, sounding an ominous note, Hitler warned before the *Reichstag*:

> Today I shall act the prophet once again. If international financial Jewry inside and outside of Europe should succeed in thrusting the nations into a world war once again, then the result will not be the

Bolshevization of the earth and with it the victory of Jewry, it will be the annihilation of the Jewish race in Europe.[65]

The Germans divided their share of Poland into two main areas. The territories to the west, comprising Danzig, West Prussia, Poznan, and upper Silesia, were designated as "incorporated" into the German Reich. These areas were reserved for settlement by Germans and ethnic Germans (*Volksdeutsche*), and they were to be cleared of all Jews, Poles, and Gypsies. The remainder of occupied Poland, including her major cities of Warsaw, Cracow, Lublin, and Radom, was designated as "the General Government."

Initially, the main apparent goal of Nazi policy was to remove the bulk of the Jewish, Polish, and Gypsy populations from the Reich territories into the General Government, and to deport Jews from small towns inside occupied Poland to centers of concentration in the larger cities.[66] Both tasks proved to be difficult, and their failure set the stage for more radical approaches later on. It is significant, however, that at this point—despite Hitler's warnings before the *Reichstag*—when the Nazis had captured so many Jews and were already at war, the extermination of the Jews had not yet become official Nazi policy.

Deportation and Concentration

The main features of the deportations as the SS envisioned it may be discerned in a *Schnellbrief* (express letter) sent by Reinhard Heydrich to the "Chiefs of all *Einsatzgruppen* of the Security Police" dated 21 September 1939. In this "strictly" secret document he distinguished between:

1) The final aim (which will require extended periods of time), and
2) The stages leading to the fulfillment of this final aim (which will be carried out in short terms). . . . *For the time being, the first prerequisite for the final aim is the concentration of the Jews from the countryside into the larger cities.* This is to be carried out with all speed.[67]

Setting aside for the moment what Heydrich meant by the distinction between the "final aim" and the "stages leading to the . . . final aim," it is clear that in the first instance the SS plan called for the removal and expropriation of about 600,000 Jews from the newly incorporated areas of the Reich and their concentration—along railway lines—in the General Government. The areas of Jewish concentration were later converted into ghettos, starting with the Lodz ghetto which was closed off in April 1940.

Since the Jewish population of the General Government was approximately 1,400,000. Heydrich's plan called for increasing that population to 2 million people.[68] By mid-March 1940, nearly 200,000 Poles and Jews had been expelled from the incorporated territories, but this was a mere fraction of what was necessary to make the policy work.[69] Moreover, by further stipulating that Jews had to be concentrated in ghettos, the plan resulted in increasing the density of the Jewish population to barely sustainable levels. People began to perish from disease and to starve in large numbers. The transfer of Jewish, Polish, and Gypsy populations from the Reich and the "incorporated" territories into the General Government created extraordinary administrative problems that required radical solutions.

As was noted, the "incorporated areas" of Poland were integrated into the administrative system of the Reich, while the General Government was to be ruled by a distinct system of its own. Taking his orders directly from Hitler himself was Hans Frank, the Governor General.[70] Except for matters relating to the army and to the Jewish Question, where he had to share power with Himmler and the SS, he ran occupied Poland as if it were his fiefdom: "Some referred to him as 'King Frank.'"[71]

Though Frank insisted on "unity of administration" throughout Poland, when it came to the Jewish Question he was challenged by Himmler and the SS. At first Frank went along with the SS policy of deporting Jews into his domain, but as the absorptive capacity of his realm became strained—by 1941 there were on the average 7.2 persons per room in the Warsaw ghetto—and the danger of widespread epidemics that might infect Germans loomed, Hitler's satrap balked.

On 12 February 1940 he went to Berlin and conferred with Göring to oppose the SS's high-handed manner and the way transports were being "shoved down their throat."[72] Apparently his protest succeeded because by 23 March 1940 the transports of Jews were halted and could proceed only with Frank's permission.[73] For the time being the deportation program was over. Though it had expelled thousands of Jews, and in the fall and winter of 1940 it would resume for a brief period, in a larger sense the deportations had failed to accomplish the goals of the SS as outlined in Heydrich's *Schnellbrief*. Deportations on such a vast scale simply could not be absorbed by the administration of the General Government.

The Dead End of Deportations

Returning for a moment to Heydrich's *Schnellbrief*, a question about the timing of the Final Solution may be posed: Did the Nazis intend to exterminate the Jews in 1939 or even earlier, or was the Final Solution as a policy of the regime formulated later? In keeping with the conception that Hitler had intended to destroy the Jews from the start and was waiting for an opportune moment to strike, some scholars take Heydrich's allusion to the "final aim" as meaning "Final Solution" or extermination. [74]

Others, influenced by the functionalist perspective, emphasize the exigencies of the machinery of destruction and the polycratic nature of authority in the Third Reich. The phrase "final solution" may in fact refer to a plan to concentrate Jews in a reservation (a term the Nazis borrowed from American usage) around Nisko near Lublin prior to expelling them further east into Soviet territory. "Death camps were a much later development," says Bauer. [75] Indeed, before the war with Russia, "the haphazardness of the deportations seems to support the assumption that at this stage the Nazis had no clear idea of what to do with the Jews." [76] As will be seen below, my own view, following that of Hilberg and Browning, attempts to transcend the intentionalist-functionalist divisions.

According to Hilberg, Heydrich's final aim was spelled out and clarified by a plan set forth by the Foreign Office in 1940 to resettle the European Jews in Madagascar, a French colony. [77] Apparently, Hitler himself had taken to the idea and confided his plan to Mussolini on 18 June and to Admiral Raeder on 30 June. [78]

This also can be inferred from a speech given by Hans Frank to his division chiefs on 12 July 1940. In that address he reported "that the Führer himself had decided that no more transports of Jews would be sent into the *Generalgouvernment*" and that the Jews might be transported to the French colony of Madagascar, "which France was to cede to Germany for that very purpose." [79] He made reference to Madagascar again in a speech to the Lublin district. Jews would be removed to Madagascar "piece by piece, man by man, Mrs. by Mrs., Miss by Miss [*Stück um Stück, Mann um Mann, Frau um Frau, Fraulein um Fraulein*]." [80] Apparently this reference to Jews created hilarity (*Heiterkeit*) in the audience, but the Madagascar plan also fell through as a solution to the Jewish problem, a casualty of the Germans' failure to conquer England. [81]

> The Madagascar plan was the last major effort to "solve the Jewish problem" by emigration. Many hopes and expectations had been pinned on this plan. . . . When the project collapsed, the entire machinery of destruction was permeated with a felling of uncertainty. No one could take the decisive step on his own, for this decision could be made only by one man: Adolph Hitler. [82]

With the collapse of the Madagascar plan, even before the war with Russia, the Nazis had created what appeared to them as an insoluble problem of what to do with the masses of Jews that the invasion of Poland had produced. With the invasion of Russia in the works by the spring of 1941, and with the expectations that some 5 million more Jews would fall into the Nazi trap, deportations and ghettoization as a solution to the Jewish problem had run into a dead end. [83]

Starvation

Starting in April 1940, confronted with the failure of the policy of expulsion and concentration, some Nazi administrators in the General Government began to debate the desirability of allowing the ghettoized Jews simply to starve to death. Thousands had already perished. Why not let the rest go the same way? Thus Ludwig Fischer, the district administrator in charge of the Warsaw ghetto, commented approvingly: "The Jews will disappear because of hunger and need, and nothing will remain of the Jewish question but a cemetery." [84]

Mass starvation was certainly a possible "solution" to the "Jewish Question." It was a policy that would be used extensively against some 2 million Russian prisoners of war at the start of the campaign against Russia. [85] Indeed, as late as April 1941, mass starvation was still being debated among some administrators who had not as yet been informed that other measures were in the works.

Thus, contrary to Fischer, Dr. Walter Emmerich, head of the economic division, argued that the ghettos were a source of productive labor and that their inhabitants (he used the term "human beings," *Menschen* [*sic!*]) had to be sustained. [86] At this late date many in the machinery of destruction, who were imbued with the Nazi creed and impatient with the "Jewish Problem," were ready to take more radical steps. Still others tried to persevere with the outdated solutions of expulsion, concentration, and labor utilization. The machinery of destruction was ready to cross the bridge toward annihilation, but it would not do so without external intervention. As Hilberg and, still more emphatically, Browning suggest, to arrive at the Final Solution the machinery of destruction needed direction from the führer himself. [87]

The Third Stage (1941–45)

Meanwhile, in pursuit of its revolutionary aims, the Hitler regime was planning dramatically to expand Germany's *Lebensraum* by launching a surprise attack on Russia. According to the Nazi creed, this would not be a conventional war of conquest; it would be an apocalyptic millenarian struggle of Aryan mankind against the seat of the world Jewish conspiracy. In this context of expanding revolutionary aims, intensifying ideological justifications, and failing alternatives, the Final Solution to the Jewish Question was implemented.

It should be noted, however, that Hitler did not leave behind a written document ordering the Final Solution—indeed, he did not work this way—nor did he or his henchmen leave detailed diaries or interviews outlining their thoughts leading to that fateful decision. [88] In order to account for the decision-making process and assess Hitler's role in it, one must turn to indirect evidence, including his directives to the army and to the activities of Himmler and Heydrich.

It was in the language used by the army rationalizing its role in the invasion of Russia that one finds the intent of the Nazi revolutionary creed, and it was in the behavior of Himmler and his deputy, Heydrich, that one detects Hitler's personal interventions in the Final Solution. As an astute historian of the period has noted: "If one wants to know what Hitler was thinking, one should look at what Himmler was doing!" [89]

On 5 December 1940 Hitler had let his generals know that a war against Russia was inevitable, given the course of the war against England and the diplomatic situation in the Balkans and Southern Europe. Two weeks later plans were set in motion for Operation Barbarossa—the invasion of Russia. [90] According to Nazi mythology, it would be an apocalyptic race war for *Lebensraum* and against the "Jewish-Bolshevist system." In this struggle the functions of the army would not be limited to military tasks alone but to the implementation of Hitler's visions of conquest and destruction. [91]

Up to preparation for the war against Russia, the German army did not play a major role in the Holocaust and in the atrocities committed against other non-Jewish civilians. Once plans for Operation Barbarossa were underway, however, this was to change radically, on the orders of the highest authorities, including Hitler himself. The army was asked not only to make room for the SS coming in its wake, but fully to cooperate, as the directives had it, in the obliteration of the "Jewish-Bolshevist system."

Thus on 30 March 1941, confiding to his diary about a meeting that he and other high-ranking military leaders had held with Hitler, General Franz Halder, chief of the General Staff, noted that according to the führer the forthcoming war against Russia would be a "[s]truggle between two opposing world outlooks. . . . The struggle must be conducted against the poison of decomposition [that is, the Jews]. This is not a question of courts-martial. . . . In the East hardness is gentle for the future."[92]

Three sets of orders reflecting Hitler's new thinking on the Jewish Question and on the direct involvement of the army in anti-Jewish policies were those given by Field Marshal Keitel on 31 March 1941; the *Kommissarbefehl* issued by General Warlimont on 6 June 1941; and the directives of Field Marshal Walter von Reichenau of 10 October 1941. Thus Keitel's orders indicated: "In the area of Army operations the *Reichsführer* SS [Himmler] will be entrusted, on behalf of the Führer, with *special tasks* for the preparation of the *political administration*—tasks entailed by the final struggle that will be carried out between two opposing political systems."[93] In the infamous *Kommissarbefehl* signed by General Walter Warlimont, the decision was made official to execute political commissars serving with Russian forces.[94]

But the orders most revealing of how far Hitler's obsessions and the Nazi creed had penetrated the army and had transformed it into an engine of genocide were those of Field Marshal Walter von Reichenau, commander-in-chief of the Sixth Army. His directive of 10 October, which was distributed to all commanding generals, read in part as follows:

> With respect to the conduct of troops toward the Bolshevist system, vague ideas are still widely prevalent. The aim of the campaign against the Jewish-Bolshevist system is the complete crushing of its means of power and the extermination of the Asiatic influence in the European cultural region. This poses tasks for the troops which go beyond the onesided routine of conventional soldiering. In the Eastern region, the soldier is not merely a fighter according to the rules of the art of war, but also a bearer of an inexorable national idea and the avenger of all bestialities inflicted upon the German people and its racial kin. Therefore, the soldier must have full understanding for the necessity of a severe but just atonement on Jewish subhumanity.[95]

The directives were Reichenau's, but the original formulations, it will be recalled, were Hitler's, as he had set them out in *Mein Kampf* and other "sacred" writings of the Nazi creed.

Thus, when war against Russia was being readied, the administrative and ideological elements were in place for radical solutions to the

Jewish Question. The SS, the party, and the civil service, by their lights, had run into a dead end. They could not deport the Jews they possessed further East, and indeed, the anticipated victory over Russia would net them 5 million more Jews. The Madagascar plan was inoperative. Jews were perishing in ghettos and threatening to infect the surrounding populations, including the Germans, with epidemics. Something had to be done. That something was genocide. It could be detected in Hitler's orders to the army and still more in the activities of the SS.

In anticipation of the war with Russia, Hitler and the true believers in the party, including Himmler and Heydrich, perceived Germany to be on the threshold of an apocalyptic struggle that would pit the Aryan Germans against the "Jewish-Bolshevist" system. It would be a war of racial survival and extermination.[96] The principal task of doing the necessary and dirty work would fall to the SS and the RSHA, but the ample cooperation of the regular army, its complicity in atrocious behavior, was a vital ingredient. The war would begin in Russia in June, and a month later it would be launched against Jewry everywhere.

Einsatzgruppen

General Keitel's order of 31 March 1941, reflecting Hitler's wishes, gave Himmler and the SS the jurisdiction to operate in Russia in the wake of the invading German army. In the first instance the task of exterminating Jews and Communists fell to *Einsatzgruppen*. These were especially designated units, coming under the jurisdiction of Heydrich's RSHA. They were made up predominantly of SS but included other police formations who were later joined by local non-German detachments.

Training for this operation began in May 1941. About three thousand men were organized into four groups—A, B, C, and D—that divided Russia geographically from north to south. They were told by Heydrich that "Judaism in the East is the source of Bolshevism and must therefore be wiped out in the accordance with the Führer's aims."[97] This was a concise summary of what needed to be done and how it was to be justified. As the army invaded Russia on 22 June 1941 in a line from the Baltic in the north to the Black sea in the south, right behind it came the four "special units."

The procedure for killing Jews was rather simple, and by now well-known. For example, in Stanislawov, a town of some 60,000 souls, half of whom were Jews, the following events transpired: On 26 July 1941 the Germans occupied the town. After a *Judenrat* was established, other leading elements of the Jewish community, especially the intelligentsia and members of the professions, were executed. One witness, an engineer, recalls that those who would be killed had been told to bring their books and assemble at Gestapo headquarters. Among this early group photographers were included, presumably because the Nazis were afraid of photographic evidence.[98]

On 12 October 1941, having previously posted placards in public, the Germans ordered the Jewish population to assemble in the center of town. Some 10,000 people showed up.[99] They were marched out of town to the new Jewish cemetery where they found units of *Einsatzgruppe* D waiting for them. Having been told to strip and to line up in front of previously dug ditches, the people were machine-gunned to death. After tumbling into the ditches their bodies were covered over with earth by Ukrainian laborers. The killing operation lasted from 11 A.M. to 7:30 P.M. The *Judenrat* was made to watch the proceedings. The shooting was halted by darkness, though it continued for a while under the headlights of trucks.[100]

A few people escaped by feigning death until nightfall. They managed to dig themselves out from among the bodies in the ditches and to climb over the 2–3 meter high wall of the cemetery. Some other Jews had survived until then because they refused to go to the original roundup. One such survivor reported that after the *Aktion*, Krueger, the Gestapo chief, sent his blood-stained tunic to the *Judenrat* for cleaning.[101] Another survivor commented dryly in Polish that, still later, the Nazis ordered the *Judenrat* to establish a theater, "but nothing came of it. No one was in the mood for entertainment."[102]

Two months after the killing operation a ghetto was established. There the remaining Jews tried to carry on as best they could and hide from attacks by marauding gangs of Nazi and local hooligans. Many perished from starvation and epidemics of typhus. On 31 March 1942 there was a roundup of Hungarian Jewish refugees, and about 5,000 local Jews who were exterminated at the Belzec death camp. In August 1942, after refusing to hand over another thousand Jews, Mordechai Goldstein, the chairman, and the rest of the *Judenrat* were hanged. On the first day of Rosh Hashana 1942, a further 5,000 Jews were sent to the Belzec extermination camp. The ghetto and the once bustling Jewish community of Stanislawov were liquidated on 22 February 1943.

In a similar manner, the *Einsatzgruppen* ravaged some 130 Russian Jewish communities. The best estimate is that 1,400,000 Jews perished by this method.[103]

The Wannsee Conference

Hitler and his Nazis believed that Jews everywhere were in league to destroy the Aryans. Hence it was not enough to conquer Russia and to destroy the Russian Jews. The world Jewish conspiracy would only raise its head somewhere else. A truly Final Solution meant the destruction of all Jews under German occupation, and if possible of all Jews from the face of the earth.

Since the war against Russia made it possible to annihilate the Jews, according to the Nazis it would be a crime not to take the opportunity provided by Fate itself. Thus would the Third Reich emerge victorious and thrive for a thousand years. Exhilarated by the extraordinary victories of the first few months of the Russian campaign and feeling itself free to act as it wished, the regime led by Hitler proceeded to the Final Solution to the Jewish Question.[104]

Thus on 17 July, in a veiled aside, Hitler told visiting Croatian Marshal Kvaternik of his intention to remove every Jew from Europe.[105] And on 31 July Heydrich obtained from Göring the authorization for what came to be known as the Wannsee conference:

> As supplement to the task which was entrusted to you in the decree dated January 24, 1939, to solve the Jewish question by emigration and evacuation in the most favorable way possible, given present conditions, I herewith commission you to carry out all necessary preparations with regard to organizational, substantive, and financial viewpoints for a total solution of the Jewish question in the German sphere of influence in Europe. . . . I further commission you to submit to me promptly an overall plan showing the preliminary organizational, substantive, and financial measures for the execution of the intended final solution of the Jewish question.[106]

Following Göring's directive, on 20 January 1942, Heydrich presided over a conference held in the office of the RSHA in Am Grossen Wannsee, 50/58 in suburban Berlin. His deputy, Adolf Eichmann, took the minutes. The conference commenced with Heydrich's announcement that Göring had appointed him "Plenipotentiary for the Preparation of the Final Solution of the European Jewish Question," and that such a task "necessitates prior joint consideration by all central agencies directly concerned with these questions, with a view to keeping policy lines parallel."[107]

Heydrich continued with a brief review of what had been accomplished to date. He pointed out that the early goals had been:

> a) Forcing the Jews out of the various areas of life of the German people;
>
> b) Forcing the Jews out of the living space of the German people.[108]

Despite many difficulties, by 31 October 1941 "approximately 537,000 were processed into emigration."[109]

He then pointed out that emigration was replaced by "evacuation of the Jews to the East. . . . However, these actions are to be regarded only as provisional options; even now practical experience is being gathered that is of major significance in view of the coming final solution of the Jewish question."[110] One assumes that the "practical experience" Heydrich alluded to was a euphemism for the experimental gassing, utilizing Zyklon B, of Russian prisoners of war, on 3 September 1941 in Bunker 11 of the Auschwitz *Stammlager*, and of the gassing of the first Jewish transports, on 8 December 1941 at Chelmno.[111]

Next, he turned to a review of European Jewish demography where he included—with the numbers under German control—population statistics on Jews in Britain, Ireland, Switzerland, and even Turkey. The total came to 11 million. "In the course of the practical implementation of the final solution, Europe is to be combed through from west to east."[112]

Before Jews were to be killed, however, their property had to be expropriated and their labor utilized for the war effort. Indeed, Jews fit for work would be "employed in road-building, in which task a large part will undoubtedly disappear through natural diminution. . . . The remnant that may eventually remain, being undoubtedly the part most capable of resistance, will have to be appropriately dealt with."[113] It is significant that in the above-quoted passage Heydrich leaves out discussing those who would not be capable of joining labor gangs, that is the old, the very young, and the ill. Presumably at this late date he did not need to go into the specifics for his knowledgeable audience.[114]

There were other issues discussed such as the setting up of a special concentration camp at Theresienstadt. This was to be a place for decorated German Jewish war veterans and old German Jews whose destruction might have hurt the sensibilities of ordinary Germans—in time most of these people were ultimately also shipped off to Auschwitz. There was also a discussion about coordinating the activities of the SS with those of the Foreign Office. The conference ended with considering what policy should be applied to mixed marriages and to *Mischlinge*.[115]

The significance of the Wannsee conference was not that it initiated the Final Solution but that it rationalized the extermination of European Jewry already in train. The conference alerted the machinery of destruction that, after the failure of the policies of deportation, annihilation was the order of the day, and it helped to coordinate the activies of the SS with the other major institutional spheres such as the party, the civil service—including the Foreign Office—industry, and the army. Moreover, by the time of the conference, many important administrative and technical problems had already been solved or were in the process of being worked out.

By October 1941, most European Jews had been rounded up in Ghettos and prevented from emigrating and escaping.[116] The personnel and technique for extermination—the use of the T-4 system of gassing—had already been or was in the process of being utilized in some death camps. Other extermination camps were in the process of construction. The gas chambers and the crematoria were either ready or in preparation for their grisly tasks.

Barely a month after Wannsee, Hitler had much to be pleased about. On 24 February 1942 in his "Message on the Anniversary of the Promulgation of the Party Program," he declared:

> My prophesy shall be fulfilled that this war will not destroy Aryan humanity but it will exterminate the Jew. Whatever the battle may bring in its course or however long it may last, that will be the final result.[117]

And a little over a month later, on 27 March 1942, Goebbels confided to his diary:

> The prophesy which the Führer made about them [the Jews] for having brought on a new world war is beginning to come true in a most terrible manner.[118]

There are some situations that are obstacles to intentions, but by the same token there are other contexts that radicalize impulses and open up new vistas of opportunity. The period 1939–41 was frustrating to the Nazi regime and to the machinery of destruction that had been given the task of deporting Jews. The General Government could not absorb further shipments, and the situation was not conducive to a solution to the Jewish question. With the start of the war against Russia, however, especially in the context of the early victories, the situation changed drastically. The war was given a new meaning, that of an apocalyptic race war, and all things became possible.

Thus in the second stage of the Nazi revolution, as the regime was prepared to carve out its portion of *Lebensraum* in the East, and when other policies dealing with the Jewish Question had failed, the Nazis arrived at the Final Solution. The ideology of racial antisemitism helped to justify a genocidal war in the east, but by the same token the war of conquest against Russia, at one and the same time, helped to radicalize anti-Jewish measures, and gave the regime the opportunity to decide in favor of total genocide.

Conclusion

This chapter concludes with a brief overview of the "twisted" road that led to the Final Solution. It briefly reviews the origins of the Holocaust in the pariah status of Jews and ends with a discussion of the process of cumulative radicalization. This was set in train by the Nazis who started with defining the "Jews" and ended with killing them.

Origins

A crucial starting point for the analysis of the Holocaust is the Christian religious tradition of anti-Judaism that led to Jew-hatred, and was a necessary condition for the construction of the Jewish pariah and hence for modern antisemitism. Modern antisemitism started out in nineteenth-century Europe as a political movement protesting Jewish emancipation and assimilation. German and other antisemites simply could not reconcile themselves to extending political and social equality to a traditional pariah group, whose assimilation they found aversive.

As the Jews began to succeed in the modern world, German antisemites raised the specter that it would not be the Jews who would be Germanized but the Germans who would be Judaized. Even before Hitler and the Nazis came to power, radical antisemites like Dühring, Fritsch, and Class found in racialism an ideological bulwark to Jewish emancipation and assimilation: there was nothing that the Jews could do or not do that would make them Germans or Europeans. They were condemned by their race to be the eternal stranger. In this manner even those Jews who had assimilated by converting to Christianity could be rooted out as foreign interlopers whose "blood" prevented them from ever becoming German or European.

Though communal resentment against Jewish assimilation was rife in nineteenth-century Germany and Europe, in the circumstances of a legitimate and viable Imperial Germany, antisemitism as a political movement had limited success in attracting supporters. This situation changed dramatically with the collapse of the Second Reich. With the emergence of a democratic republic that lacked legitimacy, revolutionary racialist antisemites like the Nazis—who under different circumstances would likely have remained a minor party—could strengthen their ranks by attracting *Volkisch* opponents to the democratic state. As discussed, it was such circumstances that made it possible for the Nazis to come to power.

The Nazis came to power during a revolutionary interregnum, after Germany had failed in creating an empire for herself rivaling that of England and had been humiliated in the Great War. Following that disaster she was governed by a government that lacked legitimacy, while the nation was deeply divided by class and social conflict. The major tasks of any revolutionary regime under the circumstances had to be to establish a legitimate government, unite the nation, and undo Germany's humiliation by expanding German power abroad.

The principal difference between the Nazis and other revolutionary movements, however, was that their initial conception of German society and the international order were guided by their ideology of racialist antisemitism in which the Jews were defined as Germany's principal domestic and international enemies. Once this conception was translated into action, it affected both domestic and international policy and led to the Final Solution.

According to this interpretation, therefore, the Final Solution was the product both of Nazi racialist antisemitism, which had some of its origins in the traditions of Christian Europe, as well as the structural opportunities and exigencies created by a revolutionary situation in Germany and by wartime conditions abroad.

Cumulative Radicalization

Most writers agree that the Nazi regime's policies toward the Jews became cumulatively radicalized, but they disagree on the causes of this process. Intentionalists like Dawidowicz and Fleming detect the impetus for radicalization in Hitler's ideology and his coming to power. His ideology dictated his regime's policies, and his intentions had always been ultimately to exterminate the Jews. Once he became the führer he had the power to act on his most cherished wishes. Because it was so radical and controversial, the decision to order the Final Solution could not be taken all at once and had to be made in increments and in secret. When

241

the opportunity presented itself at the start of the Russian campaign, however, Hitler and his followers did not hesitate to act.

As already remarked, the functionalists view the process differently.[119] From this perspective when the Nazis came to power there were no apparent plans for the Final Solution, nor has Hitler's written directive ordering the Final Solution ever been found. Indeed, until 1941 extermination did not seem to be a policy of the Third Reich. In the first instance the policy was deportation and expropriation. How did that come to be transformed into extermination?

The functionalist answer is that the decision to exterminate the Jews did not necessarily start with Hitler but was the end product of a process of radicalization that he set in motion. His ideology provided the "mandate" to solve the "Jewish Problem" and to make the Reich *Judenrein*. The SS, the party, the army, and the other institutional spheres of the Third Reich then set out to find a "solution" to the "problem" that he had set. Moreover, they competed with each other to do the führer's bidding. When they discovered that deportations would no longer work, they turned to extermination. The policy of extermination no doubt won the approval of Hitler, but he did not specifically formulate it.

As noted earlier, there is merit in both explanations, and they are not mutually exclusive, but they are both incomplete in important ways. They are not mutually exclusive because, as Browning has shown above, not only did Hitler give the mandate for the Final Solution, at crucial points he intervened in the policy process turning it to more radical paths when it seemed to get stuck. Indeed, Hitler was among the most radical of antisemites—a status in which he took pride—and he probably wished to destroy the Jews from the very start. But he was also a cunning and wily politician who knew how to dissemble and wait for an opportune moment to strike. As far as the Jews were concerned, Himmler was his fanatical and faithful spokesman, but the overall conception and the crucial orders were Hitler's. It is likely that Hitler both initiated the chain of events leading to the Final Solution and intervened at critical times to direct it into radical paths, as the intentionalists imply. He also could rely on the enthusiastic cooperation and innovative spirit of the machinery of destruction which kept the process moving and presented him with ever more radical alternatives, as the functionalists suggest.

Missing from this analysis is an explanation for the motivations of his followers. Why did the individuals making up the machinery of destruction either initiate the Final Solution or implement it with so much zeal? Where they all clinically antisemitic, as Hitler no doubt was? If one dismisses that hypothesis as improbable, were they simply cogs in a machine, obeying Hitler's authority as some psychologists suggest?[120] If so, how does one account for the enthusiastic innovative behavior at each level of the machinery of destruction? The SS and the party stalwarts were not simply obeying Hitler's orders. They were energetic, dedicated, and "creative" innovators in their search for a "solution" to the "Jewish Question." Where did their zeal come from? Why did so many believe with Himmler that killing Jews was a terribly difficult but ultimately noble task?

The answer suggested here is that following the collapse of Imperial Germany and the manner in which Weimar took its place, the ideologies of democracy, socialism, and even conservatism were discredited for many Germans as beliefs worthy of commitment. Instead, especially young and "idealistic" Germans flocked to the Hitler movement as a nationalist alternative which apparently sought Germany's welfare above mere class and factional interests.

They did not join the Nazis because of antisemitism, but the most dedicated and "idealistic" of those who joined the movement soon became imbued with the führer's own ideology. After the Nazis came to power antisemitism truly came into its own. It already was the guiding ideology of the leadership, but now it also became the creed of its followers, and an attempt was initiated by the regime to make of it the myth of political legitimation which would bind the German people to the Third Reich.

In such a situation one demonstrated one's commitment to the regime by taking seriously the racial laws and proving one's unimpeachable Aryan pedigree, and one agitated against the Jews. Indeed, the "purer" one's ancestry and the more radical one's views on the Jewish question, the more one proved one's commitment to the regime and one's faith in the führer. Thus was the personal commitment of many Germans who supported the regime joined to the task of finding a "final solution" to the "Jewish question."

On the eve of the attack on Russia, the machinery of destruction was frustrated by the policy of deportations and was driven by its own fanatics as well as opportunists to make increasingly more radical proposals as "solutions" to the "Jewish Question." Meanwhile, Hitler bid his time to destroy the Jews and intervened to direct the killing machine at crucial times when it seemed it had lost its way. With the attack on Russia, the machinery of destruction was ready to take a qualitatively more radical step toward extermination, and Hitler was ready to approve it.

243

The war against Russia transformed the Jewish Question from a problem of deportation of racially undesirable aliens into a titanic struggle between the forces of Good and Evil. The time had come for the Final Solution.

PART THREE

Conclusion

Part One discusses the problematic situations of Armenians and Jews in the Ottoman Empire and Imperial Germany, respectively, while Part Two relates the Armenian Genocide and the Holocaust to the revolutionary transformations experienced by those two old regimes. The following two chapters conclude this study. Chapter 8 stresses the differences between the Armenian Genocide and the Holocaust, since the previous seven chapters stress many of their similarities. Chapter 9 again picks up some of the major themes introduced in Chapter 1, the Introduction, and elaborates the relationship between revolution and genocide. The last chapter also introduces brief discussions of the Stalinist destruction of the Kulaks and the Cambodian "autogenocide" as further illustrations of the main points of this essay.

EIGHT

Similarities and Differences between the Armenian Genocide and the Holocaust

Up to this point I have stressed how the Armenian Genocide and the Holocaust are examples of total domestic genocide, how they resemble each other, and how they differ from other instances of mass murder. At this juncture I shall briefly sum up their common features once more, but the emphasis will be on their differences. For the most part, I stress their differences because I wish to highlight how the process of total domestic genocide makes its way under varying conditions. In addition, I want to avoid a pitfall of comparative studies which suggests that a comparison of cases necessarily implies their equivalence.

Similar Causes

Some of the similarities between the origins of the Armenian Genocide and the Holocaust have been noted earlier and may be listed:

1. As discussed in Chapters 2, 3, and 4, under the old regimes of the Ottoman Empire and Germany, Armenians and Jews were ethnoreligious minorities of inferior status that had experienced rapid social progress and mobilization in the nineteenth century. These circumstances helped to create what were known as the "Armenian Question" and the "Jewish Problem," respectively.

2. Under the old regimes, Armenians may have suffered persecution and Jews may have experienced discrimination, but in neither case was a policy of genocide formulated or implemented to solve "questions" or "problems." Genocide followed in the wake of revolutions in the Ottoman Empire and Germany.

3. As discussed in Chapter 5, following the reversals of 1908–12, the Committee of Union and Progress rejected Pan-Islam and Ottomanism as ideologies and political myths linking state to society and turned to Turkish nationalism and Pan-Turkism. The CUP identified the Turkish

ethnic group as the authentic political community, and by implication it excluded Armenians and others from the Turkish nation. Once Ottoman Turks came to view themselves not in religious but in nationalist terms, the Armenians especially were in danger of being viewed as enemies of Turkey and the Young Turk revolution. What made the Armenian situation especially dangerous was that millet's occupation of lands in Anatolia which were claimed by the Turkish nationalists to constitute the Turkish heartland. Moreover, such lands were on the border of Russia, Turkey's traditional enemy.

Similarly, a revolutionary situation in Germany allowed the Nazis to recast their society's identity and political myth. As discussed in Chapter 6, the German revolution destroyed the Weimar Republic, undermined democratic and socialist myths of legitimation, and enabled the Nazis to attain power. As pointed out in Chapter 7, once the Nazis had power they recast German political identity in terms of their racial and antisemitic ideology. This they did by excluding and expelling what they defined as "non-Aryans" and "Jews" from the newly prized "Aryan" community.

4. When the First World War broke out, the CUP enthusiastically joined the Ottoman Empire onto the side of the Germans and against the Russians. This permitted the CUP to claim that the internal Armenian enemy was in league with the external foe. Wartime circumstances then were used to justify the deportation and destruction of the Armenian community.

Similarly, the Nazis launched the Second World War in order to improve their nation's standing in the international arena, and it was under wartime circumstances that they implemented their policy of partial and total genocide. In particular, they viewed the Soviet Union as their principal foreign enemy and assumed that it was ruled by a "World Jewish Conspiracy." At the same time that they invaded Russia they put the "Final Solution" into effect.

Thus did ideological vanguards use the opportunities created by revolution and war to destroy ancient communities which were judged to be "problematic" under the old regimes and "enemies of the revolution," and "deadly threats" under revolutionary and wartime circumstances.

Significant Differences

A comparison of the Holocaust with other instances of genocide such as the Armenian Genocide may be suggestive in uncovering some of their causes and illuminating the process of genocide in general. But this demands our recognition that, although the origins of these two instances of genocide were similar in some essential ways, they were also significantly different. Indeed, there were three major differences that need to be stressed. The first was the difference in the traditional statuses of Armenians and Jews in the Ottoman Empire and Germany, respectively; the second was the specific content of the ideologies of the Nazis and the CUP; and the third was the methods of destruction, especially massacre and the death camp.

Differences in Status

It has been pointed out that Armenians and Jews were ethnoreligious communities that occupied problematic positions in the Ottoman Empire and Christian Europe, respectively. Before the dramatic changes that started to take place in the eighteenth and nineteenth centuries, the Armenians were *dhimmis* in the Ottoman Empire and the Jews were a corporate pariah caste in most of Europe. Both groups occupied distinctively inferior statuses, but the territorial situation of the Armenians in the Ottoman Empire and the stigmatized image of the Jews in Europe made for important differences in how these minorities were treated in the modern world.

Before the revolution of 1908, even under Sultan Abdul Hamid, the Armenian millet held an inferior but legitimate place in the Ottoman system of stratification. *Dhimmis* could never consider themselves the equals of Muslims, but neither were they stigmatized as "killers of God" in the same way that Jews were in Europe. This implied that until the instability generated by capitalism and nationalism *dhimmis* enjoyed a measure of tolerance and respect in the Ottoman Empire that was denied Jews in Europe. Moreover, most Armenians, except those in Istanbul, were concentrated on their ancestral lands in Anatolia or Cilicia. This gave them a further claim to the land and reinforced their autonomy as a component millet of the Ottoman system.

Following the profound changes that affected the Ottoman Empire in the nineteenth century, Armenians demanded greater autonomy and self-administration on their lands, while Ottoman Muslims came increasingly to view such demands as treachery. This view was compounded for the Ottomans especially as the Armenians were making social progress which seemed to threaten traditional hierarchies. After the revolution of 1908, Ottoman Turks became integral nationalists and claimed that the Armenian lands constituted the heartland of Turkey and that the demands of the Armenians were nothing less than sedition.

Thus certainly by the time of Abdul Hamid and especially after the Young Turk revolution there was antiminority and anti-Armenian sentiment in the Ottoman Empire and Turkey, but it manifested itself first in terms of Pan-Islam and then increasingly in terms of Turkish nationalism. Armenians, it was said, were *dhimmis* who were challenging the traditional Muslim order, or they were an alien nation in the heartland of Anatolia. Both accusations were grounds for persecution and genocide, but they differed in significant ways from European antisemitism.

After the spread of nationalism and capitalism in Western Europe, the Jews were presented with the apparent opportunity to shed their pariah status and to attain civic equality. Since they were not a separate territorial group like the Armenians in the Ottoman Empire, territorial autonomy or national self-determination seemed at first to be closed options to them. Increasingly throughout the nineteenth century, therefore, especially in Germany and France, Jews sought to acculturate and to assimilate to European society.

What they did not expect was the antisemitic reaction. The rise of the antisemitic parties in Germany, Schönerer and Lueger in Austria, and the Dreyfus affair in France were all symptoms of a European-wide rejection of Jewish assimilation and social progress. The state and the legal system may have wanted to include the Jews as citizens because the modern state had no room for separate corporate groups in the manner of Feudal Europe, but wide sections of European society would not accept Jews as their equals or as their countrymen. As discussed, the reaction took the form of racial antisemitism, an ideology that placed unbreachable obstacles to Jewish assimilation while at the same time it blamed the Jews for the ills of the modern world.

It was only after the spread of nationalism and in reaction to antisemitism that Jews themselves began to entertain notions of territorial autonomy and self-determination. Indeed, these were the circumstances making for the appearance of the Zionist movement. But the difference between the Armenians in the Ottoman Empire and Turkey, and the Jews in Europe and Germany, should be apparent. The Armenians wanted a greater degree of separation and autonomy, while at first the Jews wanted to be included. Both minorities for different reasons were denied their aspirations.

Differences in Ideology

A major difference between the Holocaust and the Armenian Genocide pertains to the distinctive ideologies of the Nazis and the Committee of Union and Progress. Hitler's pathology became the ideology of a mass movement that came to rule the most potent country in Europe. Nazi racialist ideology—what Lifton has aptly called the biomedical vision—was a form of Manicheanism that divided the world into the Aryans, carriers of the seeds of virtue and civilization, and the Jews, progenitors of evil and destruction.[1]

Enver and Talaat and the other members of the CUP did not view the Armenians in the same manner. They were not millenarian racialists. The Young Turks became nationalists, believing that without radical change the Ottoman Empire could not survive the centrifugal forces of ethnic self-determination and the pressures of the great powers. After the defeats of 1908–12, they rejected Ottomanism and Pan-Islam as rival ideologies and adopted Pan-Turkism.

The Young Turks aimed to replace the Ottoman Empire with a new Turkish national state stretching from Anatolia to Central Asia. From their perspective the Armenians had to be destroyed as a people, not because they were the carriers of an evil seed, or because they threatened to control the world, or because their destruction would bring on a thousand-year racial utopia, but because they were identified as an alien nationality, living in the heartland of Turkey and creating an obstacle to the formation of the expanded Turkish state. Once the Ottoman Empire joined Germany and Russia became a wartime enemy, the Armenians—living on both sides of the border—were identified as siding with the Russians. These were some of the ideological and structural conditions leading to the destruction of the Armenians. Thus ideology played as significant a role in the Armenian Genocide as it would play in the Holocaust, but, as one might expect, the content of the specific ideologies in the two instances were clearly distinct from each other.

The difference in ideology between the Nazis and the CUP had implications for the scope of the destruction. The project of exterminating the Jews became a twisted crusade against an imaginary evil. The result was that not only German and Austrian Jews had to be killed, but all Jews everywhere on earth were to be annihilated in order that the world might be purified and redeemed. Indeed, Jews were sentenced to death by the Nazis not only in Europe under direct German jurisdiction, but the attempt was made to carry out that verdict in places like Japan where the Germans had influence but no jurisdiction.[2] The Japanese refused to carry out the genocidal policies of their allies, but the example illustrates the difference between the Nazis' millenarian racialist vision—in essence a theodicy—and the nationalist vision of the Young Turks.

Not even the Committee of Union and Progress which had set out to destroy the Armenians in Turkey and the Ottoman Empire was motivated by such grandiose visions. Thus, for example, although Armenians were deported from most parts of the Ottoman Empire and massacred and starved en route, the Armenian populations in Lebanon and Palestine were not destroyed.[3] Possibly it was felt that these Armenians were far enough from the central areas of Turkish interest that they could be left alone.

This would have been perfectly sensible from a Turkish nationalist perspective. Moreover, because the definition of a Turk was a Muslim whose native tongue was Turkish, some Armenians who spoke Turkish fluently and had converted to Islam were able to save themselves or to be saved by sympathetic Turks.[4] Such "oversights" because they would have challenged racialist theory would not have been tolerated by the Nazis.

A major part of what made the Holocaust distinct from the Armenian Genocide, and from other cases even of total domestic genocide, were the specific intentions of the Nazi perpetrators.[5] It should be noted that this is an empirical and not only a moral or a legal observation. Moreover, it is a distinction with a difference: the Nazi worldview accounts in part for the extraordinary scope of their mass murder. They were not satisfied with deporting or killing only German Jews. All Jews in their sphere of influence, and even beyond their sphere of influence, were sentenced to death. Thus what started as a total domestic genocide became a total foreign genocide as well.

Ironically, because the intentions of the Nazis were so bizarre, that aspect of the Holocaust is less useful for a comparison with other like cases than is the Armenian Genocide. In their single-minded and murderous nationalism the Young Turks have more to teach us about current massacres and partial genocides in parts of the contemporary Third World, for instance, than does the Holocaust.

Thus, for example, recent events in Biafra, Indonesia, Burundi, Pakistan, Ethiopia, and the Sudan have a certain comparability to the Armenian Genocide of 1915. In each of these cases armed vanguards seized power after the fall or departure of a regime that had been set up by an imperial power, and they perpetrated massacres against communal groups who seemed to be opposed to the national aspirations of the dominant ethnic group. Nationalism, or ethnic chauvinism, not millenarian racialism, was the governing ideology, just as it had been in Turkey.

In the other cases cited above, however, the policy of the state was conquest or subjugation, not destruction of the communal group as such. In none of these instances did communal massacre or partial genocide add up to total domestic genocide. This may be due to the fact that in other instances of partial genocide, like Biafra, communal groups could be separated territorially, and the dominant ethnic group did not necessarily want to settle and incorporate the lands of the victims.

This should be contrasted to the Armenian Genocide in which the issue was not the incorporation or domination of the Armenians but their disappearance. The Young Turks wanted the Armenian lands, and they wanted the Armenians out of Turkey. They used total domestic genocide as the preferred method to attain their goals. It was the policy of total destruction of a national group as such that differentiates the Armenian Genocide from communal massacres and links it to the Holocaust.

Finally, it needs to be stressed that the Armenian Genocide demonstrated that radical nationalism was quite enough to justify total domestic genocide. The Nazi ideology of millenarian antisemitic racialism was certainly unique, but it is not uniquely necessary in order that a regime commit total domestic genocide.

Differences in Methods

There were some significant similarities but also differences in how both genocides were implemented. Unlike the Armenian Genocide, which evolved rapidly once the First World War started, the Holocaust as a set of policy initiatives took longer and went through at least three stages before it reached the Final Solution. As discussed in Chapter 7, these were the prewar stage (1933–39), the interim stage (1939–41), and the final stage (1941–45). Each stage can be characterized by different policy goals and distinctive but overlapping processes of victimization and destruction.

The goals and processes characterizing the first stage (1933–39) were the definition of the Jews and the Aryans, the exclusion of the former from the institutional and social life of Germany, their expropriation and their expulsion. The second interim stage (1939–41) was characterized by some indecision in the machinery of destruction. What to do with the Jews in the conquered Polish territories? Should they be deported and resettled in the East or in Madagascar, should they be exterminated? The policy of the Final Solution had not yet taken shape. In this phase Jews were being terrorized and deported from the countryside into the cities where they were concentrated in ghettos. In the third and last stage (1941–45) of the Holocaust, the Final Solution was formulated and initiated. Coinciding with the millenarian war against Russia, the decision to exterminate the Jews was implemented.

In the case of the Armenian Genocide, things moved much more swiftly. The Great War commenced in August 1914. By February 1915 Armenians in the Turkish army were disarmed and turned into labor battalions. By April the Armenian leadership was seized and the expropriations, deportations, massacres, mass shootings, and starvation of the Armenian population at large began. By 1916 some million Armenians had perished. At war's end another half-million were added to the slaughter.

The decision to kill the Armenians was taken in conjunction with the outbreak of the First World War and the danger and opportunities that wartime provided. It did not have the quality of experimentation with various solutions to the "Armenian Problem" that the Holocaust had with respect to the "Jewish Problem." Thus the first two stages of definition, expropriation, expulsion, and concentration that required extensive bureaucratic involvement on the part of the German judiciary, police, Nazi party, and SS were not present in Turkey. These stages were telescoped into one process of identification-expropriation-deportation-destruction.

Massacre and Death Camp

A number of writers have pointed to the invention of the death camp as being especially emblematic of the Holocaust.[6] Whereas other massacres and genocides may have been implemented by shootings, pogroms, and starvation, the death camp was different because it adopted modern industrial methods to the process of killing. Auschwitz Birkenau was primarily a factory for the murder of Jews and Gypsies and for their cremation. The implication here is that only a modern industrialized society like Germany could have invented and implemented this method of mass destruction.

There is an important element of truth in this view, but it overestimates the differences between the relative development of Germany and Turkey and the methods used in the two genocides. It is true that, compared to Germany, Turkey was an industrially backward country; nevertheless, it used effectively those industrial facilities that were at its disposal to carry out the genocide.

Extensive use was made of the telegram to coordinate activities and the railroad system to deport Armenians to the Syrian desert. Indeed,

Talaat himself was a former official in the telegraph office. Consequently, a hallmark of modern genocide, namely, the depersonalization and bureaucratization of the crime, could already be seen. By the same token it should not be forgotten that millions of Jews perished by shooting, forced marches, and starvation, just as the Armenians had done before them. Thus although the death camp and its extraordinary universe were a hallmark of the Holocaust, the difference in the killing process of the two genocides should not be exaggerated.

Just as the death camp is emblematic of the Holocaust, the recurrent massacre of columns of Armenian deportees as they made their way from the eastern vilayets in Turkey to the Syrian desert near Aleppo is a hallmark of the Armenian Genocide. Toynbee estimates, for example, that on the average some 50 percent of such columns were destroyed on the way.[7]

Although mass shootings and the stimulation of massacre was also utilized by the Nazis, especially in the Baltic states and the Ukraine, a much smaller percentage of Jews perished in this manner than in the death camps. Moreover, it is significant that massacre was never used in Germany itself. This suggests that there was a predisposition for massacre present in the Ottoman Empire and the Caucasus that was not available to the same degree to the Nazis in Germany and in some of the occupied countries.

One can only speculate about the reasons for such a potential for massacre. It may be noted, however, that massacres had been used against Muslims in the Russian Empire, Greece, Cyprus, and the Balkans before the onset of the Armenian Genocide. Moreover, it is significant that thousands of Turkic and non-Turkic Muslim refugees fleeing Russia and the Balkans in the nineteenth century had been resettled precisely in those areas of the eastern vilayets populated heavily by the Armenians. It follows, therefore, that they and their descendants may have been stirred by passions of revenge and displaced aggression against their helpless neighbors.[8] The CUP's role was to initiate, encourage, coordinate, and tolerate popular violence against the Armenians. In such a situation popular massacres complemented the tasks of special killing units, and there was less need for factories of destruction.

As in the CUPs destruction of the Armenians, the Nazis utilized massacre and "spontaneous" actions against Jews in the Ukraine, Hungary, Rumania, and the Baltic states. It is important to stress, however, that genocide could occur in Germany and in other "advanced" countries, even in the absence of a potential for massacre. All that was needed was a genocidal regime, a willing bureaucracy, and the acquiescence of a silent majority.

Conclusion

This chapter asserted that the Armenian Genocide and the Holocaust in being total domestic genocides were significantly different from other cases of genocide and mass destruction in the modern era. It went on to list some of their similarities and differences. The analysis pointed out that both genocides may have been the products of revolutionary transformations in the Ottoman Empire and Imperial Germany, respectively; that the victims targeted for mass murder were ethnoreligious groups of traditionally low status who had dramatically improved their social and economic positions in the modern world; and that both genocides occurred in the midst of world wars. This was said to make up their similar etiology.

There were also significant differences between the two genocides. In particular, the traditional status of Armenians and Jews in the Ottoman Empire and Europe, respectively, the intentions of the perpetrators, and the methods of destruction were singled out. Jewish pariah status in Europe with its stigmatization and long history, Nazi millenarian racialism, and the device of the death camp were significantly different from the situation of Armenian *dhimmis*, the ideology of Turkish nationalism, and the process of massacre and starvation characteristic of the Armenian Genocide.

These differences, however, did not vitiate a meaningful comparison of the two instances of total domestic genocide. To the contrary, it was precisely because the two cases varied in their etiology and methods that it was possible to gauge how total domestic genocide proceeded under distinct conditions. First, because of the difference in the social and territorial status of Armenians and Jews, the reaction to Armenian and Jewish aspirations also differed in the Ottoman Empire and in Europe. An anti-Armenian ideology equivalent to European antisemitism never appeared in the Ottoman Empire or Turkey. Second, because of the wider reach of the Nazis' millenarian racism compared to the CUP's integral nationalism, the scope of the Holocaust was broader than that of the Armenian Genocide. By the same token, because the CUP's intentions were shaped by nationalism and not racism, it is possible to assert (and warn) that the threshold for genocide, including total domestic genocide, may be ordinary, familiar, nationalism and that the mass destruction of human groups need not depend on the rise of Nazi-type ideologies. Third, a comparison of the methods of destruction demonstrates that, although the death camp was a successful adaptation to the exigencies of mass murder in the Third Reich, less sophisticated methods including repeated massacres and mass starvation can also prove to be effective in perpetrating total domestic genocide. Indeed, they have proved to be so in the contemporary world.

Finally, since genocide is a crime against humanity and not simply a historical event like the French Revolution, its occurrence raises many juridical, moral, and existential issues that a comparative empirical analysis cannot resolve. Nevertheless, by helping to identify the causes of genocide and their variations, an empirical work might help in laying the groundwork for more informed philosophical and normative discussions.[9]

NINE

Revolution and Genocide

We must crush both the interior and the exterior enemies of
the Republic, or perish with her. And in this situation, the first
maxim of our policy should be to conduct the people by reason, and the enemies of the people by terror.

Robespierre[1]

Yet the people continued to be menaced by an anti-power,
which like the nation was abstract, omnipresent, and all en-
veloping, but which was hidden where the nation was public,
individual where the nation was universal, and harmful where
the nation was good. This anti-power was thus the negative,
the inverse, the anti-principle of the nation.

François Furet[2]

Until recently the dominant image of revolution in the West has
radiated progress, power, heroism, justice, and liberty. Old regimes were
said to crumble because of their inherent incapacities to deal with the
modern world, and their destruction was explained as both necessary and
just. Revolutions were necessary because societies that wanted either to
join or to resist the modern world of states and capitalism had first to
abolish the decrepit and despotic preindustrial political, economic, social, and cultural order and the elites that governed it. Revolutions were
just because the old regimes were invariably based on patterns of domination that precluded liberty or equality.

Revolutions were also heroic struggles because, it was said, they
were led by noble, self-sacrificing, and daring vanguards that had the

courage and foresight to strike out at the old regimes when the time was ripe. Upon coming to power the revolutionaries or their epigones were able to erect a new social and political order that was more powerful, more free, and more just than the old regime, though regretfully their rule may have been punctuated by periods of violence and terror.

These images come to us through the history, literature, journalism, film, art, music, statuary, and architecture following the English, the American, the French, the Russian, and the Chinese revolutions. Indeed, in recent years the Cuban, the Algerian, the Vietnamese, and the Nicaraguan revolutions have evoked some of this imagery, at least as seen on the democratic left in the West.

It is distinctly not my purpose to debunk the revolutionary tradition and to throw my lot in with its detractors. Though the human costs of revolutions were always high, in many important instances their results were indeed to uplift the poor, educate the illiterate, open up the social structure to merit, broaden liberty and participation, strengthen the state against foreign exploitation, and help to adapt society and economy to modernization and industrialization. Still the destruction of old regimes and the rise of revolutionary vanguards to power have not always brought forth the millennium.

Actually, in some instances like the Turkish, the Stalinist, the German, the Ethiopian, and the Cambodian revolutions, the old regimes collapsed, and sometimes more moderate regimes intervened, but the visions and policies of the revolutionaries who ultimately came to power either had little to do with liberal or socialist ends or their attempts at creating a new community were so outrageously violent that the human costs of their rule far outweighed the benefits.[3]

Taking a leaf from Talmon we can see that, from the perspective of the end of the twentieth century, many revolutions, including those in the Third World, were more likely to lead to totalitarian messianic democracy than to pluralist and liberal democracy. In retrospect, even liberal and democratic revolutions demonstrated violent facets to those who were excluded from the political community.[4]

This chapter will elaborate the conceptual framework linking revolution to genocide which was first discussed in the Introduction. The first section shall briefly discuss the destruction of the Kulaks and the Cambodian "autogenocide," in order both to illustrate the hypothesis and to present some confirming evidence not based on the Armenian Genocide and the Holocaust. The second section shall examine more fully the reasons why there may be a link between revolution and genocide. The third section shall discuss some of the apparent exceptions to the pattern that genocide is linked to revolution, since it is not the case that every revolution leads to genocide nor that every genocide is a product only of revolution.

Two Illustrative and Confirming Cases

As noted in the Introduction, a comparison of the Armenian Genocide to the Holocaust suggests that under some circumstances genocide may be a by-product of revolution: once an old regime collapses and revolutionaries seize power, they are presented with an opportunity to create a new order more in keeping with their visions. To respond to the revolutionary situation and to implement their ideological desires, however, they may destroy not only the old regime's institutions but also their political opponents and the communal groups and classes that they identify with their enemies. Thus it was that after the collapse of the Ottoman and German Empires, revolutionary vanguards seized power and destroyed the Armenians and the Jews, respectively, ancient peoples that had become targets of the new regimes.

By the same token, however, genocide linked to revolution can take place against social classes and need not be directed only against a communal group or an "ethnos."[5] The destruction of the Kulaks by the Stalinist regime and the murder of the upper and middle classes in Kampuchea by the Khmer Rouge help to confirm and to illustrate that point.

The Stalinist Revolution and the Destruction of the Kulaks

The Bolsheviks were utopian revolutionaries for whom the seizure of state power in 1917 was only a first step toward an ultimate goal: the transformation of Russian society, indeed of the whole world. But the transformation of Russian society was no easy matter. After they had seized power, following the civil war (1917–21), they were confronted with a social structure that was largely inimical to them and to their ends.

The social revolution was much more difficult to engineer than the political revolution of November 1917. The Bolsheviks, largely an urban intelligentsia, were able to gain control of the cities, but the countryside and the bulk of Russian society were organized along traditional peasant lines and were not under their command. In effect, the problem of transforming Russia boiled down to what to do about the peasantry.

The Russian census of 1897 shows that, out of a population of about 105 million, there were 100 million peasants. This ratio did not change substantially when the Bolsheviks took power in 1917.[6] Though they had conquered the cities, in Russia's vast countryside they were absent or isolated. They were also resented by the peasantry for having practiced forced requisitioning during the civil war, and they were feared as intending to wrest back the land that the peasants had seized during the early phase of the revolution.

The problem of the peasantry had both an economic and a political side. The economic problem was how to raise agricultural productivity that would feed the cities and produce a surplus of commodities in order to generate desperately needed capital for industrialization. The political problem was how to solve the economic problem without at the same time creating an independent farming class that would challenge Soviet power in the countryside.

In the first instance a solution to the economic problem was attempted by the New Economic Policy (NEP) that left the expropriated lands of the old regime in the hands of the peasants and relied on market forces to bring the agricultural surplus to the cities. The NEP solution, in effect, relied on the implementation of economic policies that would be favorable to agriculture and would encourage Soviet peasants to plant a surplus and to sell it at a profit to the state. Bukharin and the "rightist opposition" favored the development of a free farming class in a context of a socialist economy and therefore viewed the measures adopted during the NEP period as a more or less permanent solution, or at least as a basis for one.[7] For Preobrazhensky and the "leftist opposition," however, NEP was perceived as a momentary stopgap measure that would have to yield to the collectivization of agriculture.

The debate between the right and the left, those who favored continuing NEP and those who wanted to abolish it, was resolved politically when Stalin came to power in 1927. His devious path to power need not delay us here. Suffice it to say that he adopted the position of the left opposition. This was in part due to economic factors such as the failed harvest of 1928 and the difficulties that the regime had with getting peasants to grow grain for the market. But economic reasons were not the primary ones for the destruction of NEP and the launching of forced draft collectivization and industrialization. The basic reasons were political and ideological. Indeed, what appeared as purely "structural" or economic obstacles to agricultural production were themselves the result of bungling and Stalinist policies seeking to implement Communist ideology and to establish state power over the countryside.[8]

Dekulakization

The Stalinists rationalized the attack on the peasantry in terms of intensifying the supposed class struggle in the countryside. They claimed that the peasantry was divided into three strata: the Kulak, the middle peasant, and the poor peasant. The Kulak was said to be a capitalist farmer who owned land, farm animals, and machinery, and hired wage labor to get his chores done. The middle peasant owned land and some means of production but did not or could not afford to hire wage labor. The poor peasant owned neither land nor means of farm production. Collectivization, in theory, was to destroy the Kulak as a class, with the help of the middle and poor peasant. The latter two classes would support collectivization because in this manner they would share in the land, the labor, and the means of production while at the same time they would help to destroy their exploiter, the supposedly hated Kulak.

This Stalinist view of the peasantry was sheer ideological fantasy. In the first place, the peasantry had supported the revolution and had even a modicum of trust in the state mainly because the peasants had seized land from the aristocratic landlords of the old regime and had been permitted to hold on to this prize during NEP. The peasantry had risen for land and peace, not for abstract Marxist slogans. Even the poor peasant who had a parcel of land clung to it and would resist any government attempt to take it away. In the second place, following the forced requisitioning that had been practiced during the civil war, the peasantry—rich, middle, and poor—was deeply suspicious of the state's intentions. In the third place, there was no clear way of distinguishing Kulaks from other peasants: If a farmer hired three other peasants to bring in his wheat on time was he a Kulak? And, last, there was no class struggle in the countryside.[9] In effect, the term "Kulak" was an ideological invention meant to crush an independent peasantry and to establish Soviet power in rural Russia.

In order to implement their scheme of collectivization, the Stalinists had to organize party, police, and army cadres to destroy the "Kulaks" and force the peasants onto collective farms. Once collectivization was set in motion, something like a war broke out in the countryside. The state's cadres would swoop down on unarmed peasant villages. Having been arbitrarily so identified, the so-called Kulaks among the villagers would be expropriated and deported to labor camps in Siberia. The rest were collectivized. Those who resisted were killed. Those who were deported perished in the millions, either on the way or in the Gulag itself

It is estimated that some 11 million peasants perished during the collectivization.[10] The mythical "Kulaks" had been destroyed and the revolution "saved."

Like the Armenians in Turkey and the Jews in Germany, millions of peasants in Russia and Ukraine were massacred, starved to death, and destroyed as a social category, not because of anything they had done or not done but because they were perceived as being essential enemies of a new postrevolutionary social and political order. The very success of some free farmers was a provocation to the revolutionary vanguard that had seized power.

Feeling themselves surrounded by foreign capitalist enemies, the Stalinists feared the Kulaks. The success of capitalist farmers raised the spectre of capitalism's ultimate triumph over communism, and it suggested an alternate vision of modernity—one that might challenge the power of the postrevolutionary state, its political myth, and its version of reality. This was the ideological motive driving the Stalinist revolution, and this is why the Kulaks had to be destroyed as a class.

A contrasting perspective minimizes the role of ideology in Stalinist motives, especially in the policy of collectivization.[11] It views Stalin's policies as deriving not from Bolshevik ideology but from the structural exigencies following the revolution and the NEP period. Accordingly, the new Soviet state, isolated in the cities, needed to impose Bolshevik rule in the countryside. Moreover, in the absence of strong market forces, the Soviet state needed to requisition agricultural surplus in order to further its policies of industrialization. Both these conditions, not ideology, led to collectivization and mass destruction of the peasantry.

One can admire the argument in its parsimonious use of variables and its avoidance of ideological and psychological elements when structural factors alone would suffice, but in this case it seems to me that the analysis stretches a point.[12] Thus the structural analysis of Stalin's collectivization program overlooks both the ideological and contingent elements in the situation. Marx and the Bolsheviks shared an ideologically rooted antagonism to the peasantry. Moreover, politics and chance played crucial roles in Stalin's coming to power.[13] Without his climb to power—not a foregone conclusion at all—it is questionable that other Bolsheviks like Trotsky and Bukharin would have perpetrated Stalin's crimes.[14] Indeed, the ruthlessness with which collectivization was carried out may be due ultimately not only to ideology but also to the paranoid personality of Stalin himself.[15]

Our analysis leaves an important point unexplained: Why did the

263

destruction of the Kulaks as a class imply the murder of so many? Indeed, following Marxist analysis it might be argued that a former Kulak who had been expropriated and had become landless was no longer a Kulak. "Objectively" he was no longer "an enemy of the state." As a landless peasant, the expropriated Kulak might be driven onto a collective farm, he might even need reeducation, but deporting him or killing him and his family implied that his social background alone, not his role in society, made him inherently an "enemy of the state."

As Gouldner points out, a major feature of the Stalinist theory of crime and punishment was based on imputing antisocial and criminal intent to individuals on the basis of their social or national background. [16] This primitive reading of Marx, which became a fundamental tenet of Stalinism, must be viewed as a primary cause of the genocide perpetrated against strata of the Russian and Ukrainian peasantry. A similar pattern appeared years later following the Cambodian revolution.

The Cambodian Revolution and Genocide

Cambodia fits the pattern of the other revolutions that have been discussed: an old regime placed in a disadvantaged position in the world arena failed to reform and was succeeded by a relatively moderate military regime which was swept aside by a radical vanguard. What followed was social revolution and genocide.

Like the Young Turks, the Stalinists, and the Nazis, the Khmer Rouge were a revolutionary vanguard that came to power following the collapse of an old regime and the failure of its moderate successor. The government of Prince Sihanouk tried to thread its way among the brutal contenders of Indochina, which at one time or another included the French, the Japanese, the Russians, the Chinese, the Americans and the Vietnamese. Using tactics born of internal weakness, the prince relied on a cunning use of timely alliances to keep Cambodia independent. When the Vietnam war spilled over into Cambodia, however, and the North Vietnamese began to use Eastern Cambodia as a refuge, his regime was doomed. With American support the Cambodian army staged a coup against the Sihanouk regime, coming to power on 18 March 1970. Despite massive bombings by the Americans, the new regime headed by Lon Nol, Sihanouk's former commander-in-chief, failed in its attempt to dislodge the Vietnamese from the eastern provinces or to defeat the Khmer Rouge. [17]

While the old regime had failed to protect the territorial integrity of the nation and was replaced by a military coup, the Khmer Rouge had managed to identify their movement with Khmer nationalism. In the eyes of many Cambodians the Lon Nol regime seemed corrupt, ineffective, and dependent on American imperialism and its strategy of massive bombing of the countryside. Only the Communists, living apparently simple, virtuous, and dedicated lives among the peasants in the northeastern and northwestern provinces, seemed to hold out hope for a regenerated and independent Cambodia. Lacking Sihanouk's legitimacy and cunning, having to fight both the Vietnamese occupiers and a civil war with the Communists, the Lon Nol regime was swept aside by more radical forces. The victorious Khmer Rouge entered Phnom Penh on 17 April 1975. This was the revolutionary background to the genocide.

"Autogenocide"

Upon seizing power, the Khmer Rouge set about destroying minority ethnic groups such as the Overseas Chinese, the Vietnamese, and the Chams, and classes such as the old nobility and the new urban commercial and professional middle classes that had flourished under Sihanouk and Lon Nol. The destruction of the ethnic groups seemed to have been based on Cambodian racism and paranoia—the sense that if drastic actions were not taken the Khmers were a doomed race destined to be submerged or destroyed, especially by the Vietnamese.[18] The destruction of classes, especially of the fledgling middle class, seemed to be based on a primitive Maoist interpretation of Marxism whereby the middle classes were a "compradore" bourgeoisie, essentially agents of foreign capitalist powers. In this case, as in the destruction of the Kulaks, the class background of a person sentenced him or her to deportation or death, usually the latter.[19]

It should also be noted that, in a manner similar to the party purges during the Stalin period in Russia, the Khmer Rouge turned upon themselves. These Khmer Rouge killings were usually initiated by the top leadership, calling itself "Angka" or "the Center."[20] The victims were the leadership and cadres in the various zones into which Cambodia had been divided. Here the reasons for the killings seemed to follow a peculiar logic that attributed failures in the economic or military spheres, not to bad planning or to lack of resources but to treacherous plots usually fomented and supported by outside powers like the Americans or to the Vietnamese. This accounts for the destruction of party cadres in the Northern and Eastern zones. Such massacres followed the Stalinist model which did not stop with the accused but included his family, colleagues, and acquaintances. These, too, had to be eliminated. Indeed, in killing everyone, the Khmer Rouge purges were relatively even more extensive and bloody than the Stalinist.

It has been estimated that out of a population of some 7 million, nearly 2 million Cambodians were killed in communal or class genocides perpetrated by the Khmer Rouge.[21] As in other cases of revolutionary genocide that we have examined in this study, the killings were carried out after the seizure of power. The Khmer Rouge tried to reconstitute society in their own image and to eliminate groups that either might have opposed their being in power or who did not fit into the new political order.[22]

Since Khmer Rouge support supposedly rested on the working class and the peasantry, the urban middle class—especially in the capital city of Phnom Penh—was identified with the corrupt, dependent, and treacherous old order that had sold out the Cambodians to the Americans and other foreign powers. The urban middle classes were viewed as the enemy, not only because they had seemed to oppose the Khmer Rouge but also because from a theoretical, ideological point of view they were a dependent bourgeoisie, dangerous domestic agents in league with foreign capitalist interests. This placed them outside the moral universe of the revolution that included only poor peasants and workers. Not only were the upper and middle classes not proletarians, in the eyes of the Khmer Rouge they had ceased being Khmer. Thus the middle class had to be eliminated. Moreover, even the city had to be gutted because it was the environment and the symbol of the decadent old order where the nobility and the hated middle class had lived and pursued their interests.

The Khmer Rouge were strongly influenced by both the Stalinist and Maoist models of revolution.[23] Despite Stalin's contempt for the peasantry, however, it is ironic that the main victims of the Cambodian revolution were not the peasants but the urban middle classes. This shows that revolutionary genocide, even when apparently following the directives of the same ideology, does not always target the same victims for elimination. Indeed, victims cannot always be predicted a priori. Sometimes these are communal groups, at other times they may be classes; sometimes they may be peasants, at other times they may be urban middle classes. The crux of the matter is not the empirical identity of the victimized groups prior to the revolution but how their identities are defined and interpreted by the revolutionary vanguard consolidating its power and pursuing its vision of a reconstituted state and society. These points will be taken up in greater detail below.

Having briefly touched on the destruction of the Kulaks and the

Cambodian "autogenocide" as possible confirmations of our main thesis, we can proceed to elaborate the explanatory framework linking total genocide to revolution that was briefly described in the Introduction. Such a framework needs to explain why certain revolutions lead to genocide while others do not, and why certain genocides are the products of revolution while others are not. In what follows I shall examine in greater detail the relationship between revolution and genocide, and in the last section try to account for some of the apparent exceptions to the relationship, that is, revolutions that do not produce genocides and genocides that are not the products of revolutions.

An Explanatory Framework Elaborated

As noted earlier, a causal analysis of genocide that limits itself to the motives and ideology of the perpetrators cannot be sufficient. Both the ideologies of the revolutionaries and the structural conditions under which they try to wield power are essential for an analysis of any policy including genocide.

Every revolution results in not only the collapse of a state's political institutions but also the loss of its legitimacy and the destruction of the political myth that links rulers to the ruled.[24] These effects have very little to do with the ideology of the vanguards vying for power during the revolutionary interregnum. Military defeat and domestic collapse had more to do with the undermining of the French, Russian, Chinese, Ottoman, German, and Cambodian old regimes, including their systems of legitimation, than the ideologies of the Jacobins, the Bolsheviks, the Maoists, the Young Turks, the Nazis, or the Khmer Rouges.

Thus every revolution creates opportunities for vanguards to seize power and to reconstruct the system of legitimacy and the political myth. Most revolutions are precipitated by and cause international tensions and war. Both of these results of revolution can be structural preconditions for genocide. We shall take these points up one at a time.

Genocide and the Recasting of Political Myth

Ideologies and political myths are basic to revolutions because, in a compelling manner, they tell the tale of the revolutionary state's origins; they identify and define the new state's true citizens, "the people,"; they target its enemies; and they formulate its goals. Revolutionary ideologies and myths are not necessarily pure fancy. Indeed, they gain credibility to the extent that the tale they tell has the semblance of historical truth, but validity is not what is at issue. For these beliefs to have profound implications in the public policy arena following a revolution, it is enough that revolutionary vanguards and their supporters firmly believe in their ideologies and myths and come to comprehend history and their own existential situation as deriving from their images and postulates. This may include a public policy of extermination or genocide.

Revolutionary myths and ideologies have implications for genocide in that every revolutionary vanguard that has achieved state power seeks to restructure the state and give it a new basis of support. To that end revolutionaries seek to persuade "the people," that is, a specially designated subset of a territorial state's inhabitants, of the revolution's justice and the new state's legitimacy.

But revolutionary vanguards need not be limited to the role of ardent wooers of something called "society," the "people," the "nation," or the "race." Having come to power in a revolutionary situation, a new regime is presented with the opportunity to shape society in its own image and to construct and redefine who is this "people" from whom this revolutionary state will seek its legitimacy. This opportunity is a structural by-product of revolutions and is largely independent of the ideology of the revolutionaries themselves. Thus the Young Turks in 1908, the Bolsheviks in 1917, the Nazis in 1933, and the Khmer Rouge in 1975 were given the opportunity to shape their respective societies by the revolutionary collapse of the various old regimes and their fragile successors. This was a structural, not an ideological or cultural, precondition for total domestic genocide.

The impulse to reconstruct and redefine the political community and to exclude from it whole categories derives in part from the exigencies of the postrevolutionary situation. This is always characterized by domestic disorder, a lack of legitimate authority, and often war. It is not enough for the revolutionary vanguard to have occupied the buildings and offices of the old regime. There are domestic and international enemies who wish to destroy it, or appear to do so, and the "people" who might support it appear as an inchoate mass.

It is the "people," that is, a segment or stratum of society at large excluding the alleged enemies of the revolution, who need to be reformed and reshaped into a collectivity of supporters of the revolutionary state. To this end they need to be given a new identity. After 1793 the Parisian revolutionary crowds became or, better yet, were recast as the "sans culottes"; after 1908 Muslim Ottomans speaking Turkish were recast as "Turks"; after 1917 Russian industrial workers were recast as "proletarians"; after 1933 non-Jewish German burghers were recast as "Aryans"; and after April 1975 some Cambodian workers and the poorest peasants were recast as *penh sith*—individuals who had full rights in the new order.[25]

The recast community is then labeled the "people," rightful heirs of kings and princes, the source of the new regime's legitimacy. It is then flattered, cajoled, and rewarded, and if need be threatened and terrorized, into playing its part in supporting the new regime and its new order. The power of revolutionary vanguards to redefine reality is not unlimited, but given their control over mass communication and education and their willingness to use police terror they can go a long way in recreating society to conform to their myths.

But recasting the political community according to a revolutionary vision implies that groups and classes, whole categories of human beings, will not fit into the postrevolutionary society. These will have to be reshaped, reeducated, reformed, or permanently excluded from the new order. Thus native Americans, "Indians," and persons of African ancestry, "Negroes," were either totally or partially excluded from or never even considered as citizens of the new Republic following the American revolution; aristocrats were excluded from the Republic following the French Revolution and became "uncitizens" in Schama's terms; Armenians were redefined and excluded from the Turkish national community following the Young Turk revolution; the Bourgeoisie was excluded from Soviet society following the Russian revolution; Jews were excluded from the Aryan racial community following the Nazi revolution; and the *bannheu*, especially those who belonged to the urban "compradore bourgeoisie," were excluded from the Kampuchean community following the Khmer Rouge revolution in Cambodia.[26]

"The Enemies of the Revolution"

Chapters 5 and 7 make the case that the conception of the "Turk" in Turkish nationalism and that of the "Aryan" in Nazi racialism had significant implications for those who were not Turkish or Aryans. "Turk" and "Aryan" were new identities fashioned in revolutionary milieus, derived from ideological premises concerning nations and races, and in need of negative counterparts. The negative counterparts to the "people-of-the-revolution" were, in Furet's terms, the "anti-power," "the enemies-of-the-revolution." Thus counterposed to the "citoyen" was the "royalist," to the "comrade" was the "bourgeois" or the "Kulak," to the "Turk" was the "Gavur," especially the Armenian, to the "Aryan *Volk Genosse*" was the Jew, and to the *"penh sith"* was the *"bannheu"* in the Cambodian revolution.

There was great variation from revolution to revolution, however, in what determined who would be labeled as "enemies-of-the-revolution" and in how they were treated. Earlier, when the experiences of Armenians and Jews in the two genocides were contrasted, it was seen that their treatment depended on the ideologies of the revolutionary regimes, on the identities of the victims, and on the wartime circumstances surrounding the Turkish and the German revolutions.

The exclusion of Jews from the Aryan political community on racial grounds and the exclusion of Armenians from the Turkish political community for nationalist reasons had somewhat different implications for the scope of the two genocides. The contrast between Jew and Aryan derived from an ideology of antisemitism and racialism, while that between Armenian and Turk originated in Turkish nationalism. The first was drawn along issues of assimilation, intermarriage, and purity of lineal descent. The second was defined by language, religion, and territory. An Armenian who spoke Turkish and converted to Islam could become a Turk. A converted Jew no matter how German in appearance, culture, or behavior, according to Nazism, could never be an Aryan German. The crime of the Armenian was to be a non-Turk occupying and appearing to claim sovereignty over the territory of the Turkish heartland. The crime of the Jew was to be a nonhuman claiming to be human. Thus the destruction of the Armenians entailed an attack on Ottoman Armenians or Armenians who lived in the projected Pan-Turkish empire, not on the world's Armenian population. Such were the territorial limits of the destruction imposed by revolutionary nationalism in the Turkish revolution. In contrast, driven by Nazi ideology, the revolution and war against the Jews was of global scope.

Those excluded from the Young Turk and the Nazi revolutions were communal groups or ethnoreligious communities that by themselves did not constitute separate socioeconomic classes. Conversely, however, the primary victims of the Stalinist and Cambodian revolutions were social classes. In the former it was largely the "Kulaks," while in the latter it was the hated *bannheu*, the "compradore bourgeoisie," although communal groups like the Chams, the Vietnamese, and the Overseas Chinese were also included among the victims. Thus we see that the identity of the victims and even the scope of the genocides differed from instance to instance. For Turkish nationalists, the victims appeared as "alien national groups"; for Nazi racists the victims appeared as "Jews" and "races"; for the Stalinists and for the Khmer Rouge the victims appeared primarily as "social classes." In each instance terms like "nation," "race," and "class" were ultimately defined by the killers themselves.[27]

Excluding a group from the postrevolutionary definition of what constitutes a member of the "people" and labeling it as "enemies of the revolution" is a necessary if not yet a sufficient condition for genocide. The probability of genocide increases considerably, however, when, in the midst of war, those who have been so excluded and labeled come to be identified with the foreign enemies of the revolutionary state. They are then said to constitute a plot, a mortal threat against the state, and violent measures against them may be proposed.

Revolution, War, and Genocide

It is striking that the Armenian Genocide, the Holocaust, the Cambodian "autogenocide," and the genocidal policies of other regimes have often followed on revolutions and have been pursued in the midst of war or civil war. The relationships between revolution and war, and war and genocide, are the topics of this section. We start with the connection between revolution and war.

As discussed above, revolutions are often the products of international crises that undermine old regimes. Later, the movements that seek and attain power after the collapse of old regimes are concerned with consolidating their positions domestically and in radically improving their country's standing in the international arena. To this end they seek foreign allies and target foreign enemies. At the same time those movements opposing the revolution also forge links to the international arena. Meanwhile states in the international arena concern themselves with the outcomes of a revolution and try to intervene in its course in order to further and protect their interests. For all these reasons revolutions can lead to wars.

Thus, for example, the National Assembly under the control of the Girondists declared war on 20 April 1792, following the threat of the Austrians and the Prussians to restore the ancien régime. It is an illusion, argues Skocpol, to suggest that this conflict was an accident that made the revolutionary regime somehow swerve off its liberal and moderate course and thrust itself into war and the Terror.

> To believe this is to suppose that the Revolution could have proceeded, let alone broken out, in a France somehow suddenly and miraculously ripped out of the context of the European state system. . . . Underlying the initial outbreaks of war (between France

and Austria) in 1792 and the recurrent outbreaks on ever wider scales thereafter were simply the long-established tensions and balance-of-power dynamics of the European state system—now interacting with . . . the unfolding revolution.[28]

Indeed, suggests Schama, it was the messianic vision of a world transformed by revolution, not only the struggle for power and interest that led to war. Thus on 20 April 1792 with Louis XVI present in the assembly, a revolutionary carried away by the moment, proclaiming himself "Orator of the Human Race," declared:

> Here is the crisis of the universe. God disentangled the primitive chaos; the French will unravel the feudal chaos . . . for free men are Gods on earth. . . . [Kings] make impious war on us with slave soldiers and extorted money; we will make a holy war with free soldiers and patriotic contributions.[29]

In the wake of the international war, the French Revolution turned radical and by 1793 had launched the Terror. But the radical phase of the Revolution, including the Terror, cannot be blamed on the war alone, for the dynamics of the Revolution had done much to precipitate that war in the first place. Some forty thousand were murdered by the Terror and conceivably more than a quarter of a million perished in the reprisals against the insurrection in the Vendée alone. One need not stigmatize the whole of the French Revolution as irredeemably genocidal, as Reynald Sécher has done, to note that its human costs were very high indeed.[30]

Wartime in turn further radicalized the French Revolution and helped spawn the Terror, if not genocide. What was true of the French Revolution was true of others as well. The Young Turk revolution that had started in 1908 as a liberal coup seeking to transform the Ottoman Empire, by 1914 had become a xenophobic anti-Western Pan-Turkic revolution seeking to create a new empire on the basis of Turkic nationality. Expecting victory over their foreign and domestic foes, the Young Turks joined the Germans in their war against Russia, and a few months after the war started they launched what came to be known as the Armenian Genocide. Similarly, after the defeat of Imperial Germany in 1918, that country was first led by a moderate liberal Weimar Republic. But the liberal phase of the German revolution was also short-lived. By 1933, the Nazis had come to power, and six years later were at war with Europe. It was in the context of that war that the Final Solution was formulated and executed.

By redefining the political community, revolutions cast certain classes and communal groups into the role of the enemies of society and the revolutionary state. When such collectivities are or can be linked to foreign enemies in wartime, the chances of their becoming targets of repression and even genocide are considerably increased. This is so for at least three reasons:

1. Wartime aggravates feelings of vulnerability and/or intensifies feelings of invincibility. In both cases it contributes an essential psychological element to the radical phases of revolutions that turn genocidal.

2. Wartime permits states to become more autonomous and independent of domestic and foreign public opinion, thereby encouraging radical solutions to social and political "problems."

3. Wartime conditions may close off other policy options, leaving genocide as a strong choice for an already radicalized regime.

Wartime conditions can aggravate feelings of vulnerability or intensify delusions of invincibility. Paradoxically, both of these emotions may encourage radical "final" solutions to political problems. Thus, for example, fearing Russian conquest, the Young Turks started to implement the measures that ended in the genocide of 1915. In the same way, expecting imminent attack by the capitalist powers, the Stalinists launched their collectivization campaign. In contrast, however, drunk with the prospect of great victories following their invasion of Russia, the Nazis started the destruction of Russian Jewry and the Final Solution. Similarly, deluded into believing that in April 1975 they had defeated not only Lon Nol but the United States as well, the Khmer Rouge launched their "autogenocide." In each case a communal group or class was seen as an essential enemy of the revolution. The decision to destroy it could be taken either as a prophylactic against internal dissension, treachery, and defeat and/or as a Final Solution to a long-standing problem, a "solution" made possible by the projected victory.

Such decisions were made easier because in wartime states feel more autonomous from internal social forces and external pressures, and hence they are ready to act as they please, at least in the domestic arena. Following the start of the First World War, the Committee of Union and Progress did not need to pay heed to the demands for autonomy made by Armenian parties or to the pressures for reform from the Great Powers. Following his overwhelming attack on Russia, Hitler could do as he predicted, which was to gain *Lebensraum* and to destroy Jewry. Following their victorious conquest of Phnom Penh, the Khmer Rouge could do as they pleased. They were unconcerned with the views of the "imperialists," or even with the views of their allies, the Chinese Communists, who had advised a more cautious approach.

Radical decisions were also more likely in war because wartime conditions seem to the perpetrators to close off other options or make them appear as too costly to implement. Before the First World War there was some discussion between the Young Turks and Armenian representatives regarding granting the Armenians greater autonomy in the Ottoman Empire. The war with Russia made such a possibility moot, at least for the Young Turks. Before the attack on Russia, there was some talk in Nazi circles about other solutions to the "Jewish Problem," such as deporting the Jews to Madagascar or to the east. The escalation of the war made the Final Solution possible and put an end to such talk. Before the collectivization campaign in Russia, there was discussion about continuing the policies of the NEP, but these were condemned as either too slow or betraying revolutionary commitments, given the expected war against the capitalist powers. Before he seized power, Pol Pot had been warned by none other than a dying Zhou Enlai not to tread the radical path of the Chinese revolution. "Don't follow the bad example of our great leap forward. Take things slowly: that is the best way to guide Kampuchea and its people to growth, prosperity, and happiness," said Zhou.[31] But once they had captured power the Khmer Rouge paid no heed to such prudent advice. Indeed, they came to the conclusion that both the Russian and the Chinese revolutions had not been radical enough because they had allowed the growth of party bureaucracy, "the experts," to undermine the revolutionary dynamism of "the reds."[32] Pol Pot and his cadres would avoid such "errors" by exterminating such "experts" and the classes from which they sprang.

The Vulnerability of the Victims

Having touched on how revolutions can predispose revolutionary vanguards in power to commit genocide, here we examine the situation of the victims: Why were they excluded from the revolutionary community? Why were they perceived as domestic enemies in wartime? And hence why were they targeted for genocide? Why they and not another group? The answers to these questions depend less on who the victims were and what they did than on what they represented to their killers.

To begin to answer these questions one should first look to the ideologies of the revolutionaries who have seized power. The integral nationalism and Pan-Turkism of the CUP, the antisemitism and racialism of the Nazis, the Marxism of the Stalinists, and the radical Maoist version of communism of the Khmer Rouge were primary sources of the stereotypes and the negative identities that targeted the Armenians, the Jews, the "Kulaks," and the Cambodian middle classes. These constructs had less to do with the real life situation of the victims than with the projected visions of their tormentors. Nevertheless, even if these were projections, the question still remains: Was there something in the structural situation of the victims that increased their vulnerability?

As noted in the Introduction (Chap. 1), Armenians and Jews were vulnerable because of their traditionally excluded or despised statuses as *dhimmis* or pariahs who experienced rapid progress and social mobilization in the prerevolutionary period. The social mobilization of excluded and despised groups outraged the sensibilities of traditional elites on the one hand and of contemporary nationalists and racists on the other hand. Traditional elites in the Ottoman Empire and Imperial Germany feared that Armenian and Jewish progress was undermining an already weakened old order. Meanwhile, Turkish nationalists and German racists balked at including traditionally despised groups in the newly formed and valued Turkish and German national and racial communities. Moreover, the rapid progress of such groups and their demands for autonomy or assimilation were viewed as further provocation.

The existence of diasporas living in Russia for both minorities may have aggravated the paranoid fears of revolutionary regimes, especially in the circumstances of impending war with that country. Russia was the enemy of the Turks in the First World War and of the Germans in both world wars. The CUP accused Ottoman Armenians of betrayal and of loyalty to the Russian side during the war. The Nazis viewed Russia and communism as the tools of the "Jewish World Conspiracy," making all Jews everywhere, especially in Russia, part of a plot to control the world and to destroy Germany and the Aryan race.

The Young Turks and the Nazis came to believe—the former while in power, the latter even before they had seized power—that the major reason for the disasters besetting their societies was the mobilization of despised minorities with connections to their enemies. Moreover, the very success of these minorities and their chance connections to the regime's enemies—at a time of war and grave crisis for both state and society—was interpreted as evidence of a plot against Germany and the Aryan race and the Ottoman Empire, respectively. In both instances the regime's belief that minorities were hatching a plot in league with foreign enemies became the construction that was used to justify genocide. It is in this context, for example, that *The Protocols of the Elders of Zion* came to be believed in Germany, while the view that the Armenians were plotting to destroy Turkey in alliance with the Russians came to be accepted in the Ottoman Empire.[33] Indeed, this view of the role of the Armenians is still widely held in Turkey and in some academic circles abroad.

Of course, neither the Jews nor the Armenians were responsible for the revolutionary crises that had beset Imperial Germany and the Ottoman Empire, nor for the climate of fear and paranoia that such crises helped to engender. In the sense that they were not responsible for the revolutionary crises, or the motives of their tormentors, Jews and Armenians may be viewed as scapegoats; nevertheless, the successful modernization and progress of each community and their cosmopolitan connections to diasporas in Russia and elsewhere fed the climate of threat and fear. Their success and international connections were the half-truths that made big lies possible. Jews and Armenians, therefore, were not simply chosen at random or because they were hated in the past the way scapegoats often are. Their identity as distinct low-status minorities, their success in the modern world, and their situation at a time of profound revolutionary crisis and war for the larger society made them available for victimization. In each case their situation was grist to the mill of the revolutionary ideology of their killers.

It may be noted in passing that in the contemporary postwar world there exist other upwardly mobile excluded groups that may be vulnerable for victimization. Among these one can single out the Overseas Chinese in Indonesia, Malaysia, and elsewhere in Asia, and the Indians and Pakistanis in Uganda and elsewhere in Africa. Although they do not exactly fit the mold of the Armenians and Jews because they did not occupy traditionally despised statuses, nevertheless such groups have been excluded on other grounds and have experienced massacre and expulsion in various parts of the world.

Referring once again to the Soviet and the Cambodian instances as confirming evidence, one notes that the distinctive victims of the Stalinists were capitalist peasants known as "Kulaks," while the Khmer Rouge attacked members of an urban social class that was defined as the "compradore bourgeoisie" or the *bannheu*. Like the Armenians and Jews, the Kulaks and the Cambodian bourgeoisie consisted of people who had apparently succeeded in adapting to the capitalist economy, who might have had commercial and other links to the capitalist and "imperialist" enemies of the revolution, and who represented a version of the modern world that was totally inimical to the visions of the revolutionaries. The situations of the Kulaks and the *bannheu* complemented the paranoid ideology of the Stalinists and the Khmer Rouge, and for that reason they were killed.

It is clearly not possible to predict with certainty which groups will be the targets of revolutionary regimes trying to refashion their societies in wartime. Nevertheless, our examples show that Armenians and Jews could not easily be made over into Turks and Germans, while the existence of Kulaks and middle classes prevented the structural and class homogenization of the Soviet Union and Cambodia, respectively. This suggests that antiliberal revolutionary regimes that reject democratic pluralism and capitalism may be especially prone to total domestic genocide.

Taking a broad historical view of revolutionary developments, it might be suggested that revolutions in England, America, and France were less likely to be genocidal than revolutions in the Ottoman Empire, Russia, Germany, China, and elsewhere. The earlier revolutions were led by aristocratic landlords against kings in powerful countries that were relatively secure in the international arena. The leaders of these revolutions were more concerned with individual political and economic liberties than with questions of national unity and class homogeneity. In contrast, the leaders of the later revolutions felt that their countries were militarily and economically at a serious disadvantage, often at the hands of states that had experienced successful revolutions of their own in the past.

Leaders of such later revolutions were more likely to feel that communal pluralism and capitalism, leading to class conflict, detracted from national unity and military readiness. Under such circumstances communal groups and classes that made for heterogeneity and political movements that stood for pluralism ran the danger of being identified as "enemies of the revolution" and becoming subject to repression and in wartime to destruction.

An instructive intermediary case is that of the French revolution. At its start it shared some of the characteristics of the English and American revolutions in that its leaders tried to strengthen the powers of the parliament against the king and of the individual against the state. When the revolution spilled into international war, however, and the future of France was at stake, national unity and even class homogeneity at the expense of individual rights became the dominant goals of the Jacobins in power. In that sense the French revolution set an ambiguous precedent for future revolutionaries. On the one hand it stood for the Rights of Man and of Citizens, on the other it represented the nation in arms. The individual rights of citizens are not always best defended by the nation in arms.

The Proposition and Its Limitations

The argument of this essay can be summed up in the following proposition:

> Total domestic genocide as we have defined it here is likely to occur only under circumstances of revolutions that lead to war and is not likely to happen in other contexts. Thus revolutions that lead to war are among the necessary but not sufficient conditions for total domestic genocide. This proposition does not imply, of course, that circumstances of revolution and war will invariably produce total domestic genocides. Also other forms of mass murder may be perpetrated without revolutions that lead to war.

Table 9.1 illustrates further the proposition and cites instances of revolutions and wars that do not lead to total domestic genocide, and of massacres, partial genocides, and total "foreign" genocides that are the products of other conditions, excluding revolutions that lead to war. As discussed, there are no cases of total domestic genocides that are not the products of revolution and war.

Some genocides, those we have called "total domestic genocides," are by-products of a wider pattern that includes revolutionary crises for the state, the ascent to power of movements that are determined to re-fashion their domestic societies according to new political myths and to transform the international system, by war if necessary. Such revolutionary regimes are likely to exclude and to victimize certain communal groups and classes, judging them as not belonging to the new political community and labeling them as "enemies of the state."

Especially vulnerable are ethnic groups and/or social classes that have traditionally been difficult to integrate into the larger society, or have been refused assimilation, at the same time as they have been successful modernizers and have had cultural or commercial connections to the foreign enemies of the regime. In wartime, or with war looming, when such a pattern appears, and other policy options of dealing with communal groups and classes are felt to disappear, genocide may be a likely outcome. Besides the Ottoman Empire and Germany, aspects of this matrix seem to have manifested themselves in Stalinist Russia, and following World War II in Cambodia, and possibly other places as well.

It is a pattern that is contingent and by no means certain. It suggests

TABLE 9.1 Instances of Genocidal and Nongenocidal Outcomes by Revolutions and Other Conditions

	Conditions		
	Total Domestic Genocide	Other Massacres, Partial and Total Genocides	Nongenocidal Repression
	Outcomes		
Revolution followed by war or threat of war	Armenian Genocide, Holocaust, genocide of the Gypsies, destruction of the Kulaks, Cambodian "autogenocide"	French Revolutionary Terror, Vendée, partial genocide of Poles, Russians, and others by Nazis, expulsion of Vietnamese Boat People	Expulsion of Cuban upper and middle classes
Other (e.g., coup, secession, civil war, revolution without war or threat of war, counterrevolution, war without revolution, colonialism)	None	Melos, Genghis Khan, colonial destruction of "native" peoples, Armenian massacres of 1894–96, Russian pogroms, massacre of Indonesian Communist party (1965), Biafra, Kurds in Iraq (1988, 1991)	Apartheid, "reservation" of "native" peoples, internment of Japanese Americans in World War II.

that revolutions that lead to wars create conditions that are potentially genocidal. Whether such conditions in fact lead to genocide depends on the ideology of the perpetrators, the identity and situation of the victims, and the other options that may be open or closed to ideological vanguards that have seized power following a revolution. In order to highlight the argument as well as its limitations we go on to discuss instances of revolutions and wars that did not produce genocide and of total and partial genocides that were not produced by revolutions.[34] A further implication of this work is that nonrevolutionary states are not likely to perpetrate total domestic genocide.

Revolutions and Wars That Did Not Produce Genocide

Some revolutions may lead to genocide because all revolutions attempt to redefine and to recast the political community, and in the process they exclude certain communal groups and classes. It is this exclusion that becomes the necessary condition for genocide, and in that sense revolutions, especially those that lead to war, can provide the circumstances under which necessary conditions for genocide are established. But the exclusion of a group or class from the moral universe of the political community is not the same as killing it and destroying its identity.

For total domestic genocide to take place a communal group or class must come to be viewed by those in power as an essential enemy of the revolutionary state and in league with its foreign foes. Moreover, the policy of destruction must appear to the perpetrators as an onerous but worthwhile task, or at worst as a necessary evil, justified by ideology, and perceived as the simplest and least costly of the policy options facing the state.

Although every revolutionary regime excludes communal groups and classes, every revolution does not lead to war; and even when it does lead to war, the regime does not necessarily identify its domestic with its foreign enemies. Instead, even when it does go to war and does identify its domestic with its foreign enemies, it may be prevented from committing genocide by lack of power, by its ideology and moral scruples, or it may choose policy options like segregation or expulsion that stop short of mass murder. Thus, although revolutions that lead to wars may be necessary, they are not both necessary and sufficient conditions for total domestic genocide.

For example, the English and the American revolutionary regimes, though they could be quite violent, did not go to war with the international system and had other means, short of genocide, for dealing with dissenters. Although the Cuban revolutionary regime singled out the upper and middle classes as enemies of the revolution, and went to war with American proxies, it did not commit genocide. Instead, it encouraged flight and emigration to the United States, thereby getting rid of its real or imagined enemies without having to resort to genocide.[35] During the Terror, the French revolutionary regime went to war, singled out leading aristocrats for execution, and attempted to destroy the aristocracy as a class, but the Jacobins lacked the power and the time to act out some of their genocidal impulses. Thus, although it was very violent, the French Revolution did not lead to a total domestic genocide in the sense that we have used the term here.[36] Similarly, the Marxist revolutionary regime in Vietnam, and the Islamic revolutionary regime in Iran did not commit total domestic genocide. These had other methods, often violent, of dealing with segments and strata that were excluded from the political community and labeled as "enemies of the revolution."[37]

It would take us too far afield to discuss all of these revolutions, but it may be noted that expulsion, social and territorial segregation, flight of minorities, and indoctrination or even destruction of political oppositions were aspects of some of these revolutions. These may have been cruel measures and violations of human rights, but they were not total genocide. In none of these revolutions was there a concerted policy of the state to destroy physically and culturally a communal group or class.

It should also be noted that certain ideologies leave much less room for moral scruples that would place a limit on revolutionary genocide. Foremost among these are racism and Stalinism. In its labeling of certain communal groups as biologically determined enemies of the political community, racism precludes indoctrination and education as a "solution" to a group's exclusion. Stalinism does the same with regard to a group's social origins. In the sense of sentencing persons to persecution and even death, not on the basis of what they have done but because of their supposed biological or social origins, racism and Stalinism are similar and potentially genocidal.

In this connection one may also note the quite extraordinary nature of Nazism as a movement and of Hitler as its leader. As a cult of death, a project to commit genocide on a worldwide scale, Nazism was the very essence, the heart of darkness, of the radical evil that is revolutionary racism. Indeed, in comparing Nazism to Stalinism it is well to remember Raymond Aron's distinction "between a philosophy whose logic is monstrous and one which can be given a monstrous interpretation."[38]

These examples call our attention to an essential indeterminacy of revolutions, if not of all human events. Why Marxism was defined in a genocidal manner in Cambodia, but not in Vietnam or Cuba, in the last analysis may have something to do with the quality of the leadership. Neither Ho nor Castro was a Pol Pot. Had another leader or group of leaders headed the Khmer Rouge, it is possible that the Cambodian revolution might have been less bloody. The point we have tried to make in this study, however, is that certain circumstances, namely, revolutionary breakdowns of old regimes, wars, and the modernization of despised groups, make it more likely although not certain for the Hitlers and the Pol Pots of this world to seize power and to make their bloody mark.

Total Genocides That Were Not the Products of Revolutions

This essay has claimed that some revolutions may lead to genocide because in creating a new order, revolutions are likely to exclude certain groups and classes from the political community, thereby establishing a necessary condition for their destruction. However, some groups are excluded from the moral universe of a political community not because of revolution but because they are perceived as foreign enemies at war with the state. Or they are viewed by colonial conquistadores and settlers as alien "pagans," "barbarians," or "savages"—people who have never been part of the political community, and given their "inferior" and "despicable" culture have no hope of joining it. Thus wars of conquest and colonization are other contexts, besides revolutions, that can lead to partial or total genocide.

Indeed, before the emergence of the nation-state the destruction of whole peoples and communities was most likely to be perpetrated by invaders from abroad who wanted to seize the territory and other resources of the victims or to convert them to their religions. We have earlier referred to Melos and Carthage, but the depredations of Tamerlane, Genghis Khan, and the Europeans in the New World also come to mind.[39] Furthermore, in the contemporary period of the state and industrialization, the creeping destruction of "primitive peoples," as modern civilization has encroached on their habitat, cannot be derived from revolution or even conquest alone.[40] These and other matters need to be discussed, but they are instances of "foreign," nondomestic genocide and thus beyond the limits of this work.

Nonrevolutionary States Are Unlikely to Commit Total Domestic Genocide

Not only revolutionaries but the defenders of the status quo or the old order may be tempted by radical policies like massacre. If in recent years, the Khmer Rouges serve as an example of a revolutionary vanguard committing genocide, then various military regimes in the contemporary Third World, such as the Indonesian military in 1965, the Nigerian military during the Biafran war, the Tutsi-dominated Burundi military against the Hutu, the Sudanese military in Southern Sudan, the Ethiopian military in Eritrea and Tigre provinces, the Pakistani military in East Pakistan, the Iraqi military against the Kurds in 1988 and 1991, and many others illustrate regimes that opposed coups, revolutions, or movements of self-determination and committed wide-scale massacres against political opponents and communal groups and classes. These, however, were not "total domestic genocides" in the limited sense we have used the term here. In none of these examples was there a concerted effort to exterminate a group or class or to implement a policy of wide-scale massacre linked to cultural destruction.[41]

Since a nonrevolutionary regime like a military junta is not concerned with redefining a new order by imposing a new political myth, it has no need to exclude groups and classes from society and the political community. Hence, such a regime is unlikely to commit total domestic genocide. What it will do, however, is aggressively maintain the established order, and to do that it may use coercion, repression, massacre, and even partial genocide against challengers. As we have seen in Chapter 2 in the example of the Abdul Hamid regime, states may initiate or tolerate pogroms and massacres as a way to maintain an old order. But, as we have suggested earlier, massacre, and even partial genocide, are not the same as total genocide, unless these turn into a policy of extermination or become part of a plan to destroy the cultural and social identity of a group. A brief description of the Nigerian-Biafran civil war helps to illustrate this point.

Nigeria-Biafra

It is estimated that more than 1 million Biafrans, mostly Ibos, perished in the Nigerian-Biafran civil war that lasted from 1967 to 1970. The war had been preceded by a military coup in January 1966 that had been led by Ibo officers, and by pogroms against Ibos in Northern Nigeria, where some 10,000 people had been massacred in September of 1966.[42] These massacres were the primary reason for the secession of Biafra in 1967.

The large numbers of dead during the civil war was only in part due to military casualties, including bombing raids. Mass death was the product of mass starvation that was caused by disruption of agriculture in the affected regions, on the one hand, and by the decision of the Federal Military Government (FMG) to blockade Biafra, on the other hand. Even more than the massacres of September, it was the decision to blockade

Biafra and to obdurately refuse to lift the deadly blockade that was the basis of the accusations of genocide against General Gowon and the FMG.[43]

The FMG replied that the blockade would be lifted immediately once Biafra surrendered. Led by the able and charismatic Colonel Ojukwu the Biafrans bravely held out to the end. They fought on because they believed that their secession would succeed, bringing a legitimate and effective government as a result. If Biafra failed they were convinced that they would be massacred just as their kin had been in the North and in other parts of Nigeria. Thus hope and fear kept the Biafrans fighting, and the determination to maintain Nigerian unity kept up Nigerian pressure and continued the dying.

One can accuse the FMG of a callous disregard of human life in its pursuit of Nigerian unity, but I do not think that the term *total domestic genocide* fits its policies. The FMG wanted to prevent a secession, not to commit genocide. Indeed, in the midst of war it was already making plans to reintegrate the Ibos into the Nigerian state. Thus, for example, in a 1970 interview General Gowon was asked why the FMG refused to decorate Nigerian commanders in their war against the Biafrans. He replied that he wanted to spare embarrassment to Ibo officers who would be commingled with other ethnic groups in the Nigerian military following the conclusion of the civil war.[44] Indeed, after the war Ibos were largely reintegrated, if not welcomed, into the Nigerian army and society.[45] The victims of their policies were not treated in a like manner by the Young Turks, the Stalinists, the Nazis, or the Khmer Rouges. The Nigerian-Biafran war was a political and human disaster that included massacre and mass death, but the term *total domestic genocide* does not fit its reality.

The point of this example is not to excuse the Nigerian regime or governments like it that pursue or permit mass death as a policy of the state. Like the Abdul Hamid regime in 1894–96 against the Armenians, the Nigerian military perpetrated massacres or permitted partial genocide against unarmed defenseless civilians—men, women, and small children—but they did not set out to eliminate whole categories of the Nigerian social structure. A policy of massive state repression, even one leading to massacres and partial genocide, implies a different policy process and has different origins than revolutionary total genocide. The former wants to restore or maintain an old order, the latter wants to create a new world.

Although nonrevolutionary and counterrevolutionary states may commit massacre, or produce mass death that may appear as genocide-in-part, only revolutionary states are likely to commit total domestic genocide, or what the UN has called "genocide-in-whole." By the same token, it should be noted that there is nothing in principle preventing a regime that started out to crush a coup, a revolution, or a secession, itself becoming revolutionary and setting out to refashion the social structure by eliminating one of its communal groups or classes. In that event the pattern of revolutionary genocide may appear in the wake of counterrevolution or of a war of secession.

Conclusion

Since the Second World War many more people have been killed as victims of domestic massacres and partial or total genocides than by international war. State-perpetrated massacres and genocide are a greater danger to the world community than war itself. The outcome of the recent Gulf War only reinforces this view. By the same token, as this study has tried to demonstrate, total domestic genocide, the extermination or attempted destruction of a communal group or class, has been a relatively rare occurrence, because revolutions leading to wars are rare as well. Stable legitimate regimes—unless they are destroyed by revolution and war—are not likely perpetrators of total domestic genocide. Notwithstanding, this does not imply that men and women of good will should oppose all revolutions because of the inherent danger that they might turn out badly.

Some tyrannies can be overthrown only by revolutions. In order that tyrannical regimes not be replaced by genocidal ones, however, future revolutionaries will need to heed the lessons of the past: the revolutionary regime will always have its enemies, and there will likely be communal groups and classes from the old regime that cannot easily be integrated into the new order. The moral danger is that revolutionaries will identify such poorly integrated collectivities with the enemies of the revolution and, especially in wartime, that they will target such groups for repression and genocide. This violence against the victims of the revolution will be explained as necessary to the establishment of the new order. Revolutions fought in the name of justice must not abandon justice as the principle of governance. No one made this point better than Albert Camus.

For four bitter years he had been editor of *Combat*, the journal of the secret French resistance against the Nazis. On 25 August 1944, as the Allies and the Resistance were about to recapture Paris from the oppressor, Camus wrote:

Nothing is given to men [and women] and the little they can conquer is paid with unjust deaths. But man's greatness lies elsewhere. It lies in his decision to be stronger than his condition. And if his condition is unjust, he has only one way of overcoming it, which is to be just himself. [46]

NOTES

Preface

1. Peter Gay, in Karl Dietrich Bracher, *The German Dictatorship* (New York: Holt, Rinehart and Winston, 1970), vii.

Chapter One

1. Karl Marx, from *The Eighteenth Brumaire of Napoleon* (London, 1869). Cited in Lewis S. Feuer, ed., *Karl Marx and Friedrich Engels: Basic Writings on Politics and Philosophy* (New York: Doubleday, 1959), 320.

2. Isaiah Berlin, *Four Essays on Liberty* (London: Oxford University Press, 1969), 120.

3. The major point of departure for the comparative study of genocide including the Holocaust is Leo Kuper's *Genocide: Its Political Uses in the Twentieth Century* (New Haven: Yale University Press, 1981). Among other recent significant contributions are those of Helen Fein, *Accounting for Genocide* (New York: Free Press, 1979), 3–30, and "Genocide: A Sociological Perspective," *Current Sociology* 38, no. 1 (Spring 1990): 1–126; Frank Chalk and Kurt Jonassohn, eds., *The History and Sociology of Genocide* (New Haven: Yale University Press, 1990); Ervin Staub, *The Roots of Evil: The Origins of Genocide and Other Group Violence* (Cambridge: Cambridge University Press, 1989); Israel W. Charny, ed., *Toward the Understanding and Prevention of Genocide* (Boulder and London: Westview Press, 1984); Barbara Harff and Ted Robert Gurr, "Toward Empirical Theory of Genocides and Politicides: Identification and Measurement of Cases since 1945," *International Studies Quarterly* 32 (1988): 359–71; Irving Louis Horowitz, *Taking Lives: Genocide and State Power* (New Brunswick, N.J., and London: Transaction Books, 1982); Jack Nusan Porter, ed., *Genocide and Human Rights* (Washington, D.C.: University Press of America, 1982); Richard L. Rubenstein, *The Age of Triage* (Boston: Beacon Press, 1983); Isidor Walliman and Michael N. Dobkowski, eds., *Genocide and the Modern Age* (New York: Greenwood Press, 1987); and Florence Mazian, *Why Genocide?* (Ames: Iowa State University Press, 1990).

4. Some of the writers who have blazed a trail in comparing the Holocaust to the Armenian Genocide are Kuper, *Genocide*; Helen Fein, "A Formula for Genocide: A Comparison of the Turkish Genocide (1915) and the German Holocaust (1939–1945)," *Comparative Studies in Sociology* 1 (1978): 271–93, and *Accounting*, 3–30; Vahakn N. Dadrian, "The Convergent Aspects of the Armenian and Jewish Cases of Genocide: A Reinterpretation of the Concept of Holocaust," *Holocaust and Genocide Studies* 3, no. 2 (1988): 151–70; Hrair R. Dekmejian, "Determinants of Genocide: Armenians and Jews as Case Studies," in Richard G. Hovannisian, ed., *The Armenian Genocide in Perspective* (New Brunswick, N.J.: Transaction Books, 1986), 85–96; Staub, *The Roots of Evil*; and Mazian, *Why Genocide?*. Some of these works are discussed below. Also see Fein, "Genocide: A Sociological Perspective," 69–75.

5. See United Nations. *Yearbook of the United Nations, 1948–49* (New York: Columbia University Press, 1949), 959–60.

6. See Chalk and Jonassohn, *The History and Sociology of Genocide*, 57–222.

7. This will be discussed more fully in Chap. 9.

8. Theda Skocpol, ed., *Vision and Method in Historical Sociology* (Cambridge: Cambridge University Press, 1984), 374–75. Though I depart in certain respects from her strict structural perspective, as will be seen below, my work has been especially influenced by Theda Skocpol's *States and Social Revolutions* (Cambridge: Cambridge University Press, 1979). Other examples of comparative historical research that have been influential are those of S. N. Eisenstadt, *The Political System of Empires* (New York: Free Press, 1963); Barrington Moore, Jr., *Social Origins of Dictatorship and Democracy* (Boston: Beacon Press, 1966); and Charles Tilly, *The Formation of National States in Western Europe* (Princeton: Princeton University Press, 1975). For an insightful overview of writings in comparative history see Raymond Grew, "The Case for Comparing Histories," *American Historical Review* 85, no. 4 (1980): 763–78; and Skocpol, *Vision and Method*, above.

9. Skocpol, *Vision and Method*, 376.

10. Though this is not the place to argue philosophy of history and philosophy of science, it may be suggested that all general laws are bounded by historical contexts, and that especially in social science those propositions that are not so bounded tend to be either self-evident or trivial. Indeed, in the last few years a number of comparative political scientists, including Gabriel Almond, have called on their field to "take the historical cure" in order to overcome the malaise of general theory building. See his "Approaches to Developmental Causation," in Scott C. Flanagan and Robert J. Mundt, eds., *Crisis, Choice, and Change* (Boston: Little Brown, 1973), 1–42. At a deeper level of analysis see the controversy between Carl G. Hempel and Michael Scriven in Patrick Gardner, ed., *Theories of History* (Glencoe: Free Press, 1959), 344–56 and 443–75.

11. In an important study, Harff and Gurr, "Toward Empirical Theory of Genocides and Politicides," have identified some forty-four episodes of what they call "genocides and politicides." Since their work deals with genocides following the Second World War, they do not include the Holocaust and the Armenian Genocide. Moreover, for their purposes they do not need to distinguish, as this essay does, between the destruction of part of a group and a whole group.

12. In narrowing our sample to cases of total genocide alone, we are following a procedure used by Theda Skocpol, for example, in her study of the French, Russian, and Chinese revolutions. There she focuses her attention on the complex phenomenon of social revolutions rather than broadening her sample to include allied phenomena such as political revolutions, riots, and acts of violence in general. See her disagreement with Harry Eckstein on this point in her *States and Social Revolutions*, 33–34.

13. All major works on the origins of the Holocaust have emphasized the ideology of antisemitism as either the most important or one of the most important factors. For studies that have stressed ideology see, for example, Leon Poliakov, *Harvest of Hate* (New York: Waldon Press, 1979); George L. Mosse, *The Crisis of German Ideology: Intellectual Origins of the Third Reich* (New York: Grosset and Dunlap, 1964); Lucy S. Dawidowicz, *The War against the Jews* (New York: Holt, Rinehart and Winston, 1975); and Eberhard Jäckel, *Hitler's World View* (Cambridge, Mass.: Harvard University Press, 1981). Major works that have stressed factors other than ideology are Raul Hilberg, *The Destruction of the European Jews* (Chicago: Quadrangle, 1961; new ed. 1985); Helen Fein, *Accounting for Genocide*; Jacob

Katz, *From Prejudice to Destruction* (Cambridge, Mass.: Harvard University Press, 1980); and Yehuda Bauer, *A History of the Holocaust* (New York: Franklin Watts, 1982).

The most important work on the Holocaust that stresses the role of bureaucracies and other organizations is that of Hilberg, above. See also Hannah Arendt's *Eichmann in Jerusalem* (New York: Viking Press, 1969). The "functionalist" position is spelled out by Tim Mason, "Intention and Explanation: A Current Controversy about the Interpretation of National Socialism," in Gerhard Hirschfeld and Lothar Ketternacker, eds., *Der Führerstaat: Mythos und Realität* (Stuttgart: Klett-Cotta, 1981): 21–40, and Hans Mommsen, "The Realization of the Unthinkable: 'The Final Solution of the Jewish Question' in the Third Reich," in Gerhard Hirschfeld, ed., *The Policies of Genocide* (London: Allen & Unwin, 1986), 93–144.

For judicious discussions of the recent controversy between the "intentionalists" and "functionalists" see especially Christopher R. Browning, *Fateful Months* (New York and London: Holmes and Meier, 1985), and "Beyond 'Intentionalism' and 'Functionalism': A Reassessment of Nazi Jewish Policy, 1939–1941" (Paper presented at the annual meeting of the American Historical Association, Washington, D.C., December 1987). See also Ian Kershaw, *The Nazi Dictatorship* (London: Edward Arnold, 1985). For an informative historiographical essay on the Holocaust that discusses the controversy see Michael R. Marrus, *The Holocaust in History* (Hanover, N.H.: University Press of New England, 1987).

14. Among scholar who have contended—where they have not denied its occurrence—that the genocide was provoked by the Armenians themselves are Stanford J. Shaw and Ezel Kural Shaw, *History of the Ottoman Empire and Modern Turkey*, vol. 2, *Reform, Revolution, and Republic The Rise of Modern Turkey, 1808–1975* (Cambridge: Cambridge University Press, 1977); William L. Langer, *The Diplomacy of Imperialism* (New York: Alfred A. Knopf, 1935); and Bernard Lewis, *The Emergence of Modern Turkey* (Oxford: Oxford University Press, 1961), 356. As will be seen below and in Chap. 5 (this vol.), Lewis does not deny that a genocide occurred, but he sees it as stemming from the provocative aspirations and actions of Armenian nationalism. For a critique of the Shaws's approach see Richard G. Hovannisian, "The Critic's View: Beyond Revisionism," *International Journal of Middle East Studies* 9 (August 1978): 337–86. For a reply to Hovannisian see Stanford J. Shaw and Ezel K. Shaw, "The Authors Respond," *International Journal of Middle East Studies* 9 (August 1978): 386–400. See also Gwynne Dyer, "Turkish 'Falsifiers' and Armenian 'Deceivers': Historiography and the Armenian Massacres," *Middle Eastern Studies* 12 (1976): 99–107. For a critique of Dyer see Gerard G. Libaridian, "Objectivity and the Historiography of the Armenian Genocide," *Armenian Review* 31 (Spring 1978): 79–87. For more extensive essays on the literature pertaining to the denial of the Armenian Genocide see the articles by Marjorie Housepian Dobkin, Richard G. Hovannisian, and Vigen Guroian, in Hovannisian, ed., *The Armenian Genocide in Perspective*; Leo Kuper, *Genocide*, 101–19 and 219–20; and Roger W. Smith, "Denial of the Armenian Genocide," in Israel W. Charny, ed., *Genocide: A Critical Bibliographic Review*, vol. 2 (New York: Facts on File, 1991), 63–85.

15. See especially Kuper, *Genocide*; Fein, *Accounting for Genocide*; Horowitz, *Taking Lives*; Roger W. Smith, "Human Destructiveness and Politics: The Twentieth Century as an Age of Genocide," in Isidor Walliman and Michael N. Dobkowski, eds., *Genocide and the Modern Age* (New York: Greenwood Press, 1987), 21–40; Barbara Harff, "The Etiology of Genocides," 41–61. Other writers singling out the modern state as a potentially "terrorist" regime capable of severe repression including genocide are Michael Stohl and George

Lopez, eds., *The State as Terrorist* (New York: Greenwood Press, 1984). The classic statement on totalitarianism was made by Hannah Arendt, *The Origins of Totalitarianism* (New York: Meridian Press, 1958).

16. Dawidowicz, *The War against the Jews*, 190–91.

17. See Norman Cohn, *Warrant for Genocide* (New York: Harper and Row, 1967).

18. Dawidowicz, *The War against the Jews*, 95.

19. See n. 13 above.

20. Dawidowicz, *The War against the Jews*; and Gerald Fleming, *Hitler and the Final Solution* (Berkeley and Los Angeles: University of California Press, 1982).

21. In his work Arno J. Mayer, *Why Did the Heavens Not Darken? The Final Solution in History* (New York: Pantheon Books, 1988), also sees the conflict with Russia as leading up to the Final Solution, but his argument differs from that of the intentionalists and functionalists. He views the Nazis' antisemitism as deriving from Hitler's and the upper class's anti-Bolshevism.

He traces the timing of the Final Solution to the Germans' realization in late 1942 and early 1943 that their attempt at conquering Russia would likely fail and that annihilating the Jews could be their major accomplishment. As other critics have pointed out, Mayer's work is not persuasive because Hitler's antisemitism and racialism cannot be subsumed under his anti-communism. The Final Solution did not commence in 1943, by which time most Jews had already been killed, but in 1941, when the Germans invaded the Soviet Union. The dates are significant because they demonstrate that it was not Hitler's fear of defeat but his conviction of imminent victory that drove him to the Final Solution. On this and allied points please see Chap. 7 (this vol.).

22. These points are made both by Hilberg, *Destruction of European Jews*; and Arendt, *Eichmann in Jerusalem*.

23. See n. 14 above.

24. Lewis, *The Emergence of Modern Turkey*.

25. Leo Kuper, *Genocide*; and *The Prevention of Genocide* (New Haven: Yale University Press, 1985).

26. Smith, "Human Destructiveness," 21.

27. Horowitz, *Taking Lives*; also see n. 15 above.

28. Arendt, *The Origins of Totalitarianism*, 462.

29. Ibid., 464.

30. There is documentary evidence that the Nazis had ambitious plans not only to exterminate the Jews during the war but also to transform the ethnic and racial composition of Europe following the war. The methods to be used were colonization, deportation, and extermination. Some of these conceptions were spelled out in Heinrich Himmler's speeches and in the *Generalplan Ost*. See Czesław Madajczyk, "General Plan Ost and the Fate of the Jews," in Yehuda Bauer et al., eds., *Remembering for the Future: Working Papers and Addenda*, vol. 3, *The Impact of the Holocaust and Genocide on Jews and Christians* (Oxford: Pergamon Press, 1989), 298–313; Himmler's "Reflections on the Treatment of Peoples of Alien Races in the East," in Yehuda Bauer, *A History of the Holocaust*, 351–54; and "Himmler's Summation, October 4, 1943," in Lucy S. Dawidowicz, ed., *A Holocaust Reader* (New York: Behrman House, 1976), 138–40. On the so-called euthanasia program targeting non-Jewish Germans, especially deformed and retarded children, see Dawidowicz's discussion of the T-4 program in her *The War against the Jews*, 175–81. Also see Chap. 7 (this vol.).

31. This was implied in J. L. Talmon's analysis of the French Revolution. See his

The Origins of Totalitarian Democracy (London: Mercury Books, 1961). Robert W. Tucker makes the connection between totalitarian and revolutionary regimes quite explicit. See his *The Soviet Political Mind* (New York: W. W. Norton, 1971), 3–48. Tucker does not want to abandon the idea of totalitarianism. What he wants is to subsume it under the concept of revolutionary movement regimes and to stress the personality and ego defensive needs of the dictator in the formulation of policy.

32. See Fein, *Accounting for Genocide*; and "Lives at Risk" (Working Paper of the Institute for the Study of Genocide, John Jay College of Criminal Justice, New York, March 1990); Harff, "The Etiology of Genocides"; Mazian, *Why Genocide?*; and Staub, *The Roots of Evil*.

33. Fein, *Accounting*, 9.

34. Ibid., 8.

35. See her "Scenarios of Genocide: Models of Genocide and Critical Responses," in Israel W. Charny, ed., *Toward the Understanding and Prevention of Genocide*, 18.

36. Harff, "Etiology," 43.

37. The concepts of social mobilization and its close kin, modernization, have been variously used in the literature. By social mobilization, Karl W. Deutsch means "the process in which major clusters of social, economic, and psychological commitments are eroded or broken and people become available for new patterns of socialization and behavior." See his "Social Mobilization and Political Development." *American Political Science Review* 55 (1961): 493–514. According to Lerner, modernization refers to a system of interacting variables including industrialization, urbanization, literacy, and political participation that has characterized social change in the contemporary period. See his classic *The Passing of Traditional Society* (New York: Free Press, 1958). It is apparent that social mobilization is dependent on modernization in the above sense. It should be noted also that other meanings of these terms exist and that these concepts have come in for some heavy criticism. See, for example, Dean C. Tipps, "Modernization Theory and the Comparative Study of Societies: A Critical Perspective," *Comparative Studies in Society and History* 15 (1973): 199–226. In this context it is suggested that in the nineteenth century in the Ottoman Empire and Imperial Germany, respectively, Armenians and Jews were more likely than the majority Muslims or Germans to enter into industrial and commercial professions, and to become urban, literate, and politically aware.

38. See the discussion of the destruction of the Kulaks and the Cambodian "autogenocide" in Chap. 9. On the fate of the Gypsies in Nazi Europe see, for example, Leita Kaldi, "Gypsies and Jews: Chosen People," in Charny, *Toward the Understanding*, 113–18, and Donald Kenrick and Grattan Puxon, *The Destiny of Europe's Gypsies* (London: Cox and Wyman, 1972).

39. See Fein, "Scenarios of Genocide Past and Future," in Charny, *Toward the Understanding*, 18–22, and Chalk and Jonassohn, *The History and Sociology of Genocide*, 29–32.

40. Raphael Lemkin, *Axis Rule in Occupied Europe* (Washington, D.C.: Carnegie Endowment for International Peace, 1944; repr., New York: Howard Feritg, 1973), 79.

41. See Yehuda Bauer, "The Place of the Holocaust in Contemporary History," in Jonathan Frankel, ed., *Studies in Contemporary Jewry* (Bloomington: Indiana University Press, 1984), 201–34, and Kuper, *Genocide* and *The Prevention of Genocide*. For an enlightening discussion of genocide and the prevention of genocide under international law see Louis René Beres, "Reason and Realpolitik: International Law and the Prevention of Genocide," in Charny, *Toward the Understanding*, 306–23.

42. See United Nations, 959–60.

43. This essay assumes that society is horizontally stratified into classes and vertically segmented into communal or ethnic groups. Following Weber, classes may be based on wealth, status, or power. Communal groups, by contrast, are based primarily on ascriptive criteria like religion, language, nationality, or race. Members of such groups share a common identity and culture extending throughout their life cycle. As a rule, especially in modern industrial societies, communal segments are themselves stratified by class. Although communal segments and classes can be analytically detected in most societies, such groups and the conflicts based on them are not everywhere equally salient. Communal groups have also been called "ethnic groups," and the societies where they have played distinctive roles have been called "culturally plural." There is a vast literature on communal groups and culturally plural societies; indeed, there is also controversy in the usage of these terms. For classic statements see J. S. Furnivall, *Colonial Policy and Practice* (London: Cambridge University Press, 1948), and Leo Kuper and M. G. Smith, eds., *Pluralism in Africa* (Berkeley and Los Angeles: University of California Press, 1969). For a significant recent contribution see Donald L. Horowitz, *Ethnic Groups in Conflict* (Berkeley and Los Angeles: University of California Press, 1985).

44. For a discussion of some of the episodes of partial genocide see especially Kuper, *Genocide;* and Harff and Gurr, "Toward Empirical Theory of Genocides and Politicides." On the gassing of the Kurds in Iraq see Thomas L. Friedman, *From Beirut to Jerusalem* (New York: Farrar, Strauss, and Giroux, 1989), 90–91.

45. See Kuper, *Genocide,* 19–39, 138–60.

46. For more extended discussion of these two cases see Chap. 9.

47. See Bauer, "The Place of the Holocaust," 214, in which he makes the suggestion, followed here, that genocide and Holocaust be defined by continua. Bauer and other scholars, however, have not emphasized the third dimension; nevertheless, geographical and political scope are significant, I believe, in differentiating the Holocaust from other kinds of total genocides or exterminations. Thus the Final Solution was not to be limited to Germany alone, or to Eastern Europe, or indeed even to Europe. It was designed to encompass the world as a whole. This made the intended geographical scope of the Holocaust wider than any other genocide.

48. Frank Chalk and Kurt Jonassohn have a most suggestive definition of genocide that leaves open as a variable the type of group that may be victimized by genocide. Thus Chalk defines genocide as "a form of one-sided mass killing in which a state or other authority intends to destroy a group, as that group and membership in it are defined by the perpetrator." See his "Definitions of Genocide and Their Implications for Prediction and Prevention," in Bauer et al., eds., *Remembering for the Future,* vol. 3, *The Impact of the Holocaust and Genocide on Jews and Christians,* 69; and Chalk and Jonassohn, *The History and Sociology of Genocide,* 23.

It may also be suggested that the destruction or undermining of some aspect of a group's social identity that does not include the killing of some or all of its members not be called "massacre" or "genocide." There are other terms such as "forced assimilation" or what Lemkin called "denationalization" that are more applicable. See Lemkin, 79.

49. By way of contrast Bauer wishes to limit the meaning of genocide to the destruction of communal, that is, racial, religious, national, or ethnic groups as such and to exclude from his definition the destruction of classes. This leads him explicitly to exclude

the "autogenocide" in Cambodia and the destruction of the Kulaks under the Stalin regime from his definition of genocide. See his "The Place of the Holocaust," 213–14.

50. Although Kuper in *Genocide* makes a strong case for including the destruction of political groups in a definition of genocide, Lawrence J. Leblanc disagrees. See his "The United Nations Genocide Convention and Political Groups: Should the United States Propose an Amendment?" *Yale Journal of International Law* 13, no. 2 (1988): 293.

51. I am grateful to Helen Fein for pointing this out.

52. It may be argued that, in the extreme instance wherein every member of a group is killed, in effect its social identity is also destroyed. Nevertheless, perpetrators of total genocide have seldom been satisfied with biological destruction alone. They have also set out to extirpate evidence of the hated group's identity from the culture and social structure of the larger society. Thus typically if, as in the Armenian and Jewish instances, the targeted group was also a religious community, it was not enough to kill its members: its churches and synagogues had to be razed and its holy texts burned. If it was a separate language group, traces of its tongue had to be eliminated from the language of the perpetrators. Indeed, for the Nazis the Final Solution was meant not alone to kill Jews but to eliminate forever the hated "Jewish spirit" from the world. See Saul Friedländer, "On the Possibility of the Holocaust: An Approach to a Historical Synthesis," in Yehuda Bauer and Nathan Rotenstreich, eds., *The Holocaust as Historical Experience* (New York: Holmes and Meier, 1981), 2.

53. Cf. this approach with Bauer, "The Place of the Holocaust," and Kuper, *Genocide*. Bauer calls "genocide" what I have called "partial genocide," and he calls "Holocaust" what I have called "total genocide." As noted above, he excludes classes and political groups from his definition. Kuper also makes an implicit distinction between partial and total genocide. He calls the former "genocidal massacre" and the latter "genocide." See, for example, his *Genocide*, 55.

54. See John Paden, "Communal Competition, Conflict and Violence in Kano," in Robert Melson and Howard Wolpe, eds., *Nigeria: Modernization and the Politics of Communalism* (East Lansing: Michigan State University Press, 1971), 113–44; John de St. Jorre, *The Brothers' War* (Boston: Houghton Mifflin, 1972), 65–122. Also see Chap. 9 (this vol.).

55. See Kaldi, "Gypsies and Jews: Chosen People"; Kenrick and Puxon, *The Destiny of Europe's Gypsies*.

56. Bauer's suggestion that genocide and holocaust be viewed as lying on a continuum of intended destruction is especially apt when considering the classification of the Armenian Genocide. It was a policy of destruction that may be located on a dimension between the Holocaust and other instances of total genocide. Indeed, in Bauer's terms both the Holocaust and the Armenian Genocide should be viewed as instances of what he calls "holocaust." See Bauer, "The Place of the Holocaust," 214–17. See also Dadrian, "The Convergent Aspects." Utilizing different criteria from those cited here, Dadrian makes a strong case that the Armenian Genocide should be viewed as largely indistinguishable from the Holocaust.

57. Thus, for example, the Nazis attempted to have Jewish refugees who had found shelter in Japan deported to the death camps. Though they failed in this endeavor to extend the Final Solution beyond Europe, their very effort illustrates the worldwide scope of the Holocaust. See Marvin Tokayer and Mary Swartz, *The Fugu Plan: The Untold Story of the Japanese and the Jews in World War II* (New York: Paddington, 1979).

58. Here one can note the difference in approach between this study's definition of genocide and that of Steven T. Katz. Convinced that the Holocaust was unique and essentially incomparable, Katz seems to define genocide in the manner that we have defined the Holocaust: it means the complete extermination of a group and the destruction of its identity in all of its aspects. Not surprisingly, given his definition, he discovers that there is no other genocide that compares to the Holocaust and that it is in effect a unique and incomparable event. See his "Essay: Quantity and Interpretation—Issues in the Comparative Historical Analysis of the Holocaust," *Holocaust and Genocide Studies* 4, no. 2 (1989): 127–48.

59. Theda Skocpol, *States and Social Revolutions*. See esp. her introduction where she lays out her "structural perspective," 3–43.

60. Ibid., 4.

61. Terms like "political myth," "ideology," and "identity" have been used in many ways and have multiple meanings that cannot be fully discussed or cited here. On the concept of "political myth," see Harold D. Lasswell and Abraham Kaplan, *Power and Society* (New Haven: Yale University Press, 1950), 116. Cf. this to Gaetano Mosca's "the political formula," in his *The Ruling Class* (New York: McGraw-Hill, 1939), 70. On the relationship of ideology to political crisis see David Apter, "Ideology and Discontent" and Clifford Geertz, "Ideology as a Cultural System," both in David Apter, ed., *Ideology and Discontent* (New York: Free Press, 1964), 15–46 and 47–76, respectively. On the concept of "political identity," see especially Lucian W. Pye, "Identity and the Political Culture," in Leonard W. Binder, ed., *Crises and Sequences in Political Development* (Princeton: Princeton University Press, 1971), 101–34.

62. Skocpol, 23.

63. A good example of this pattern—one with which Skocpol explicitly disagrees—is that of the Stalinist state scrapping the New Economic Policy and deciding on a murderous policy of collectivization and dekulakization. See Chap. 9 (this vol.) for a more extended discussion of this point.

64. The distinction between comparativists and particularists derives from an earlier essay by Yehuda Bauer, "'Unique and Universal': Some General Problems Arising Out of Holocaust Research" (Hebrew University, Jerusalem n.d., Mimeographed). Bauer changed and elaborated his views in later works. See esp. his "The Place of the Holocaust," and "Is the Holocaust Explicable?" in Bauer et al., eds., *Remembering for the Future*, vol. 2, *The Impact of the Holocaust on the Contemporary World*, 1967–75. For other recent attempts devoted to the historicity of the Holocaust see Michael R. Marrus, "Recent Trends in the Historicity of the Holocaust," *Holocaust and Genocide Studies* 3, no. 3 (1988): 257–65; and Henry R. Huttenbach, "Locating the Holocaust on the Genocide Spectrum: Towards a Methodology of Definition and Categorization," *Holocaust and Genocide Studies* 3, no. 3 (1988): 289–304.

65. Jacob Katz, "Was the Holocaust Predictable?" in Yehuda Bauer and Nathan Rotenstreich, 33.

66. Friedländer, "On the Possibility of the Holocaust: An Approach to a Historical Synthesis," in Bauer and Rotenstreich, 1.

67. In the same vein see Raul Hilberg, "The Anatomy of the Holocaust," and "The Significance of the Holocaust," in Henry Friedlander and Sybil Milton, eds., *The Holocaust: Ideology, Bureaucracy, and Genocide* (Millwood, N.Y.: Kraus International, 1981), 85–102, esp. 94. See also Emil L. Fackenheim's foreword to Yehuda Bauer's *The Jewish Emergence from*

Powerlessness (Toronto: University of Toronto Press, 1979), vii–xiv. Similar points are made by Robert A. Pois, "The Holocaust and the Ethical Imperative of Historicism," *Holocaust and Genocide Studies* 3, no. 3 (1988), 267–72; and Steven Katz, "Essay: Quantity and Interpretation."

A seminal attempt arguing the historical uniqueness of the Holocaust, while avoiding mystification, was made by Alice L. and A. Roy Eckardt, "The Holocaust and the Enigma of Uniqueness: A Philosophical Effort at Practical Clarification," in Irene G. Shur and Franklin H. Littell, eds., *Reflections on the Holocaust, The Annals of the American Academy of Political and Social Science* 450 (1980): 165–74. For a pointed critique of the Eckardts' view see Pierre Papazian, "A 'Unique Uniqueness'?" *Midstream* 30, no. 4 (April 1984): 14–25. For a balanced discussion of the issues raised by the assertion of uniqueness, see Alan Rosenberg, "Was the Holocaust Unique?: A Peculiar Question?" in Walliman and Dobkowski, *Genocide and the Modern Age*, 145–62.

68. Lucy S. Dawidowicz, *The Holocaust and the Historians* (Cambridge, Mass.: Harvard University Press, 1981), 14.

69. Saul Friedländer, "On the Possibility of the Holocaust," 2.

70. Jean-Paul Sartre, *Jean-Paul Sartre on Genocide* (Boston: Beacon Press, 1968), 57.

71. For a perceptive discussion of how the issue of the comparability of the Holocaust has divided German historians and raised important issues about the German past, see Charles S. Maier, *The Unmasterable Past* (Cambridge, Mass.: Harvard University Press, 1988). I am deliberately omitting from the category of comparativists those neo-Nazi, antisemitic, and apologetic writings that have purposely gone out of their way to trivialize and/or to justify the Holocaust. Indeed, one of the reasons that some historians are suspicious of those who want to "compare" the Holocaust derives from the existence of this kind of literature.

Chapter Two

1. An earlier version of this chapter appeared as "A Theoretical Inquiry into the Armenian Massacres of 1894–96," *Comparative Studies in Society and History* 24, no. 3 (1982): 481–509.

2. Great Britain, House of Commons, *Correspondence Relating to the Asiatic Provinces of Turkey*, Sessional Papers, 1895, vol. 109, pt. 1, c. 7894. Constantinople, 31 August 1894.

3. These were Kurdish cavalry recruited and organized by the Porte and named after Sultan Abdul Hamid II. By 15 December 1892 there were thirty-three such regiments each numbering about 500 men. Their commanding officer was Zeki Pasha, a Circassian who was later decorated for his repression of the Armenians at Sassoun. See below and Christopher J. Walker, *Armenia: The Survival of a Nation* (New York: St. Martin's Press, 1980), 134.

4. Great Britain, House of Commons, *Correspondence Relating to the Asiatic Provinces of Turkey*, Sessional Papers, 1895, vol. 109, pt. 1, c. 7894, "Events at Sassoun, and Commission of Inquiry at Moush," inclosure 2 in no. 60, Van, 6 November 1894.

5. Ibid.

6. Ibid.

7. Ibid.

8. Ibid.

9. Johannes Lepsius, *Armenia and Europe* (London: Hodder and Stoughton, 1897), 3;

Great Britain, *Correspondence*, Sessional Papers, c. 7894, inclosure 49, Sir Philip Currie to the Earl of Kimberley, 23 November 1894.

10. Great Britain, inclosure 49, 23 November 1894.

11. Ismail Kemal Bey suggests that the sultan may have used the occasion to precipitate a massacre. See his *The Memoirs of Ismail Kemal Bey* (London: Constable & Co., 1920), 264.

12. See Lepsius, *Armenia and Europe*, 77–79.

13. William L. Langer, *The Diplomacy of Imperialism* (New York and London: Alfred A. Knopf, 1935), 324.

14. Richard G. Hovannisian, *Armenia on the Road to Independence* (Berkeley and Los Angeles: University of California Press, 1967), 28.

15. See Roderic H. Davison, *Reform in the Ottoman Empire, 1856–1876* (Princeton: Princeton University Press, 1963), 414–15, and Stanford J. Shaw and Ezel Kural Shaw, *History of the Ottoman Empire and Modern Turkey*, vol. 2 (Cambridge: Cambridge University Press, 1977), 205.

16. See Louise Nalbandian, *The Armenia Revolutionary Movement: The Development of Armenian Political Parties through the Nineteenth Century* (Berkeley and Los Angeles: University of California Press, 1963), 206n. 54.

17. Hovannisian, *Armenia on the Road to Independence*, 28.

18. Lepsius, *Armenia and Europe*, 330–31. Hovannisian cites these data in *Armenia on the Road to Independence*, 267n. 15. For the sake of accuracy, the Lepsius data would have been better reported to the nearest thousand or even ten thousand. This holds equally for the data reported by A. W. Terrell, the American ambassador to the Porte, who cited a figure of 37,095 as of 4 February 1896. See United States of America, National Archives, Record Group 59, *Despatches from United States Ministers to Turkey, 1818–1906*, microfilm publication M46, roll 61, enclosure 796. It should be noted that Terrell's figures do not cover the period following February 1896.

19. Shaw and Shaw, 204–5.

20. Roderic H. Davison, "Nationalism as an Ottoman Problem and the Ottoman Response," in William W. Haddad and William Ochsenwald, eds., *Nationalism in a Non-National State: The Dissolution of the Ottoman Empire* (Columbus: Ohio State University Press, 1977), 25–56.

21. Lepsius, *Armenia and Europe*, 76. Lepsius, whose work is a major source on the massacres, was a German historian and theologian. He took a lifelong interest in Armenian affairs and was the editor of the forty-volume German Foreign Ministry series, *Die Grösse Politik der Europaischen Kabinette*, and of *Deutschland und Armenien, 1914–1918* (Potsdam: Tempelverlag, 1919). Ulrich Trumpener, *Germany and the Ottoman Empire, 1914–1918* (Princeton: Princeton University Press, 1968), discusses his activities at the time of the massacres. René Pinon, who was then professor at the École des Sciences Politique, wrote the following appreciation [my translation]: "Johannes Lepsius, Doctor of Theology, has acquired a respected reputation in German science as a specialist on the Armenian questions. His book on the massacres of 1894–1895 established him as an authority. At the same time that he is a scholar, Lepsius is also a man of action and a missionary. He is President of the German Mission to the Orient, and of the German-Armenian society. His philological and historical studies, his long field trips into Armenia and into other parts of the Ottoman Empire, give a particular weight to his judgements." See René Pi-

non, "Preface," *Rapport secret sur les massacres d'Arménie*, by Johannes Lepsius (1919; rpt. Paris: Payot, 1966), 3–5.

22. Lepsius, *Armenia and Europe*, 79.

23. G. H. Fitzmaurice to Sir Philip Currie, "Massacres in Ourfa (October 28 and 29 and December 28 and 29)," extract from *Blue Book, Turkey no. 5* (1896). This is also known as Great Britain, House of Commons, *Correspondence Relating to the Asiatic Provinces of Turkey. Reports by Vice Consul Fitzmaurice, from Birejik, Ourfa, Adiman, Behesni*, Sessional Papers, 1896, vol. 106, c. 8100. Also quoted in Lepsius, *Armenia and Europe*, 157–58. For a similar observation see Sir Edwin Pears, *The Life of Abdul Hamid* (1917; rpt. New York: Arno Press, 1973), 233–34.

24. See Lepsius, *Armenia and Europe*, 47, and C. M. Hallward's report in Great Britain, *Correspondence*, Sessional Papers, c. 7894, inclosure 2 in no. 60, Van, 6 October 1894.

25. Lepsius, 37.

26. Shaw and Shaw, 302.

27. See Vahakn N. Dadrian, "Factors of Anger and Aggression in Genocide," *Journal of Human Relations* 19, no. 3 (1971): 394–417. For an introduction to the concepts and to the literature see Stanley Milgram and Hans Toch, "Collective Behavior of Crowds and Social Movements," in Gardner Lindsey and Elliot Aronson, eds., *The Handbook of Social Psychology* (Reading, Mass.: Addison-Wesley, 1969), 507–611.

28. On Abdul Hamid's extensive use of the spy system see Ahmed Emin, *Turkey in the World* (New Haven: Yale University Press, 1930), 32–33.

29. Shaw and Shaw, 203.

30. Ibid. A search through the works of Davison, Langer, Lewis, Nalbandian, Hovannisian, Lepsius, and Arnold Toynbee, as well as through the consular reports, nowhere confirmed the thesis that the Hnchakists planned an Armenia from which Muslims were to be driven or killed.

31. See Nalbandian, *Armenian Revolutionary Movement*.

32. Ibid., 119.

33. Hovannisian, 16.

34. Sarkis Atamian, *The Armenian Community* (New York: Philosophical Library, 1955), 118–19.

35. Roderic H. Davison, "The Armenian Crisis," *American Historical Review* 53, no. 10 (1948): 483.

36. Atamian, *Armenian Community*, 118–19, 138. Dadrian questions this assertion. Letter received from Vahakn N. Dadrian, 2 October, 1979.

37. Shaw and Shaw, 202.

38. Lepsius, *Armenia and Europe*, 35.

39. Ibid., 76–77.

40. A brief methodological point is in order here: despite writers like Edwin Pears who argue that Abdul Hamid was a sadist and insane, for our purposes it is not necessary to probe the ego-defensive functions of the sultan's ideology and actions. As will be seen, given the prevailing ideology concerning *dhimmis* and given the sultan's position and power, we can account for his attitudes and intentions without resorting to depth psychology. See Pears, *Life of Abdul Hamid*, and Fred. I. Greenstein, *Politics and Personality* (New York: Norton, 1975).

41. For a discussion of the millet system and of the role of *dhimmis* in it, see among others H. A. R. Gibb and Harold Bowen, *Islamic Society and the West* (New York: Oxford University Press, 1965); B. Lewis, Ch. Pellat, and J. Schacht, eds., *The Encyclopedia of Islam*, new ed. (London: Luzak & Co., 1961), 227–31; Benjamin Braude and Bernard Lewis, eds., *Christians and Jews in the Ottoman Empire* (New York: Holmes and Meier, 1982). That sacred principles were involved in Abdul Hamid's own mind becomes clear in the sultan's attempts to reinstate the caliphate and to make the Ottoman Empire the center of world Muslim culture. See Shaw and Shaw, 259–60.

42. The conscription was a practice whereby Orthodox Christian boys (most Armenians and Jews were excluded) were recruited as slaves for the sultan's household or for the army. Though at first resented, in time it became a gateway to high position. After the sixteenth century the practice was discontinued. Gibb and Bowen, *Islamic Society*, 210.

43. In the case of the Bulgarians, "so complete was their absorption in the Greek millet that in the first place there is actually no mention of them by name in Ottoman official documents . . . and in the second their very existence as a people was almost unknown in Europe even to students of Slavonic literature as late as the beginning of the nineteenth century." Gibb and Bowen, 234.

44. Gibb and Bowen, 232.

45. Hovannisian, 25.

46. Though Armenians were barred from bearing arms and defending themselves by force, in practice, as we have seen in Sassoun, some Armenian communities had recourse to weapons. These always had to be smuggled and hidden. When used, they endangered the community because of Hamidiye repression.

47. "Christians came to be regarded as the natural allies of the external enemy." Gibb and Bowen, 232.

48. See Roderic H. Davison, "Turkish Attitudes Concerning Christian-Muslim Equality in the Nineteenth Century," *American Historical Review* 59, no. 4 (July 1954): 844.

49. This point is made by many writers, most notably Bernard Lewis in his classic study, *The Emergence of Modern Turkey* (New York: Oxford University Press, 1961), also the excellent essay by Davison, "Nationalism as an Ottoman Problem."

50. See Davison, *Reform*, 418.

51. Shaw and Shaw, 213.

52. Ibid., 212.

53. Kemal, *Memoirs of Ismail Kemal Bey*, 255.

54. See Davison, *Reform*, 404–8.

55. See Hovannisian, 13–15.

56. Great Britain, *Correspondence*, Sessional Papers, c. 7894; inclosure 1 in no. 35, 4 November 1894.

57. Ibid.

58. Kemal, *Memoirs*, 255–56.

59. Hovannisian, 1. Also see H. J. Sarkiss, "The Armenian Renaissance 1500–1863," *Journal of Modern History* 9 (December 1937): 433–48.

60. According to the figures of the Armenian patriarchate, in the six vilayets, by 1901–2, there were 483 Armenian schools, staffed by 897 teachers, educating 29,054 boys and 7,785 girls. For the empire as a whole, there were 903 Armenian schools, 2,088 teachers, and a student population of 59,513 boys and 21,713 girls. See the report by Arnold Toynbee in Bryce, *The Treatment of the Armenians in the Ottoman Empire, 1915–1916*;

Documents Presented to Viscount Grey of Fallodon, Secretary of State for Foreign Affairs (London: H.M.S.O., 1916), 662–63. For education data on the empire as a whole, including Muslim students, see Shaw and Shaw, 112, table 2.2; 113, table 2.3; 244, table 3.15.

61. See Nalbandian, 52.

62. Vahakn N. Dadrian notes that "even though they represented a mere 12 percent of the total population of the Ottoman Empire . . . the Armenians dominated the fields of banking and money lending . . . moreover, by the second half of the nineteenth century, clothing manufacturing, mining, shipping, and milling were mostly controlled by Armenians." See his "The Structural and Functional Components of Genocide: A Victimological Approach to the Armenian Case," in Israel Drapkin and Emilio Viano, eds., *Victimology* (Lexington, Mass.: Lexington Books, D. C. Heath and Co., 1975), 127.

In a private correspondence, however, Richard G. Hovannisian has noted,

> Your thesis of difficulties for minorities at times of upward mobility is, of course, logical and seems borne out of many other instances. In the Armenian case, too, the threshold of tolerance decreased while corruption and anarchy increased, creating explosive circumstances. Yet also in the Armenian experience it should be remembered that there was not just one national experience in the empire. . . . The Armenians of Constantinople and the coastal city, together with those in the bureaucracy, were experiencing rapid economic and cultural upward mobility. And while the same could be said on a more retarded basis for those of the interior provinces in matters of education, cultural endeavors, and national consciousness, this was not always true economically. Many regions in the eastern provinces were actually more impoverished at the end of the nineteenth century than ever before. The large migration of peasants toward the cities was in part due to that impoverishment, together with the growing physical insecurity caused by the breakdown of authority and unbridled raids. This disparity does not necessarily detract from your thesis but notice should be given to it. (Letter received on 25 September 1979)

In response to Hovannisian it may be noted that defenders of a hierarchical and exclusivist order can be outraged by the progress of even a fraction of a minority that is supposed to know its place. Its advance violates the principles of hierarchy and exclusion and can be seen as a harbinger of change that is anathema to conservatives, reactionaries, or integral nationalists. In a similar vein, as will be seen in Chap. 3 (this vol.), not every Jew in Europe or Germany experienced rapid progress, but the few that did were enough to outrage the sensibilities of many Germans and Europeans.

63. George Hughes Hepworth, *Through Armenia on Horseback* (New York: E. P. Dutton, 1898), 339.

64. Recalling the definitions in Chap. 1, the question arises whether the massacres of 1894–96 should be called "massacre" or "pogrom," or "partial genocide." The massacres were too extensive to be simply called a "pogrom," but neither were they a "total genocide," nor even quite a "partial genocide." These were not a total genocide in that the Porte had no intention of exterminating the Armenians or destroying the millet. Neither were they quite a partial genocide in that, although many victims perished, there was no concerted effort by the sultan or the Porte to destroy the identity or the major traditional institutions of the Armenians. What the regime wanted was to cut the Armenians down to size, to restore an old millet to its proper place. Thus on the three dimensions that

range from massacre through partial genocide to total genocide, it seems that the Armenian massacres occupy a position between "massacre" and "partial genocide."

65. Shaw and Shaw, 205.

66. Vahakn N. Dadrian clearly suggests that the massacres of 1894–96 were a prelude to the genocide of 1915. See his "A Theoretical Model of Genocide with Particular Reference to the Armenian Case," *Armenian Review* 31 (February 1979): 119–20.

Chapter Three

1. See Heinrich von Treitschke's "A Word About Our Jews," excerpted in Richard S. Levy, *Antisemitism in the Modern World: An Anthology of Texts* (Lexington, Mass.: D. C. Heath, 1991), 72.

2. Bertolt Brecht, *Selected Poems*, trans. H. R. Hays (New York: Grove Press, 1959), 127.

3. The literature on antisemitism is vast. For a suggestive definition and discussion of antisemitism see Levy, 1–30. For an influential and arresting discussion of antisemitism see Gavin I. Langmuir, *Toward a Definition of Antisemitism* (Berkeley: University of California Press, 1990), and *History, Religion and Antisemitism* (Berkeley: University of California Press, 1990). It will be apparent that although I learned much from Langmuir, Levy, and others, my understanding of antisemitism differs somewhat from theirs.

4. Fritz Stern, *The Politics of Cultural Despair* (Berkeley: University of California Press, 1961).

5. *The Origins of Totalitarianism* (New York: Meridian Books, 1958), vii.

6. Ismar Schorsch, "German Antisemitism in the Light of Post-War Historiography," *Leo Baeck Institute Yearbook* 19 (1974): 257–72; Uriel Tal, *Christians and Jews in Germany: Religion, Politics, and Ideology in the Second Reich* (Ithaca: Cornell University Press, 1975).

7. See H. H. Gerth and C. Wright Mills, *From Max Weber* (New York: Oxford University Press, 1958), 188–90. Also see Werner J. Cahnman, "Pariahs, Strangers and Court-Jews: A Conceptual Clarification," *Sociological Analysis* 35, no. 3 (1974): 154–66.

8. Erik H. Erikson uses the term to mean that part of a person's identity that he or she actively must reject in order to survive his "identity crisis" and become a mature member of his own society. He stretches the concept in connection with the white racist's view of blacks, but it can be extended as well to apply to the antisemite's view of Jews. See his "The Concept of Identity in Group Relations," in Talcott Parsons and Kenneth B. Clark, eds., *The Negro American* (Boston: Beacon Press, 1966), 227–53.

9. In a noteworthy essay, "The Jew as Pariah: A Hidden Tradition," in Hannah Arendt, *The Jew as Pariah: A Collection of Essays and Letters Written from 1942–1966*, ed. Ron H. Feldman (New York: Grove Press, 1978), 67–90, Arendt suggested that for assimilated Jews only a stance of rebellion and resistance could counter the hazards of self-stigmatization. Despite her earlier warnings ("The Jew as Pariah" was written in 1944), she herself came close to the danger she cautioned against. See esp. her *Eichmann in Jerusalem* (New York: Viking Press, 1963).

10. Rosemary R. Ruether, *Faith and Fratricide* (Minneapolis: Seabury Press, 1974). Ruether's views differ from that of Flannery who argued that Christian anti-Judaism was based on a body of prejudice incorporated from pagan sources and on a faulty hermeneutics of scripture. See Edward H. Flannery, *The Anguish of the Jews: Twenty-Three Centuries of Antisemitism* (New York: Paulist Press, 1965). Similarly, Baum averred that Christianity could not be intrinsically antisemitic. He later changed his mind and subscribed to

Ruether's views. See Gregory Baum, *Is the New Testament Anti-Semitic?* (New York: Paulist Press, 1965), and Baum's introduction to Ruether, *Faith and Fratricide*, 1–22. Also see his "Catholic Dogma after Auschwitz," in Alan T. Davies, ed., *Antisemitism and the Foundations of Christianity* (New York: Paulist Press, 1979), 137–50. It should be noted as well that Ruether had been strongly influenced by the works of James Parkes. See esp. his *The Conflict of the Church and the Synagogue* (New York: Atheneum, 1969).

11. Salo Baron, "Ghetto and Emancipation: Shall We Revise the Traditional View?" *Menorah Journal* 14, no. 6 (June): 515–26; David Biale, *Power and Powerlessness in Jewish History* (New York: Schocken Books, 1986).

12. Jacob Katz, *Out of the Ghetto* (New York: Schocken Books, 1978), 16–17.

13. Ruether, 121.

14. Ibid., 94.

15. Ibid., 95.

16. Gregory Baum. "Introduction," to Reuther, *Faith and Fratricide*, 12–13, has noted that according to this view,

> [t]he Jews were attached to the letter, to externals, to the shell, while the Christians were open to the spirit, the inward content, the deeper meaning of God's promises. The Christians troubled by the Jewish refusal, tried to find in the Scriptures the prediction of the "blindness" of Israel. They read the history of Israel as a series of failures and infidelities, which had now climaxed in the rejection of Jesus as the one who fulfilled the scriptural promises.

17. See his *Eight Orations against the Jews*, 6.2–3. Cited in Ruether, 147. Although 1,500 years intervened between St. Chrysostom and Pastor Stoecker (see Chap. 4, this vol.), it is pertinent to note that the Catholic saint and the Lutheran pastor were both concerned, at different times, to degrade the status of the Jews. Accusations of deicide also persisted well into our own era. It should be noted as well that John Chrysostom is quoted here, not in order to suggest that his writings alone underpinned anti-Judaism, but to call attention to an anti-Jewish tradition in Christianity that was one of the crucial elements shaping later Judeophobia and modern antisemitism.

18. The view of the Jews as blind to the truth and of the Church as superceding the synagogue is graphically expressed and symbolically condensed in a pair of thirteenth-century statues representing the Church and the Synagogue outside of the Bamberg cathedral in Germany. A similar pair stands outside of the church of St. Severin in Bordeaux. The Church is represented as a noble and proud maiden. She is crowned and holds the Ecclesia in one hand and a staff in the other. In contrast the Synagogue is portrayed as blindfolded, her crown fallen and her staff broken.

19. See Erikson, "The Concept of Identity in Group Relations."

20. Baum, "Introduction," 12–13.

21. Flannery, 49.

22. Ibid., 50.

23. Ruether, 186.

24. For the connection between lepers and Jews see Leon Poliakov, *The History of Antisemitism* (New York: Schocken Books, 1974), 104–5. See also Joshua Trachtenberg, *The Devil and the Jews* (New Haven: Yale University Press, 1944).

25. The Roman emperor of the East, Theodosius II (408–50 C.E.), compiled what came to be known as the Theodosian Code (C.Th.). It was the official collection of

imperial statutes beginning with those promulgated by Constantine. The Code was incorporated into Western Roman law by emperor Valentinian III. Esp. chaps. 8 and 9 of book 16 of the Code refer to the Jews.

26. Flannery, 53–54.

27. This became an important prohibition because in an economy that was based on slave labor, Jews were placed under a heavy disadvantage as landowners and owners of latifundia. Ruether noted, "Jews were not immediately eliminated from agriculture, but these laws began a trend that was eventually to bias Jewish economic life toward trade and exclude them from their normal participation in landholding and agriculture." See Ruether, 188.

28. Flannery, 55.

29. Ruether, 192.

30. See Jeremy Cohen, *The Friars and the Jews* (Ithaca: Cornell University Press, 1982).

31. It should be noted that Robert Chazan does not view the Crusade of 1096 as necessarily causing a major decline in Jewish life of the period, but he does see it as introducing a new kind of militant persecution that sought the total destruction of Judaism as a faith and of Jews as a people. See his *European Jewry and the First Crusade* (Berkeley: University of California Press), 219.

32. Note that Langmuir, 301–2, defines antisemitism as "all instances in which people, because they are labeled Jews, are feared as symbols of subhumanity, and hated for threatening characteristics they do not in fact possess." He dates such "chimerical" fear and hatred to 1350. What Langmuir calls "antisemitism" I prefer to call "Jew-hatred" or Judeophobia. I use the term "antisemitism" in a more limited manner to refer to a modern ideology concerning the workings of the world in which the Jews play a dominant, conspiratorial, controlling, and nefarious role.

33. Poliakov, *The History of Antisemitism*, 53.

34. Ruether, 213.

35. Ibid., 213–14. Also Trachtenberg, *The Devil and the Jews*. It should also be noted in this context that because of the ambiguous legacy of Martin Luther, the Reformation in Germany only helped to reenforce the negative medieval stereotype of the Jew. On this point see Larry E. Axel, "Christian Theology and the Murder of the Jews," *Encounter* (Indianapolis) 40 (Spring 1979): 129–41, and Mark U. Edwards, Jr., *Luther's Last Battles* (Ithaca: Cornell University Press, 1983), 115–42. Edwards argues that, with regard to the Jews, especially the Luther of *On the Jews and Their Lies* should be understood as a man of his times. That Luther's legacy had catastrophic consequences for antisemitism and the Holocaust is stressed by Axel.

36. Peter G. J. Pulzer, *The Rise of Political Anti-Semitism in Germany and Austria* (New York: John Wiley, 1964), 7.

37. In 1848 the Frankfurt Assembly extended to Jews equal rights of German citizenship. By 1849 all states except Bavaria followed suit. With the failure of the liberal revolution, Jewish emancipation was temporarily rescinded. As Germany approached unification, however, Jewish rights were restored. The Jews of Baden were freed in 1862 and those of Württemberg in 1864. On 3 July 1869 the Emancipation Law of the North German Confederation abolished all discriminatory laws and regulations based on religious distinctions. With unification in 1871, Jews were extended equality in all states including Bavaria.

38. This pattern was not unique to Jews but was characteristic, as we have seen in Chaps. 1 and 2 of other modernizing groups such as the Armenians and the Ibos. For classic theoretical discussions of modernization and social mobilization see Daniel Lerner, *The Passing of Traditional Society* (New York: Free Press, 1958), and Karl W. Deutsch, "Social Mobilization and Political Development," *American Political Science Review* 55 (1961): 493–514.

39. Arthur Ruppin, *The Jews in the Modern World* (London: Macmillan, 1934), 24.

40. Ibid., 29.

41. Ibid., 31–32.

42. Ibid., 37.

43. Paul R. Mendes-Flohr and Jehuda Reinharz, eds., *The Jews in the Modern World* (New York: Oxford University Press, 1980), 533.

44. These figures and the percentages are based on and derived from Pulzer, 10.

45. See Mendes-Flohr and Reinharz, table 9, 533.

46. Ruppin, 306.

47. Ibid., 309.

48. George L. Mosse, "Jewish Emancipation: Between *Bildung* and Respectability," in Jehuda Reinharz and Walter Schatzberg, eds., *The Jewish Response to German Culture* (Hanover, N.H.: University Press of New England, 1985), 1–16.

49. Simon Kuznets, "Economic Structure and Life of the Jews," Louis Finkelstein, ed., *The Jews* (New York: Harper Brothers, 1960), 1066, points out, for example, that since a modernizing minority like the Jews may represent a large fraction of the urban and industrial population, it may find itself caught in the cleavage between the rural and urban sectors of society. This may have been one source of friction between Poles and Jews; another may have been the simple fact of economic and social competition in the modern urban and industrial sphere of society itself.

50. One need not exaggerate the tolerance extended to Jews in the United States to point out that organized political antisemitism never did materialize there as it did in Germany and the rest of Europe in the nineteenth century. For a somewhat different view that draws a parallel between the two countries see Gordon Mork, "German Nationalism and Jewish Assimilation—the Bismarck Period," *Leo Baeck Institute Yearbook* 22 (1977): 81–91.

51. Ruppin, table 13, 136.

52. See, for example, the works of the socialist-Zionist leader Ber Borochov. *Nationalism and the Class Struggle* (Westport, Conn.: Greenwood Press, 1937), 59, who opened his critique of Jewish economic development with the following: "The socioeconomic structure of the Jewish people differs radically from that of other nations. Ours is an an anomalous, abnormal structure." Antisemites from Marr to Hitler also argued that the economic structure of the Jews was abnormal, but they blamed alleged Jewish cupidity for that, while the Zionists singled out the lack of an autonomous and independent Jewish homeland.

53. Ruppin, 133.

54. Monika Richarz, "Jewish Social Mobility in Germany during the Time of Emancipation, 1790–1871," *Leo Baeck Institute Yearbook* 20 (1975): 69–78.

55. Ibid., 72.

56. Ibid., 73.

57. Ibid., 74.

58. Ibid., 77.

59. Ruppin, table 13, 136.

60. See Frederic W. Grunfeld, *Prophets without Honour* (New York: Holt, Rinehart and Winston, 1979).

61. For a comparison of the relative development or mobilization of Western European as against Eastern European Jews see Ruppin; Jacob Lestschinsky, "The Economic and Social Development of the Jewish People," *Jewish Encyclopedic Handbooks* (New York: Central Yiddish Cultural Organization, 1946), 361–90; Celia S. Heller, *On the Edge of Destruction* (New York: Columbia University Press, 1977); and Calvin Goldscheider and Alan S. Zuckerman, *The Transformation of the Jews* (Chicago: University of Chicago Press, 1984).

62. Because they show the inner personal and ideological tensions created by modernity, the autobiographies and biographies of Gershom Scholem and Isaac Deutscher are especially instructive. On Scholem see *On Jews and Judaism in Crisis* (New York: Schocken Books, 1978), *From Berlin to Jerusalem* (New York: Schocken Books, 1988), and David Biale, *Gershom Scholem: Kabbalah and Counter History* (Cambridge, Mass.: Harvard University Press, 1979). See Isaac Deutscher, *The Non-Jewish Jew* (London: Oxford University Press, 1968). Also see Jehuda Reinharz, *Fatherland or Promised Land: The Dilemma of the German Jew, 1893–1914* (Ann Arbor: University of Michigan Press, 1975).

63. German antisemites used the term "Judaization" with great frequency. Reflected in the concept was their fear that Jews had inordinate, indeed controlling power in Germany, and that the spirit or culture of Judaism and the Jews was displacing the German spirit or culture. For an insightful discussion see Steven E. Aschheim, "'The Jew Within': The Myth of 'Judaization' in Germany," in Reinharz and Schatzberg, *The Jewish Response to German Culture*, 212–41, and the discussion below.

64. Among other outstanding treatments of racial antisemitism, besides those already cited, are George Mosse, *Toward the Final Solution: A History of European Racism* (New York: Howard Fertig, 1978), and Jacob Katz, *From Prejudice to Destruction* (Cambridge, Mass.: Harvard University Press, 1980), 303–17.

65. See Heller, *On the Edge of Destruction*.

66. For a further discussion of the Marxist or socialist assessment of antisemitism see Chap. 4 (this vol.); and Paul W. Massing *Rehearsal for Destruction: A Study of Political Anti-Semitism in Imperial Germany* (New York: Howard Fertig, 1967); and Richard S. Levy, *The Downfall of the Anti-Semitic Parties in Imperial Germany* (New Haven: Yale University Press, 1975). In *On the Jewish Question*, Marx identifies Jews with the spirit of capitalism and expresses his animus toward Jews without examining their historical role as pariahs in European society. Indeed, some writers, including Aschheim, 219–24, imply that Marx's essay should be treated as part of the antisemitic canon.

67. The *Mittelstand* refers to the vast stratum of the "middle estate," a term harking back to preindustrial society, which in Germany existed between the peasantry and the bourgeoisie. It excluded the nobility and the working class and included various categories of small merchants, artisans, teachers, white-collar workers, and officials of the middle and lower ranks of the civil service. Levy, *Downfall*, 19, notes that "the term masqueraded as sociological, but its real significance was ideological."

68. For a discussion of Stoecker see Chap. 4 (this vol.).

69. Shulamit Volkov, "Antisemitism as a Cultural Code: Reflections on the History and Historiography of Antisemitism in Imperial Germany," *Leo Baeck Institute Yearbook* 23 (1978): 24–46.

70. Aschheim, 214.

71. See Levy, *Antisemitism in the Modern World*, 2 and 74–96, and Moshe Zimmerman, *Wilhelm Marr: The Patriarch of Antisemitism* (New York: Oxford University Press, 1986), 112–15.

72. Levy, *Antisemitism in the Modern World*, 84.

73. Pulzer, 51.

74. Levy, 80.

75. Also see Stoecker's speech "What We Demand of Modern Jewry" which is analyzed in Chap. 4 (this vol.).

76. One should not exaggerate the enthusiasm that most Europeans had for Jewish emancipation. As will be seen in Chap. 4 (this vol.), the liberals and the socialists supported it, but not out of a respect for Jews and Judaism or a desire for pluralism. Indeed, supporters of Jewish emancipation hoped that it would lead to an accelerated pace of Jewish assimilation and hence to a disappearance of the Jewish pariah. For further discussion of this point see Chap. 4; and Katz, *From Prejudice to Destruction*, 129–38 and 147–222.

77. Cited in Mendes-Flohr and Reinharz, *The Jew in the Modern World*, 273.

78. See Claude Lanzmann, *Shoah* (New York: Pantheon, 1985), 99–100.

79. See, for example, Jan Karski, *Story of a Secret State* (Boston: Houghton Mifflin, 1944); Alexander Dallin, *German Rule in Russia, 1941–1945* (London: Macmillan, 1957): Jan Gross, *Polish Society under German Occupation* (Princeton: Princeton University Press, 1979); and Michael Berenbaum, *A Mosaic of Victims: Non-Jews Persecuted and Murdered by the Nazis* (New York: New York University Press, 1990).

Chapter Four

1. August Bebel, *Sozialdemokratie und Antisemitismus* (1906), 38, quoted in Paul W. Massing, *Rehearsal for Destruction: A Study of Political Anti-Semitism in Imperial Germany* (New York: Howard Fertig, 1967), 197.

2. By "populism" I mean a doctrine of majority rule that pays little heed to minority rights. Movements advocating populism have tended to mobilize middle-class and especially lower-middle-class groups. See Seymour Martin Lipset, *Political Man* (Baltimore: Johns Hopkins University Press, 1981), 131–79 and 488–503. The concept of *Völkisch* ideology as developed by Mosse is closely allied to the notion of populism, but it goes beyond it by, for example, linking it to integral nationalism and racism. Disagreeing with Lipset, Hamilton notes that the social basis of Nazi appeal far transcended the populism of the *Mittelstand* and the peasantry, unlike that of the antisemitic parties in Imperial Germany. See George L. Mosse, *The Crisis of German Ideology* (New York: Grosset and Dunlap, 1964), and Richard F. Hamilton, *Who Voted for Hitler?* (Princeton: Princeton University Press, 1982).

3. See Massing, *Rehearsal*; Peter G. J. Pulzer, *The Rise of Political Anti-Semitism in Germany and Austria* (New York: John Wiley, 1964); Hans-Ulrich Wehler, *The German Empire, 1871–1918* (Leamington Spa/Dover, N.H.: Berg, 185); Karl D. Bracher, *The German Dictatorship* (New York: Holt, Rinehart and Winston, 1970); and Shulamit Volkov, "Antisemitism as a Cultural Code: Reflections on the History and Historiography of Antisemitism in Imperial Germany," *Leo Baeck Institute Yearbook* 23 (1978): 25–46.

4. Craig notes that despite its seeming limitations, the *Reichstag* had powers of debate, of review, and over the budget that might have been used to extend its authority.

Bismarck needed it as a counterweight to the crown and to the aristocracy that, despite his best efforts to secure their privileges, never quite trusted him. See Gordon A. Craig, *Germany: 1866–1945* (New York: Oxford University Press, 1978), 48. As to the chancellor, he was appointed by the emperor and was responsible only to him. The chancellor's main tasks were to appoint officials to the imperial bureaucracy and to conduct foreign policy. A telling feature of this regime was that by law the emperor of Germany was king of Prussia, and in most cases he appointed his chancellor as minister president of Prussia.

5. Following the revolution of 1848, the National Assembly, the first in Prussian history, was elected by universal manhood suffrage. By early December 1848, however, the king's powers had been restored and the assembly scattered. Though rejecting the call of the liberals to form a constitutional monarchy, to everyone's surprise Frederick William IV granted a constitution that safeguarded some basic freedoms and called for the convening of a Prussian parliament of two houses. The upper body was to be composed of hereditary members, nobles, princes, and the king's appointees; while the lower house was to be selected on the basis of universal manhood suffrage. In May 1849, the king revised the constitution and the suffrage so that representation to the lower house was so weighted in favor of the property-owning classes that 15 percent of the population had control over two-thirds of the seats. "This system, which was to last until 1918, would serve as a barrier to democratic reform and social legislation in behalf of the masses." See Craig, *Germany*, 93.

6. Not only did the constitution of the Second Reich subvert principles of equality, it did not include a bill of rights or a declaration of fundamental liberties. This was a far cry from American and French constitutional practice, but it was equally distant from the German constitution of 1849 that did include provisos for civil liberties. See Craig, *Germany*, 41. Wehler refers to Imperial Germany under Bismarck as "an autocratic, semi-absolutist sham constitutionalism . . . [ruled by] a Bonapartist dictator." See his *The German Empire*, 55. For a critique of the Marxian concept of "Bonapartism," as applied to Imperial Germany, see David Blackbourn and Geoff Eley, *The Peculiarities of German History* (New York: Oxford University Press, 1984), 149–52.

7. Craig, 144.

8. The above synopsis of developments in Imperial Germany is based on Wehler, 1985. It is a view that was earlier formulated by Thorstein Veblen, *Imperial Germany and the Industrial Revolution* (New York: Viking Press, 1954); Alexander Gerschenkron, *Bread and Democracy in Germany* (New York: Howard Fertig, 1966); and Ralf Dahrendorf, *Society and Democracy in Germany* (Garden City, N.Y.: Anchor Books, 1969). Other writers who have based their analyses of Imperial Germany on the notion that it was a faulted society in the above sense are Bracher, *The German Dictatorship*, and Craig, *Germany*. For a theoretical statement relating crises of participation to the institutionalization of the state and the processes of modernization see Samuel P. Huntington, *Political Order in Changing Societies* (New Haven: Yale University Press, 1968). For a critical view see Blackbourn and Eley, *Peculiarities*. For a perspective that is in turn critical of Blackbourn and Eley see Gordon A. Craig's review of Blackbourn and Eley, "The German Mystery Case," *New York Review of Books* (January 1986): 20–24.

9. See Wehler, *Empire*, 14–20; Gustav Stolper, *The German Economy: 1870 to the Present* (New York: Harcourt, Brace, Jovanovich, 1967); David S. Landes, *The Unbound Prometheus* (Cambridge: Cambridge University Press, 1972); and Martin Kitchen, *The Political Economy of Germany, 1815–1914* (London: Croom Helm, 1978).

10. Volker Rittberger, "Revolution and Pseudo-Democratization: The Formation of the Weimar Republic," in Gabriel A. Almond, Scott C. Flanagan, and Robert G. Mundt, eds., *Crisis, Choice and Change* (Boston: Little, Brown, 1973), 290; and Landes, *Prometheus*, 329–31.

11. Koppel S. Pinson, *Modern Germany* (New York: Macmillan, 1954), 221.

12. See Craig, *Germany*, 186. Literacy as a factor in development was stressed by Daniel Lerner, *The Passing of Traditional Society* (New York: Free Press, 1958). A link between literacy and industrialization in Imperial Germany was the establishment and spread of technical institutes like the Beuth Technical Institute founded in Berlin in 1821. See Wehler, 19.

13. Rittberger, "Revolution," 289.

14. Craig, 146.

15. Ibid., 156.

16. Ibid., 179.

17. Indeed, between 1891 and 1913 trade union membership grew by nearly 1000 percent, and between 1906 and 1914 the membership of the SPD increased by 183 percent. Such growth in the numbers and potential power of the working class resulted in greater union militancy and in increased pressure on the regime to expand participation. These conclusions can be verified in part by the increased number of strikes and lockouts and by the growth of electoral support for the SPD between 1890 and the First World War. See Rittberger, 304–8.

18. See Carl E. Schorske, *German Social Democracy, 1905–1917* (Cambridge, Mass.: Harvard University Press, 1955); Peter Gay, *The Dilemma of Democratic Socialism* (New York: Collier Books, 1962); Guenther Roth, *The Social Democrats in Imperial Germany* (Totowa, N.J.: Bedminster Press, 1963), 163–71.

19. Richard S. Levy, *The Downfall of the Anti-Semitic Parties in Imperial Germany* (New Haven: Yale University Press, 1975), 14, 67–90.

20. Massing, *Rehearsal*; Bracher, *Dictatorship*; Wehler, *Empire*.

21. Massing, 66.

22. Levy, 89.

23. Pinson, 166.

24. Craig, 98–100.

25. Massing, 128.

26. Craig, 63.

27. Ibid., 69.

28. Ibid., 96.

29. On liberal antipathy toward Jews and Judaism see esp. Uriel Tal, *Christians and Jews in Germany: Religion, Politics, and Ideology in the Second Reich* (Ithaca: Cornell University Press, 1975), and Jacob Katz, *From Prejudice to Destruction* (Cambridge, Mass.: Harvard University Press, 1980).

30. Levy, 182.

31. Ibid., 181.

32. Pinson, 181.

33. Thus Massing notes, "This vexation with Jews and Liberals was not entirely without cause. . . . The Berlin liberal press, with which many Jews were associated, had crusaded against Conservative and Catholic 'enemies of the Reich,' helping to make 'ultramontane' one of the most popular epithets of the period, blending, as it did, enlight-

ened liberal opposition to established dogma with nationalistic hostility to an authority seated 'beyond the mountain, in the Vatican.'" See his *Rehearsal,* 18.

34. In a private correspondence (4 January 1988), Professor Levy remarked that "the Center was a better defender of liberalism in Imperial Germany than the liberals. The failure of the imperial antisemites had much to do with their inability to penetrate the Catholic and the proletarian masses." Without questioning the personal motives of prominent Catholic statesmen such as Windthorst and Lieber, it needs to be pointed out, however, that the Center's opposition to the antisemitic parties was based less on philo-semitism or matters of principle than on political self-defense for Catholics who like the Jews were a minority. See Levy, 189. Indeed, when the political currents shifted under the Nazis, Catholic areas no less than Protestant gave them their support and were equally indifferent to the fate of the Jews. See Ian Kershaw, *Popular Opinion and Political Dissent in the Third Reich: Bavaria, 1933–1945* (Oxford: Clarendon Press, 1983), 224–78 and 358–86.

35. See Massing, 155; Levy, 130–65; George L. Mosse, *Masses and Man: Nationalist and Fascist Perceptions of Reality* (New York: Howard Fertig, 1980), 284–316; Robert Wistrich, *Socialism and the Jews* (Rutherford, N.J.: Fairleigh Dickinson University Press, 1982); and Steven E. Aschheim, "'The Jew Within': The Myth of 'Judaization' in Germany," in Jehuda Reinharz and Walter Schatzberg, eds., *The Jewish Response to German Culture* (Hanover, N.H.: University Press of New England, 1985), 212–41.

36. Quoted in Massing, 160.

37. Ibid., 181.

38. Ibid.

39. Thus of the forty-four antisemitic deputies who were elected to the *Reichstag* between 1887 and 1912, forty-one were of *Mittelstand* origin. While the Center was able to aggregate the Catholic peasant vote, Protestant peasants, especially in Hesse, were susceptible to antisemitic appeals. It should, of course, be noted that although these two classes were more likely to vote for the antisemitic parties than were other strata, only a minority did so. By the same token, a majority of the *Mittelstand* and the peasantry were likely to be Judeophobic, anti-Jewish, or possibly even antisemitic in their private attitudes and views. Indeed, for the most part, the nonpolitical party pressure groups that based their support on the lower-middle class and the peasantry were antisemitic in their views. See, for example, Massing's (139) discussion of the German Federation of Salaried Commercial Employees and of the Agrarian League. Had the peasants and the lower-middle class fully supported and voted for the antisemitic parties, these would not have failed as badly as they did. For a critical review of the role of the *Mittelstand* in Imperial Germany, see David Blackbourn, "The *Mittelstand* in German Society and Politics," *Social History* 4 (1977): 409–33.

40. Massing, *Rehearsal;* Levy, *Downfall;* and Craig, *Germany.*

41. Levy, 15.

42. Levy, 16.

43. Massing, 11.

44. Ibid., 51–12.

45. Levy, 32.

46. In this group, Levy (29) includes Paul de Lagarde, Eugen Dühring, and Friedrich Lange. I would not include de Lagarde on the same list with Fritsch. Though both men had given up on the *Kaiserreich's* being able to deal with the Jewish question, de Lagarde turned away from political solutions altogether. Fritsch, on the other hand,

though contemptuous of parliament, had not abandoned the possibility that less conventional means, not excluding violence, might work. Following Fritz Stern, *The Politics of Cultural Despair* (Berkeley: University of California Press, 1961), I would prefer to call de Lagarde a "cultural pessimist," while reserving the term "revolutionary" for those who, at the very least, advocated revolutionary means toward political ends.

47. Levy, 235–36.

48. Ibid., 30.

49. For histories of the antisemitic parties the reader is directed to the excellent studies of Massing, Pulzer, and esp. Levy.

50. In a private correspondence (4 January 1988), Professor Levy suggests that "the antisemites tried to constitute an independent political force as well as to ally with the Conservatives. Distrust of the 'democratic' (I like 'populist' better, too) dangers of the movement was variable, however. The *Bund der Landwirte* was much more tolerant, for example, than the DKP. Bismarck became disenchanted early. But the degree of toleration was relative to the perceived position of those who attempted to use the unruly antisemites. . . . Still it is not perhaps as clearly a linear process of disenchantment on the part of the elite as you suggest in your synopsis." That the process of disenchantment was not linear can be seen from the career of Pastor Stoecker as set forth below. For a discussion of the career of Liebermann von Sonnenberg, whose career parallels that of Stoecker and who was equally as important as the pastor, see Levy.

51. Massing, 24. Also see Levy, 18.

52. Massing, 25.

53. Ibid., 278.

54. Ibid.

55. Ibid, 279.

56. Ibid.

57. Ibid., 280.

58. Ibid., 281.

59. Ibid.

60. Ibid., 282.

61. Ibid.

62. Ibid., 283.

63. Ibid., 285.

64. Ibid.

65. Ibid.

66. For a discussion of the concept of "Judaization" in German discourse see Aschheim. Also see the discussion in Chap. 3 (this vol.).

67. Massing, 286.

68. Ibid.

69. Ibid.

70. Ibid., 287.

71. Ibid., 29.

72. For a fascinating history of the relationship between Bismarck and Bleichröder see Fritz Stern, *Gold and Iron: Bismarck, Bleichröder, and the Building of the German Empire* (New York: Vintage Press, 1979).

73. Massing, 38.

74. Ibid., 38–39.

75. Ibid., 52.

76. Ibid., 76.

77. Ibid., 58.

78. Ibid., 125.

79. Wehler, *Empire*, coined the terms explicitly, but Bracher, *Dictatorship*, relies on this concept as well. It should be noted, however, that elite manipulation was but one of the many sources that Bracher found for the phenomenon of antisemitism.

80. Wehler, 91.

81. Ibid., 92.

82. Ibid., 94.

83. Levy, 255–65.

84. The thesis that antisemitism was a form of social imperialism and negative integration manipulated by the upper, to distract the lower, classes is based on an elitist view of social and political causality that may neglect the independent existence of the lower classes and their impact on social relations. For a general discussion of this point see Geoff Eley, *From Unification to Nazism: Reinterpreting the German Past* (Boston: Allen and Unwin, 231–53).

85. Levy, 249–50.

86. Heinrich Class became the leader of the Pan-German League in 1908.

87. Erich Goldhagen, "The Mad Count: A Forgotten Portent of the Holocaust," *Midstream* (February 1976): 61–63.

88. Shulamit Volkov, "Antisemitism as a Cultural Code."

89. Volkov, 35. It should be noted that in a later essay Volkov makes a strong case for distinguishing the antisemitism of Imperial Germany from its Nazi variation. She stresses that the difference does not lie in the content of the ideology alone but in the context in which it was formulated and in the purposes to which it was harnessed. This is very much the point that I am trying to stress in this chap. and in Chaps. 6 and 7 (this vol.). See her "The Written Matter and the Spoken Word: On the Gap between Pre-1914 and Nazi Anti-Semitism," in François Furet, ed., *Unanswered Questions: Nazi Germany and the Genocide of the Jews* (New York: Schocken Books, 1989), 33–53.

90. Levy, 249.

91. Ibid., 255.

92. Ibid., 250.

93. Ibid., 260.

94. Ibid., 261.

95. Ibid., 263.

96. Ibid., 262.

97. Ibid.

98. Ibid.

Chapter Five

1. Parts of this chapter have appeared earlier under the title, "Provocation or Nationalism: A Critical Inquiry into the Armenian Genocide of 1915," in Richard G. Hovannisian, ed., *The Armenian Genocide in Perspective* (New Brunswick, N.J.: Transaction Books, 1986), 61–84. This was reprinted in Frank Chalk and Kurt Jonassohn, eds., *The History and Sociology of Genocide* (New Haven: Yale University Press, 1990), 266–90.

2. Arnold Toynbee, *Acquaintances* (London: Oxford University Press, 1967), 241–42.

3. Quoted in Uriel Heyd, *Foundations of Turkish Nationalism: The Life and Teachings of Ziya Gökalp* (London: Luzac, 1950), 124.

4. Roderic H. Davison, *Turkey: A Short History* (Englewood Cliffs, N.J.: Prentice-Hall, 1968), 109.

5. For precursors and background to the Young Turks, see Serif Mardin, *The Genesis of Young Ottoman Thought* (Princeton: Princeton University Press, 1962); Bernard Lewis, *The Emergence of Modern Turkey* (Oxford: Oxford University Press, 1961); Feroz Ahmad, *The Young Turks* (Oxford: Clarendon Press, 1969); Ernest E. Ramsaur, Jr., *The Young Turks* (Beirut: Khayats, 1965).

6. Arnold J. Toynbee, "A Summary of Armenian History Up to and Including 1915," in Viscount J. Bryce, *The Treatment of Armenians in the Ottoman Empire: Documents Presented to Viscount Grey of Fallodon, Secretary of State for Foreign Affairs* (London: H.M.S.O., 1916), 591–653. There is a vast literature on the Armenian genocide; besides Toynbee's fundamental work, one should cite Johannes Lepsius, *Deutschland und Armenien* (Potsdam: Tempelverlag, 1919), and Henry Morgenthau, *Ambassador Morgenthau's Story* (Garden City, N.Y.: Doubleday, 1918). A major recent contribution is that of Vahakn N. Dardian, "Genocide as a Problem of National and International Law: The World War I Armenian Case and Its Contemporary Legal Ramifications," *Yale Journal of International Law* 14, no. 2 (Summer 1989): 221–334. Other important studies that complement or amplify Toynbee are Richard G. Hovannisian, *Armenia on the Road to Independence* (Berkeley and Los Angeles: University of California Press, 1967); Yves Ternon, *Les Arméniens: Histoire d'un Génocide* (Paris: Editions du Seuil, 1977); Hovannisian, *The Armenian Genocide in Perspective;* Christopher J. Walker, *Armenia: The Survival of a Nation* (London: Croom Helm, 1980; New York: St. Martin's Press, 1981); and Gerard J. Libaridian, "The Ultimate Repression: The Genocide of the Armenians," in Isidor Walliman and Michael N. Dobkowski, eds., *Genocide in the Modern Age* (New York: Greenwood Press, 1987), 203–36. For an informative bibliographic essay see Richard G. Hovannisian, "The Armenian Genocide," in Israel W. Charny, ed., *Genocide: A Critical Bibliographic Review* (New York: Facts on File, 1988), 89–116, and Richard G. Hovannisian, *The Armenian Holocaust: A Bibliography Relating to the Deportations, Massacres, and Dispersion of the Armenian People, 1915–1923* (Cambridge, Mass.: Armenian Heritage Press, 1980).

7. See n. 14, chap. 1.

8. Toynbee, 640.

9. Dadrian, "Genocide as a Problem," 266.

10. Toynbee, 640.

11. Esp. in the eastern *vilayets*, some of the Muslim villagers themselves had been driven out of Russia and the Balkans. This is significant because it sheds light on the motives of such villagers. See Hovannisian, *Armenia on the Road*, 13, and Stanford J. Shaw and Ezel Kural Shaw, *The History of the Ottoman Empire and Modern Turkey*, vol. 2 (Cambridge: Cambridge University Press, 1977), 203.

12. See Dadrian, "Genocide as a Problem," 275; Walker, *Survival*, 197; and Jacob M. Landau, *Pan-Turkism in Turkey* (London: C. Hurst, 1981; Hamden, Conn.: Archon Books, 1981), 53.

13. Dadrian, 274–75.

14. Ibid., 277.

15. Toynbee, 643. Consider as well the testimony of survivors like Kerop Bedoukian, *The Urchin: An Armenian's Escape* (London: J. Murray, 1978). Compare such accounts with the following from Shaw and Shaw (315): "Specific instructions were issued for the army to protect the Armenians against nomadic attacks and to provide them with sufficient food and other supplies to meet their needs during the march and after they were settled . . . [T]he Armenians were to be protected and cared for until they returned to their homes after the war." It should be noted that this description is given without any discussion of disconfirming evidence, including that of Toynbee above.

16. Toynbee, 648.

17. Ibid., 649. In a private correspondence, Professor Alan Fisher of Michigan State University has suggested that the Ottoman census may have underestimated the total population of whatever group because the census counted the number of households only. Thus the 1.1 million figure that Toynbee uses may be low, both because of the Ottoman desire to underestimate the size of the Armenian millet and because of the reasons cited by Fisher. See also n. 23 below.

18. Toynbee, 649. He estimates that the number of refugees plus the populations of Smyrna and Constantinople who escaped the deportations was 350,000, and the number of non-Apostolic (Gregorian) Armenians, plus converts to Islam, plus those who escaped or were spared was 250,000. This gives him a figure of 600,000 for the number who were spared or escaped. That apparently there were categories of Armenians who were spared the deportations and the massacres were points stressed by Professor Yehuda Bauer in his "Unique and Universal: Some General Problems Arising Out of Holocaust Research," an undated mimeographed publication from Hebrew University. He used these points to suggest that the Armenian Genocide was less inclusive than the Holocaust. Later Bauer changed his mind, referring to both events as "holocausts." See Yehuda Bauer, "The Place of the Holocaust in Contemporary History," in Jonathan Frankel, ed., *Studies in Contemporary Jewry* (Bloomington: Indiana University Press, 1984), 201–34. Moreover, Aram Andonian, in *The Memoirs of Naim Bey* (London: Hodder & Stoughton, 1920), suggests that a significant part of the Armenian population of Constantinople was not spared, and Marjorie Housepian, *The Smyrna Affair* (New York: Harcourt Brace Jovanovich, 1966), documents how the Armenian population of Smyrna was massacred in 1922. This information could not be available to Toynbee who was acquainted with reports no later than Spring 1916.

19. Ibid., 650.

20. Ibid.

21. Ibid., 651.

22. Andonian, xiii–xiv. An important authentication of the Andonian documents is provided by Vahakn N. Dadrian, "The Naim-Andonian Documents on the World War I Destruction of the Ottoman Armenians: The Anatomy of Genocide," *International Journal of Middle East Studies* 18 (1986): 311–60.

23. Johannes Lepsius, *Le rapport sécret sur les massacres d'Arménie* (Paris: Payot, 1918; repr., Paris: Payot, 1966). Dickran Boyajian in *Armenia: The Case for a Forgotten Genocide* (Westwood, N.J.: Educational Book Crafters, 1972), 287, and others dispute the 1 million figure and suggest that 1.5 million Armenians perished. It may be that the higher figure reflects all the victims from 1915 to 1923. A recent estimate is provided by Justin McCarthy, *Muslims and Minorities* (New York and London: New York University Press, 1983). He cites a figure of 1,465,418 Anatolian Armenians for 1912 and 880,880 for 1922. He

concludes, therefore, that "[a]lmost 600,000, 40% of their population had died" in the period of the First World War and after (130). Like other historians supporting the prov- ocation thesis, which will be discussed below, he assumes that such deaths were not due to a premeditated genocide but to a civil war between Muslims and Armenians (119). For a detailed critique of McCarthy's statistical analysis, see Levon Marshalian, "Population Statistics on Ottoman Armenians in the Context of Turkish Historiography," *Armenian Review* 40, no. 4 (Winter 1987): 1–59.

24. Morgenthau, 351–52.

25. Dadrian, "Genocide as a Problem," 262.

26. Ibid., 279.

27. J. F. Willis, *Prologue to Nuremberg: The Politics and Diplomacy of Punishing War Crimi- nals of the First World War* (Westport, Conn.: Greenwood, 1982), 181. Quoted in Dadrian, 281.

28. Dadrian, 281–90.

29. Ibid., 292–93.

30. Ibid., 295.

31. *Takvimi Vekayi*, no., 3540, 5 May 1919, 8; quoted in Dadrian, 296n.280.

32. Ibid., 4; in Dadrian, 297.

33. Ibid., 6; in Dadrian, 299.

34. Dadrian, 298.

35. *Takvimi Vekayi*, no. 3540, 6; quoted in Dadrian, 299. Drawing a parallel between the CUP's "Responsible Secretaries" and Nazi *Gauleiters*, Dadrian notes that they were selected by the Central Committee and invested with powers at the local level superced- ing that of the government itself. See Dadrian, 302 and n.313. What the relationship might have been between the "Responsible Secretaries" and Enver's Special Organization is not clear.

36. *Takvimi Vekai*, no. 3540, 6; in Dadrian, 300.

37. Dadrian, 300.

38. *Takvimi Vekayi*, no. 3540, 7; in Dadrian, 300.

39. Ibid., 8; in Dadrian, 300.

40. Ibid., 7; in Dadrian, 301.

41. Dadrian, 305. Also see *Takvimi Vekayi*, no. 3540, 14.

42. *Takvimi Vekayi*, no. 3604, 22 July 1919, 217–20; in Dadrian, 307.

43. Dadrian, 307–8.

44. It should be noted, however, that some of the principal architects of the Ar- menian Genocide were later assassinated by Armenians seeking to "avenge" their crimes. This includes Talaat, Dr. Shakir, and Jemal. Enver was killed in battle on 4 August 1922. Dr. Nazim was hanged by the Kemalist regime for conspiring against the life of Mustafa Kemal, not for his role in the genocide. See Dadrian, 310n.358.

45. In his later works such as *The Western Question in Greece and Turkey* (London: Constable, 1922) and *Acquaintances* (London: Oxford University Press, 1967), Toynbee was to repudiate some of his own denunciations of the Young Turk regime, and like Bernard Lewis in *The Emergence of Modern Turkey*, he came to see why the CUP may have felt threatened by Armenian (and Greek) self-determination. Nevertheless, as the quote below shows, he never denied the validity of his earlier findings. For a discussion of Toynbee's position regarding the Armenian Genocide see Norman Ravitch, "The Arme- nian Catastrophe," *Encounter* 57 (1981): 69–84.

46. Toynbee, *Acquaintances*, 241–42.

47. Michael J. Arlen, *Passage to Ararat* (New York: Ballantine Books, 1975), 201. Also see Dickran Kouymjian, "The Destruction of Armenian Historical Monuments as a Continuation of the Turkish Policy of Genocide," in Permanent People's Tribunal, *A Crime of Silence: The Armenian Genocide* (London: Zed Books, 1985), 173–85.

48. Lewis, *The Emergence of Modern Turkey*, 356.

49. Lewis, 210–11.

50. In Walker, *Armenia: The Survival of a Nation*, 181.

51. Roderic H. Davison, "The Armenian Crisis, 1912–1914," *American Historical Review* 53 (1948): 482.

52. See Hovannisian, *Armenia on the Road to Independence*, 38–39.

53. Davison, "The Armenian Crisis," 483.

54. Ibid., 484.

55. Ibid.

56. Ibid., 484–85.

57. See Ahmed Emin, *Turkey in the World War* (New Haven: Yale University Press, 1930), 212–23. Cf. with Hovannisian, *Armenia on the Road to Independence*, 46–47.

58. Emin, 220.

59. Ibid.

60. Cf. with Himmler's summation of 4 October 1943: "We had the moral right, we had the duty toward our people to kill this people which wanted to kill us." In Dawidowicz, *A Holocaust Reader*, 133.

61. *Osmanischer Lloyd*, 26 February 1915; quoted in Walker, *Armenia: The Survival of a Nation*, 199.

62. Ahmad, *The Young Turks*, 153.

63. Hovannisian, 1.

64. Lewis, *The Emergence of Modern Turkey*, 1.

65. Roderic H. Davison, *Reform in the Ottoman Empire, 1856–1876* (Princeton: Princeton University Press, 1963).

66. Davison, *Turkey: A Short History*, 117.

67. Ibid.

68. For works on Pan-Turkism and Turanism see, among others, Ahmed Emin, *Turkey in the World War*, 87–100; Alexander Henderson, "The Pan-Turanian Myth Today," *Asiatic Review* (January 1945): 88–92; Gotthard Jaschke, "Der Freiheitkampf des türkischen Volkes," *Die Welt des Islams* 14 (1932): 6–21; Jacob M. Landau, *Pan-Turkism in Turkey* (London: C. Hurst, 1981); Gerard Libaridian, "The Ideology of the Young Turk Movement," in The Permanent People's Tribunal, *The Crime of Silence: The Armenian Genocide*, 37–49. For a discussion relating "Pan" movements to racism, and in the European context to antisemitism, see Hannah Arendt, *The Origins of Totalitarianism* (New York: Meridian Books, 1958).

69. Davison, *Turkey*, 112.

70. Salwyn J. Schapiro, *The World in Crisis* (New York: McGraw-Hill, 1950), 134, 136–37; Anthony D. Smith, *Theories of Nationalism* (London: Duckworth, 1971), 16.

71. George Mosse, *The Crisis of German Ideology: The Intellectual Origins of the Third Reich* (New York: Grosset and Dunlap, 1964).

72. Unlike Lewis, Dadrian does not see the CUP as having any redeeming features or liberal motives. Indeed, basing his information on French consular reports, Dadrian

suggests that as early as 1910 the CUP was contemplating a massacre against Christian minorities. See his "Genocide as a Problem," 253.

73. Uriel Heyd, *Foundations of Turkish Nationalism: The Life and Teachings of Ziya Gökalp* (London: Luzac, 1950), 29.

74. Ibid., 36.

75. Ibid., 37. On the other hand, Professor Dadrian notes, "There is no evidence that Gökalp, though tried, was ever convicted and sentenced. . . . Before the trials could be completed, he, along with others, [was] deported to Malta. Since he never occupied the post of a Minister, Responsible Secretary, or Inspector, he was excluded from this trial series." Personal correspondence, 30 March 1990, 2.

76. Heyd, 132.

77. Ibid., 113.

78. Ibid., 111.

79. Ibid.

80. Ibid., 63.

81. Ibid., 132.

82. Ibid., 57.

83. Ibid., 124.

84. Landau, *Pan-Turkism in Turkey*, 52.

85. Ibid., 55.

86. Ibid., 51; Emin, *Turkey in the World War*, 63–77; also see Ulrich Trumpener, *Germany and the Ottoman Empire, 1914–1918* (Princeton: Princeton University Press, 1968).

87. Landau, 53–54.

88. Ibid., 52–53.

89. Morgenthau, *Ambassador Morgenthau's Story*, 336.

90. Ibid., 339.

Chapter Six

1. Quoted in Theodor Abel, *The Nazi Movement: Why Hitler Came to Power* (New York: Atherton Press, 1966), 69.

2. From Joseph Goebbels, *Der Angriff*, 30 April 1928. Quoted in Karl D. Bracher, *The German Dictatorship* (New York: Holt, Rinehart and Winston, 1970), 141.

3. For a discussion of Nazism as a revolutionary phenomenon see David Schoenbaum, *Hitler's Social Revolution: Class and Status in Nazi Germany* (Garden City, N.Y.: Doubleday, 1963); Ralf Dahrendorf, *Society and Democracy in Germany* (Garden City, N.Y.: Anchor Books, 1969); Timothy Mason, "The Legacy of 1918 for National Socialism," in Anthony Nichols and Erich Matthias, eds., *German Democracy and the Triumph of Hitler* (New York: St. Martin's Press, 1971), 215–39; Juan J. Linz, "Some Notes toward a Comparative Study of Fascism in Sociological and Historical Perspective," in Walter Laqueur, ed., *Fascism: A Reader's Guide* (Berkeley: University of California Press, 1976), 3–124; and Jeremy Noakes, "Nazism and Revolution," in Noel O'Sullivan, ed., *Revolutionary Theory and Political Reality* (New York: St. Martin's Press 1983), 73–100.

Much of the disagreement in categorizing Nazism as a revolutionary movement stems from varying conceptions of revolution. Most writers would agree that social revolutions entail profound transformations of the political and class structures. Their disagreement hinges in part on their assessment of what happened to the German class structure under the Nazis. Thus Dahrendorf seeing the Nazis as limiting and finally destroying the power of the Junkers judged them to be revolutionary in the above sense. Furthermore, because he viewed the Junkers as obstacles to German modernization, he suggested that by helping to eliminate the aristocracy the Nazis helped to modernize the German class structure.

Schoenbaum, Noakes, and Mason would disagree with this judgment. Their assessment was that, in effect, the Nazis left the class structure more or less intact, and it was the defeat of Germany that ultimately ushered in the transformation of the class structure. Linz and Noakes, however, stressed the political aspects of the Nazi revolution, especially the undermining of the German state and its substitution with Hitler as the führer.

As noted in Chap. 1 and in the discussion above, this essay does not limit revolution to the transformation of the class structure. Its interpretation of the German revolution follows more closely that of Linz and Noakes than of the other writers listed above.

4. Following Crane Brinton, *The Anatomy of Revolution* (New York: Vintage Press, 1952), one may view the Nazi revolution as the radical phase of the German revolution and Weimar as its moderate phase. It should be noted, however, that this essay does not rely on Brinton's model of revolution. Moreover, it should also be noted that in the view of some Marxist writers it was the "November Revolution" and the formation of the Weimar Republic that was "revolutionary," and the role of the Nazis was "counterrevolutionary." See R. Palme Dutt, *Fascism and Social Revolution* (London: Martin Lawrence, 1934); and Nicos Poulantzas, *Fascism and Dictatorship* (London: Verso Press, 1979). For an insightful discussion of the issue see Eugen Weber, "Revolution? Counterrevolution? What Revolution?" in Walter Lauquer, ed., *Fascism: A Reader's Guide* (Berkeley: University of California Press, 1976), 435–68.

From our perspective, however, the November Revolution, as will be seen, and the Weimar Republic that it brought in its wake were two brief episodes in an emerging revolutionary interregnum that did not cease until the end of the war. During this interregnum, the Nazis were one of the political formations and revolutionary vanguards that struggled for power.

Again as in n. 3 above, the difference in usage derives from a difference in understanding of what is meant by revolution and what that term implies. In much of the liberal and Marxist traditions revolutionary transformations of the political and social orders are inherently progressive. Revolutions produce regimes and social structures that, in the long run, broaden human freedom and promote human justice. This volume makes no such assumptions. Some revolutions, like the English, American, and French, and possibly the Russian, Chinese, and Cuban, may be viewed as progressive in the above sense, but the German revolution in its Nazi phase, the Turkish revolution in its Pan-Turkish phase, and the Cambodian revolution in its Khmer Rouge phase, for example, were distinctively not progressive, neither were they simply counterrevolutions whose aim was the restoration of the old regimes.

5. See the discussion below and Louis L. Snyder, *The Weimar Republic* (Princeton: D. Van Nostrand, 1966), 118.

6. Thus on 8 August Rawlinson's Fourth British Army tore into the Germans at Amiens, and by September allied armies were advancing all along the front. In the East, first the Bulgars and then the Turks sued for peace. While the Austrians, after losing 150,000 men in attempting to breach the Piave line against the Italians, informed the Germans that they could fight no longer. Thus the notion that the Germans lost the war

because of treachery at home was nonsense. They lost the war because by the summer and fall of 1918 they were overwhelmed on the Western Front. See Gordon A. Craig, *Germany: 1866–1945* (Oxford: Oxford University Press, 1978), 395.

7. Craig, 395.

8. Ibid., 397.

9. The *Freikorps* were unofficial military formations that were led by officers and Non-Commissioned Officers who recruited volunteers often from among their own former troops. It was such units under the overall command of General Walther Luttwitz who marched into Berlin and crushed the Spartakists revolt. In the process they captured and later murdered Karl Liebknecht and Rosa Luxemburg, the fiery and popular leaders of the Communist left. Craig (409) has noted,

> These brutal murders inflicted a wound upon the German working-class from which it did not recover. . . . The memory of Liebknecht and Luxemburg was to be one of the most potent factors in preventing a true reunion of the left even when Adolf Hitler was standing at the gates.

Freikorps veterans would come to play an important role in the staffing and organization of the NSDAP. See Robert G. L. Waite, *Vanguard of Nazism: The Free Corps Movement in Postwar Germany* (Cambridge, Mass.: Harvard University Press, 1952); Gerald Feldman, *Army, Industry, and Labor* (Princeton: Princeton University Press, 1966); and Richard F. Hamilton, *Who Voted for Hitler?* (Princeton: Princeton University Press, 1982), 309–60.

10. As can be seen from table 6.1, this was a triumph for the SPD and for the parties of what came to be known as the Weimar coalition (SPD, DDP, and Center).

11. For an important study pertaining to President Wilson's motivations during the Versailles Treaty negotiations see Alexander George and Juliette George, *Woodrow Wilson and Colonel House* (New York: J. Day Co., 1956).

12. Craig, 356.

13. Snyder, 39.

14. Ibid., 16. By an ironic coincidence, it was the democratic forces, both inside and outside of Germany, that heedlessly cooperated to absolve the German militarists for her defeat. Thus, as Snyder points out, the allies themselves must be held partly responsible for the turn of events. First they signed the armistice at a time when not a single inch of German territory had been occupied—this encouraged the view among the Germans that they had not truly been defeated. The second error stemmed from President Wilson's refusal to deal with the military masters of Wilhelminian Germany. This strengthened Ludendforff's hand and made it possible for him to evade the symbolic but all important act of surrender. The odium of defeat was borne by the civilian leaders alone.

15. Snyder, 108.

16. Ibid., 118.

17. Ibid., 117n.9.

18. There were other features of the constitution such as the system of proportional representation and article 48 which though not challenging the legitimacy of the state as such helped to undermine Weimar indirectly. See Craig, 416–17.

19. Craig, 420; Thomas Childers, *The Nazi Voter* (Chapel Hill: University of North Carolina Press, 1983), 93, 171, 242.

20. Craig, 420.

21. Ibid., 421.
22. Ibid., 424.
23. Ibid., 396.
24. Childers, 23.
25. William S. Allen, *The Nazi Seizure of Power* (New York: Franklin Watts, 1984).
26. Despite its Marxist rhetoric, which so terrified the middle classes, the SPD continued the trade unionist, revisionist, and democratic socialist politics of its prewar days. With the rise of Revisionism, though it still ritualistically articulated a variety of Marxist and revolutionary ideology, the SPD increasingly became a trade unionist and moderate party. See Allen, 54.
27. Allen, 54.
28. Ibid.
29. Craig, 502.
30. Allen, 34.
31. Thus referring to Northeim, his case study, Allen (296–97) noted:

> The most important factor in the victory of Nazism was the active division of the town along class lines. Though there was cohesion in Northeim before the Nazis began their campaigns leading to the seizure of power, the cohesion existed within the middle class or within the working class and did not extend to the town as a whole. The victory of Nazism can be explained to a large extent by the desire on the part of Northeim's middle class to suppress the lower class and especially its political representatives, the Social Democratic party. . . . In many ways the actions and beliefs of Northeimers during the last years of the Weimar era were the same as if World War I had never ended. It was in this sort of atmosphere that the SPD might seem treasonable and the Nazi[s] reasonable.

What was true for Northeim in particular was true for much of Germany in general, with the exception of Berlin and some other urban centers.
32. Karl D. Bracher, *The German Dictatorship* (New York: Holt, Rinehart and Winston, 1970), 130.
33. Ibid., 198.
34. Ebert's agreement with Groener came under severe strain soon after the fateful phone call. On 16 December a Congress of Workers' and Soldiers' Councils assembled in Berlin. To the relief of the chancellor and his colleagues, the congress did not provide an umbrella for a leftist putsch. On the contrary, the workers' representatives elected an executive that was in large part composed of Majority Socialists, and they ratified Ebert's plan for the election and convocation of a National Constituent Assembly. On one subject alone did the congress place Ebert in a difficult position. It insisted that Field Marshal von Hindenburg be dismissed and that the army be disbanded and replaced by a popular militia (*Volkswehr*).

Hearing of the plan Groener and his chief aide, Major Kurt von Schleicher, called on Ebert after the congress had adjourned. The military officers warned the new chancellor that the agreement of 9 November between the regime and the army would be revoked if he accepted the provisions of the congress. Claiming that the resolutions of the congress would not apply to the field army, Ebert's answers were ambiguous and dilatory. See Craig, 406. In the final analysis the left's recommendations on army reform were not implemented, and the Independent Socialists withdrew from the Council of People's Representatives. Indeed, Ebert's discussion left the army untouched, even as it divided the left and weakened support for the Republic. Also see Bracher, 71.

35. Craig, 463.

36. Bracher, 110.

37. Craig, 463.

38. Bracher (192) remarked:

> The slogan of legal revolution offers the key to the character and development of the National Socialist power seizure. National Socialist propagandists, politicians, and constitutional experts all along emphasized that although Hitler's takeover was the beginning of a revolution that would profoundly affect all aspects of life, it was a completely legal, constitutional process.

Bracher points out that this was a pseudolegal seizure of power that was meant to destroy the legal and constitutional system upon which it had relied.

39. From *Der Angriff*, 30 April 1928, in Bracher, 141.

40. Childers (16) remarked: "In spite of the convulsive changes in the political and economic environment, the parties of the Bismarckian, Wilhelminian, and Weimer eras remained firmly entrenched along [the] lines of social, religious, and regional cleavage."

41. The main policy difference between the two was that under Gustav Stresemann the DVP was willing to cooperate, even if reluctantly, with the parties of the Weimar coalition, including the SPD. Indeed, Stresemann became chancellor between August and November 1923, and the DVP joined twelve out of the twenty-one cabinets of the Republic. By way of contrast, the DNVP was uncompromisingly opposed to the Republic and would not serve in any cabinet with the SPD. It joined only four of the twenty-one Weimar cabinets.

42. This is a point stressed by Pinson, 413; Craig, 505–6; and Childers, 39.

43. Hamilton, 242.

44. Alan Bullock, "The German Communists and the Rise of Hitler," in International Council for Philosophy and Humanistic Studies, ed., *The Third Reich* (London: Weidenfeld and Nicolson, 1955), 508.

45. Ibid., 509.

46. The Great Depression was the precipitating crisis that destroyed the Weimar Republic and swept the Nazis into power. It would be a mistake, however, to blame the Great Depression as such for the rise of the Nazis. The economic crisis alone could not have led to such radical consequences without the prior undermining of Weimar by the widely felt illegitimacy of its inception and by the endemic class cleavages of German society. Indeed, in legitimate and stable regimes like the United States, England, and the Scandinavian countries, the economic crisis of 1929 never threatened to undermine the state. Thus the Great Depression should be viewed as a crucial phase in the longer sequence making up the German revolutionary interregnum. For parallel views see Hamilton, 6.

47. There is a large literature on Hitler's psychopathology and its relations to antisemitism. See esp. William C. Langer, *The Mind of Adolf Hitler* (New York: New American Library, 1972); Rudolph Binion, *Hitler among the Germans* (New York: Elsevier, 1976); and Robert G. L. Waite, *The Psychopathic God* (New York: Signet, 1977).

48. Sarah Gordon, *Hitler, Germans and the "Jewish Question"* (Princeton: Princeton University Press, 1984), 53–54. She suggests that, in addition to Hitler, principally Julius Streicher and Alfred Rosenberg were dedicated antisemites from the start. "Yet surprisingly few of the top Nazi leaders were virulent anti-Semites before 1925. None of the more prominent men in the Nazi party joined it primarily because of anti-Semitism." Among these she lists Goebbels, Himmler, Goering, and Eichmann.

49. Allen, 84.

50. Meir Michaelis, *Mussolini and the Jews* (Oxford: Clarendon Press, 1978); and Zeev Sternhell, "Fascist Ideology," in Walter Laqueur, *Fascism: A Reader's Guide* (Berkeley: University of California Press, 1976), 315–78.

51. *The Nazi Movement* was a study that had been conducted in 1932 and published in 1934. It was based on 681 life histories of Nazi party members; of these 581 remain. Abel's survey provided the basis of two reanalyses of the data by Peter H. Merkl. See the latter;'s *Political Violence under the Swastika* (Princeton: Princeton University Press, 1975); and *The Making of a Stormtrooper* (Princeton: Princeton University Press, 1980). According to Gordon (54–55), the missing 100 records were seized by the FBI and appear to be lost.

52. Abel, *The Nazi Movement*, 6.

53. Gordon, 56.

54. Abel (164) noted that 60 percent of his respondents—all Nazis—made "no reference whatsoever to indicate they harbored anti-Semitic feelings," while nearly 4 percent expressed open disapproval of Nazi antisemitism. Since in his 1934 study Abel did not indictae what indices he used to measure antisemitism and did not tabulate his data, it is difficult to compare his specific findings to that of Merkl and Gordon above.

55. Abel, 120.

56. This figure is derived from Merkl's *Stormtrooper* (247), a reworking of the Abel data. By collapsing columns 4 and 5 of his table 5.7, one arrives at a subsample of 268 respondents. Of these, 185 indicated that the reasons for their first political involvement were primarily due to factors as discussed above.

57. Abel, 25.

58. Ibid., 28.

59. Ibid., 69.

60. Ibid., 138.

61. Ibid., 151.

62. Ibid., 153.

63. Hamilton, 323.

64. Hamilton makes this point as part of his broader critique of the view—expressed by Lipset and others—that Nazism appealed primarily to the middle class and especially to the *Mittelstand*. Hamilton's work is nicely complemented and refined by Childers, *The Nazi Voter*, who demonstrates which strata of the various classes were most likely to support the Nazis in the various elections held during the Weimar period. Also see Seymour Martin Lipset, *Political Man* (Baltimore: Johns Hopkins University Press, 1981), 127–82. Also see the discussion below.

65. Abel, 129.

66. Ibid., 130.

67. Ibid., 173.

68. Ibid.

69. Ibid., 143.

70. Bracher, *Dictatorship*; Lipset, *Political Man*, 127–82; and Linz, "Some Notes," 3–124.

71. Lipset, 135.

72. Ibid.

73. Ibid., 134.

74. Ibid., 489.

75. Ibid., 134.

76. See, for example, Poulantzas, *Fascism and Dictatorship*.

77. Lipset, 145.

78. Note that, when we compare the percentages of the total vote received in 1928 and 1930, the ratio for the conservative DNVP was .49, while for the DVP it was .56, and for the DDP it was .72. In other words, in that crucial election, the DNVP, which according to Lipset should have held on to its support because of the antagonism of the upper-class conservatives to the parvenue Nazis, in fact lost votes at a faster rate than did the liberal parties! My explanation for this phenomenon is that supporters of the DNVP—the successor of the Conservatives from Imperial Germany—were even more opposed to Weimar and the SPD than were those of the liberal parties, and it was that opposition—even at the risk of revolutionary transformation—which shifted them to the Nazis when the time seemed opportune.

That in 1932 the DNVP was able to recoup some of its losses may be explained by noting that the second election of 1932 followed an earlier electoral triumph of the Nazis. Off-year elections that follow a major sweep are likely to restore some support for the losing parties. By the time of the second election of 1932 the DNVP became the only viable alternative to the Nazis on the right, which may explain why the DVP did not experience a similar upsurge.

Following the work of Rudolf Heberle, *Social Movements* (New York: Appleton-Century-Crofts, 1951), 28–30, Lipset (140) points out that the rate of defections from the DNVP was highest in border areas of Germany where German nationalism may have been strongest. Thus defections from the DNVP were more pronounced among nationalists, argues Lipset, than upper-class especially aristocratic conservatives. Lipset's analysis has been recently challenged by Hamilton, 24–31.

79. That was seen quite clearly from the Abel, Merkle, and Gordon studies discussed above.

80. Linz, 4–5.

81. The Catholic middle class from the days of the *Kulturkampf* had voted for the Center party. That party was traditionally an expression of the Catholic minority interest, and on communal grounds its supporters were relatively impervious to the Nazi appeal in the early years of the Weimar Republic.

82. Linz, 7.

83. See, for example, Ian Kershaw, "The Persecution of the Jews and German Popular Opinion in the Third Reich," *Leo Baeck Institute Yearbook* 26 (1981): 261–89; and *Popular Opinion and Political Dissent in the Third Reich: Bavaria 1933–1945* (Oxford: Clarendon Press, 1983), 224–78 and 358–86. Also see Allen, 84; and Sebastian Haffner, *The Meaning of Hitler* (Cambridge, Mass.: Harvard University Press, 1983).

84. Dawidowicz, *The War against the Jews*.

Chapter Seven

1. "First Decree for Implementation of the Law for the Restoration of the Professional Civil Service, April 11, 1933," cited in Lucy S. Dawidowicz, *A Holocaust Reader* (New York: Behrman House, 1976), 41.

2. Primo Levi, *Survival in Auschwitz* (New York: Collier Books, 1961), 22.

3. Adolf Hitler, *Mein Kampf*, trans. Ralph Manheim (New York: Houghton Mifflin, 1971), 286.

4. Ibid., 290.

5. Ibid., 292.

6. Eberhard Jäckel, *Hitler's World View* (Cambridge, Mass.: Harvard University Press, 1981), 96–97.

7. Hitler, 397.

8. Ibid., 398.

9. Jäckel, 98–99.

10. Hitler, 300.

11. Jäckel, 104.

12. See Norman Cohn, *Warrant for Genocide* (New York: Harper and Row, 1967).

13. Jäckel, 52.

14. Ibid., 58–59.

15. Hitler, 661–62.

16. It should be noted that by turning against Russia, Hitler broke with the *Weltpolitik* of Imperial Germany which saw herself in colonial competition with England and France. He gave at least three reasons for this change in policy: first, an anti-British "colonial" policy would result in an alliance of Britain and France against Germany; second, it would scatter the *Volk*, when the task of domestic and foreign policy was to assure that the Aryans would not mix with lesser breeds and remain the master race rooted to its own "soil"; third, to pursue an anti-British colonial policy would entail an alliance with Russia, but this could not be contemplated because Russia was the seat of the world Jewish conspiracy. See Hitler, 641–67; and Jäckel, 27–46.

17. Hitler, 654–55.

18. Ian Kershaw, *The "Hitler Myth"* (Oxford and New York: Oxford University Press, 1989).

19. Ibid., 251.

20. Ibid., 250.

21. See Franklin Littel and Hubert Locke, eds., *The German Church Struggle and the Holocaust* (Detroit: Wayne State University Press, 1974).

22. See George L. Mosse, *Nazi Culture* (New York: Grosset and Dunlap, 1966), for examples of how the Nazi creed had penetrated various aspects of German culture including the spheres of the family, religion, literature, education, industrial relations, the state, and science—especially biology. Also see the important discussion of the Nazi political myth by Uriel Tal, "On Structures of Political Theology and Myth in Germany Prior to the Holocaust," in Yehuda Bauer and Nathan Rotenstreich, eds., *The Holocaust as Historical Experience* (New York and London: Holmes and Meier, 1981), 43–74. Tal argues that the Nazi political myth achieved certain structural similarities to messianic Christianity, with the führer in the role of messiah and the Aryans as the new Chosen People. By making this parallel to religion, the Nazis were able to tap powerful sources of emotions among the Germans. Neither Mosse nor Tal, however, explain why it was that

following the Great War and the rise of Weimar the Germans were especially vulnerable to such messianic appeals. It may be suggested that espeically middle-class Germans who rejected the legitimacy of rule by the SPD were vulnerable to such mythic appeals, especially as these were articulated in the language of German nationalism. See also James M. Rhodes, *The Hitler Movement: A Modern Millenarian Revolution* (Stanford: Hoover Institution Press, 1980).

23. See Raul Hilberg, *The Destruction of the European Jews* (Chicago: Quadrangle Books, 1967; new ed., New York: Holmes and Meier, 1985); and Hannah Arendt, *Eichmann in Jerusalem* (New York: Viking Press, 1963).

24. Hilberg, 31–39.

25. From 30 June 1934, the SS (*Schutzstaffel* or Defense Corps) replaced the SA (*Sturmabteilung* or Storm Troops) as the paramilitary elite corps of the Nazi party. At the start of the war, the SS comprised one-quarter of a million men and women. When the Nazis came to power, the SS was given jurisdiction over the concentration camp system. Later it was given the mandate to solve the Jewish Question and to implement the Final Solution.

Since 1929 the SS had been headed by Heinrich Himmler. In 1936 he became *Reichsführer* (Reichleader), heading both the SS and the German police. In 1934 on Hitler's orders the intelligence and surveillance functions of the SS were officially transferred to the SD (*Sicherheitsdienst* or Security Service) and placed under the jurisdiction of Reinhard Heydrich, Himmler's deputy. On 27 September 1939, following Himmler's initiative, the SD and the Gestapo (*Geheime Staatspolizei* or Secret State Police), and other police units, were amalgamated into one organization known as the RSHA (*Reichssicherheitshauptamt* or Reich Security Main Office) headed by Heydrich. In March 1941, the RSHA was given the principal task of organizing the *Einsatzgruppen* (Special Forces) for the massacre of Russian Jews. In June 1941, the RSHA was given the mandate to coordinate and carry out the Final Solution.

26. Hilberg, 39.

27. Dawidowicz, *Holocaust Reader*, 74.

28. See esp. Karl A. Schleunes, *The Twisted Road to Auschwitz* (Urbana: University of Illinois Press, 1970).

29. Lucy S. Dawidowicz, *The War against the Jews* (New York: Holt, Rinehart and Winston, 1975), 68.

30. Karl D. Bracher, *The German Dictatorship* (New York: Holt, Rinehart and Winston, 1970), 197.

31. On 11 April 1933, a law clarifying what was meant by the term "non-Aryan" was promulgated. It was called "First Decree for Implementation of the Law for the Restoration of the Professional Civil Service." Section 3 part 1 read as follows: "A person is to be regarded as non-Aryan if he is descended from non-Aryan, especially Jewish, parents or grandparents. It is enough for one parent or grandparent to be non-Aryan. This is to be assumed especially if one parent or one grandparent was of the Jewish faith." See Dawidowicz, *Holocaust Reader*, 41.

Thus by 11 April 1933, if one had even one grandparent who was a Jew one was considered to be non-Aryan and outside of the protection and privileges of the German Aryan community. By 1935 the definition of who was a Jew was reformulated as part of the "Nuremberg Laws."

In Section 3 part 2 of the same law there was a qualifying clause inserted that stipulated that men who had fought at the front or who had had a father or son killed fighting for Germany during the war would be exempt from the Aryan clause. This was inserted at the insistence of President Hindenburg and was deleted in 1935, a year after the "old gentleman" had passed away. Christopher R. Browning has noted that Jews who had been hired under the *Kaiserreich* also were not dismissed until Hindenburg died in 1934. From a personal correspondence, 18 August 1989.

32. Dawidowicz, *Holocaust Reader,* 39.

33. Raul Hilberg, *Documents of Destruction* (Chicago: Quadrangle Books, 1971), 17.

34. Dawidowicz, *War against the Jews,* 80.

35. Gordon A. Craig, *Germany: 1866–1945* (New York: Oxford University Press, 1978), 683–84.

36. Mommsen points out that the rally at Nuremberg had originally been called to make use of the Abyssinian crisis in order to announce a more assertive posture in foreign affairs. When that plan fell through Hitler and the party turned once again to the "Jewish Question." See Hans Mommsen, "The Realization of the Unthinkable: The 'Final Solution of the Jewish Question' in the Third Reich," in Gerhard Hirschfeld, ed., *The Policies of Genocide* (London: Allen and Unwin, 1986), 103.

37. Dawidowicz, *Holocaust Reader,* 45.

38. In effect the law of 15 September 1935 created a new honorary category of citizen, the *Reichsbuerger* that was limited only to Aryans; nevertheless, Jews still retained their status as *Staatsangeghöriger,* which allowed them to keep their passports. The law stripping them of all legal rights was decreed in November 1941. Browning, personal correspondence, 18 August 1989.

The law of 15 September 1935 also left unclear what to do about persons of mixed ancestry, that is, people who were partly of "German blood" and partly of "Jewish blood." To the question of *Jüdische Mischlinge* the "First Decree to the Reich Citizenship Law" addressed itself. It was promulgated on 14 November 1935 and read as follows: "A Jew is anyone descended from at least three grandparents who are fully Jewish as regards race" (article 5, para. 2). A "Jewish *Mischling* is anyone who is descended from one or two grandparents who are fully Jewish as regards race. . . . A grandparent is deemed fully Jewish without further ado if he has belonged to the Jewish religious community" (article 2, para. 2). According to this law, any *Mischling* who was a Jew (by religion or married to a Jew) was also to be considered a Jew (article 5, para. 2). See Dawidowicz, *Holocaust Reader,* 46.

It should be noted that the *Mischling* category was resisted by elements in the party who wanted to lump *Mischlinge* with Jews, but Dr. Bernhard Loesener, a former customs official who was the author of the law, successfully fought for his version of the law on the grounds that persons of "mixed blood," were they to be excluded from the "Aryan" category and pooled with the "Jews," would strengthen the Jewish pool with German blood [*sic*]. Moreover, 45,000 men would be lost to the army should the *Mischlinge* be classified as "Jews." The upshot of the *Mischling* definition was that this category of persons was not treated as Jewish during the Holocaust. See Hilberg, *Destruction,* 47.

Though in 1942 and later as well there were threats made either to sterilize or to exterminate the *Mischlinge,* these threats were not carried out. Surprisingly, they suffered only slight discrimination. Thus on the seemingly arbitrary whim of a minor official, an "expert" on the Jewish Question, approximately 107,000 Germans of some Jewish ancestry managed to survive the war while 125,000 labeled as "Jews" were m Hilberg, *Destruction*, 268–77.

Christopher R. Browning writes about Loesener: "He was a disaffected unlike so many others who made the claim, clung to his position to prevent wo from happening]. . . . He fought a long battle with the SS to preserve the *Misc* gory against Heydrich's and others' attempts to widen the pool of victims. . . arrested in 1944 for hiding members of the July conspiracy but somehow surv war." Personal correspondence, 18 August 1989.

39. See, for example, the discussion in Gordon Craig, *The Germans* (New Yor. Putnam, 1982), 126–46; and George L. Mosse, *German Jews beyond Judaism* (Bloomi Indiana University Press, 1985). Also see Chap. 4 (this vol.); and the works of H Arendt and Gershom Scholem (also in this vol.).

40. Dawidowicz, *A Holocaust Reader*, 47–48.

41. Dawidowicz, *The War against the Jews*, 91.

42. Hilberg, *Documents*, 17–18.

43. Hilberg, *The Destruction of the European Jews*, 49.

44. Hannah Arendt, *The Origins of Totalitarianism* (New York: Meridian Book 1958), 355–56.

45. Hitler, *Mein Kampf*, 403–4. See also Robert J. Lifton, *The Nazi Doctors* (New York: Basic Books, 1986), 24.

46. Lifton, 25–27.

47. Dawidowicz, *War against the Jews*, 176–77.

48. Ibid., 177.

49. Browning, personal correspondence, 18 August 1989.

50. Dawidowicz, 179. Yehuda Bauer suggests that the number may have been as high as 275,000 and that the killing lasted until after the war and possibly even later. See his *A History of the Holocaust* (New York: Franklin Watts, 1982), 208.

51. See Uwe Dietrich Adam, "The Gas Chambers," in François Furet, ed., *Unanswered Questions* (New York: Schocken Books, 1989), 138; and Ian Kershaw, *Popular Opinion and Political Dissent in the Third Reich* (Oxford: Clarendon Press, 1983), 334–40.

52. Bauer, *A History of the Holocaust*, 109.

53. Craig, *Germany*, 709.

54. Hilberg, *Destruction*, 23–60.

55. Bauer, *A History*, 108.

56. Hilberg, 23–28.

57. Ibid., 24.

58. See Nuremberg Trial Document PS-1816 quoted in Bauer, *History*, 111.

59. Ibid., 111.

60. Ibid., 111.

61. Ibid., 111.

62. A side effect of the policy of "Aryanization" was the acceleration of the process of industrial and monopoly concentration in the Third Reich. By driving out Jewish competition, expropriation allowed non-Jewish firms to concentrate production still further and to realize larger profits. See Craig, *Germany*, 636; and Hilberg, *Destruction*, 61.

63. Bauer, *History*, 109.

64. Hilberg, 54.

65. *Stenographische Berichte des Reichstags (1939)*, 16B, cited in Jäckel, *Hitler's World View*, 61. Professor Richard S. Levy has suggested that "Hitler's 'prophesies' were often in reality the announcement of his intentions." But he concludes that "[t]he thrust of his denunication seems to be that Jews must be seen as the embodiment of all Germany's enemies, both capitalists and communists. Almost all Germans, with the exception of the shattered Left, could unite behind this notion." Personal correspondence, 28 August 1989.

66. The SS plan also made provisions for the establishment of a system of indirect rule through "Councils of Jewish Elders" (*Jüdische Ältestenräte*) which were to be made responsible to the German authorities "for the exact and punctual execution of all directives issued or yet to be issued." See Dawidowicz, *Reader*, 60. In conjunction with these councils Jews were to be concentrated in ghettos from which they were forbidden to leave except that "economic necessities are always to be considered in this connection," Dawidowicz, 62.

The *Schnellbrief* continued that Jewish property had to be "Aryanized," except in those eventualities where "some Jewish trader here and there" might be of use to the army. "In such cases, however, prompt Aryanization of these enterprises is to be sought and the emigration of the Jews is to be completed later." See Dawidowicz, 62. On the role of the Jewish councils see especially Isaiah Trunk, *Judenrat* (New York: Stein and Day, 1977).

67. Dawidowicz, *Holocaust Reader*, 59.

68. See Hilberg, *Destruction*, 137 and 130–34.

69. Commencing on 1 December 1939—the delay was due to the army insisting that the "clean up" be postponed until after the conclusion of military operations—about 200,000 people, Jews, Poles, Gypsies and others were deported from the Reich to occupied Poland. See Hilberg, *Destruction*, 138; and Christopher R. Browning, "Beyond 'Intentionalism' and 'Functionalism': A Reassessment of Nazi Jewish Policy from 1939 to 1941" (Paper presented at the American Historical Association meeting, Washington, D.C., December 1987), 6. Note that Browning cites figures of 175,000 Poles and 300,000 Jews who might have been deported or fled into the General Government. SS figures cite a total of 261,517 persons deported between December 1939 and January 1941. These do not distinguish between Poles and Jews. See Christopher R. Browning, "Nazi Resettlement Policy and the Search for a Solution to the Jewish Question," *German Studies Review* 9, no. 3 (October 1986): 497–519.

These measures were carried out with great brutality and extensive loss of life. At this stage of Nazi policy, while the Polish peasantry and working class were expelled to the east, the leadership class and the intelligentsia were systematically murdered. See also Jan Gross, *Polish Society under German Occupation* (Princeton: Princeton University Press, 1979).

70. His other titles included *Reichminisster* without portfolio, *Reichsleiter* (leader) of the party, and President of the German Academy of Law [*sic*]. In short, notes Hilberg, he was a "top Nazi in every respect." *Destruction*, 131. Richard S. Levy notes that Frank's appointment as Governor General of Poland may have been a demotion because he was denied ready proximity to Hitler. Personal correspondence, 28 August 1989.

71. Besides his personal staff, Frank headed fourteen principal divisions akin to ministries. These included Interior, Justice, Education, Propaganda, Railways (Ostbahn), the Postal Service, and so on. At the same time he was head of a territorial administrative

system based on four *Gouverneure*, each heading a separate district. These included Cracow, Lublin, Radom, and Warsaw. Galicia became the fifth district in August 1941, after the invasion of Russia. See Hilberg, *Destruction*, 132–33.

72. Hilberg, 138.

73. Ibid., 139.

74. Dawidowicz, *Holocaust Reader*, 55–56. She suggests that the idea for the Final Solution was first broached by Hitler in a letter to Adolf Gemlich dated 16 September 1919. See her *Holocaust Reader*, 30. According to Christopher R. Browning, Heydrich's *Endziel* referred to expulsion not extermination. See his "Nazi Ghettoization Policy in Poland: 1939–1941," *Central European History* 19, no. 4 (1987), 343–68.

75. Bauer, 151.

76. Ibid., 152.

77. Hilberg, *Destruction*, 260.

78. Browning, "Beyond 'Intentionalism' and 'Functionalism,'" 7–8.

79. Hilberg, 141.

80. Ibid.

81. Ibid., 261. Also see Leni Yahil, "Madagascar—Phantom of a Solution to the Jewish Question," in Bela Vago and George L. Mosse, eds., *Jews and Non-Jews in Eastern Europe, 1918–1945* (New York: John Wiley, 1974), 315–34.

82. Hilberg, *Destruction*, 260–261.

83. Browning, 15.

84. Ibid., 12.

85. Ibid., 13.

86. Ibid.

87. Hilberg, 261; and Browning, 14–15.

88. Christopher R. Browning, "The Decision Concerning the Final Solution," in François Furet, ed., *Unanswered Questions*, 99.

89. Browning, "Beyond 'Intentionalism' and 'Functionalism,'" 10.

90. Craig, *Germany*, 727–28.

91. For Hitler's relations to the army see Craig, *Germany*, 729–30; and Eberhard Jäckel, *Hitler in History* (Hanover and London: University Press of New England, 1984), 38: "He won the army's support from one juncture to the next only by flattering and obliging its leaders and not least by corrupting them. He corrupted them personally by cash awards and grand decorations, but above all and principally by making them his accomplices." The spectacular military victories of the early years no doubt also had their effect in convincing the old elites in the army and elsewhere of the validity of the Nazi worldview. See Browning, "Beyond 'Intentionalism' and 'Functionalism,'" 16–17. Also see Christian Streit, "The German Army and the Policies of Genocide," in Hirschfeld, *The Policies of Genocide*, 1–14.

92. Dawidowicz, *The War against the Jews*, 163.

93. International Military Tribunal 26:53–58 (henceforth IMT); cited by Dawidowicz, *Holocaust Reader*, 68.

94. Dawidowicz, *War against the Jews*, 64–65.

95. IMT 25, 81–86; cited in Dawidowicz, *Holocaust Reader*, 70–72.

96. "As the Nazis prepared to confront and destroy Bolshevism in 1941, neither the Russian communists nor Russian Jews could wait; both would have to be eliminated,

for ultimately they were one—the political and biological manifestations of the same 'Jewish-Bolshevik' conspiracy." See Browning, "Beyond 'Intentionalism' and 'Functionalism,'" 15.

97. Dawidowicz, 167.

98. See the testimony in Polish of Mosze Apollo, *Yad Vashem Archives*, 03/3646, 1973.

99. *Encyclopedia Judaica*, vol. 15, 339.

100. See the testimony in Polish of Symon Baron, *Yad Vashem Archives*, 661/46 from 03/1153, 1949, and personal correspondence from Professor Christopher R. Browning, 18 August 1989.

101. My father, William J. Melson (a.k.a. Wolf Mendelsohn), in a taped interview (Cambridge, Mass., 1978).

102. Symon Baron.

103. Hilberg, *Destruction*, 256; and Bauer, *History*, 200.

104. Browning, like Hilberg above, suggests that only Hitler himself could have given the order for the Final Solution. See his "Beyond 'Intentionalism' and 'Functionalism,'" 21–22: "[The] euphoria of victory emboldened and tempted an elated Hitler to dare ever more drastic policies."

105. Browning, 18.

106. IMT 26:266–67; cited in Dawidowicz, *Holocaust Reader*, 72–73.

107. Dawidowicz, 74.

108. Ibid.

109. Ibid., 75.

110. Ibid., 76.

111. Adam, "The Gas Chambers."

112. Dawidowicz, 78.

113. Ibid.

114. Bauer, *History*, 205.

115. At Wannsee, the secretary of state, Dr. Stuckart, recommended that *Mischlinge* be sterilized. His suggestion was debated inconclusively at two subsequent conferences. Meanwhile, at Auschwitz experiments were conducted on some of the prisoners, but the doctors never did succeed in discovering a technique for mass sterilization. "The upshot of their failure was that, after all the discussion and controversy, the *Mischlinge* were neither deported nor sterilized." See Hilberg, *Destruction*, 273; and Dawidowicz, *Holocaust Reader*, 81. Also see n. 38 above.

116. For example, by 13 October 1941, Spanish Jews in France were prevented from being expelled to Spanish Morocco. This is significant because had the policy of expulsions and deportations still been in effect—as some writers claim—such Jews would not have been restrained from leaving Europe. By then what was wanted was the destruction of Jews, not their expulsion. The Spanish Jews were slated for extermination with all the rest. See Browning, "The Decision Concerning the Final Solution," 107–8. Browning adds, however, that in order to avoid complications and protests from neutral countries like Spain and Turkey, "the Foreign Office advised that these be given a chance to withdraw their Jews. Spain, after some delay, exercised this option." Personal correspondence, 18 August 1989.

117. *Keesings Archiv der Gegenwart* (1942), 5409; cited in Jäckel, *Hitler's World View*, 63.

118. Cited in Jäckel, 133n.43.

119. See Dawidowicz, *The War against the Jews;* and Mommsen, "The Realization of the Unthinkable: The 'Final Solution of the Jewish Question' in the Third Reich." Browning is especially illuminating in helping to resolve the controversy. See his "The Decision Concerning the Final Solution," and "Beyond Intentionalism and Functionalism: A Reassessment of Nazi Jewish Policy from 1939 to 1941." Also helpful are Michael R. Marrus, *The Holocaust in History* (Hanover and London: University Press of New England, 1987), 31–54; and Ian Kershaw, *The Nazi Dictatorship* (London: Edward Arnold, 1985), 61–105.

120. See for instance Stanley Milgram, *Obedience to Authority* (New York: Harper and Row, 1974).

Chapter Eight

1. See Robert J. Lifton, *The Nazi Doctors* (New York: Basic Books, 1986); and esp. Eberhard Jäckel, *Hitler's World View,* (Cambridge, Mass.: Harvard University Press, 1981).

2. See Marvin Tokayer and Mary Swartz, *The Fugu Plan: The Untold Story of the Japanese and the Jews in World War II* (New York: Paddington, 1979).

3. See Avedis K. Sanjian, *The Armenian Communities in Syria under Ottoman Dominion* (Cambridge, Mass.: Harvard University Press, 1965), 274–88.

4. See, for example, the survivor's memoir of Kerop Bedoukian, *Some of Us Survived* (New York: Farrar, Straus, Giroux, 1978).

5. This point was earlier stressed by Yehuda Bauer in the essay "Is the Holocaust Explicable?" which first appeared in Yehuda Bauer et al. eds., *Remembering for the Future,* vol. 2, *The Impact of the Holocaust in the Contemporary World,* 1967–75.

6. See Alan Rosenberg, "Was the Holocaust Unique?" in Isidor Walliman and Michael N. Dobkowski, eds., *Genocide and the Modern Age* (New York and London: Greenwood Press, 1987), 145–62.

7. See Arnold Toynbee, "A Summary of Armenian History up to and Including 1915," Viscount J. Bryce, *The Treatment of the Armenians in the Ottoman Empire: Documents Presented to Viscount Grey of Fallodon, Secretary of State for Foreign Affairs* (London: H.M.S.O., 1916), 650.

8. See Vakakn N. Dadrian, "Factors of Anger and Aggression in Genocide," *Journal of Human Relations* 19, no. 3 (1971): 394–417.

9. Franklin H. Littel refers to the Holocaust as an epochal event and sees it as creating a crisis of meaning for all persons and institutions, including Jews and Christians, churches and universities. See his "Fundamentals in Holocaust Studies," *Annals of the American Academy of Political and Social Science,* 450 (July 1980): 213–17. For a bitter but moving Jewish religious response to the Holocaust see Richard L. Rubenstein, *After Auschwitz* (Indianapolis: Bobbs-Merrill, 1966). For similar sentiments articulated by writers on the Armenian Genocide see Dadrian, "The Convergent Aspects"; and Leo Hamalian, "The Armenian Genocide and the Literary Imagination," in Richard G. Hovannisian, ed., *The Armenian Genocide in Perspective* (New Brunswick, N.J.: Transaction Press, 1986), 153–66.

Chapter Nine

1. Speech to the National Convention, 1792.

2. François Furet, "The Terror," in François Furet and Mona Ozouf, eds., *A Critical Dictionary of the French Revolution* (Cambridge, Mass.: Harvard University Press, 1989), 138.

3. On the Stalinist and Cambodian revolutions see below. On Ethiopia, see, for

example, Robert D. Kaplan, *Surrender or Starve: The Wars behind the Famine* (Boulder and London: Westview Press, 1988).

4. See J. L. Talmon, *The Origins of Totalitarian Democracy* (London: Mercury Books, 1961), 251.

5. A report to the UN Human Rights Commission noted that the mass murder, which had occurred in Cambodia, was comparable to the depradations of the Nazis and that it represented "nothing less than autogenocide." See UN Document E/CN, 4/SR, 1510. This was cited in David Hawk's "Pol Pot's Cambodia: Was It Genocide?" in Israel W. Charny, ed., *Toward the Understanding and Prevention of Genocide* (Boulder and London: Westview Press, 1984), 52.

6. Alvin W. Gouldner, "Stalinism: A Study of Internal Colonialism," in Maurice Zeitlin, ed., *Political Power and Social Theory* (Greenwich, Conn.: Jai Press, 1980), 215.

7. On Bukharin see Stephen F. Cohen, *Bukharin and the Bolshevik Revolution* (New York: Alfred A. Knopf, 1973). On how Bukharin differed with Stalin and represented an alternative path to Socialist development see Cohen's *Rethinking the Soviet Experience* (New York: Oxford University Press, 1985), 71–92.

8. Jerry F. Hough has pointed out that the grain crisis of 1928 "was a consequence of unfavorable price policy with respect to grain products. . . . An adjustment of prices within the agricultural sector might well have solved the grain marketing problems rather easily, but the Bolshevik leadership certainly did not understand this." See his "Introductory Remarks" to James R. Millar and Alec Nove, "Was Stalin Really Necessary?" *Problems of Communism* 25, no. 4 (July–August 1976): 53. But Alec Nove points out that collectivization was due not just to a misunderstanding of economic policy but to a Bolshevik ideology that regarded the market as an enemy. See his "The 'Logic' and Cost of Collectivization," in Millar and Nove, 55–59.

9. Robert Conquest notes: "[T]he naming of the kulak enemy satisfied the Marxist preconceptions of the Party activist. It presented a flesh-and-blood foe accursed by history. . . . And it provided a means of destroying the leadership of the villagers, which might have greatly strengthened the resistance . . . to collectivization. See his *The Harvest of Sorrow* (New York: Oxford University Press, 1986), 118–20. Moshe Lewin remarks: "The indiscriminate nature of the dekulakization operation, and the fact that it turned into a series of violent reprisals against whole sectors of the broad mass of the peasantry, were an inevitable consequence of the vagueness attaching to the term 'kulak.'" See his *Russian Peasants and Soviet Power* (New York: W. W. Norton, 1975), 490.

10. Conquest estimates that by 1937 some 11 million peasants perished due to the dekulakization campaign and the mass death produced by famine, especially in Ukraine, that was one of its results. To this figure he adds another 3.5 million as an estimate of those who perished in the Gulag after 1937, which brings him to a total of 14.5 million dead. See Conquest, 299–301 and 306. This is a conservative figure compared to that of Gouldner, for example, who estimated that 20 million peasants perished between 1929 and 1939. See Gouldner, *Stalinism*, 215. Cohen, *Rethinking* (95), cites a figure of 20 million for the period of Stalin's rule. These statistics are considerably higher than Hough's who estimated that 3.5 million peasants perished during the period of collectivization, "most probably the product of the famine of 1932–1933." See Jerry F. Hough and Merle Fainsod, *How the Soviet Union Is Ruled* (Cambridge, Mass.: Harvard University Press, 1979), 152. A quite extraordinary figure of 61,911,000 victims of "democide," which includes genocide, massacres, slave labor, and deportations is suggested by R. J. Rummel for the

period 1917–1987. See his *Lethal Politics: Soviet Genocides and Mass Murder, 1900–1987* (New Brunswick, N.J.: Transaction Press, 1990); cited in Helen Fein, "Genocide: A Sociological Perspective," *Current Sociology* 38, no. 1 (Spring 1990): 76.

Conquest makes a further distinction between the dekulakization campaign which applied to all Soviet peasants, and the state-induced famine which especially devastated the Ukraine between 1932 and 1933. In effect, he estimates that some 7 million peasants perished of famine, of which some 6 million were Ukrainians. Indeed, he makes the case that the Soviet state's attack on the Ukrainian peasantry was meant not only as a measure to eliminate a class but to destroy Ukranian nationalism. This would suggest that at the same time that a class genocide was launched against the Soviet peasantry, a national or ethnic genocide-in-part was perpetrated against the Ukrainians. On these points see Lyman H. Legters, "The Soviet Gulag: Is it Genocidal," in Israel W. Charny, ed., *Toward the Understanding and Prevention of Genocide* (Boulder and London: Westview Press, 1984), 60–66; and James E. Mace, "The Man-Made Famine of 1933 in the Soviet Ukraine: What Happened and Why?" in Charny, 67–83.

11. See Theda Skocpol, *States and Social Revolutions* (Cambridge: Cambridge University Press, 1979), 220–25.

12. See Jerome L. Himmelstein and Michael S. Kimmel, "States and Social Revolutions: The Implications and Limits of Skocpol's Structural Model," *American Journal of Sociology* 86, no. 5 (1981): 1153.

13. See David Mitrany, *Marx against the Peasant* (New York: Collier Books, 1961).

14. See Cohen, *Rethinking*.

15. See Robert C. Tucker, *The Soviet Political Mind* (New York: W. W. Norton, 1971), 67–71.

16. See Gouldner, "Stalinism," 233–35.

17. See Elizabeth Becker, *When the War Was Over* (New York: Simon and Schuster, 1986), 129–216; and Timothy Carney, "The Unexpected Victory," in Karl D. Jackson, ed., *Cambodia 1975–1978: Rendezvous with Death* (Princeton: Princeton University Press, 1989), 13–36.

18. Becker, 253–63; and David Hawk, "The Photographic Record," in Jackson, *Cambodia*, 212–13.

19. Karl D. Jackson, "Ideology of Total Revolution," in Jackson, *Cambodia*, 42–45; Jackson notes: "What is distinctive about the Khmer Rouge is not that they reserved positions of power for themselves and decreased the power of the former elite; what is distinctive is that they entered Phnom Penh with a plan for forthrightly exterminating entire social categories and destroying all of the institutions of pre-1970 Cambodian society," 51. On the class composition of the victims see Becker, 245.

20. Becker, 179.

21. David Hawk, "Pol Pot's Cambodia" (51), estimates that from 1975 to 1978, out of a population of some 7 million, between 1 and 3 million Cambodians perished as a result of Khmer Rouge policies.

22. For contrary views on the origins of the violence in Cambodia see William Shawcross, *Sideshow: Kissinger, Nixon, and the Destruction of Cambodia* (New York: Simon and Schuster, 1979). Shawcross, in particular, has stressed the Nixon administration's massive bombing policy between 1969 and 1973 as a major cause. Though that policy may have been misconceived and immoral, its consequences cannot account for the specific measures taken by the Khmer Rouge, in particular their attack on the urban middle classes

and the ethnic minorities. Nor can it explain why the level of violence increased rather than decreased after the Khmer Rouge seizure of power. See Karl D. Jackson, "The Ideology of Total Revolution," 37. There also exists an apologetic literature that denies the genocidal intent of the Khmer Rouge and blames "imperialist powers" and the "imperialist" press for self-serving distortions. See, for example, Noam Chomsky and Edward S. Herman, *After the Cataclysm: Postwar Indochina and the Reconstruction of Imperial Ideology* (Nottingham: Spokesman, 1979). For a balanced assessment see Leo Kuper, *Genocide* (New Haven: Yale University Press, 1981), 158–60.

23. Kenneth M. Quinn, "Explaining the Terror," in Jackson, *Cambodia,* 219–31, 234–36.

24. For a discussion of these terms please see Chap. 1.

25. Jackson, 52.

26. For the term "uncitizens," see Simon Schama, *Citizens: A Chronicle of the French Revolution* (New York: Alfred A. Knopf, 1989), 859.

> Suddenly, subjects were told that they had become Citizens; an aggregate of subjects held in place by injustice and intimidation had become a Nation. From this new thing, the Nation of Citizens, justice freedom and plenty could be not only expected but required. By the same token, should it not materialize, only those who had spurned their citizenship, or who were by their birth or unrepentant beliefs incapable of exercising it, could be held responsible. Before the promise of 1789 could be realized, then, it was necessary to root out Uncitizens.

For the expression *bannheu,* see Jackson, 52.

27. It should be noted that identifying a group as a separate race excludes its members more thoroughly than if it were defined as a class. Presumably a person can change his class identification by losing an old position or gaining a new one. Revolutionary myths and ideologies that stress the class membership of its members should in principle be less bloody than revolutions that stress ethnic or racial background. In practice there is very little difference, especially in Stalinist revolutions that define a person by his or her social origins.

28. Skocpol, *States and Social Revolutions,* 186.

29. The revolutionary was Anacharsis Cloots. Following his outburst "[in] a flat, faltering voice Louis XVI then read the formal declaration of war as though it were a death sentence upon himself. Which indeed it was." See Schama, *Citizens,* 597.

30. See Reynald Sécher, *Le génocide Franco-Français: La Vendée-Vengé* (Paris: Presses Universitaires de France, 1986); and Schama, *Citizens,* 791.

31. Quinn, 220.

32. The Khmer revolutionaries reckoned that since they could not wait to reform the bourgeoisie or even to use it for their own ends, the simplest solution was to destroy it. Apparently there were at least two reasons for this drastic decision: first, the Khmer Rouge were intent on achieving the promised land of pure communism in the shortest possible time; and, second, the bourgeoisie was too large and the Khmer Rouge cadres were too few and too inexperienced to try to integrate and reform it. Had they not destroyed the bourgeoisie, reckoned the Khmer Rouge, the perfect communist society would have been delayed in Kampuchea, and their cadres would have been overwhelmed. A new class of "experts," just as in China, would have risen to displace the "reds" and to strangle the revolution. See Jackson, "The Ideology of Total Revolution," 57–58.

33. Norman Cohn, *Warrant for Genocide* (New York: Harper and Row, 1967).

34. The examples discussed below are apparent deviations from the main proposition, and methodologically they need to be discussed in a full exposition of the argument. They support the hypothesis that revolutions that lead to wars are among the necessary but not the sufficient conditions for total domestic genocide, although some revolutions that have led to wars did not produce genocide, and some genocides have been caused by other factors than revolutions that led to wars. For deviant case analysis see Paul F. Lazarsfeld and Morris Rosenberg, eds., *The Language of Social Research* (Glencoe: Free Press, 1955), 167–74; Morris Zelditch, Jr., "Intelligible Comparisons," in I. Vallier, ed., *Comparative Methods in Sociology* (Berkeley: University of California Press, 1971), 267–307; and Theda Skocpol, *Vision and Method in Historial Sociology* (Cambridge: Cambridge University Press, 1984), 356–91.

35. It is estimated that between 1960 and 1974 some 584,875 Cubans either fled or were forced out by the Castro regime. Indeed, this was a way of "exporting" the opposition. See Jorge I. Dominguez, *Cuba: Order and Revolution* (Cambridge, Mass.: Harvard University Press, 1978), 139–40.

36. I hesitate to call the French Revolution "genocidal" in the sense that we have been using the term here. Though thousands of aristocrats were killed and there were scattered attempts to do away with the aristocracy as a class, most aristocrats including their families remained unharmed, and the destruction of that class never became an articulated policy of the terror. As to the massacres in the Vendée, they may be seen as "genocidal massacres" in the sense that Kuper uses the term, or "genocide-in-part" as the UN uses it, but these were not part of a policy of extermination or total domestic genocide such as was launched against the Jews, the Armenians, the Kulaks, and the Khmer upper and middle classes. It may be that the Jacobins, who were in power only briefly during the Terror of 1793 and 1794, did not have sufficient time to establish their dominance over France in the manner that the Nazis controlled Germany and the Stalinists dominated Russia. Without a mass party and institutional power, some of their genocidal impulses could not be translated into policy. See also Colin Lucas, *The Structure of the Terror* (New York: Oxford University Press, 1973); and the article on the Terror by Furet in Furet and Ozouf, *Critical Dictionary*, 1989, 137–50.

37. From the perspective of this study one could view the Baha'is as an endangered category in Iran, especially when that Muslim revolutionary country was at war with Iraq. The Baha'is could be viewed as being especially dangerous to the Iranian revolution because they challenged the validity of the Shiite revolutionary myth. Indeed, Leo Kuper viewed the Baha'is as a "hostage" group in Iran whose persecutions recall the "early stages in the German genocide against the Jews." See his *The Prevention of Genocide* (New Haven: Yale University Press, 1985), 152. Kuper himself suggests that the Baha'is may have been spared destruction by the intervention of the world community, including the United Nations (163–64). It may also be suggested that although Iran was at war with Iraq it was hard put to connect the Baha'is to the Iraqi regime.

38. See Raymond Aron's *Clausewitz* (New York: Simon and Schuster, 1986), 369; cited by Charles S. Maier, *The Unmasterable Past* (Cambridge, Mass.: Harvard University Press, 1988), 78.

39. See the bibliographic essay by Frank Chalk and Kurt Jonassohn, "The History and Sociology of Genocidal Killings," in Israel W. Charny, ed., *Genocide: A Critical Bibliographic Review* (New York: Facts on File, 1988), 39–58.

40. See Chalk and Jonassohn (53) on the genocidal effects of some colonialism. See also Eric R. Wolf, "Killing the Achés," in Richard Arens, ed., *Genocide in Paraguay* (Philadelphia: Temple University Press, 1976), 47–57; and Lyndall Ryan, *The Aboriginal Tasmanians* (Vancouver: University of British Columbia, 1981). The destruction of native peoples in the New World, Africa, and Oceania has run the gamut from unintended mass death due to the spread of epidemics by Europeans, through genocidal massacres, and includes exterminations or total genocide as we have used the term here.

41. In 1965 the Indonesia military destroyed the Communist party of Indonesia (PKI) and massacred thousands of its supporters. Beyond that horror, the bloodletting against the party became the occasion on some islands for the massacre of communal groups like the non-Muslims in Aceh and the Overseas Chinese in East Java. Indeed, it is estimated that between 250,000 and 500,000 people were killed and some 200,000 were arrested. See Harold Crouch, *The Army and Politics in Indonesia* (Ithaca and London: Cornell University Press, 1978), 155. By the same token, however, the Indonesian military did not set out to transform Indonesian society by destroying the social classes supporting the PKI; nor with the exception of some commanders was it intent on exterminating communal groups like the Chinese. Once the PKI was crushed and the pogroms were under control, the army established an authoritarian statist regime, and the classes and communal groups that had supported the PKI were allowed to live. This was not extermination or total genocide as we have used the term here. It was, however, genocide-in-part according to the UN convention.

Similarly, in the Tutsi-dominated regime's destruction of the Hutu uprising of 1972, the army managed to massacre as many as 100,000 Hutu, but once the threat of Hutu revolution passed, the Hutu were subjugated but not exterminated. See René Lemarchand and Martin David, *Selective Genocide in Burundi* (London: Minority Rights Group, 1974).

42. See John de St. Jorre, *The Brothers' War: Biafra and Nigeria* (Boston: Houghton Mifflin, 1972), 86.

43. The Biafrans used the threat of genocide to prolong the war and to appeal for international support. See John J. Stremlau, *The International Politics of the Nigerian Civil War* (Princeton: Princeton University Press, 1977).

44. Mike Wallace and Harry Reasoner interviewers, "Nigeria-Biafra" (New York: CBS News, 1970), film. Also see portion of Gowon's speech promising amnesty to all secessionists in J. Isawa Elaigwu, *Gowon* (Ibadan: West Books, 1985), 135–43.

45. Jean Herskovits points out, for example, that in the presidential elections of 1979 every political party fielded an Ibo either as a presidential or as a vice-presidential candidate. See her "Democracy in Nigeria," *Foreign Affairs* (Winter 1979/80): 324.

46. Albert Camus, *Resistance, Rebellion, and Death* (New York: Alfred A. Knopf, 1961), 39–40.

SELECTED BIBLIOGRAPHY

This selected bibliography lists most, though not all, of the major works that were consulted in this study, including some works that do not appear in the notes. It is divided into four main sections: I. Theory, Methodology, and Historiography; II. The Armenian Massacres of 1894–96 and the Genocide of 1915–23; III. Antisemitism and the Holocaust; IV. Other Revolutions or Genocides.

I. THEORY, METHODOLOGY, AND HISTORIOGRAPHY

Adorno, Theodor W., Else Frenkel-Brunswik, Daniel J. Levinson, and R. Nevitt Sanford. *The Authoritarian Personality.* New York: Harper and Row, 1950.

Almond, Gabriel A. "Approaches to Developmental Causation." In Gabriel A. Almond, Scott C. Flanagan, and Robert J. Mundt, eds., *Crisis, Choice, and Change,* 1–42.

Almond, Gabriel A., Scott C. Flanagan, and Robert J. Mundt, eds. *Crisis, Choice, and Change.* Boston: Little, Brown, 1973.

Apter, David, ed. *Ideology and Discontent.* New York: Free Press, 1964.

Arendt, Hannah. *The Origins of Totalitarianism.* New York: Meridian Books, 1958 [1951].

Aron, Raymond. *Clausewitz.* New York: Simon and Schuster, 1986.

Barkun, Michael. *Disaster and the Millennium.* New Haven: Yale University Press, 1974.

Bauer, Yehuda. "'Unique and Universal': Some General Problems Arising Out of Holocaust Research." Hebrew University. Mimeo. n.d.

———. "The Place of the Holocaust in Contemporary History." In Jonathan Frankel, ed., *Studies in Contemporary Jewry,* 201–34. Bloomington: Indiana University Press, 1984.

———. "Is the Holocaust Explicable?" In Bauer et al., eds., *Remembering for the Future,* vol. 2, *The Impact of the Holocaust on the Contemporary World,* 1967–75.

Bauer, Yehuda, et al., eds. *Remembering for the Future: Working Papers and Addenda.* 3 vols. Oxford: Pergamon Press, 1989.

Beres, Louis René. "Reason and Realpolitik: International Law and the Prevention of Genocide." In Charny, ed., *Toward the Understanding and Prevention of Genocide,* 306–23.

———. "Genocide, State and Self." *Denver Journal of International Law and Policy* 18, no. 1 (Fall 1989): 37–57.

Berger, Peter L., and Thomas Luckmann. *The Social Construction of Reality.* New York: Anchor Books, 1967.

Berlin, Isaiah. *Four Essays on Liberty.* London: Oxford University Press, 1969.

Binder, Leonard W., ed. *Crises and Sequences in Political Development.* Princeton: Princeton University Press, 1971.

Brinton, Crane. *The Anatomy of Revolution.* New York: Vintage Press, 1957.

Bibliography

Camus, Albert. *Resistance, Rebellion, and Death.* New York: Alfred A. Knopf, 1961.

Carsten, F. L. *The Rise of Fascism.* Berkeley and Los Angeles: University of California Press, 1982.

Chalk, Frank. "Definitions of Genocide and Their Implications for Prediction and Prevention." In Bauer et al., eds., *Remembering for the Future,* vol. 3, *The Impact of the Holocaust and Genocide on Jews and Christians,* 67–79.

Chalk, Frank, and Kurt Jonassohn, eds. *The History and Sociology of Genocide.* New Haven: Yale University Press, 1990.

Charny, Israel W. *How Can We Commit the Unthinkable? Genocide: The Human Cancer.* Boulder: Westview Press, 1982.

———, ed. *Toward the Understanding and Prevention of Genocide.* Boulder and London: Westview Press, 1984.

———, ed. *Genocide: A Critical Bibliographic Review.* Vol 1. New York: Facts on File, 1988.

———, ed. *Genocide: A Critical Bibliographic Review.* Vol. 2. New York: Facts on File, 1992.

Dadrian, Vahakan N. "Factors of Anger and Aggression in Genocide." *Journal of Human Relations* 19, no. 3 (1971): 394–417.

———. "The Structural-Functional Components of Genocide: A Victimological Approach to the Armenian Case." In Drapkin and Viano, eds. *Victimology,* 123–35.

———. "The Convergent Aspects of the Armenian and Jewish Cases of Genocide: A Reinterpretation of the Concept of Holocaust." *Holocaust and Genocide Studies* 3, no. 2 (1988): 151–70.

Dawidowicz, Lucy S. *The Holocaust and the Historians.* Cambridge, Mass.: Harvard University Press, 1981.

Dekmejian, Hrair R. "Determinants of Genocide: Armenians and Jews as Case Studies." In Hovannisian, ed., *The Armenian Genocide in Perspective,* 85–96.

Deutsch, Karl W. "Social Mobilization and Political Development." *American Political Science Review* 55 (1961): 493–514.

Dobkin, Marjorie Housepian, "What Genocide? What Holocaust? News from Turkey, 1915–1923: A Case Study." In Hovannisian, ed., *The Armenian Genocide in Perspective,* 97–110.

Drapkin, Israel, and Emilio Viano, eds. *Victimology.* Lexington, Mass.: D. C. Heath, 1974.

Dutt, Palme R. *Fascism and Social Revolution.* London: Martin Lawrence, 1934.

Dyer, Gwynne. "Turkish 'Falsifiers' and Armenian 'Deceivers': Historiography and the Armenian Massacres." *Middle Eastern Studies* 12, no. 1 (1976): 99–107.

Eckardt, Alice L., and A. Roy Eckardt. "The Holocaust and the Enigma of Uniqueness: A Philosophical Effort at Practical Clarification." In Shur and Littel, eds., *Reflections on the Holocaust,* 165–74.

Eisenstadt, S. N. *The Political System of Empires.* New York: Free Press, 1963.

———. *Revolution and the Transformation of Societies.* New York: Free Press, 1978.

Erikson, Erik H. "The Concept of Identity in Group Relations." In Parsons and Clark, *The Negro American.*

Fein, Helen. "A Formula for Genocide: A Comparison of the Turkish Genocide (1915) and the German Holocaust (1939–1945)." *Comparative Studies in Sociology* 1 (1978): 271–93.

———. *Accounting for Genocide.* New York: Free Press, 1979.

336

————. "Scenarios of Genocide: Models of Genocide and Critical Responses." In Charny, ed., *Toward the Understanding and Prevention of Genocide*, 3–31.

————. "Genocide: A Sociological Perspective." *Current Sociology* 38, no. 1 (Spring 1990): Preface–126.

Friedländer, Saul. "On the Possibility of the Holocaust: An Approach to a Historical Synthesis." In Bauer and Rotenstreich, eds., *The Holocaust as Historical Experience*, 1–22.

Furnivall, J. S. *Colonial Policy and Practice*. London: Cambridge University Press, 1948.

Gardner, Patrick, ed. *Theories of History*. Glencoe, Ill.: Free Press, 1959.

Geertz, Clifford. "Ideology as a Cultural System." In Apter, ed., *Ideology and Discontent*, 47–76.

Gerth, H. H., and C. Wright Mills. *From Max Weber: Essays in Sociology*. New York: Oxford University Press, 1958.

Goldstone, Jack. "Theories of Revolution: The Third Generation." *World Politics* 32 (1980): 425–53.

Greene, Thomas H. *Comparative Revolutionary Movements*. Englewood Cliffs, N.J.: Prentice-Hall, 1974.

Greenstein, Fred I. *Politics and Personality*. New York: W. W. Norton, 1975.

Greenstein, Fred I., and Nelson W. Polsby, eds. *Handbook of Political Science*. Vol. 3. *Macropolitical Theory*. Reading, Mass.: Addison-Wesley, 1975.

Grew, Raymond. "The Case for Comparing Histories," *American Historical Review* 85, no. 4 (1980): 763–78.

Guroian, Vigen. "Collective Responsibility and Official Excuse Making: The Case of the Turkish Genocide of the Armenians." In Hovannisian, ed., *The Armenian Genocide in Perspective*, 135–52.

Gurr, Ted Robert. *Why Men Rebel*. Princeton: Princeton University Press, 1970.

Hagen, E. E. *On the Theory of Social Change*. Homewood, Ill.: Dorsey Press, 1962.

Harff, Barbara. "The Etiology of Genocides." In Walliman and Dobkowski, *Genocide and the Modern Age*, 41–61.

Hempel, Carl G. "The Function of General Laws in History." In Gardner, ed., *Theories of History*, 344–56.

Hermassi, Elbaki. "Toward a Comparative Study of Revolutions." *Comparative Studies in Society and History* 18, no. 2 (April 1976): 211–35.

Horowitz, Donald L. *Ethnic Groups in Conflict*. Berkeley and Los Angeles: University of California Press, 1985.

Horowitz, Irving L. *Taking Lives: Genocide and State Power*. New Brunswick and London: Transaction Books, 1982.

Hovannisian, Richard G. *The Armenian Holocaust: A Bibliography Relating to the Deportations, Massacres, and Dispersion of the Armenian People, 1915–1923*. Cambridge, Mass.: Armenian Heritage Press, 1978.

————. "The Critic's View: Beyond Revisionism." *International Journal of Middle East Studies* 9 (1978): 337–86.

————. "The Armenian Genocide and Patterns of Denial." In Hovannisian, ed., *The Armenian Genocide in Perspective*, 111–34.

Huntington, Samuel P. *Political Order in Changing Societies*. New Haven: Yale University Press, 1968.

———. "The Change to Change." *Comparative Politics* 3 (1971): 283–322.

Huttenbach, Henry R. "Locating the Holocaust on the Genocide Spectrum: Towards a Methodology of Definition and Categorization." *Holocaust and Genocide Studies* 3, no. 3 (1988): 289–304.

Katz, Jacob. "Was the Holocaust Predictable?" In Bauer and Rotenstreich, eds., *The Holocaust as Historical Experience*, 23–42.

Katz, Steven. "Essay: Quantity and Interpretation—Issues in the Comparative Historical Analysis of the Holocaust." *Holocaust and Genocide Studies* 4, no. 2 (1989): 127–48.

Kuper, Leo. *The Pity of It All.* Minneapolis: University of Minnesota Press, 1976.

———. *Genocide: Its Political Uses in the Twentieth Century.* New Haven: Yale University Press, 1981.

———. *The Prevention of Genocide.* New Haven: Yale University Press, 1985.

Kuper, Leo, and M. G. Smith. *Pluralism in Africa.* Berkeley and Los Angeles: University of California Press, 1969.

Laqueur, Walter, ed. *Fascism: A Reader's Guide.* Berkeley and Los Angeles: University of California Press, 1976.

Lasswell, Harold D. and Abraham Kaplan. *Power and Society.* New Haven: Yale University Press, 1950.

Lazarsfeld, Paul F., and Morris Rosenberg, eds. *The Language of Social Research.* Glencoe: Free Press, 1955.

Leblanc, Lawrence J. "The United Nations Genocide Convention and Political Groups: Should the United States Propose an Amendment?" *Yale Journal of International Law* 13, no. 2 (1988): 268–96.

Lemkin, Raphael. *Axis Rule in Occupied Europe.* New York: Howard Fertig, 1973 [1944].

Lerner, Daniel. *The Passing of Traditional Society.* New York: Free Press, 1958.

Libaridian, Gerard J. "Objectivity and the Historiography of the Armenian Genocide." *Armenian Review* 31 (Spring 1978): 79–87.

Lijphart, Arend. "Comparative Politics and the Comparative Method." *American Political Science Review* 65 (1971): 682–93.

———. "The Comparative Cases Strategy in Comparative Research." *Comparative Political Studies* 8, no. 2 (1975): 158–77.

Linz, Juan J. "Totalitarian and Authoritarian Regimes." In Greenstein and Polsby, eds., *Handbook of Political Science*, vol. 3, *Macropolitical Theory*, 175–412.

———. "Some Notes toward a Comparative Study of Fascism in Sociological and Historical Perspective." in Laqueur, *Fascism: A Reader's Guide*, 3–124.

Linz, Juan J., and Alfred Stepan, eds. *The Breakdown of Democratic Regimes.* Baltimore: Johns Hopkins University Press, 1978.

Lipset, Seymour Martin. *Political Man.* Baltimore: Johns Hopkins University Press, 1981.

Lipset, Seymour, and Stein Rokkan, eds. *Party Systems and Voter Alignments.* New York: Free Press, 1967.

McClelland, David A. *The Achieving Society.* Princeton: Van Nostrand, 1961.

Maier, Charles S. *The Unmasterable Past.* Cambridge, Mass.: Harvard University Press, 1988.

Marrus, Michael R. *The Holocaust in History.* Hanover, N.H.: University Press of New England, 1987.

―――. "Recent Trends in the Historicity of the Holocaust." *Holocaust and Genocide Studies* 3, no. 3 (1988): 257–65.

Marx, Karl. *The Eighteenth Brumaire of Napoleon*. London: 1869. Cited in Lewis S. Feuer, ed., *Karl Marx and Friedrich Engels: Basic Writings on Politics and Philosophy*. New York: Doubleday, 1959.

Mazian, Florence. *Why Genocide? The Armenian and Jewish Experiences in Perspective*. Ames: Iowa State University Press, 1990.

Melson, Robert. "Revolutionary Genocide: On the Causes of the Armenian Genocide of 1915 and the Holocaust." *Holocaust and Genocide Studies* 4, no. 2 (1989): 161–74.

Milgram, Stanley. *Obedience to Authority*. New York: Harper and Row, 1974.

Moore, Barrington, Jr. *Social Origins of Dictatorship and Democracy*. Boston: Beacon Press, 1966.

Mosca, Gaetano. *The Ruling Class*. New York: McGraw-Hill, 1939.

Nolte, Ernst. *Three Faces of Fascism*. New York: Holt, Rinehart and Winston, 1965.

Oberschall, Anthony. *Social Conflict and Social Movements*. Englewood Cliffs, N.J.: Prentice-Hall, 1973.

Papazian, Pierre. "A 'Unique Uniqueness' "? *Midstream* 30, no. 4 (April 1984): 14–25.

Parsons, Talcott, and Kenneth B. Clark. *The Negro American*. Boston: Beacon Press, 1966.

Pois, Robert A. "The Holocaust and the Ethical Imperative of Historicism." *Holocaust and Genocide Studies* 3, no. 3 (1988): 267–72.

Porter, Jack Nusan, ed. *Genocide and Human Rights*. Washington, D.C.: University Press of America, 1982.

Poulantzas, Nicos. *Fascism and Dictatorship*. London: Verso Editions, 1979.

Pye, Lucian W. "Identity and the Political Culture." In Binder, ed., *Crises and Sequences in Political Development*, 101–34.

Rogger, Hans, and Eugen Weber, eds. *The European Right: A Historical Profile*. Berkeley and Los Angeles: University of California Press, 1965.

Ronen, Dov. *The Quest for Self-Determination*. New Haven: Yale University Press, 1979.

Rosenberg, Alan, "Was the Holocaust Unique?: A Peculiar Question?" In Walliman and Dobkowski, eds., *Genocide and the Modern Age*, 145–62.

Royal Institute of International Affairs. *Nationalism*. London: Frank Cass, 1963.

Rubenstein, Richard L. *The Age of Triage*. Boston: Beacon Press, 1983.

Sartre, Jean Paul. *Jean Paul Sartre on Genocide*. Boston: Beacon Press. 1968.

Schapiro, Salwyn J. *The World in Crisis*. New York: McGraw-Hill, 1950.

Schorsch, Ismar. "German Antisemitism in the Light of Post-War Historiography." *Leo Baeck Institute* 19 (1974): 257–72.

Scriven, Michael. "Truisms as the Grounds for Historical Explanations." In Patrick Gardner, ed., *Theories of History*, 443–75.

Shaw, Stanford J., and Ezel Kural Shaw. "The Authors Respond." *International Journal of Middle East Studies* 9 (1978): 386–400.

Skocpol, Theda. *States and Social Revolutions*. Cambridge: Cambridge University Press, 1979.

―――, ed. *Vision and Method in Historical Sociology*. Cambridge: Cambridge University Press, 1984.

Smith, Anthony D. *Theories of Nationalism*. London: Duckworth, 1971.

Smith, Roger W. "Denial of the Armenian Genocide." In Charny, ed., *Genocide: A Critical Bibliographic Review*. Vol. 2, 63–85.

————. "Human Destructiveness and Politics: The Twentieth Century as an Age of Genocide." In Walliman and Dobkowski, eds., *Genocide and the Modern Age*, 21–40.

————. "Genocide and Denial: The Armenian Case and Its Implications." *Armenian Review* 42, 1/165 (Spring 1989): 1–38.

Sowell, Thomas. *The Economics and Politics of Race: An International Perspective.* New York: Morrow, 1983.

Staub, Ervin. *The Roots of Evil: The Origins of Genocide and Other Group Violence.* New York: Cambridge University Press, 1989.

Sternhell, Zeev. "Fascist Ideology." In Laqueur, *Fascism: A Reader's Guide*, 315–78.

Stohl, Michael, and George Lopez, eds. *The State as Terrorist.* Westport, Conn.: Greenwood Press, 1984.

Talmon, J. L. *The Origins of Totalitarian Democracy.* London: Mercury Books, 1961.

Tilly, Charles, ed. *The Formation of National States in Western Europe.* Princeton: Princeton University Press, 1975.

————. "Revolutions and Collective Violence." In Greenstein and Polsby. eds., *Macropolitical Theory*, 483–555.

Tipps, Dean C. "Modernization Theory and the Comparative Study of Societies: A Critical perspective." *Comparative Studies in Society and History* 15 (1973): 199–226.

Trimberger, Ellen Kay. *Revolution from Above: Military Bureaucrats and Development in Japan, Turkey, and Peru.* New Brunswick, N.J.: Transaction Press, 1978.

Tucker, Robert W. *The Soviet Political Mind.* New York: W. W. Norton, 1971.

Turner, Henry Ashby, Jr., ed. *Reappraisals of Fascism.* New York: Franklin Watts. 1975.

United Nations, *Yearbook of the United Nations, 1948–49.* New York, 1949.

Walliman, Isidor, and Michael N. Dobkowski, eds. *Genocide and the Modern Age.* New York: Greenwood Press, 1987.

Weber, Eugen. *Varieties of Fascism.* Princeton: Princeton University Press, 1964.

————. "Revolution? Counterrevolution? What Revolution?" In Laqueur, ed., *Fascism: A Reader's Guide*, 435–68.

Wilson, Bryan. "Millenialism in Comparative Perspective." *Comparative Studies in Society and History* 6 (1963): 93–114.

Zagorin, Perez. "Prolegomena to the Comparative History of Revolution in Early Modern Europe." *Comparative Studies in Society and History* 18. no. 2 (April 1976): 151–74.

Zelditch, Morris, Jr. "Intelligible Comparisons." In I. Vallier, ed., *Comparative Methods in Sociology*, 267–307. Berkeley: University of California Press, 1971.

II. The Armenian Massacres of 1894–96 and the Genocide of 1915–23

A. Primary Sources

Bryce, Viscount J. *The Treatment of the Armenians in the Ottoman Empire: Documents Presented to Viscount Grey of Fallodon, Secretary of State for Foreign Affairs.* London: H.M.S.O., 1916.

Great Britain. House of Commons. *Correspondence Relating to the Asiatic Provinces of Turkey.* Sessional Papers, 1895, vol. 109, pt. 1, c. 7894.

————. *Correspondence Relating to the Asiatic Provinces of Turkey. Reports by Vice Consul Fitzmaurice, from Birejik, Ourfa, Adiman, Behesni.* Sessional Papers, 1896. vol. 106, c. 8100.

United States. National Archives. Record group 59. *Despatches from United States Ministers to Turkey. 1818–1906* Microfilm publication M46, roll 61, enclosure 796.

B. Secondary Sources

Ahmad, Feroz. *The Young Turks.* Oxford: Clarendon Press, 1969.

Andonian, Aram. *The Memoirs of Naim Bey.* Newtown Square, Pa.: Armenian Historical Research Association, 1965 [1920].

Arlen, Michael J. *Passage to Ararat.* New York: Ballantine Books, 1975.

Atamian, Sarkis. *The Armenian Community.* New York: Philosophical Library, 1955.

Bardakjian, Kevork. *Hitler and the Armenian Genocide.* Cambridge, Mass.: Zoryan Institute, 1985.

Bedoukian, Kerop. *The Urchin: An Armenian's Escape.* London: J. Murray, 1978.

Berkes, Niyazi. *Turkish Nationalism and Western Civilization.* New York: Columbia University Press, 1959.

Boyajian, Dickran. *Armenia: The Case for a Forgotten Genocide.* Westwood, N.J.: Educational Book Crafters, 1972.

Braude, Benjamin, and Bernard Lewis, eds. *Christians and Jews in the Ottoman Empire.* Vol. 1. *The Central Lands.* New York: Holmes and Meier, 1982.

Dadrian, Vahakn N. "A Theoretical Model of Genocide with Particular Reference to the Armenian Case." *Armenian Review* 31 (February 1979): 116–36.

———. "The Naim-Andonian Documents on the World War I Destruction of the Ottoman Armenians: The Anatomy of Genocide." *International Journal of Middle East Studies* 18 (1986): 311–60.

———. "Genocide as a Problem of National and International Law: The World War I Armenian Case and Its Contemporary Legal Ramifications." *Yale Journal of International Law* 14, no. 2 (Summer 1989): 221–334.

Davis, Leslie A. *The Slaughterhouse Province: An American Diplomat's Report on the Armenian Genocide, 1915–1917.* Edited by Susan K. Blair. New Rochelle, N.Y.: Aristide D. Caratzas, 1989.

Davison, Roderic H. "The Armenian Crisis, 1912–1914." *American Historical Review* 53, no. 10 (1948): 481–505.

———. "Turkish Attitudes Concerning Christian-Muslim Equality in the Nineteenth Century." *American Historical Review* 59, no. 4 (1954): 844–64.

———. *Reform in the Ottoman Empire.* Princeton: Princeton University Press, 1963.

———. *Turkey: A Short History.* Englewood Cliffs, N.J.: Prentice-Hall, 1968.

———. "Nationalism as an Ottoman Problem and the Ottoman Response." In Haddad and Ochsenwald, eds., *Nationalism in a Non-National State: The Dissolution of the Ottoman Empire,* 25–56.

Djemal Bey, Ahmed. *Memories of a Turkish Statesman.* London: Hutchison, 1922.

Emin, Ahmed. *Turkey in the World War.* New Haven: Yale University Press, 1930.

Gibb, H. A. R., and Harold Bowen. *Islamic Society and the West.* New York: Oxford University Press, 1965.

Gökalp, Ziya. *The Principles of Turkism.* Leiden: E. J. Brill, 1968.

Gürün, Kamuran. *The Armenian File: The Myth of Innocence Exposed.* New York: St. Martin's Press, 1985.

Haddad, William W., and William Ochsenwald, eds., *Nationalism in a Non-National State.* Columbus, Ohio: Ohio State University Press, 1977.

Henderson, Alexander. "The Pan-Turanian Myth Today." *Asiatic Review* (January 1945): 88–92.

Hepworth, George Hughes. *Through Armenia on Horseback*. New York: E. P. Dutton, 1898.

Heyd, Uriel. *Foundations of Turkish Nationalism: The Life and Teachings of Ziya Gökalp*. London: Luzac, 1950.

Housepian, Marjorie. *The Smyrna Affair*. New York: Harcourt Brace Jovanovich, 1966.

Hovannisian, Richard G. *Armenia on the Road to Independence*. Berkeley and Los Angeles: University of California Press, 1967.

———, ed. *The Armenian Genocide in Perspective*. New Brunswick, N.J.: Transaction Press, 1986.

———. "The Armenian Genocide." In Charny, ed., *Genocide: A Critical Bibliographic Review*. Vol. 1. 89–116.

———. *The Armenian Genocide: History, Politics, Ethics*. London: Macmillan; and New York: St. Martins, 1992.

Jaschke, Gotthard. "Der Freiheitkampf des türkischen Volkes." *Die Welt des Islams* 14 (1932): 6–21.

Kedourie, Elie. *England and the Middle East: The Destruction of the Ottoman Empire, 1914–1921*. London: Bowes and Bowes, 1956.

Kemal, Ismail. *The Memoirs of Ismail Kemal Bey*. London: Constable & Co., 1920.

Landau, Jacob M. *Pan-Turkism in Turkey*. London: C. Hurst, 1981.

Lang, David Marshall. *Armenia: Cradle of Civilization*. London: George Allen and Unwin, 1980.

Langer, William L. *The Diplomacy of Imperialism*. New York: Alfred A. Knopf, 1935.

Lepsius, Johannes, *Armenia and Europe*. London: Hodder and Stoughton, 1897.

———. *Deutschland und Armenien, 1914–1918*. Potsdam: Tempelverlag, 1919.

———. *Rapport secret sur les massacres d'Arménie*. Paris: Payot, 1966 [1919].

Lewis, Bernard. *The Emergence of Modern Turkey*. New York: Oxford University Press, 1961.

———. "The Ottoman Empire and Its Aftermath," *Journal of Contemporary History* (London) 15, no. 1 (January 1980): 27–35.

Lewis, B., Ch. Pellat, and J. Schacht, eds. *The Encyclopedia of Islam*. New ed. London: Luzak & Co., 1961.

Libaridian, Gerard J. "The Ultimate Repression: The Genocide of the Armenians." In Walliman and Dobkowski, eds., *Genocide in the Modern Age*, 203–36.

McCarthy, Justin. *Muslims and Minorities*. New York and London: New York University Press, 1983.

Mardin, Serif. *The Genesis of Young Ottoman Thought*. Princeton: Princeton University Press, 1962.

Marshalian, Levon. "Population Statistics on Ottoman Armenians in the Context of Turkish Historiography." *Armenian Review* 40, no. 4 (Winter 1987): 1–59.

Melson, Robert. "A Theoretical Inquiry into the Armenian Massacres of 1894–1896," *Comparative Studies in Society and History* 24, no. 3 (1982): 481–509.

———. "Provocation or Nationalism: A Critical Inquiry into the Armenian Genocide of 1915." In Hovannisian, *The Armenian Genocide in Perspective*. 61–84.

Morgenthau, Henry. *Ambassador Morgenthau's Story*. New York: Doubleday, 1918.

Nalbandian, Louise. *The Armenian Revolutionary Movement: The Development of Armenian Political Parties through the Nineteenth Century*. Berkeley and Los Angeles: University of California Press, 1963.

Pears, Edwin. *The Life of Abdul Hamid*. 1917; repr., New York: Arno Press, 1973.

Permanent People's Tribunal. *A Crime of Silence: The Armenian Genocide*. London: Zed Books, 1985.

Pinon, René. "Preface." In Lepsius, *Rapport secret sur les massacres d'Arménie*, 1966.

Ramsaur, Ernest E., Jr. *The Young Turks*. Beirut: Khayats, 1965.

Ravitch, Norman. "The Armenian Catastrophe." *Encounter* 57 (1981): 69–84.

Sanjian, Avedis K. *The Armenian Communities in Syria under Ottoman Dominion*. Cambridge, Mass.: Harvard University Press, 1965.

Sarkiss, H. J. "The Armenian Renaissance 1500–1863." *Journal of Modern History* 9 (December 1937): 433–48.

Shaw, Stanford J., and Shaw, Ezel Kural. *History of the Ottoman Empire and Modern Turkey*. 2 vols. Cambridge: Cambridge University Press, 1: 1976, 2: 1977.

Suny, Ronald Grigor. *Armenia in the Twentieth Century*. Chico, Calif.: Scholars Press, 1983.

Toynbee, Arnold J. "A Summary of Armenian History Up to and Including 1915." In Bryce, *The Treatment of Armenians in the Ottoman Empire*.

———. *Acquaintances*. London: Oxford University Press, 1967.

———. *The Western Question in Greece and Turkey*. New York: Howard Fertig, 1970 [1922].

Trumpener, Ulrich. *Germany and the Ottoman Empire, 1914–1918* Princeton: Princeton University Press, 1968.

Walker, Christopher J. *Armenia: The Survival of a Nation*. London: Croom Helm; New York: St. Martin's Press, 1980.

III. ANTISEMITISM AND THE HOLOCAUST

A. Primary Sources

Melson, Nina J. (Ponczek). Interview by author, Cambridge, Mass., Summer 1978. Tape recording.

Melson, William J. (a.k.a. Wolf Mendelsohn). Interview by author, Cambridge, Mass., Summer 1978. Tape recording.

Yad Vashem Archives. Testimony of Mosze Apollo (in Polish), 03/3646. Jerusalem, 1973.

———. Testimony of Symon Baron (in Polish), 661/46 from 03/1153. Jerusalem, 1949.

B. Secondary Sources

Abel, Theodor. *The Nazi Movement: Why Hitler Came to Power* New York: Atherton Press, 1966.

Adam, Uwe Dietrich. "The Gas Chambers." In Furet, *Unanswered Questions*, 134–54.

———. "Nazi Actions Concerning the Jews between the Beginning of World War II and the German Attack on the USSR." In Furet, *Unanswered Questions*. 84–95.

Allen, William S. *The Nazi Seizure of Power*. New York: Franklin Watts, 1984.

Almog, Shmuel, ed. *Antisemitism through the Ages*. Oxford: Pergamon Press, 1988.

Arendt, Hannah. *Eichmann in Jerusalem*. New York: Viking Press, 1963.

———. *The Jew as Pariah*. Edited by Ron H. Feldman. New York: Grove Press, 1978.

Aschheim, Steven E. "'The Jew Within': The Myth of 'Judaization' in Germany." In Reinharz and Schatzberg, eds., *The Jewish Response to German Culture*, 212–41.

Axel, Larry. "Christian Theology and the Murder of the Jews." *Encounter* (Indianapolis) 40 (Spring 1979): 129–41.

Baron, Salo. "Ghetto and Emancipation: Shall We Revise the Traditional View?" *Menorah Journal* 14, no. 6 (1928): 515–26.

————. *The Jewish Community: Its History and Structure to the American Revolution*. 3 Vols. Philadelphia: Jewish Publication Society, 1942.

Bauer, Yehuda. *The Holocaust in Historical Perspective*. Seattle: University of Washington Press, 1982.

————. *The Jewish Emergence from Powerlessness*. Toronto: University Press of Toronto, 1979.

————. *A History of the Holocaust*. New York: Franklin Watts, 1982.

Bauer, Yehuda, and Nathan Rotenstreich, eds. *The Holocaust as Historical Experience*. New York: Holmes and Meier, 1981.

Baum, Gregory. *Is the New Testament Anti-Semitic?* New York: Paulist Press, 1965.

————. "Introduction." In Reuther, *Faith and Fratricide*, 1–22.

————. "Catholic Dogma after Auschwitz." In Davies, ed., *Antisemitism and the Foundations of Christianity*, 137–50.

Berghahn, Volker R. *Modern Germany: Society, Economy, and Politics in the Twentieth Century*. Cambridge: Cambridge University Press, 1982.

Biale, David. *Gershom Scholem: Kabbalah and Counter History*. Cambridge, Mass.: Harvard University Press, 1979.

————. *Power and Powerlessness in Jewish History*. New York: Schocken Books, 1986.

Binion, Rudolph. *Hitler among the Germans*. New York: Elsevier, 1976.

Blackbourn, David, and Geoff Eley. *The Peculiarities of German History*. Oxford: Oxford University Press, 1984.

Borochov, Ber. *Nationalism and the Class Struggle*. Westport, Conn.: Greenwood Press, 1937.

Bracher, Karl D. *The German Dictatorship*. New York: Holt, Rinehart and Winston, 1970.

Browning, Christopher R. *Fateful Months*. New York and London: Holmes and Meier, 1985.

————. "Nazi Resettlement Policy and the Search for a Solution to the Jewish Question." *German Studies Review* 9, no. 3 (October 1986): 497–519.

————. "Nazi Ghettoization Policy in Poland: 1939–1941." *Central European History* 19, no. 4 (1987): 343–68.

————. "Beyond 'Intentionalism' and 'Functionalism': A Reassessment of Nazi Jewish Policy," 1939–1941 (Paper presented at the American Historical Association meeting, Washington, D.C., December 1987).

Bullock, Alan. *Hitler: A Study in Tyranny*. New York: Harper and Row, 1962.

Childers, Thomas. *The Nazi Voter*. Chapel Hill and London: University of North Carolina Press, 1983.

Cohn, Norman. *The Pursuit of the Millennium*. New York: Harper Torchbooks, 1961.

————. *Warrant for Genocide*. New York: Harper and Row, 1967.

Craig, Gordon A. *Europe since 1815*. Hindsdale, Ill.: Dryden Press, 1974.

————. *Germany: 1866–1945*. New York and Oxford: Oxford University Press, 1978.

————. *The Germans*. New York: G. P. Putnam, 1982.

————. "The German Mystery Case." *New York Review of Books*, 30 January 1986, 20–24.

Dahrendorf, Ralf. *Society and Democracy in Germany*. New York: Doubleday, 1969.

Davies, Alan T., ed. *Antisemitism and the Foundations of Christianity*. New York: Paulist Press, 1979.

Dawidowicz, Lucy S. *The War against the Jews*. New York: Holt, Rinehart, and Winston, 1975.

————. *A Holocaust Reader*. New York: Behrman House, 1976.

Deutscher, Isaac. *The Non-Jewish Jew*. London: Oxford University Press, 1968.

Donat, Alexander. *The Holocaust Kingdom*. New York: Holt, Rinehart and Winston, 1965.

Eckardt, A. Roy. *Elder and Younger Brother: The Encounter of Jews and Christians.* Philadelphia: Schocken, 1973.

Edwards, Mark U., Jr. *Luther's Last Battles.* Ithaca: Cornell University Press, 1983.

Eley, Geoff. *Reshaping the German Right.* New Haven: Yale University Press, 1980.

———. *From Unification to Nazism: Reinterpreting the German Past.* Boston and London: George Allen and Unwin, 1986.

Eyck, Erich. *A History of the Weimar Republic.* 2 vols. Cambridge, Mass.: Harvard University Press, 1962.

Feldman, Gerald. *Army, Industry, and Labor.* Princeton: Princeton University Press, 1966.

Fest, Joachim C. *Hitler.* New York: Vintage Books, 1975.

Finkelstein, Louis, ed. *The Jews: Their History, Culture, and Religion.* 4 Vols. New York: Harper Brothers, 1960.

Flannery, Edward H. *The Anguish of the Jews: Twenty-Three Centuries of Antisemitism.* New York: Paulist Press, 1965.

Fleming, Gerald. *Hitler and the Final Solution.* Berkeley and Los Angeles: University of California Press, 1982.

Friedlander, Henry, and Sybil Milton. *The Holocaust: Ideology, Bureaucracy, and Genocide.* Millwood, N.Y.: Kraus International, 1981.

Friedländer, Saul. "From Antisemitism to Extermination." In Furet, *Unanswered Questions,* 3–31.

Furet, François. *Unanswered Questions.* New York: Schocken Books, 1989.

George, Alexander, and Juliette George. *Woodrow Wilson and Colonel House.* New York: J. Day Co., 1956.

Gerschenkron, Alexander. *Bread and Democracy in Germany.* New York: Howard Fertig, 1966.

Goebbels, Josef. From *Der Angriff,* 30 April, 1928. Also see p. 141, Bracher, *The German Dictatorship.* 1970.

Goldhagen, Erich. "Obsession and Realpolitik in the Final Solution." *Patterns of Prejudice* (Great Britain) 12, no. 1 (1978): 1–16.

Goldscheider, Calvin, and Alan S. Zuckerman. *The Transformation of the Jews.* Chicago: University of Chicago Press, 1984.

Gordon, Sarah. *Hitler, Germans, and the "Jewish Question."* Princeton: Princeton University Press, 1984.

Grunfeld, Frederic W. *Prophets without Honour.* New York: Holt, Rinehart, and Winston, 1979.

Gutman, Yisrael. *The Jews of Warsaw, 1939–1943.* Bloomington: Indiana University Press, 1982.

Haffner, Sebastian. *The Meaning of Hitler.* Cambridge, Mass.: Harvard University Press, 1983.

Hamilton, Richard F. *Who Voted for Hitler?* Princeton: Princeton University Press, 1982.

Heberle, Rudolf. *From Democracy to Nazism.* Baton Rouge: Louisiana State University Press, 1945.

Heller, Celia S. *On the Edge of Destruction.* New York: Columbia University Press, 1977.

Hilberg, Raul. *Documents of Destruction.* Chicago: Quadrangle Books, 1971.

———. "The Anatomy of the Holocaust" and "The Significance of the Holocaust." In Friedlander and Milton, *The Holocaust: Ideology, Bureaucracy, and Genocide,* 85–102.

————. *The Destruction of the European Jews.* Chicago: Quadrangle, 1967; new ed., New York: Holmes and Meier, 1985.

Himmler, Heinrich. "Himmler's Summation, October 4, 1943." In Dawidowicz, *A Holocaust Reader,* 138–40.

————. "Reflections on the Treatment of Peoples of Alien Races in the East." In Bauer, *A History of the Holocaust,* 351–354.

Hirschfeld, Gerhard, ed. *The Policies of Genocide.* London: Allen and Unwin, 1986.

Hirschfeld, Gerhard, and Lothar Ketternacker, eds. *Der Führerstaat: Mythos und Realität.* Stuttgart: Klett-Cotta, 1981.

Hitler, Adolf. *Mein Kampf.* Translated by Ralph Manheim. New York: Houghton Mifflin, 1971.

Jäckel, Eberhard. *Hitler's World View.* Cambridge, Mass.: Harvard University Press, 1981.

————. *Hitler in History.* Hanover and London: University Press of New England, 1984.

Kaldi, Leita. "Gypsies and Jews: Chosen People." in Charny, *Toward the Understanding and Prevention of Genocide,* 113–18.

Kater, Michael H. *The Nazi Party.* Cambridge, Mass.: Harvard University Press, 1983.

Katz, Jacob. *From Prejudice to Destruction.* Cambridge, Mass.: Harvard University Press, 1980.

Kenrick, Donald, and Grattan Puxon. *The Destiny of Europe's Gypsies.* London: Cox and Wyman, 1972.

Kershaw, Ian. *Popular Opinion and Political Dissent in the Third Reich: Bavaria 1933–1945.* Oxford: Clarendon Press, 1983.

————. *The Nazi Dictatorship.* London: Edward Arnold, 1985.

————. *The "Hitler Myth": Image and Reality in the Third Reich.* Oxford and New York: Oxford University Press, 1989.

Kitchen, Martin. *The Political Economy of Germany, 1815–1914.* London: Croom Helm, 1978.

Kren, George, and Leon Rapaport. *The Holocaust and the Crisis of Human Behavior.* New York: Holmes and Meier, 1980.

Kuznets, Simon. "Economic Structure and Life of the Jews." In Finkelstein, *The Jews,* 1597–1666.

Landes, Davis S. *The Unbound Prometheus.* Cambridge: Cambridge University Press, 1972.

Langer, Walter C. *The Mind of Adolf Hitler.* New York: New American Library, 1972.

Lanzmann, Claude. *Shoah.* New York: Pantheon, 1985.

Lestschinsky, Jacob. "The Economic and Social Development of the Jewish People." *Jewish Encyclopedic Handbooks.* 361–90. New York: Central Yiddish Cultural Organization, 1946.

Levi, Primo. *Survival in Auschwitz.* New York: Collier Books, 1961.

Levy, Richard S. *The Downfall of the Anti-Semitic Political Parties in Imperial Germany.* New Haven: Yale University Press, 1975.

————, *Antisemitism in the Modern World.* Lexington, Mass.: D. C. Heath, 1991.

Lifton, Robert J. *The Nazi Doctors.* New York: Basic Books, 1986.

Littel, Franklin H. *The Crucifixion of the Jews.* New York: Harper and Row, 1975.

Littel, Franklin H., and Hubert Locke, eds. *The German Church Struggle and the Holocaust.* Detroit: Wayne State University Press, 1974.

Loewenberg, Peter. "The Psychohistorical Origins of the Nazi Youth Cohort." *American Historical Review* 76, (December 1981): 1457–1502.

Madajczyk, Czesław. "*Generalplan Ost* and the Fate of the Jews, 1941–1943." In Bauer et al., eds., *Remembering for the Future*, vol. 3, 298–313.

Maier, Charles S. *Recasting Bourgeois Europe*. Princeton: Princeton University Press, 1975.

Marx, Karl. *On the Jewish Question*. Translated by Helen Lederer. Cincinnati: Hebrew Union College, 1958.

Mason, Timothy W. "The Legacy of 1918 for National Socialism." In Nichols and Matthias, eds., *German Democracy and the Triumph of Hitler*, 215–39.

———. "Intention and Explanation: A Current Controversy about the Interpretation of National Socialism." In Hirschfeld and Ketternacker, eds., *Der Führerstaat: Mythos und Realität*, 21–40.

Massing, Paul W. *Rehearsal for Destruction: A Study of Political Anti-Semitism in Imperial Germany*. New York: Howard Fertig, 1967.

Mayer, Arno J. *Dynamics of Counterrevolution in Europe*. New York: Harper and Row, 1971.

———. *Why Did the Heavens Not Darken? The Final Solution in History*. New York: Pantheon Books, 1988.

Mendes-Flohr, Paul R., and Jehuda Reinharz, eds. *The Jew in the Modern World: A Documentary History*. New York: Oxford University Press, 1980.

Merkl, Peter H. *Political Violence under the Swastika*. Princeton: Princeton University Press, 1975.

———. *The Making of a Stormtrooper*. Princeton: Princeton University Press, 1980.

Michaelis, Meir. *Mussolini and the Jews*. Oxford: Clarendon Press, 1978.

Mommsen, Hans. "The Realization of the Unthinkable: 'The Final Solution of the Jewish Question' in the Third Reich." In Hirschfeld, ed., *The Policies of Genocide*, 93–144.

Mork, Gordon R. "German Nationalism and Jewish Assimilation—the Bismarck Period." *Leo Baeck Institute Yearbook* 22 (1977): 81–91.

Mosse, George L. *The Crisis of German Ideology: Intellectual Origins of the Third Reich*. New York: Grosset and Dunlap, 1964.

———. *Nazi Culture*. New York: Grosset and Dunlap, 1966.

———. *Toward the Final Solution*. New York: Howard Fertig, 1978.

———. *German Jews beyond Judaism*. Bloomington, Ind.: University Press, 1985.

Nichols, Anthony J. *Weimar and the Rise of Hitler*. New York: St. Martin's Press, 1979.

Nichols, Anthony J., and Erich Matthias. *German Democracy and the Triumph of Hitler*. New York: St. Martin's Press, 1971.

Noakes, Jeremy. "Nazism and Revolution." In O'Sullivan, ed., *Revolutionary Theory and Political Reality*, 73–100.

O'Sullivan, Noel, ed. *Revolutionary Theory and Political Reality*. New York: St. Martin's Press, 1983.

Parkes, James. *The Conflict of the Church and the Synagogue: A Study in the Origins of Anti-Semitism*. New York: Atheneum, 1969.

Phelps, Reginald H. "'Before Hitler Came': Thule Society and Germanen Orden." *Journal of Modern History* 35, no. 3 (September 1963): 245–61.

Pinson, Koppel S. *Modern Germany*. New York: Macmillan, 1954.

Poliakov, Leon. *The History of Anti-Semitism*. New York: Schocken, 1965.

———. *Harvest of Hate*. New York: Holocaust Library and Schocken Books Inc., 1979 [1954].

Pulzer, Peter G. J. *The Rise of Political Anti-Semitism in Germany and Austria*. New York: John Wiley, 1964.

Bibliography

Reinharz, Jehuda, and Walter Schatzberg, eds. *The Jewish Response to German Culture.* Hanover and London: University Press of New England, 1985.

Rhodes, James M. *The Hitler Movement: A Modern Millenerian Revolution.* Stanford: Hoover Institution Press, 1980.

Richarz, Monika. "Jewish Social Mobility in Germany during the Time of Emancipation, 1790–1871." *Leo Baeck Institute Yearbook* 20 (1975): 69–78.

Rittberger, Volker. "Revolution and Pseudo-Democratization: The Formation of the Weimar Republic." In Almond, Flanagan, and Mundt, *Crisis, Choice, and Change,* 285–392.

Ruether, Rosemary. *Faith and Fratricide.* New York: Seabury Press, 1974.

Ruppin, Arthur. *The Jews in the Modern World.* London: Macmillan, 1934.

Sachar, Howard. *The Course of Modern Jewish History.* New York: Dell, 1958.

Schleunes, Karl A. *The Twisted Road to Auschwitz.* Urbana: University of Illinois Press, 1970.

Schoenbaum, David. *Hitler's Social Revolution: Class and Status in Nazi Germany.* Garden City, N.Y.: Doubleday, 1963.

Scholem, Gershom. *On Jews and Judaism in Crisis.* New York: Schocken Books, 1976.

Shur, Irene G., and Franklin H. Littel, eds. *Reflections on the Holocaust.* Special ed. of *Annals of the American Academy of Political and Social Science* 450 (1980).

Snyder, Louis L. *The Weimar Republic.* Princeton: D. Van Nostrand, 1966.

Sombart, Werner. *The Jews and Modern Capitalism.* Glencoe, Ill.: Free Press, 1951.

Stern, Fritz. *The Politics of Cultural Despair.* Berkeley and Los Angeles: University of California Press, 1961.

————. *Gold and Iron: Bismarck, Bleichröder, and the Building of the German Empire.* New York: Vintage, 1979.

Stokes, Lawrence. "The German People and the Destruction of the European Jews." *Central European History* 6, no. 2 (June 1973): 167–91.

Tal, Uriel. *Christians and Jews in Germany: Religion, Politics, and Ideology in the Second Reich.* Ithaca: Cornell University Press, 1975.

————. "On Structures of Political Theology and Myth in Germany Prior to the Holocaust." In Bauer and Rotenstreich, eds., *The Holocaust as Historical Experience,* 43–76.

Tokayer, Marvin, and Mary Swartz. *The Fugu Plan: The Untold Story of the Japanese and the Jews in World War II.* New York: Paddington, 1979.

Trachtenberg, Joshua. *The Devil and the Jews: The Medieval Conception of the Jews and Its Relation to Modern Anti-Semitism.* New Haven: Yale University Press, 1944.

Treitschke, Heinrich von. "A Word about Our Jews." 1881. In Levy, ed., *Antisemitism in the Modern World,* 67–73.

Trunk, Isaiah. *Judenrat.* New York: Stein and Day, 1977.

Vago, Bela, and George L. Mosse, eds. *Jews and Non-Jews in Eastern Europe.* New York: John Wiley, 1974.

Veblen, Thorstein. *Imperial Germany and the Industrial Revolution.* 1915; rep. New York: Viking. 1954.

Volkov, Shulamit. "Antisemitism as a Cultural Code: Reflections on the History and Historiography of Antisemitism in Imperial Germany." *Leo Baeck Institute* 23 (1976) 25–46.

————. "The Written Matter and the Spoken Word: On the Gap between Pre-1914 and Nazi Antisemitism." In Furet, *Unanswered Questions,* 33–53.

Waite, Robert G. L. *Vanguard of Nazism: The Free Corps Movement in Postwar Germany.* Cambridge, Mass.: Harvard University Press, 1952.

——. *The Psychopathic God: Adolf Hitler.* New York: Signet, 1977.

Wehler, Hans-Ulrich. *The German Empire, 1871–1918.* Leamington, N.H.: Berg, 1985.

Wiesel, Elie. *Night.* New York: Avon 1969.

Yahil, Leni. "Madagascar—Phantom of a Solution to the Jewish Question." In Vago and Mosse, eds., *Jews and Non-Jews in Eastern Europe*, 315–34.

——. *The Holocaust: The Fate of European Jewry.* New York: Oxford University Press, 1990.

Zimmerman, Moshe. *Wilhelm Marr: The Patriarch of Antisemitism.* New York: Oxford University Press, 1986.

IV. OTHER REVOLUTIONS OR GENOCIDES

Arens, Richard, D., ed. *Genocide in Paraguay.* Philadelphia: Temple University Press, 1976.

Becker, Elizabeth. *When the War Was Over.* New York: Simon and Schuster, 1986.

Berenbaum, Michael. *A Mosaic of Victims: Non-Jews Persecuted and Murdered by the Nazis.* New York: New York University Press, 1990.

Beres, Louis R. "After the Gulf War: Prosecuting Iraqi Crimes under the Rule of Law." *Vanderbilt Journal of Transnational Law* 261, no. 3 (1991): 487–503.

Cohen, F. Stephen. *Rethinking the Soviet Experience.* New York: Oxford University Press, 1985.

Conquest, Robert. *The Harvest of Sorrow.* New York: Oxford University Press, 1986.

Crouch, Harold. *The Army and Politics in Indonesia.* Ithaca: Cornell University Press, 1978.

Dallin, Alexander. *German Rule in Russia, 1941–1945.* London: Macmillan, 1957.

Dominguez, Jorge I. *Cuba: Order and Revolution.* Cambridge, Mass.: Harvard University Press, 1978.

Elaigwu, J. Isawa. *Gowon.* Ibadan: West Books, 1985.

Fein, Helen. "Lives at Risk." Working Paper of the Institute for the Study of Genocide, John Jay College of Criminal Justice, New York, March 1990.

Friedman, Thomas L. *From Beirut to Jerusalem.* New York: Farrar, Strauss, and Giroux, 1989.

Furet, François. *Interpreting the French Revolution.* Cambridge: Cambridge University Press, 1986.

Furet, François, and Mona Ozouf, eds. *A Critical Dictionary of the French Revolution.* Cambridge, Mass.: Harvard University Press, 1989.

Gouldner, Alvin W. "Stalinism: A Study of Internal Colonialism." In Maurice Zeitlin, ed., *Political Power and Social Theory.* Greenwich, Conn.: Jai Press, 1980.

Gross, Jan. *Polish Society under German Occupation.* Princeton: Princeton University Press, 1979.

Harff, Barbara, and Ted Robert Gurr. "Toward Empirical Theory of Genocides and Politicides: Identification and Measurement of Cases since 1945." *International Studies Quarterly* 32 (1988): 359–71.

Hawk, David. "Pol Pot's Cambodia." In Charny, *Toward the Understanding and Prevention of Genocide*, 51–59.

Herskovits, Jean. "Democracy in Nigeria." *Foreign Affairs* (Winter 1979/80): 314–35.

Hough, Jerry, and Merle Fainsod. *How the Soviet Union Is Ruled.* Cambridge, Mass.: Harvard University Press, 1979.

Bibliography

Jackson, Karl D., ed. *Cambodia, 1975–1978: Rendezvous with Death.* Princeton: Princeton University Press, 1989.

Kaplan, Robert D. *Surrender or Starve: The Wars behind the Famine.* Boulder and London: Westview Press, 1988.

Lemarchand, René, and Martin David. *Selective Genocide in Burundi.* London: Minority Rights Group, 1974.

Lewin, Moshe. *Russian Peasants and Soviet Power.* New York: W. W. Norton, 1975.

Lucas, Colin. *The Structure of the Terror.* New York: Oxford University Press, 1973.

Melson, Robert, and Howard Wolpe. "Modernization and the Politics of Communalism: A Theoretical Perspective." *American Political Science Review* 64, no. 4 (1970): 1112–30.

———, eds. *Nigeria: Modernization and the Politics of Communalism.* East Lansing: Michigan State University Press, 1971.

Mitrany, David. *Marx against the Peasant.* New York: Collier Books, 1961.

Paden, John. "Communal Competition, Conflict and Violence in Kano." In Melson and Wolpe, *Nigeria: Modernization and the Politics of Communalism,* 113–144.

Quinn, Kenneth M. "Explaining the Terror." In Jackson, *Cambodia, 1975–1978,* 215–40.

Rummel, R. J. *Lethal Politics: Soviet Genocides and Mass Murder, 1900–1987.* New Brunswick, N.J.: Transaction Press, 1990.

Ryan, Lyndall. *The Aboriginal Tasmanians.* Vancouver: University of British Columbia, 1981.

St. Jorre, John de. *The Brothers' War: Biafra and Nigeria.* Boston: Houghton Mifflin, 1972.

Schama, Simon. *Citizens: A Chronicle of the French Revolution.* New York: Alfred A. Knopf, 1989.

Sécher, Reynald. *Le génocide Franco-Français: La Vendée-Vengé.* Paris: Presses Universitaire de France, 1986.

Shawcross, William. *Sideshow: Kissinger, Nixon, and the Destruction of Cambodia.* New York: Simon and Schuster, 1979.

Stremlau, John J. *The International Politics of the Nigerian Civil War.* Princeton: Princeton University Press, 1977.

Tucker, Robert C. *The Soviet Political Mind.* New York: W. W. Norton, 1971.

Wolf, Eric R. "Killing the Achés." in Arens, *Genocide in Paraguay.*

Wytwycky, Bohdan. *The Other Holocaust.* Washington, D.C.: Novak Report, 1980.

INDEX

Index

356